JUDGMENT
AND DECISION
MAKING

JUDGMENT AND DECISION MAKING

J. FRANK YATES

The University of Michigan

1990

PRENTICE HALL *Englewood Cliffs, New Jersey 07632*

Library of Congress Cataloging-in-Publication Data

Yates, J. Frank (Jacques Frank)
    Judgment and decision making / J. Frank Yates.
      p.   cm.
    Includes bibliographical references.
    ISBN 0-13-511726-7
    1. Judgment. 2. Decision-making.   I. Title.
  BF447.Y37 1990
   153.4'6--dc20   89-36468
                                                          CIP

Editorial/production supervision
  and interior design: **Susan E. Rowan**
Cover design: **Diane Saxe**
Manufacturing buyer: **Ray Keating**

 © 1990 by Prentice-Hall, Inc.
A Division of Simon & Schuster
Englewood Cliffs, New Jersey 07632

Printed in the United States of America
10 9 8 7 6 5 4 3 2 1

ISBN 0-13-511726-7

PRENTICE-HALL INTERNATIONAL (UK) LIMITED, *London*
PRENTICE-HALL OF AUSTRALIA PTY. LIMITED, *Sydney*
PRENTICE-HALL CANADA INC., *Toronto*
PRENTICE-HALL HISPANOAMERICANA, S.A., *Mexico*
PRENTICE-HALL OF INDIA PRIVATE LIMITED, *New Delhi*
PRENTICE-HALL OF JAPAN, INC., *Tokyo*
SIMON & SCHUSTER ASIA PTE. LTD., *Singapore*
EDITORA PRENTICE-HALL DO BRASIL, LTDA., *Rio de Janeiro*

For Hali, Zacky,
and my mother

Contents

9   *Expected Utility 240*

10   *Cousins of Expected Utility 282*

11   *Expected Value Versus Risk 306*

12   *Personal Representations: Their Character 331*

Preface

For a long time, there was little general interest in the psychology of judgment and decision making. This is no longer true; these days few areas of psychology attract more attention. Judgment and decision psychology's growing appeal is largely due to the careful and dramatic demonstrations of principles reported by several investigators over the past decade or so. Those demonstrations have convinced many people that judgment and decision making represent an area of study that is interesting and important in its own right. The demonstrations are compelling from a practical point of view, too. They suggest that the rules governing our judgment and decision behavior could be seriously flawed. Those rules might lead us to act in ways that leave us significantly worse off than we need be.

Despite current fascination with judgment and decision making, the subject is surprisingly rarely taught. In part, this is because many of the major developments in the field are recent; all new research takes some time to find its way into the curriculum. But there are other explanations, too. Those who have actually tried to teach judgment and decision psychology report a serious impediment to their efforts: a shortage of reading material suitable for their students. Much of the relevant scholarly literature requires a background in mathematics and statistics that many instructors realize their students do not have. On the other hand, students in fields that *do* rely on formalisms, for example, engineering and management science, sometimes find the behavioral judgment and decision making literature opaque for other reasons. Because they often have had little exposure to psychology, they have a hard time synthesizing individual research reports into a coherent whole.

Judgment and Decision Making was written in response to the need for a comprehensive and integrative text that is accessible to a broad audience. It is intended for use primarily by juniors and seniors and by beginning graduate and professional students. It should be suitable as a principal source in an introductory course on judgment and decision behavior. Depending on the instructor's aims and on students' backgrounds, the book easily can be supplemented by articles from the scholarly literature, including those cited in the book itself. *Judgment and Decision Making* can also serve as a complement to the texts normally used in professional school courses that emphasize normative procedures, for example, courses in decision analysis, operations research, management information systems, clinical diagnosis, auditing, finance, and planning.

Most of the material in this book was drawn from lectures and discussions in classes I have taught at the University of Michigan and Peking University. It gives me great pleasure to acknowledge the lessons hundreds of my students have given me. Our spirited conversations, their challenging questions, and their unique viewpoints have led me to insights that otherwise would never have dawned on me. I have also benefited greatly from the ideas and criticisms of many colleagues. I especially appreciate the time and effort the following friends contributed in reviewing several drafts of the book's chapters: Bruce Carlson, Shawn Curley, Ju-whei Lee, Keith Levi, Linda McDaniel, Karen Siegel-Jacobs, Eric Stone, Sy Veniar, and Mark Young. My reviewers have saved me from the embarrassment of seemingly countless mistakes; I take full responsibility for the errors that remain. Special thanks are due to Albert Cain, chairman of the Michigan Psychology Department, for his support and encouragement throughout the preparation of the book. Important financial assistance was provided by the Arthur F. Thurnau Trust and the Psychology Department Enrichment Fund. My greatest debt is to the world-wide community of judgment and decision researchers whose work I have attempted to describe. I thank them sincerely and ask their forgiveness for any failures on my part to represent their discoveries faithfully.

J. F. Y.

JUDGMENT
AND DECISION
MAKING

1

An Overview

DECISIONS
>   The decision concept   Decision types

AIMS
EMPHASES
PLAN
SOME SUGGESTIONS
SUMMARY
KEY TERMS
ADDITIONAL READING
EXERCISES AND STUDY QUESTIONS

At the time, it seemed like a pretty good idea.

—Many of Us

Consider the following excerpt from the Ann Arbor *News* (Miller, 1986, December 12, p. A1):

> When more than 250 angry parents gathered Dec. 4 to watch the Willow Run Board of Education lay off 23 teachers and cut into the very muscle of its school programs, the first question that should have been on the minds of everyone was why.
>
> Why didn't the school district see this coming? Why didn't the district make deeper cuts last spring when it laid off 17 teachers? Why couldn't the 177-student loss be predicted, and why did 290 students leave the district in the past two years? Why didn't Superintendent _____ heed the words of his administrative crew who predicted at least a 40-student drop this year?
>
> The district's 1985–86 budget was a comedy of errors. Willow Run started the year with a healthy $900,000 surplus and ended $117,000 in the hole. Why didn't it see the insurance premium skyrocketing? And why were heating, electricity, workers's compensation, computer, substitute pay and other costs grossly underbudgeted?

The Willow Run school budget crisis illustrates the subject of this book, human judgment and decision making, as well as its significance. The school board and superintendent were the district's primary decision makers. Their major decision tasks included such duties as budgeting, hiring staff, authorizing programs, and approving contracts. Clearly, many of their decisions went awry. As suggested by the newspaper account, a series of misjudgments was a significant contributor to those decisions. As a consequence of the decisions, the quality of students' education suffered. Teachers were left jobless in the middle of the year. Local property values stagnated because of the adverse publicity. And, eventually, the superintendent resigned amid the controversy.

The purpose of this chapter is to provide you with an overview of judgment and decision behavior and how they will be approached in this book. The first section defines what we mean by the term "decision." The second outlines the book's aims, while the third describes its emphases, including its focus on a particular kind of judgment. The fourth section previews the remaining chapters. The fifth and final substantive section offers some suggestions for how you can gain the most from your reading.

DECISIONS

Everybody knows what a decision is. After all, each of us makes decisions all day long. We choose which clothes to wear in the morning. We pick a route to take to work. We plan how much money to withdraw from the bank and set aside for food, entertainment, and incidentals. On some days, we even make "monumental" decisions, for example, what job to take, what car to buy, whether or not to get married, and to whom. Some of us actually get paid to make, advise, or influence significant decisions for other people. For example, lawyers recommend remedies for their clients' legal troubles. Physicians suggest alternative therapies for their patients' illnesses. Money managers select stock portfolios for their clients' funds. Sales representatives encourage customers to purchase the goods they happen to offer. Counselors help students select their courses, majors, and careers.

The decision concept

Although we all have a sense of how the word decision is used in everyday life, careful study demands more precision. By a **decision** we will mean an action taken with the intention of producing favorable outcomes. A decision is said to be **successful** if it indeed does bring about outcomes at least as satisfying as would have been yielded by any other action the decision maker might have pursued; otherwise, the decision **fails**. An unsuccessful decision results from one or more **decision errors** committed while the decision was being deliberated. Suppose you chose to take the Clark Drive route to work one icy morning and arrived an hour late because the roadway was so slick that traffic had to move at a snail's pace. Had you taken the Oak Boulevard route, you would have found the streets cleared by road crews and could have gotten to work on time. Somewhere during your consideration of how to get to your job, you made a decision error, an error that may or may not have been preventable.

Decision types

All decisions share several common features: They are conscious. They are voluntary. They are intended to bring about outcomes the decision maker prefers over other outcomes. However, we will find it useful to distinguish three types of decisions: choices, evaluations, and constructions. These types differ according to the nature of the action the decision maker takes.

Choices In a **choice** situation, the decision maker is confronted with a well-defined set of alternatives. The usual task is to choose one of them. Sometimes, however, the decision maker is allowed to select two or more alternatives from an even larger collection of options. An example: "Brenda Summers" owns a small business. To increase her company's efficiency, she has decided to acquire a personal computer. The issue now is which particular computer to buy. She has narrowed the possibilities to three machines: the "HAL Standard," the "Orange Valencia," and the "Multicomp II." She must make a choice. Another example is in college admissions. There more than one alternative is picked. The college must assemble an entire freshman class from the pool of applicants, which is usually much larger than the number of spaces available.

Evaluations **Evaluation** situations focus on one alternative at a time. The decision maker's task is to indicate the worth of that alternative. For such an action to constitute a decision instead of an idle pronouncement, the indication of worth must have at least the *potential* of affecting outcomes the decision maker cares about. Evaluations are commonly expressed in either of two ways. In one mode of expression, the decision maker uses some form of verbal or quantitative analogy to indicate worth. For instance, the decision maker might say that the alternative is "good" rather than "excellent." Or it might be given a rating of 4 on a 5-point scale. In the other mode of expression, the decision maker characterizes worth by acknowledging indifference between the given alternative and some desirable or undesirable object, for example, a monetary gift or penalty. Thus, if given the option, the decision maker would not care whether the alternative or the object were received.

Again consider Ms. Summers's deliberations about personal computers. When asked by a colleague to evaluate the HAL Standard, she says, "It's a very good machine." This statement is a legitimate decision rather than casual conversation if Ms. Summers believes that it might affect her colleague's computer purchases. That is because his satisfaction with those purchases would affect his regard for her opinion. Suppose Ms. Summers carefully examines the Orange Valencia computer and then announces that she would pay as much as $2500 for it, but no more. That $2500 maximum buying price is an evaluation of the Orange Valencia. In effect, Ms. Summers has indicated that she is indifferent between keeping her $2500 and exchanging it for the computer.

Constructions   In a **construction** situation, the decision maker has at his or her disposal a set of limited resources. The task is to use those resources to construct *the* most satisfactory alternative. Brenda Summers's personal computing problem once more provides an illustration. Ms. Summers's chore is much bigger than simply selecting a computing machine. Eventually, she must accumulate several other pieces of hardware, too, including a video monitor to allow her to see her work as she does it, a printer to produce permanent copies of her results, and perhaps an extra disk drive to increase the system's capacity to do all the work she requires. She must also acquire the programs or software that constitutes the instructions her computer follows in doing her work (writing letters and reports, keeping inventory, and compiling financial records). There are scores of different pieces of equipment Ms. Summers might buy. The shelves of local computer stores are also filled with programs for each of the tasks Ms. Summers needs performed. Thus, from this broader perspective, we see that Ms. Summers is actually faced with a construction decision. Her aim is to assemble the most suitable personal computing system she can, consisting of various items of machinery and the programs for running them. She must do this within such constraints as her budget and her office space.

Relationships among the decision types   The kinds of decisions distinguished here are not completely independent of one another. In many respects, choice is the most fundamental type of decision. When an evaluation is made in terms of indifferences, the decision maker indicates explicitly that a reliable choice cannot be made between the alternative being evaluated and the object used for expressing that evaluation. When a construction decision is made, it is intended that the alternative that is constructed would be chosen over any other alternative that might be assembled. Moreover, we would expect that, if one alternative is chosen over another, it would also be evaluated more highly, and conversely. For instance, if Ms. Summers evaluates the Multicomp II computer more highly than the HAL Standard, we would think that, if allowed to choose, she would pick the Multicomp II. As we will see, in actual practice, people do not always behave this way. Such anomalies are one reason the distinctions among decision types are worth retaining. They also suggest why decision behavior is interesting and important to comprehend.

AIMS

Our aims in studying decision behavior are threefold. Foremost, we seek to understand *how* people make decisions. In situations like that which faced the Willow Run officials, what information is taken into account in anticipating what will happen in the future? How is that information synthesized into specific predictions and ultimate decisions, for example, how many people to hire and which ones? In other circumstances, for example, medicine, would the same mechanisms be employed? If not, how would those alternative mechanisms differ? Exactly what is it that determines which decision procedures will be applied and which will not?

Our second goal concerns decision *quality*. Typically, how good *are* people's decisions and the cognitions that underlie them? Is the Willow Run case an oddity? Or are decision errors widespread? Are there important distinctions among various errors? What are the foundations of specific errors?

Our third aim in examining decision making is its *improvement*. If decision behavior is at least sometimes deficient, can it be made better? Can we reduce the frequency and magnitude of decision errors? Granted, the Willow Run officials missed the boat on their forecasts of enrollments and costs. But nobody is perfect. The procedures used by Willow Run might have been basically sound, but simply ran into a little bad luck that *any* approach would have suffered. On the other hand, there just might exist forecasting methods that are less susceptible to error.

Two general strategies for improving decision-related behavior have been taken. In the first, the person is taught better ways of performing various tasks. In the second, the individual abdicates the role of decision maker. One way this is done is by turning over chores to someone who is presumably more expert. We do this routinely when we ask our physicians which treatments for our ailments are most likely to succeed. After all, as laypersons, what do *we* know about medicine? In the alternative form of the abdication approach, we assign tasks to machines. There is nothing to prevent a bank from allowing its loan officers to assess credit risks from unstructured client interviews. On the other hand, the bank could require loan applicants to supply certain background information that is then used by a computer program to calculate risks of loan defaults. The implicit and explicit suggestions for improving decisions that are offered throughout this book represent both strategies.

EMPHASES

People's decisions are dictated by several factors. In the case of choice, one contributing factor is simply which alternatives happen to come to mind: You cannot choose to buy the house for sale on Pearl Street unless that possibility is brought to your awareness. Value is a consideration in all decisions, given our definition of the decision concept. You might be inclined toward the house on Pearl Street partly because you like its Tudor styling; you value its appearance. Your best friend, who despises Tudor architecture, might reject the house out of hand because of how it looks. We could continue citing various determinants of decision behavior. And several will receive attention in this book as we try to understand the kinds of decisions distinguished above. But one of them will have special emphasis: judgment.

A **judgment** is an opinion about what is (or will be) the status of some aspect of the world, for example, the number of students who will enroll in a school district. We normally think of opinions as being a peculiarly human province. But not all judgments come from people. In today's technological world, many judgments are generated by other means, such as computers. For instance, in projecting the sales of a car it might produce, an automobile company augments its marketing experts' personal judgments with estimates made according to statistical forecasting techniques.

Judgment is a major class of cognitive activity, on a par with learning and perception. As such, it is interesting and important in its own right. However, it is the role of judgment in decision making that motivates our interest in the subject. Judgments form the cornerstone of most decisions. The quality of those decisions can be no better than the quality of the judgments supporting them. To wit, the Willow Run school board's unfortunate overhiring of teachers was largely predicated on an overestimate of the district's school-age population.

Sometimes our judgmental statements seem like definitive pronouncements of fact. For instance, television and radio announcers often say such things as, "No rain tomorrow, folks!" Such **deterministic** judgments fail to acknowledge the possibility that anything other than the predicted weather conditions might actually prevail. Despite the commonness of deterministic judgment, even the most myopic individuals realize that there is uncertainty in the great majority of decision situations that arise. For example, the Willow Run superintendant surely recognized that the district's utility costs could lie anywhere in a range of possibilities. As we will see, there are significant practical advantages to explicitly acknowledging the uncertainty in decision situations. That is why this book devotes special attention to understanding people's **likelihood judgments**, which qualify the chances of an event's occurrence, for example, "There's a 60% chance of precipitation in Chicagoland tonight, neighbors!"

There is an implication in acknowledging that this book has special emphases, for example, judgments and decisions in the presence of uncertainty: Certain other topics are de-emphasized. This is necessary because otherwise the book would be too long. You should be aware of the existence and importance of the topics we are unable to discuss in depth. Among the major ones are these:

Decision in certainty. Although uncertainty is pervasive, there are in fact circumstances where decisions are made in certainty, or at least where the uncertainty is ignored. For instance, most shoppers probably do not recognize uncertainty in the choice between two shirts to buy. Among the issues that *are* acknowledged, however, is the conflict between the strengths and weaknesses of the alternatives, for example, the superior styling of one shirt cast against the better price of the other (see Shapira, 1981).

Deterministic judgment. Adults normally realize that they can seldom perfectly anticipate the events that have significance for their decisions. Thus, their judgments about those events are implicitly likelihood judgments. Nevertheless, they often report their opinions deterministically. For example, your doctor might say, "You have nothing more serious than a cold," when she is not nearly as convinced of that diagnosis as she sounds. And how often on the 6:30 news have we heard such statements as, "The President's chief economic advisor says that the unemployment rate will be 6.3% next month"? Although we are unable to explore deterministic judgment, the subject is fascinating and has been studied extensively (for example, Castellan, 1977; Goldberg, 1970).

Social decision making. We make many of our decisions alone. For instance, any school superintendant must personally make countless administrative decisions every day. However, lots of decisions are made in the presence of others or are made by groups, for example, by a school board. Such social decisions ultimately must rest on what individuals do. That is why it is not unreasonable that the present book focuses almost exclusively on the processes governing individual behavior. But there is no question that those processes are moderated by the influences of others and that group decision processes are a distinct entity in themselves. Although we do not have the space to discuss these topics, a good deal is understood about them (see, for example, Brandstatter, Davis, and Stocker-Kreichgauer, 1982; Hammond and others, 1975; Kaplan and Miller, 1983).

PLAN

Judgment and Decision Making has two parts. The first, consisting of Chapters 2 to 7, examines likelihood judgment, which, as argued above, is one of the most crucial decision contributors. Chapters 8 to 13 comprise the second part of the book. There the focus is pointedly on how the person actually arrives at a decision, including the integration of judgments with other considerations.

Chapter 2 is called *Assessment*. It discusses the problem of determining just how likely a person thinks an event is. When your real estate agent says that there is about a 40% chance that mortgage rates will decline in the winter, what assurance do you have that that is what he really thinks? Are there ways of probing his mind that should give you greater confidence that you are using his expertise to the fullest?

Chapter 3, *Analysis*, like Chapter 2, is methodological. Suppose that *two* real estate agents give their opinions about interest rate changes. Being human, they are bound to disagree, at least sometimes. Whose judgments should you follow? Naturally, you would want to act on the predictions made by the agent who is usually more accurate. But there is the rub: What does it mean to say that one person's likelihood judgments are more accurate than another's? Chapter 3 describes several commonly recognized concepts and aspects of accuracy and how they can be measured.

In Chapter 4, *Accuracy*, we get to the description of actual judgment behavior. In that chapter specifically, we examine the characteristic accuracy of likelihood judgments made under several conditions. For instance, relative to conventional standards, just how accurate are the typical weather forecaster's predictions? How about physicians' medical diagnoses? How about our own judgments in everyday life?

Accuracy concerns the extent to which likelihood judgments correspond to what happens in the real world. This is clearly an important feature of judgment quality. However, it is not the *only* quality dimension. Another is consistency. Good judgments ought not contradict one another. Nor should they conflict with accepted principles of rationality. Chapter 5, *Coherence*, discusses concepts of consistency for likelihood judgments, as well as the consistency typically observed in people's real judgment behavior.

Chapters 6 and 7 get behind the indications in previous chapters about the goodness of people's likelihood assessments: How are those judgments formed in the first place? Two classes of judgment procedures are recognized. Chapter 6, *Formal Procedures*, focuses on judgment mechanisms that are analogous to what a logician or statistician might do in solving a problem. They involve applying accepted relational principles to derive desired conclusions from assumed facts. These procedures are distinctive in that they do not require us to consider the substance of the given situation. Suppose we *assume* that "All A's are B's," and are told that "X is an A." Then, according to conventional rules of logic, we should conclude that "X is a B," too. It is irrelevant whether A's are cows, B's are animals, and X is Elsie, or that A's are items of furniture, B's are desks, and X is your dining room table. It is also immaterial whether the assignments agree or disagree (as in the second set of correspondences) with reality.

By contrast, in the judgment mechanisms examined in Chapter 7, *Substantive Procedures*, the content of the given situation is paramount. Substantive judgment processes rest on presumptions about how nature actually produces certain classes of events. In a specific situation, the individual evaluates the chances for an event's occurrence according to those presumptions and the current facts. For instance, in a court case, a juror might judge the likelihood of the defendant's guilt by the extent to which the defendant's personality fits the juror's stereotype of a person who "is capable of committing this kind of crime."

Chapter 8, *Bedrock Principles*, is the first of the "decision" chapters. It discusses concepts that have become the very foundations—the bedrock—of the field of decision making under uncertainty. Those principles do a poor job of describing how people actually decide. But they are essential background for making sense out of real decision behavior.

Without doubt, *the* dominant idea in the history of scholarship on decision making is expected utility, the subject of Chapter 9. Expected utility principles deal directly with the central problem of integrating uncertainty and value, for example, in choosing between a business proposition that has a 50% probability of a $5000 profit and one offering a lesser 20% chance of a more substantial $10,000 return. As we will see, people's decisions deviate systematically from the demands of expected utility principles. However, those principles are important partly because they capture many notions of what is considered rational. They also serve as a point of departure for other theories of decision, theories that often better account for what people really do. Chapter 10, *Cousins of Expected Utility*, discusses competing theories that are very closely related to expected utility theories, "cousins," as it were. Chapter 11, *Expected Value versus Risk*, examines points of view that are more distant, but still owe a debt to concepts related to expected utility.

A personal representation is a given individual's own characterization of a decision situation. Different representations can yield radically different decisions. For instance, two staff recruiters might make conflicting hiring recommendations because they see different things in the same job candidates. Such examples highlight the fact that a complete understanding of decision behavior requires an understanding of how people represent the decision situations that confront them. Chapter 12, *Personal Representations: Their Character*, discusses various features that decision representations often have in common. Chapter 13, *Personal Representations: Their Contents and Moderation*, catalogs some of the considerations that are thought to be contained in many representations, regardless of the context, for example, anticipated regret. That chapter also reviews the influences various factors such as stress have on how a person represents a given decision situation.

SOME SUGGESTIONS

It is recommended that you approach each chapter as follows (see Robinson, 1962): First, examine the chapter outline. This should give you some idea of the issues addressed by the chapter. Next, you might peruse the expressions listed in the *Key Terms* section. These expressions correspond to fundamental concepts introduced in the chapter. Thoroughly understanding those terms should be one of your goals. Many students find it useful to next go through the chapter inspecting the tables and figures. Often, this not only clarifies the issues, but even resolves some of them. Reading the chapter summary will settle even more.

Throughout your preliminary survey of the chapter, you should do more than seek to understand what the author is trying to communicate. You should also pose questions of your own that you believe the chapter might answer. In general, reading is more effective—to say nothing of being more enjoyable—when we put the material in our own terms, when we use it to solve problems in our own lives. Thus, for instance, in the present chapter, it would be to your advantage to think about judgment and decision problems with special interest to yourself (Try it!): "How accurately did I anticipate what it would be like going to school here?" "With my major, how easily will I find a good job when I graduate?" "If I get married next month, will I be satisfied 10 years from now?" "Is my financial advisor right when he says that I will 'probably' be better off putting my savings in a mutual fund rather than government bonds?" "Why am I using this advisor in the first place? Is he *really* better than the guy down the street?" "Should I apply to medical school at Harvard, or would I be wasting my time and money?"

You should next read the chapter carefully. The task should go especially smoothly if, while reading, you actively search for answers to the questions you have asked. More than likely, you will have had only a vague understanding of the summary upon first reading it. The summary will make much more sense when you reread it after studying the "meat" of the chapter; it should put the basic ideas in a nice, compact capsule. At that point you should also be able to define, illustrate, and use the expressions in the *Key Terms* section.

To test and solidify your understanding, you should attempt the items in the chapter's *Exercises and Study Questions* section. The exercises have fairly well agreed upon right and wrong answers. They concern concepts or procedures that people often need to practice in order to master fully. Study questions normally demand the reader to go beyond the material in the text: What are the implications of specific principles? How might certain phenomena be explained? How could those hypothesized explanations be tested? Answers to selected items are at the back of the book. Others can be obtained by writing the publisher.

Judgment and Decision Making is an introduction to the subject. The text is largely an interpretation of original research reported in scholarly journals. As such, it should provide a good understanding of many basic judgment and decision principles. You might want more, however. Perhaps you are considering a career as a researcher in decision behavior. Or maybe you want to develop ways of making better judgments and decisions in some practical setting, for example, counseling, health care, business, or engineering. Then you will need to go beyond the foundation you build by studying this text. You must immerse yourself in the original literature. As a first step in that direction, you might examine firsthand the sources cited in each chapter. Going further, you could use the chapter's *Additional Reading* section. The references included there discuss specialized and often more advanced topics related to those introduced in the chapter.

Much of contemporary scholarship on human decision making is rooted in such fields as measurement theory, economics, and engineering.

Those areas use mathematics and statistics extensively to model how people ought to behave, as well as how they in fact behave. Over time, mathematics has become a dominant language for analyzing and discussing judgment and decision making. Unfortunately, many people are put off by that language. Some complain that the language is difficult to understand and that it obscures what is really important psychologically. **Judgment and Decision Making** tries to avoid this problem by expressing concepts in ordinary prose. Whenever possible, however, translations of these ideas into the formalisms that researchers normally use are provided, too. This is important because the reader should recognize the field for what it really is. And, as we hope you will become convinced, mathematical expression is often quite useful; it can clarify issues that remain murky when discussed in mere words.

One comment on conventions: This is not a work of fiction, at least not intentionally so. Nevertheless, to illustrate various ideas, the book is replete with fictional characters and places, as well as real ones. When the distinction between the real and the imaginary is not obvious, the names of fictional people and entities appear in quotation marks the first time they are mentioned.

If you feel uncomfortable with math, do not despair. The book requires that the reader have nothing more than a knowledge of elementary algebra. At various points, certain statistical concepts are required to understand particular principles. If you have had an introductory course in statistics, these essential concepts will be familiar to you already. Regardless, every concept is explained to the extent necessary for understanding the relevant psychological ideas. A few sections of the book explore topics that involve more algebraic detail than is characteristic of the rest of the text. These sections are marked "Optional." You can omit them without losing any sense of continuity or without being unable to understand what follows. If you have had extensive experience with mathematics and statistics, the formalisms used in **Judgment and Decision Making** will strike you as elementary. If so, you should just read past their explanations and get right to the psychology. That is what the book is *really* about.

SUMMARY

Decisions are actions people take with the intention of producing favorable outcomes. Three decision types are distinguished. Choices are decisions in which the person selects one or more alternatives from a well-defined larger set of options. Evaluations are indications of the worth of individual alternatives. Constructions are decisions in which an individual tries to assemble *the* most satisfactory alternative possible.

This book is about human decision making, particularly in the presence of uncertainty. Special emphasis is placed on one of the most significant contributors to decision behavior—judgment. Shortcomings in judgments are a prime example of decision errors, which are specific behaviors that are responsible for failed decisions.

KEY TERMS

Choice
Construction
Decision
Decision error
Decision failure
Deterministic judgment
Evaluation
Judgment
Likelihood judgment

ADDITIONAL READING

Abelson and Levi (1985); Arkes and Hammond (1987); Dawes (1988); Einhorn and Hogarth (1981); Kahneman, Slovic, and Tversky (1982); Nisbett and Ross (1980); Pitz and Sachs (1984); von Winterfeldt and Edwards (1986).

EXERCISES AND STUDY QUESTIONS

1. What is the fundamental problem in judging decision quality illustrated by the cartoon shown in Figure 1.1E? Explain. Can you think of a reasonable approach to dealing with this problem?

Adam®   **by Brian Basset**

Figure 1.1E. © Copyright 1984 Universal Press Syndicate. Reprinted with permission. All rights reserved.

2. Some decision theorists maintain that it makes no sense to speak of good and bad decisions, only of good and bad decision *procedures*. Other theorists disagree. Offer arguments for each view.
3. Describe an everyday situation in which a person tries to construct the most satisfying alternative, but fails. Speculate about why the attempt does not succeed.
4. "Veronica Herbert" is the president of "Peerless Industries," a manufacturer of industrial solvents. Peerless's major competitor is "Peak Enterprises." "Peter

Salters" is Veronica Herbert's vice president for planning. One day she says to him, "I'm thinking about having us market Product X20. To make a decent profit, though, we need to be the sole source of such cleansers. Is Peak going to sell something as good as X20 within the next couple of years?" Mr. Salters responds, "I'd say there's about a 60% chance they will, Veronica." Exasperated, she cries out, "For Pete's sake, Pete! Can't you ever just say either 'Yes' or 'No?' Why do you always have to be so wishy-washy?" Thereafter, whenever Ms. Herbert asks whether something is going to happen, Mr. Salters does in fact respond simply "Yes" or "No." What do you see as the advantages and disadvantages of what Ms. Herbert has forced Mr. Salters to do?

2

Assessment

A pinch of probably is worth a pound of perhaps.

—James Thurber

Overheard one morning: "Boy, what a gorgeous day! Isn't it great, just being alive? Why don't we go on a picnic?" Every now and then, we all experience this kind of zest for life. Suppose you are the one feeling good about just being on the planet. You and your friends do decide to drive all the way to a distant park for a picnic. If the weather remains good, you will have a grand time. If it rains, your day will be ruined. Not only will you get soaked, but you will have foregone all the other things you might have done.

If you were clairvoyant, you would *know* whether rain was in store. You would, of course, then act accordingly. Alas, being mortal, you are not blessed with clairvoyance. Nevertheless, you have *opinions* about the weather. And the more sure you are that the skies will be fair, the more inclined you are to go on your picnic. Conversely, the more certain you are that it will rain, the more strongly you feel you had better do something else with your day.

We routinely make judgments about how likely it is that various events will happen. As in your picnic dilemma, those judgments have profound effects on our decisions. In the next several chapters, we will examine numerous issues concerning **likelihood judgments**, that is, opinions about how certain it is that various events will occur. The present chapter is about method: How can we accurately assess people's opinions, including our own? This is an important question because we cannot begin to study—and thus understand—how people think about uncertainty unless we can measure their likelihood judgments. The issue has practical significance, too. We often make decisions not on the basis of our own likelihood judgments, but those of others, for example, experts. You might easily distrust your own opinion about whether or not it will rain on your picnic. Instead, you would rather rely on forecaster "Verna Green's" Channel 4 weather report. But what is the best way for Ms. Green to tell you what her opinion is?

The first section of this chapter describes the fundamental distinction between two major classes of likelihood judgment assessment procedures. The second and third sections, respectively, present and illustrate variations of these basic approaches. The final section discusses considerations we should take into account in choosing among techniques for measuring people's opinions.

BASIC APPROACHES

During the Late, Late Show one night, "Pete Shorter," the owner of "Jiffy Transmission Exchange," appears on the television screen and shouts:

> I'm *convinced* that, even *90 days* after they drive out the door, virtually *all* our customers are *completely* satisfied with the rebuilt transmissions we sell them!

During the next commercial break, "Jack Price," the owner of "Sudden Service Transmissions," comes on and yells the following:

> If, within 90 days after the work is done, you aren't *fully* satisfied with the rebuilt transmission we sell you, we'll refund your money and give you another transmission—absolutely FREE!

Both of these sales pitches reflect how sure the company owners are that their transmissions will work for at least three months. Their differences illustrate the distinction between two major approaches to likelihood judgment assessment.

In the **statement approach**, opinion is conveyed by a **likelihood statement**, an explicit pronouncement of a person's degree of certainty that an event will happen. As an example, Pete Shorter says he is "convinced" that any Jiffy transmission will last a long time. Presumably, however, he is less sure than if he said he was convinced that nearly all his customers are satisfied after 120 rather than only 90 days.

We can imagine Jack Price saying in his next round of ads, "Talk is cheap, Jiffy! Put your money where your mouth is!" In effect, that is what Sudden Service has done. Mr. Price is so sure that any of *his* transmissions will last 90 days that he is willing to act on that opinion. In addition, it is reasonable to assume that he is even more certain of Sudden Service's transmission quality than if he had only promised replacement, without a refund. We thus *infer* Jack Price's opinion from his decision—the decision to offer Sudden Service's particular guarantee. Such conclusions are characteristic of the second assessment strategy, the **inference approach**.

Each assessment strategy has many variations. In the next section we examine several statement procedures, also known as direct methods (Spetzler and Staël von Holstein, 1975). The section after that discusses inference or indirect techniques.

STATEMENT METHODS

Verbal reports

Verbal reports are the simplest way to express likelihood opinions. The person uses ordinary, everyday language to indicate degrees of certainty in an event's occurrence, for example, the term "convinced" in the case of Jiffy Transmission Exchange's advertisement. Various professions favor some words rather than others, for example, "odds on," "expected," and "suggests" in medicine (Bryant and Norman, 1980); "probable," "reasonably possible," and "remote" in accounting (Chesley, 1982); and "one must consider," "it could be," and "meaningful chance" in political forecasting (Beyth-Marom, 1982). In all instances, though, it is implicitly assumed that there is at least a rough consensus about the relative likelihoods of events labeled with particular expressions. For example, Beyth-Marom (1982) found that political analysts generally agreed that an event described as having a "meaningful chance" was more likely than an event that "one must consider."

Rankings

Sometimes people convey their likelihood judgments comparatively. That is, they report that one event it is more, equally, or less likely than some other event. Such **likelihood rankings** are also called **qualitative likelihood judgments**. Experts frequently use these statements to convey likelihood assessments to the public. For example, transportation authorities often reassure skittish air travelers as follows: "You are much more likely to get killed in a car accident than in a plane crash. Nevertheless, you drive all the time, right?" We sometimes abbreviate likelihood rankings as follows: (Die in car accident) $>_L$ (Die in airplane crash). The symbols $>_L$, $<_L$, and $=_L$ denote greater, lesser, and equal judged relative likelihoods, respectively.

Ratings

Likelihood ratings are similar to verbal reports. The judge attaches one of several specified labels to an event. As in the case of verbal reports, there is an assumed consensus about the implied relative chances of events given different labels. There are two major differences between ordinary verbal labels and ratings, however. The first is that the list of available labels in a rating procedure is usually more restricted. The other is that the consensus about the implied likelihood ordering of rating labels is stronger.

The following is an example of a likelihood rating scale:

Using the statements listed below, please indicate your opinion about Mayor Burn's chances of being reelected next week (check one):

_____ Very sure he will be reelected
_____ Moderately sure he will be reelected
_____ Unsure whether he will be reelected or defeated
_____ Moderately sure he will be defeated
_____ Very sure he will be defeated

The respondent in the given political survey picks the one expression that most closely corresponds to his or her opinion that Mayor Burn will be reelected. People usually find it easy and natural to answer such questions.

In other rating scales, the label the person attaches to each event is numerical, or at least analogous to a number. For instance, the scale shown in this next illustrative survey item requires a number between 1 and 10 to signify the strength of certainty in the target event's occurrence:

Please circle the number below which corresponds to your belief that the U.S. unemployment rate will be lower 6 months from now than it is today:

Certain That NOT Lower   1 2 3 4 5 6 7 8 9 10   Certain That Lower

Another example of a rating scale is common in the world of finance. A bond is a type of financial security. More precisely, a bond is a certificate promising that on a specified date the issuer of the bond will pay the bond holder a specified sum of money. For instance, if your grandmother gave you a $100 U.S. savings bond on your tenth birthday, then when the bond matured, you were entitled to receive $100 from the U.S. Treasury Department. Bonds are issued by businesses as well as governments. They are actually a means of borrowing funds. In essence, when we buy bonds, we are lending our money to the organization selling those bonds.

Not all bonds are repaid; sometimes the issuers default, leaving the bondholders with worthless pieces of paper. Thus, it is important that prospective bond purchasers have some idea of the chances that bond issuers will indeed repay their debts. There are several bond rating services that, effectively, offer their opinions about what those chances are. The ratings they publish can be interpreted in large measure as ratings of the likelihood that bond issuers will pay the interest on their bonds and repay the bonds at their maturity.

Standard & Poor's is a leading bond rating service. They characterize their rating system as follows (Standard & Poor's, 1985, April, p. 37):

> A Standard & Poor's debt rating is a current assessment of the creditworthiness of an obligor (for example, the bond seller) with respect to a specific obligation (for example, bond)....
> The ratings are based, in varying degrees, on the following considerations:
> '   1. Likelihood of default—capacity and willingness of the obligor as to the timely payment of interest and repayment of principal in accordance with the terms of the obligation....

These are the potential ratings, from best to worst: AAA, AA, A, BBB, BB, B, CCC, CC, C, and D. Note that (p. 37):

> Debt rated 'AAA' has the highest rating assigned by Standard & Poor's. Capacity to pay interest and repay principal is extremely strong.

The following is said about other categories (p. 37):

> Debt rated 'BB,' 'B,' 'CCC,' or 'CC' is regarded, on balance, as predominantly speculative with respect to capacity to pay interest and repay principal....
> Debt rated 'D' is in default, and payment of interest and/or repayment of principal is in arrears.

As an example, in April 1985, Standard & Poor's gave an AA rating to a certain African Development Bank bond and a BBB rating for a particular issue by American Can International Corporation. Other considerations are involved, but it is reasonable to conclude that Standard & Poor's thought the chances of repayment were better for the African Development bonds.

Probability judgments

Probability judgments are very similar to likelihood ratings. They, like some ratings, involve the assignment of numbers to events corresponding to their perceived chances of occurrence. Unlike ordinary ratings, however, probability judgments must conform to several specific and restrictive rules.

Suppose the letter A is used to denote the event of interest, for example, "It will rain this afternoon," to make things concrete. A **probability judgment** for event A, abbreviated as $P'(A)$, is a likelihood statement that satisfies the following conventions:

1. $P'(A)$ is between 0 and 1, that is, $0 \le P'(A) \le 1$. In other words, $P'(A)$ is a proportion. Sometimes probability judgments are expressed as percentages. For example, saying there is a 75% chance of rain is the same as saying $P'(\text{Rain}) = 0.75$.

2. $P'(A) = 0$ means the person believes there is no chance of event A occurring. For instance, $P'(\text{Rain}) = 0$ would indicate that the person is certain there will be no rain.

3. $P'(A) = \frac{1}{2}$ means the person feels that event A is just as likely to occur as not occur; for example, $P'(\text{Rain}) = 0.50$ would mean that the person thought the chances of rain and no rain were even.

4. $P'(A) = 1$ indicates that the person is absolutely sure that event A will happen. So, if you say you are 100% certain of rain, this would imply that there is no doubt in your mind that rain is coming.

5. Intermediate values of $P'(A)$ represent intermediate degrees of certainty in event A's occurrence. Thus, if you say $P'(\text{Rain}) > \frac{1}{2}$, this means that you think it is more likely than not that we will see rain. A value of $P'(\text{Rain}) < \frac{1}{2}$ would mean the opposite. The higher the stated value of $P'(A)$ is, the more certain the person is that event A will happen.

Several other terms are often used to describe probability judgments. One of these expressions is *probability estimate*. Unfortunately, this suggests that the person is trying to identify a true probability. But in most decision situations, there is no such thing. For example, what is the true probability that it will rain tomorrow afternoon? Other common terms for probability judgments are *subjective probabilities* and *personal probabilities*. As we will see in Chapter 5, the word "probability" has a precise meaning in mathematics. So referring to people's probability judgments as probabilities might be construed as a claim that those statements have the properties mathematicians attribute to probabilities. They may or may not possess those properties.

In practice, probability judgments are reported in a variety of ways. In the most straightforward method, the person simply reports a number, for example, "I'm 60% sure that AT&T stock will be selling at a higher price this time next year." Another technique is "frequentistic" in character. A diagnosing physician might say, "If I saw a hundred cases just like this one, I'd expect the patient's tumor to be malignant in 45 of them," implying a 45% probability judgment that the current patient's tumor is malignant.

FIGURE 2.1.   Alternative settings of a wheel-of-fortune or probability wheel.

Yet another class of probability judgment response methods uses *randomized reference devices.* Consider the wheels-of-fortune shown in Figure 2.1. Each wheel is actually an alternative setting of a single wheel-of-fortune, or *probability wheel* (Spetzler and Staël von Holstein, 1975). The wheel is such that the proportion of its surface area that is dark can be varied continuously from 0% to 100%. Suppose we ask football fan "Joe Pro Stevens" the following: "Joe, adjust the dark area of the wheel so that you think it's just as likely that the AFC will win next Sunday's Super Bowl as that the spinner would stop on the dark area of the wheel-of-fortune." Imagine that Joe Pro sets the wheel so that 54% of its area is dark, as in the middle panel of Figure 2.1. We would then conclude that, for Joe Pro,

$$P'(\text{AFC wins}) = 54\%$$

Notice that percentages were never explicitly mentioned anywhere in the procedure.

Odds judgments

"Local experts say the odds are 10 to 1 that the conservatives will maintain control of City Council in next Tuesday's election." Such statements appear commonly in newspapers. What do they mean?

The **odds** for an event are the number of times the event is more likely to occur than to not occur. An **odds judgment** is a person's *opinion* of the relative chances of an event's occurrence—relative to the chances of the event *not* occurring. So, in the City Council example, local experts feel it is 10 times more likely that the conservatives will win the next election than that they will lose or tie with their opponents.

Let us adopt the standard notation for probabilities and odds. The probability for event A would be $P(A)$; its odds would be $\Omega(A)$. The **complement** of an event includes all possibilities other than those contained in the event itself. If A is the event of interest, we can designate the complement of event A by A^c. For instance, if A is "Pass the final examination," then A^c is "Fail the final." According to the above definition, the following relationship must hold between odds and probabilities:

$$\Omega(A) = \frac{P(A)}{P(A^c)}$$

or, equivalently, according to one particular rule of probability theory (Chapter 5),

$$\Omega(A) = \frac{P(A)}{1 - P(A)}$$

Suppose $P(\text{Pass}) = 80\%$. Then, according to that probability theory rule, $P(\text{Fail}) = 1 - P(\text{Pass}) = 20\%$. Accordingly, the odds on passing would be $\Omega(\text{Pass}) = 80\%/20\% = 4$, or 4 to 1.

Note that, while we have denoted probabilities by P, we have represented probability *judgments* by P'. We can similarly distinguish odds and odds judgments by Ω and Ω', respectively. If a person's probability and odds judgments satisfied the same probability theory rule referred to above, we would observe the following:

$$\Omega'(A) = \frac{P'(A)}{P'(A^c)} = \frac{P'(A)}{1 - P'(A)}$$

Of course, the relationship between probability and odds judgments can be turned around:

$$P'(A) = \frac{\Omega'(A)}{1 + \Omega'(A)}$$

For instance, for the local City Council election, the experts said that Ω'(Conservatives win) = 10. This should imply that P'(Conservatives win) = 10/11 = 0.91, approximately.

Probability judgments for quantities

"Copper Star Productions" is managing an upcoming music festival. An important issue is how many people will actually attend the event. Anticipating the crowd size is significant because Copper Star must make contracts for various services. If they employ only a few food vendors and the crowd is large, patrons might become upset, even unruly. Besides, such a situation would represent a lost opportunity for a substantial profit. On the other hand, if Copper Star hires hordes of vendors but only a small audience materializes, they will "lose their shirts" paying the vendors and getting stuck with spoiled food.

"Jerry Reed" and "Steve Houston" are Copper Star's co-owners. Each has his own opinions about what the crowd size C will be. They both recognize that C could take on any number of values; C is a **random variable**. Nevertheless, they certainly do not think that all crowd sizes are equally likely. Instead, each believes that C has a good chance of being in some ranges, but not in others. Their opinions about potential crowd sizes can be represented as **judged probability distributions**.

Figure 2.2a is a graphical depiction of Jerry Reed's judged probability distribution for the festival audience; Figure 2.2b shows Steve Houston's distribution. We thus see that the opinions of Copper Star's owners are very different. Mr. Reed's distribution indicates that he expects the crowd to be small, whereas Mr. Houston's distribution implies the opposite view. However, each distribution recognizes the *possibility* of both large and small crowds.

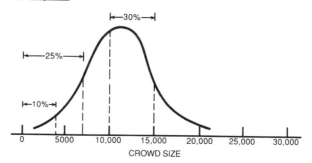

FIGURE 2.2. Judged probability distributions for the size of a music festival crowd size: (a) Jerry Reed's, (b) Steve Houston's.

The essential information in each distribution is the probability that C falls between any two points, which is the area under the curve between those points. Suppose we specify two potential crowd sizes, say 10,000 and 15,000 people. We then ask one of the Copper Star owners to state $P'(10{,}000 \leq C \leq 15{,}000)$. If we asked Jerry Reed, he should report $P'(10{,}000 \leq C \leq 15{,}000) = 30\%$. However, Steve Houston ought to say $P'(10{,}000 \leq C \leq 15{,}000) = 18\%$. The interval [10,000, 15,000], along with the judged probability that C is contained in that range, is called a **credible interval.** For Jerry Reed, [10,000, 15,000] is a 30% credible interval. It is an 18% credible interval for Mr. Houston. Standard methods for discovering people's opinions about the chances of quantities assuming various values are requests for statements about credible intervals.

The fractile method A **fractile** is a point in a probability distribution below which a specified proportion of the distribution exists. For example, the 0.10 fractile (also called the 10th percentile) of the distribution has the following interpretation: The person believes there is a 10% chance that the actual value of the quantity is equal to or less than that amount. Equivalently, the person feels that there is a 90% chance that the actual value will be *greater* than that amount. To be concrete, suppose a banker says that 12.3 percentage points is the 10th percentile of her judged probability distribution for the local home mortgage interest rate six months from now. This means that she thinks there is a 10% chance that the actual rate will be 12.3 points or lower. If R is the actual mortgage rate in six months, then the banker's judgment can be characterized as $P'(R \leq 12.3 \text{ points}) = 0.10$.

In the **fractile method** for eliciting a judged probability distribution, the person is asked to report fractiles spanning almost the entire distribution. To obtain the 10th percentile of Jerry Reed's judged probability distribution for the music festival audience, we might ask something like the following. "Mr. Reed, please give me a crowd size figure that has this property: In your mind you are 90% sure that the *actual* number of people attending your event will be more than that figure." If his report is faithful to the distribution shown in Figure 2.2a, he should respond, "Oh…, I'd say about 4000 folks." A typical application of the fractile method might require the person to describe, say, the 0.01, 0.25, 0.50, 0.75, and 0.99 fractiles.

The cumulative probability method   In each stage of the fractile method, we would specify to Jerry Reed a certain probability p. We would then ask him to report to us the crowd size c_p, such that he feels the probability is p that no more than that many people will show up at the music festival; that is, $p = P'(C \leq c_p)$, where C is the actual crowd size. Probability p is known as a **cumulative probability**, since it represents the cumulative probability that the pertinent quantity will assume any of the values at or below the stated point, the p fractile. Instead of asking for crowd sizes corresponding to specific cumulative probabilities, we could reverse the procedure. We would present Mr. Reed with various numbers of people. We would then ask for his probability judgment that the actual audience size will be no greater than each of those numbers.

Imagine that we apply this **cumulative probability method** with Steve Houston. At one point in the procedure we ask, "What's the probability that the festival will attract no more than 20,000 people, Mr. Houston?" True to his judged probability distribution shown in Figure 2.2b, he says, "About 45%, I'd guess." In response to the question, "What's the probability that the festival will have no more than 25,000 patrons?" he responds, "Mmm…, I'd say somewhere around 70%." These two cumulative probability judgments could be written briefly as

$$P'(C \leq 20,000) = 0.45$$

and

$$P'(C \leq 25,000) = 0.70$$

respectively. In both the fractile and cumulative probability methods, we end up with what ought to be equivalent results. For various possible values q, the person indicates the judged probability that the actual value of the quantity Q will be that amount or less, that is, $P'(Q \leq q)$.

INFERENCE METHODS

Inferences from choices

George is on his way home from work at 9:45 one night. Only then does he remember that his kids need milk for tomorrow's breakfast. ("Rats!") He is midway between the only two markets in the area, Quikstop and Zippy. He knows that one of the stores closes at 9:30, the other at 10. And, as luck would have it, he cannot remember which store closes when. If he heads off to the store that closes at 10, everything will be fine. But if he goes to the store that is already closed, tomorrow's breakfast will be a dismal affair; there will not be enough time left to make it to the store with the 10 P.M. closing time.

Figure 2.3 illustrates the alternatives as **tree diagrams**. We see that the significant potential consequences of the alternatives are identical, "Milk" and "No Milk." So George has only one basis for choice, the relative chances of the stores being open until 10. If George thinks Quickstop is more likely to have the 10 P.M. closing time, he will go to Quickstop. He makes the opposite choice if he thinks Zippy is more likely to be open until 10. If, in his mind, the stores are equally likely to be open late, he will be indifferent between the alternatives. So we can infer George's likelihood judgments from his choice behavior: If he goes to Quickstop without hesitation, we conclude that

$$(\text{Quickstop open until } 10) >_L (\text{Zippy open until } 10)$$

A trip to Zippy would indicate that

$$(\text{Zippy open until } 10) >_L (\text{Quickstop open until } 10)$$

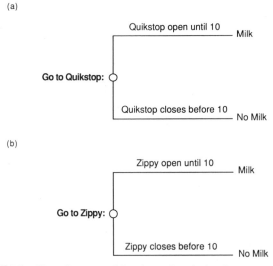

FIGURE 2.3.   Tree diagrams of the alternatives facing George, going to Quikstop versus going to Zippy.

Suppose George cannot make a firm choice, and thus tosses a coin to decide which store to try. We then infer that

$$(\text{Quickstop open until } 10) =_L (\text{Zippy open until } 10)$$

The case of George and his milk decision demonstrates the method of inferring likelihood judgments from choices. In this technique, the person is faced with a special pair of **prospects**, which is the term for alternatives in which the outcomes are uncertain. These prospects are special in two ways. First, each involves the same two potential outcomes, one of which is preferred over the other, for example, milk versus no milk. Second, in one of the prospects, the preferred outcome is contingent on one of the focal events; the less-preferred outcome results from the complement of that event. For instance, in the Zippy option, George's kids would have milk for breakfast if Zippy were open; otherwise, they would not. The other special prospect has a similar structure, except that the outcomes depend on the second focal event and its complement, for example, whether Quikstop is either open or closed. Since the only possible significant difference between the options is the relative likelihood of the focal events, that is the sole potential basis for choice.

Inferences from indifferences

Suppose George's milk crisis were not real, but instead occurred in a dream. We can then imagine a more interesting situation arising. We pick up the dream at a point where George has chosen to go to Quikstop. All of a sudden—Poof!—a strange milkman appears on the scene! The following bizarre conversation ensues:

MILKMAN: I see you need some milk. May I offer my services?

GEORGE: Uh, …, sure. I'm glad you came along. But what are you doing out selling milk on the street, at this time of night, no less?

MILKMAN: Well, I'm not really an ordinary milkman. Why don't we get on with it, OK? And don't worry about time: I'll make it stand still. I have here a big urn. As you can see, I also have some stacks of poker chips. There are 300 red chips and 700 white chips. I'll put them into the urn and let you pick one chip at random. If you draw a red chip, I'll let you buy a gallon of milk from me, even though you'll have to walk the same distance as from here to Quikstop to do so. Understand? [This lottery is shown in Figure 2.4a.]

GEORGE: It's weird, but it seems clear enough.

MILKMAN: Now, which would you rather do, play this lottery or go to Quikstop?

GEORGE: I think I'd better go to Quikstop. See ya!

MILKMAN: No! Wait, hold your horses! Let me change things a bit. Suppose I put 700 red chips and 300 white chips in the urn. [This lottery is depicted in Figure 2.4b.] *Now* which would you prefer? Would

(a)

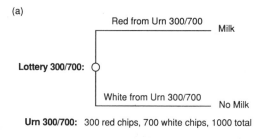

Red from Urn 300/700 —— Milk

Lottery 300/700: ○

White from Urn 300/700 —— No Milk

Urn 300/700: 300 red chips, 700 white chips, 1000 total

(b)

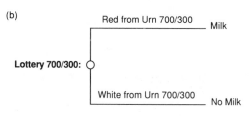

Red from Urn 700/300 —— Milk

Lottery 700/300: ○

White from Urn 700/300 —— No Milk

Urn 700/300: 700 red chips, 300 white chips, 1000 total

(c)

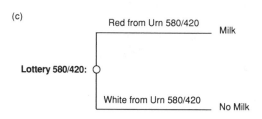

Red from Urn 580/420 —— Milk

Lottery 580/420: ○

White from Urn 580/420 —— No Milk

Urn 580/420: 580 red chips, 420 white chips, 1000 total

Figure 2.4. Some lotteries presented to George by the mystical milkman.

	you rather play the lottery, or would you still rther go to Quikstop?
GEORGE:	Hey, that's a pretty good deal! I'll play the lottery! Let's do it.
MILKMAN:	Not so fast! Let me have you consider some other lotteries.

    The milkman offers George a series of lotteries in which the proportion of red chips in the urn generally ascends from 30%, as in the first lottery, and descends from 70%, as in the second. In each case, George either strongly rejects or accepts the lottery. Finally, however, the conversation gets to this point:

MILKMAN:	How about this one? This time the urn will have 580 red chips and 420 white ones. [This lottery is illustrated in Figure 2.4c.] What's your pleasure?

GEORGE: Actually, you know, I don't feel strongly one way or the other. I'm indifferent.

MILKMAN: Great! Why don't you toss a coin to decide if you'll play this lottery or go on your way to Quikstop?

And the dream ends.

What can we conclude from George's conversation with the mystical milkman? George was indifferent between the prospect shown in Figure 2.3a and the lottery represented in Figure 2.4c. According to the reasoning of the previous method, George must feel it is just as likely that Quikstop is open until 10 P.M. as that a red chip would be drawn from the urn in the lottery. George—and most other people, too—considers the probability of drawing a red chip from the urn to be 58% = 580/1000. So we conclude that, for George,

$$P'(\text{Quickstop open until 10}) = 0.58$$

A **canonical event** is one for which there is a general consensus about its probability. Selecting a red chip at random from an urn of known composition is an example of a canonical event. Everyone would agree that the probability of selecting a red chip would be the proportion of red chips in the urn. The mystical milkman led George through an application of the method of inferring judgments from indifferences. In this technique, a prospect is constructed in which a preferred outcome depends on the event in question. The person expresses indifference between this prospect and a similarly structured one in which the preferred outcome depends on a canonical event, for example, a red chip being picked from an urn, getting a head on a coin toss, drawing an ace from a deck of cards. We infer that the person's probability judgment for the focal event must be the same as the canonical event probability.

There are other procedures for inferring people's likelihood judgments from their decisions. Several of these techniques rely on the person making decisions according to a certain type of decision principle. One example appears in Chapter 8 (pp. 232–35).

CONSIDERATIONS IN SELECTING ASSESSMENT PROCEDURES

We have reviewed several ways a person's opinion about an event's chances of occurrence might be assessed. On what bases should we decide which to use in a given situation? Wallsten and Budescu (1983) discuss various ways of evaluating assessment procedures. Here we examine some of the most important.

Value-induced biases

"Don't bring me no bad news!" sang the Wicked Witch of the West in the Broadway musical, "The Wiz." If the Wicked Witch's messengers express their opinions in terms of likelihood judgments, we should expect those reports to be **biased**, to deviate systematically from the messengers' actual opinions. Similar biases might affect real people's indicated likelihood judgments.

Radiologists are physicians who make diagnoses on the basis of X-rays and other body images. Wallsten (1981) analyzed radiologists' probability judgments that patients' lesions were malignant, that is, cancerous, rather than resulting from less serious conditions. Those probability judgments were substantially higher than they should have been. Wallsten interprets these results as evidence of a **value-induced bias**. That is, the radiologists might have biased their true opinions of cancer upward, because of the importance of diagnosing cancer. The reason for this bias may be that, if a patient really does have cancer, that condition should be treated. If a radiologist reports a high probability that a tumor is malignant, then an attending physician is more likely to treat for cancer than if a low probability is indicated.

It does not seem that the likelihood judgment assessment procedures discussed in this chapter should differ from one another in their susceptibility to value-induced biases, although the issue has not been studied thoroughly. However, there exist other techniques, called *proper scoring rules*, that are expressly intended to reduce such effects as value-induced biases. These methods are discussed briefly in Chapter 8 (pp. 232–35).

Usefulness in decision making

"Keith and Sally Collins" own a citrus farm. The weather is expected to turn very cold tomorrow night, possibly below freezing. The Collinses could simply ignore the threat. Or they could take precautions, for example, by placing smudge pots throughout the orchards in preparation for heating their trees in the event of a freeze. It would cost $1000 to hire emergency workers to put in place and eventually remove the smudge pots from the orchards. If the temperature does fall below freezing, it will cost an additional $4000 to fuel the burners the whole night. On the other hand, if their trees are caught in a freeze unprotected, the Collinses figure that they stand to lose $15,000.

The situation facing the Collinses is summarized in the **payoff matrix** shown in Table 2.1. The rows of the matrix describe the alternatives available to the Collinses, either act to protect their trees or do nothing. The columns are defined by the pertinent events, freezing and nonfreezing temperatures. The cells of the matrix indicate the amounts of money the Collinses stand to lose, depending on their choice and the actual temperature.

Sally Collins phones the local radio station to request a forecast. Suppose the forecaster says, "Yes, it *is* quite possible we'll have a freeze tomorrow night, Mrs. Collins." Now, should the Collinses put the smudge pots in their orchards or not? It is not obvious what the appropriate action is, given that the forecaster expressed his opinion in words. Even if the forecaster had said something like, "On our standard freeze warning scale, the chance of a

TABLE 2.1 Payoff Matrix (Costs) for Citrus Farmers
Keith and Sally Collins

	TEMPERATURE	
ACTION	FREEZING	NOT FREEZING
Protect trees	$5000	$1000
Do nothing	$15,000	$0

freeze is rated 'moderate,'" it would still be unclear what the Collinses should do.

Consider one particular approach to the Collinses's decision problem, an approach we examine in more detail in Chapters 8 and 9. A preview is sufficient for the moment. The **expected value (EV)** of a prospect is the sum of the values, for example, costs, of the potential outcomes, each weighted by its probability. Suppose the probability of a freeze is denoted by p, and the probability of no freeze by $1 - p$. Then the expected value of the Collinses protecting their trees can be written as

$$EV(\text{Protect}) = p(\$5000) + (1 - p)(\$1000)$$

$$= \$4000p + \$1000$$

Similarly, the EV of doing nothing can be shown to be

$$EV(\text{Do nothing}) = \$15,000p$$

The **expected value choice principle** says that a decision maker should always select the available alternative that has the best expected value. As we will see in Chapter 8, one rationale for this principle is that it sometimes promises that the decision maker will be better off "in the long run." The Collinses want to minimize their costs. Thus, in the present case, the Collinses should prepare to protect their orchards only if

$$EV(\text{Protect}) \leq EV \text{ (Do nothing)}$$

If you work through the algebra, you will see that this is equivalent to saying that the trees should be protected if p, the probability of a freeze, is such that

$$p \geq p_t = \tfrac{1}{11} \approx 9.1\%$$

Critical values like p_t are sometimes called **threshold probabilities**, since they define boundaries, or thresholds, between probabilities which imply that different actions ought to be taken.

Obviously, for the Collinses to apply the expected value choice principle, they need a freeze forecast in probability form. If the local weather service announces a freeze probability judgment of at least 9.1%, the Collinses will prepare for a freeze. If that judgment is lower, they will not. Because they permit people to apply decision rules like the expected value choice principle, precise likelihood assessments, including probability and odds judgments, are especially attractive.

Communication clarity

Bryant and Norman (1980) assembled 30 verbal expressions of likelihood. Those expressions are commonly found in the medical reports physicians use to communicate among themselves about their patients. Bryant and Norman asked physicians to indicate how they would interpret each of the expressions in terms of probability judgments for the presence of disease. Suppose a physician in the study read a report in which a radiologist said something like, "On the basis of my examination of the X-ray, there is a *significant chance* that Patient X has Disease D." The physician was supposed to indicate what the radiologist felt was the probability the patient had Disease D when he or she wrote "significant chance."

Figure 2.5 displays the means and standard deviations for the physicians' responses to several of the expressions presented by Bryant and Norman.[1] The remarkable thing about the standard deviation bands around the means for the expressions represented in the figure is that they all include 0.5. For example, the band for "significant chance" extends from about 35% to approximately 77%. This implies that many of the physicians interpreted "significant chance" to mean that the patient was more likely to have the

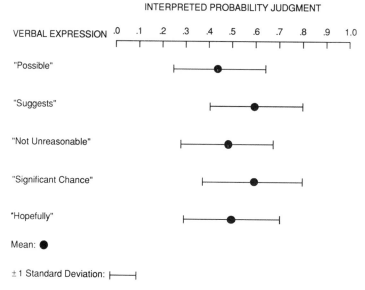

Figure 2.5.   Means and standard deviations of probability judgments physicians believed to correspond to verbal expressions of uncertainty commonly used in medicine. Adapted from information appearing in *The New England Journal of Medicine*, Volume 302, 1980, page 411, "Expressions of probability: Words and numbers," by G. D. Bryant and G. R. Norman, with permission from the publisher.

[1]For variables distributed according to a normal, bell-shaped curve, 68% of all cases fall between one standard deviation below the mean and one standard deviation above the mean.

disease than to not have it. On the other hand, another large number of respondents interpreted the expression to have the opposite meaning.

The Bryant and Norman study, as well as numerous others (for example, Beyth-Marom, 1982; Kong and others, 1986), highlights what most see as a serious deficiency of verbal reports of likelihood opinion—their lack of clarity in communication. Quantitative expressions, for instance, probability judgments, are thought to be much less susceptible to multiple interpretations.

Indication of full, true opinion

What really *is* a person's true opinion about what is going to happen? Some maintain that an opinion is purely something in the individual's head. Since as far back as the time of the philosopher Ramsey (1931), others have argued that the most important opinions are those that manifest themselves in the person's decisions. From this latter perspective, the best techniques for assessing likelihood opinions are inference methods. If we are indeed interested in opinions in terms of their roles in decision making, then inference methods do seem advantageous. But consider the following.

Figure 2.6a shows Urn 1, which contains 100 balls, 50 of them red and 50 of them white. As suggested, Lottery Red 1 is such that the player wins $100 if a red ball is drawn at random from Urn 1; otherwise, the player wins

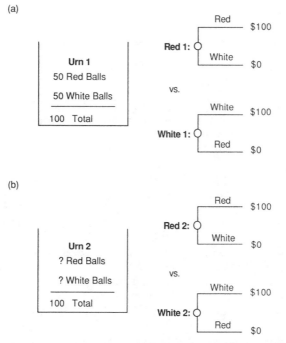

FIGURE 2.6. Lotteries contrasting (a) unambiguous and (b) ambiguous uncertainty.

nothing. Lottery White 1 is similar, except that the $100 prize is contingent upon drawing a white ball from Urn 1. Lotteries Red 2 and White 2 in Figure 2.6b are identical to Lotteries Red 1 and White 1, except that balls are to be drawn from Urn 2. That urn also contains 100 red and/or white balls. However, the numbers of balls of each color are unspecified.

Most people are indifferent between Lotteries Red 1 and White 1 and between Lotteries Red 2 and White 2. According to the method of inferring judgments from choices, we would conclude that, for these people,

$$\text{(Red from Urn 1)} =_L \text{(White from Urn 1)}$$

and

$$\text{(Red from Urn 2)} =_L \text{(White from Urn 2)}$$

Translated into probability judgments, we might expect

$$P'(\text{Red from Urn 1}) = P'(\text{White from Urn 1}) = 0.50$$

and

$$P'(\text{Red from Urn 2}) = P'(\text{White from Urn 2}) = 0.50$$

But now, suppose a person (for example, yourself) is offered a choice between Lotteries Red 1 and Red 2. Most choose Lottery Red 1. (Did you?) By the above reasoning, we infer

$$\text{(Red from Urn 1)} >_L \text{(Red from Urn 2)}$$

Since the event "White from Urn 1" is the complement of "Red from Urn 1," and "White from Urn 2" is the complement of "Red from Urn 2," we also conclude that

$$\text{(White from Urn 2)} >_L \text{(White from Urn 1)}$$

Nevertheless, when asked to choose between Lotteries White 1 and White 2, most people prefer Lottery White 1, contradicting the previous inference.

Ellsberg (1961) brought attention to the lotteries and typical choice patterns described above.[2] As he noted, those choices imply likelihood judgments that do not qualify as even qualitative, that is, ordinal probabilities. Thus, what should be equivalent applications of the choice inference method do not yield the same orderings of event likelihoods. Ellsberg argued that the source of the difficulty is the difference in the types of uncertainty involved in drawing balls from Urns 1 and 2. In Urn 1, the uncertainty is clear-cut. In contrast, in Urn 2, the uncertainty is vague or **ambiguous**. Many practical situations differ in the ambiguity they contain, too. Imagine a certain surgical procedure, which has been performed in thousands of previous operations. Forty percent of the time, the procedure has succeeded. A new technique has never been tried, but expert surgeons expect the same

---

[2]The patterns are sometimes called instances of the **Ellsberg Paradox.**

success rate. Clearly, there is more ambiguity associated with this second procedure than the first.

Some decision theorists contend that ambiguity differences should be ignored. However, other observers suggest that it would be useful to accompany all reports of likelihood opinions by indications of the ambiguity perceived to be contained in the relevant situations. For example, Diamond and Forrester (1983) recommend two-part probability judgments, such as those illustrated in the cartoon in Figure 2.7. Some people see verbal rather than quantitative expressions of opinion as attractive because they seem to allow for the communication of ambiguity in the events being considered.

SUMMARY

Likelihood judgments are opinions about the chances of various events occurring. These opinions guide many of our decisions. Accurate assessment of likelihood judgments is essential if we wish to understand the nature of judgment processes. It is important on practical grounds because often our decisions are predicated on the likelihood judgments of experts. We can take full advantage of their expertise only if we can discover their true opinions.

There are two basic strategies for assessing likelihood judgments, the statement approach and the inference approach. In statement methods, the person makes an explicit pronouncement of his or her degree of certainty in an event's occurrence. In inference procedures for assessing likelihood judgments, an individual's opinions about the chances of events occurring are inferred from decisions in specially structured situations.

Several considerations should be taken into account in choosing a method of assessing likelihood judgments. Among these considerations are susceptibility to biases, usefulness in decision making, communication clarity, and the indication of full, true opinion.

Figure 2.7. Cartoon illustrating two-part probability judgments. Reprinted with permission from the NAS, Inc.

KEY TERMS

Ambiguous uncertainty
Canonical event
Complement
Credible interval
Cumulative probability
Ellsberg Paradox
Expected value
Expected value choice principle
Fractile
Fractile method
Inference methods
Likelihood judgment
Likelihood ranking
Likelihood rating

Likelihood statement
Odds
Odds judgment
Payoff matrix
Probability distribution
Probability judgment
Prospect
Qualitative judgment
Random variable
Threshold probability
Tree diagram
Value-induced bias
Verbal report

ADDITIONAL READING

Chesley (1978); Samson and Thomas (1986); Schaefer and Borcherding (1973); Seaver, von Winterfeldt, and Edwards (1978); Selvidge (1980); Swets and others (1986); Wallsten and others (1986); Winkler (1972, Chapter 2).

EXERCISES AND STUDY QUESTIONS

1. In this chapter, we saw that in its ads, Sudden Service Transmissions was willing to offer a 90-day, money-back, free-replacement guarantee on its mufflers. The ads for Jiffy Transmissions do not promise such a guarantee. Should we therefore conclude that Sudden Service is more certain that its transmissions will last 90 days than is Jiffy?

2. Quantitative likelihood judgments seem to offer much more information than qualitative likelihood judgments. So one naturally wonders why the latter would be used rather than the former. Offer one or more arguments in favor of qualitative judgments.

3. On Tuesday, Dan said that he thought the Yankees have a 25% chance of winning the American League pennant. He also said that the Blue Jays have a 15% chance of being league champions. On Wednesday, Dan was asked outright which team he felt had the better chance of winning the pennant, the Yankees or the Blue Jays. He picked the Blue Jays. Can you think of any plausible reason for the apparent inconsistency in Dan's judgments? Design a study that would test your hypothesis.

4. According to a prominent foreign affairs expert, the odds are 0.25 that the prime minister of Outer Inland will be replaced by his party. What does this mean in terms of probability?

5. Use the fractile method to elicit a friend's judged probability distribution for the daily rate for a private room at a local hospital. Request the following fractiles: $q_{0.10}, q_{0.25}, q_{0.50}, q_{0.75}, q_{0.90}$, where $q_{0.10}$ for instance, denotes the 0.10 fractile

or 10th percentile. Apply the cumulative probability method to assess the same judged distribution. Intuitively, would you expect the results from the two methods to be equivalent? Are your results in fact consistent with each other?

6. Some see value-induced biases in physicians' judgments as a good thing. After all, they seem to assure that the patient will be treated for serious illnesses, if there is even the slightest chance that those illnesses are present. However, there are drawbacks to such biases, too. Describe one or more of them.

7. Bruce is an active member of the State University Booster Club. State is playing North University on Saturday. You want to know Bruce's actual opinion about State's chances. To find out, you first construct Gamble 1, which is such that Bruce wins $10 if State wins, and nothing if State loses. You then find that Bruce is indifferent between Gamble 1 and Gamble 2, which promises $10 if a red poker chip is drawn at random from an urn containing 650 red and 350 white chips, and nothing otherwise. You therefore conclude that, for Bruce, P'(State wins) = 65%. There is reason to suspect that your inference is in error. In what way, and why?

8. According to statistics reported by Lichtenstein and others (1978), the yearly death rate from tornadoes in the United States is about 0.000044, that is, 44 per million. The rate for deaths from appendicitis is 0.00044. You belong to the "Appendicitis Society," which promotes appendicitis prevention. You are considering two different ways of reporting the seriousness of appendicitis. First, you could announce, "This year 44 in every 100,000 Americans will die of appendicitis." Or, you might report, "The death rate from appendicitis is 10 times that from tornadoes."

   (a) Which report do you present, and why?

   (b) What does this example suggest about how people think about uncertainty?

9. (a) Construct tree diagrams representing the alternative actions available to the Collinses in the situation described on pages 28–29.

   (b) What are the expected values (that is, costs) of the alternatives, assuming that the probability of a freeze is 25%?

   (c) Compute the expected values of the options when the probability of a freeze is 5%.

   (d) Sally Collins calls two local weather forecasters. The first says that the probability of a freeze is 25%. The other says the chance of a freeze is only 5%. What should she do?

10. "John Cook" is the city manager for the town of "Southern Meadow." Two ambulance companies, "Fuller Ambulance Co." and "Sumpter Transport, Inc.," have applied for the contract to provide emergency medical services for the town. The charges proposed by the firms are essentially the same. So Mr. Cook concluded that the *sole* basis for choice should be the promptness of each company's response to emergencies. The companies agreed to an experiment conducted by Mr. Cook. On randomly selected occasions, Mr. Cook made test calls to the firms and recorded the time it took them to arrive at the scenes of simulated emergencies. Care was taken to be sure that each firm had to respond to emergencies under virtually identical conditions, for

example, time of day and distance. To simplify his analysis, Mr. Cook grouped together arrival times that were approximately the same. He found that 25% of Fuller's arrival times were about 12 minutes, while the remaining 75% of those times were in the neighborhood of 8 minutes. In contrast, 30% of Sumpter's arrival times were about 15 minutes, 50% were 9 minutes, and 20% were approximately 3 minutes.

(a) Construct tree diagrams of the alternatives between which Mr. Cook must choose.

(b) What are the expected values of the arrival times for the competing companies?

(c) On the basis of your answer to part (b), what decision should Mr. Cook make, and why?

(d) Can you think of any rational reason for objecting to the decision indicated in part (c)? Explain. (*Note:* You cannot contest Mr. Cook's desire that the sole basis for choice should be arrival time.)

3

Analysis

If all errors were clearly stated, they would perish by themselves.

—Vauvenargues

"Stuart Prentice" is seriously ill. There are two treatments for his illness. The one that is generally more effective is surgical. The other requires that he take heavy doses of medication. As with many such procedures, the surgical treatment involves some risk of perioperative death. That is, the patient could "die on the table" during the operation. The severity of the risk depends on the patient's condition. "Dr. Robinson" says that, in Mr. Prentice's case, the risk of perioperative death is "negligible." On the other hand, "Dr. Jefferson" feels that the risk is "substantial." Whom should Mr. Prentice believe? Suppose that Dr. Robinson's judgments about such matters are usually more accurate than Dr. Jefferson's. Then this is one reason Mr. Prentice should base his treatment decision on Dr. Robinson's opinion instead of Dr. Jefferson's. But exactly what does the term "accurate" mean as it applies to likelihood judgments, and how can we measure such accuracy? These questions are the subject of the present chapter.

We saw in Chapter 2 that people's judgments sometimes concern discrete events, for example, "survive surgery" versus "die in surgery." Other judgments are about quantities, for instance, how long we might be disabled during rehabilitation from surgery. The first section of this chapter discusses how to measure the overall accuracy of likelihood judgments for events, for example, how to determine whether Dr. Robinson's judgments about surgical outcomes indeed are usually more accurate than Dr. Jefferson's. As it turns out, accuracy is not a simple concept; there are several different ways a person's judgments can be accurate or inaccurate. The second section describes what various accuracy components are and how they can be characterized. The third section is devoted to the problem of measuring the accuracy of judgments about quantities. This chapter is mainly methodological. However, the techniques we examine also force us to make important conceptual distinctions that might otherwise go unnoticed.

OVERALL ACCURACY OF EVENT JUDGMENTS

We previously learned that verbal statements of likelihood, such as "negligible" and "substantial," are problematic because different people interpret them in different ways. Mr. Prentice's dilemma illustrates another difficulty: It is not obvious how to evaluate the accuracy of opinions expressed in words. In contrast, there are several well-established ways of measuring the accuracy of probability judgments. Here we focus on one such measure, which applies to judgments about events. (In a later section, we consider judgments concerning quantities.) Properly applied and interpreted, measures like these could assist Stuart Prentice in deciding whether he should accept the opinion of Dr. Robinson or that of Dr. Jefferson.

The probability score

Picture yourself as a counselor at a certain college. You try to give students good advice about how well they would do in various courses, considering such factors as their aptitudes and previous course work. But you are unsure how good your predictions really are. As a first step in your plan to find out, you decide to make your predictions explicit, as probability judgments of the form $P'(A)$, where the target event A is "Will earn a grade of B or better." That is, for every course taken by each of your counselees, you record your probability judgment that the student will earn a grade of at least a B. Now how can you quantify the accuracy of your assessments? Here is where our fantasy becomes outlandish but instructive: Imagine that you have a friend in the counseling office named Merlin. Unlike yourself, Merlin is blessed with the gift of clairvoyance. You ask Merlin to make probability judgments for the same cases you do. Suppose that you can measure how close your judgments are to Merlin's. Since Merlin is clairvoyant, his judgments are perfectly accurate. Thus, the closeness of your judgments to Merlin's is also a measure of how accurate your judgments happen to be.

Real clairvoyants like Merlin do not exist. However, the approach suggested above is essentially the one implicit in the measure of probability judgment accuracy that is most commonly used, the probability score. (Two other measures are described in Problem 2 of the *Exercises and Study Questions*.) So let us continue:

(a) Consider an occasion when the target event A may or may not occur. We can abbreviate your probability judgment as $f = P'(A)$; for example, $f = 0.65$ when you think there is a 65% probability that "Mary Smith" will earn a grade of B or better in Chemistry 100.

(b) Since Merlin is a clairvoyant, he reports either of only two different probability judgments, 1 and 0; the former when the target event A is going to happen, the latter when it is not. The convention is to call the clairvoyant's judgment the **outcome index** d, where

$$d = 1, \quad \text{if event } A \text{ occurs}$$

$$= 0, \quad \text{if event } A \text{ does not occur}$$

Thus, if Mary Smith indeed is destined to earn a B or better in her chemistry course, Merlin reports $d = 1$. If otherwise, he indicates $d = 0$.

(c) Our measure of closeness between your judgment and Merlin's is the **probability score (PS)**, also known as the **quadratic score** and the **Brier (1950) score**:

$$PS(f, d) = (f - d)^2 \tag{3.1}$$

So, if Mary Smith is going to do well in chemistry, the probability score for your 65% probabilistic prediction is

$$PS(f, d) = (0.65 - 1)^2 = (-0.35)^2 = 0.1225$$

If not, your judgment earns a score of

$$PS(f, d) = (0.65 - 0)^2 = (-0.65)^2 = 0.4225$$

The previous example suggests how specific values of PS can be interpreted. Since PS is the squared difference between your judgments and those of the clairvoyant, the smaller PS is, the better. Table 3.1 illustrates more completely how PS reflects probability judgment accuracy. The first column in the table lists various probability judgments you might report, going all the way from 100% certainty that a student will earn a grade of B or better down to 0%, that is, absolute certainty that the student will *not* achieve such a grade. The second column shows the resulting probability scores when the target event does in fact occur, that is, when Merlin the clairvoyant says that the student will get a B or better. The third column lists the scores when lower grades are earned. We thus see that probability scores are bounded by 0 and 1:

$$0 \qquad\qquad \leq PS \leq \qquad\qquad 1$$

(perfect accuracy)   (counterperfect accuracy)

with lower scores denoting better accuracy. The lower extreme indicates perfect accuracy, the same as the clairvoyant's. The largest possible value is associated with counterperfect accuracy. This score would be achieved by a diabolical clairvoyant who, unlike a benevolent clairvoyant such as your friend Merlin, always reports probability 100% for the target event when it is not going to occur and 0% when it is.

Since there are no real clairvoyants like Merlin, how can PS have any practical value as an accuracy measure? Suppose we are content with measuring accuracy *after* the event of interest does or does not occur instead of before. Then the probability score is quite sufficient. After the fact, we

TABLE 3.1 Potential Probability Scores, Given Your Judgment (f) and the Clairvoyant's Judgment (d), That Is, Whether the Target Event A = "B or Better" Ultimately Occurs

$f = P'(A)$	PROBABILITY SCORE (PS)	
	$d = 1$: A OCCURS	$d = 0$: A DOES NOT OCCUR
1.0	0.00	1.00
0.9	0.01	0.81
0.8	0.04	0.64
0.7	0.09	0.49
0.6	0.16	0.36
0.5	0.25	0.25
0.4	0.36	0.16
0.3	0.49	0.09
0.2	0.64	0.04
0.1	0.81	0.01
0.0	1.00	0.00

know what the clairvoyant *would* have said and can proceed to calculate *PS* as indicated. Take the case of Mary Smith. Suppose you wait until the term is over and find that Mary got a C in Chemistry 100. You would then know that, had Merlin really existed, he would have reported $d = 0$. And, since you had indicated $f = P'$(B or better) = 65%, the probability score for your judgment is found to be 0.4225, as we saw before.

The mean probability score

We are all cursed with inconsistency. Continuing your role as a counselor, we can easily imagine that sometimes your grade predictions are good, earning probability scores close to 0. But at other times, your judgments are far off the mark, yielding high values of *PS*. Despite this inconsistency, there is some level of accuracy that is characteristic of how good your judgment usually is. The average value of *PS* over a large number of occasions is an indication of such typical judgment quality. Table 3.2 illustrates the approach, although you should recognize that, in a more realistic situation, many more judgments would be required to permit generalizations.

You make probabilistic grade predictions for one course for each of ten counselees, that is, of the form $f = P'$(B or better). Column 2 of the table lists your predictions. After the term is over, you learn the students' actual grades, which are indicated in column 3. A benevolent clairvoyant would have made the probability judgments shown in column 4, the outcome index column. The calculations of the probability scores for judgments about the individual counselees are shown in columns 5 and 6. The row labeled "Sum" shows the sums of the values listed in the various columns. For the moment, the only sum of interest is the last one, for the *PS* column. We want the average probability score. There are several different averages for any

TABLE 3.2   Probability Score Computational Example for Ten Counselees

(1) COUNSELEE	(2) f	(3) ACTUAL GRADE	(4) d	(5) $f - d$	(6) $PS = (f - d)^2$
1	0.6	B or better	1	−0.4	0.16
2	0.3	Less than B	0	0.3	0.09
3	0.5	Less than B	0	0.5	0.25
4	0.4	B or better	1	−0.6	0.36
5	0.8	B or better	1	−0.2	0.04
6	0.6	Less than B	0	0.6	0.36
7	0.7	B or better	1	−0.3	0.09
8	0.6	B or better	1	−0.4	0.16
9	0.5	B or better	1	−0.5	0.25
10	0.2	Less than B	0	0.2	0.04
Sum	5.2	—	6	−0.8	1.80
Mean	0.52	—	0.60	−0.08	0.18
Exp'n	$\bar{f}$	—	$\bar{d}$	Bias	$\overline{PS}$

$d = 1$ when target event "B or better" actually occurs; $d = 0$ otherwise. $f = P'$ (B or better) = probability judgment for the target event.

quantity. The mean or arithmetic average is simply the sum of all the values of the quantity, divided by the number of values. Thus, the **mean probability score**, expressed as $\overline{PS}$, is just the sum of all the pertinent individual probability scores divided by the total number of judgments. So, in the present case, we find that your mean probability score was

$$\overline{PS} = \frac{1.80}{10} = 0.18$$

Interpreting probability scores: Some standards

Was your mean probability score of 0.18 a good one? Or was your judgment deficient? These questions highlight the need for standards that can be used in interpreting probability scores. If we could establish such standards, we could then answer questions about goodness comparatively, that is, relative to these standards.

Extreme standards   We have already discussed two standards. One is set by a benevolent clairvoyant (Merlin), who always earns $PS = 0$. The other is set by a diabolical clairvoyant, who says $P'(A) = 0\%$ whenever the target event A is due to occur and $P'(A) = 100\%$ when it is not, hence earning the score $PS = 1$ on every occasion. As illustrated in Figure 3.1, since $PS = 0.50$ bisects the full range of possible PS values, you might expect that this

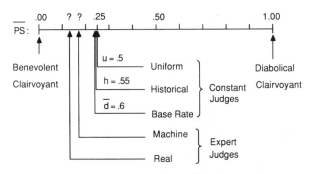

FIGURE 3.1.   Some standards for interpreting probability scores. See text for explanation.

intermediate value is another meaningful standard for $\overline{PS}$, with smaller scores being "good" and larger ones "bad." In fact, however, we have to work especially hard to earn an average probability score as high, that is, as poor, as 0.50. So $\overline{PS} = 0.5$ is not a useful standard of comparison.

Constant judges One class of fictional judges does provide important standards. These are various kinds of constant judges. A **constant judge** is an individual who, on every occasion that arises, reports the same, constant opinion. Imagine, for example, that Sherry is another counselor in your office whom you browbeat into making probabilistic grade predictions. Her heart is not in the task. So in every case she reports $P'(\text{B or better}) = 0.75$. That is, she says that there is a 75% chance that every student will earn a grade of B or better in every course. Sherry is a constant judge.

One particular constant judge has special significance. Suppose that today is Harry's first day as a counselor. Nevertheless, he too is asked to make grade predictions. Harry reasons to himself as follows:

> I don't know beans about how to predict what these students will do. So let's see what makes sense for me to do. Now, in every case, there are two possibilities. The student will either get a grade that's a B or better or he won't. Since I have no idea what might happen, I should say that both possibilities are equally likely.

Thus, on every occasion, Harry reports u= $P'(\text{B or better}) = 0.5$. Harry is assuming the role of a **uniform judge**, who behaves as if all the possible events in a given situation have the same probability. In the present discussion, since we are only concerned with cases in which a single target event A and its complement A^c are distinguished, this implies that $P'(A) = P'(A^c) = \frac{1}{2}$. You should be able to convince yourself that, for the uniform judge, over all occasions, $\overline{PS} = 0.25$, as indicated graphically in Figure 3.1. (Using Equation 3.1, what PS does the uniform judge earn if A occurs? If A^c occurs?)

What could be easier than behaving as if we knew nothing and then predicting like the uniform judge? Such a question suggests that the uniform could not be an especially useful standard. In fact, it is. As we will see, the accuracy of real people's probability judgments often falls short of that achieved by the uniform judge. Your value of $\overline{PS} = 0.18$ is distinctly better than that of the uniform judge. But let us consider some other constant judges against which you might compare yourself.

Another kind of constant judge examines previous records concerning the target event A. This individual then notes the proportion of times in the past that the target event has occurred. We symbolize such a proportion by h and call it the **historical base rate**. Then, on every occasion in the future, our **historical judge** reports $h = P'(A)$ as his or her probability judgment for the target event. For instance, suppose that Catherine looked in the archives at your college and found that 55% of all course grades were B or better, that is, h = 55%. Then when, for every course elected by her counselees, she indicates $P'(\text{B or better}) = 0.55$, she is behaving like a historical judge.

How good a mean probability score will a historical judge earn? The answer to this question is most easily understood in terms of another base rate besides the historical base rate. Refer to Table 3.2. Note that six out of your ten counselees earned grades of at least a B. Thus, in that sample of ten occasions, the target event occurred 60% of the time. This 60% is an example of a **sample base rate**, the proportion of target event occurrences in a given sample of occasions. Recall that the outcome index d takes on the value 1 when the target event happens and 0 otherwise. You should convince yourself that this implies that the base rate for a given sample is simply the mean outcome index for that sample, denoted $\bar{d}$, and as illustrated in Table 3.2.

Consider an arbitrary constant judge, such as Sherry above. Suppose we denote this person's constant judgment as c; for example, $c = P'$(B or better) = 0.75 for Sherry. We can show that the mean probability score earned by such a constant judge for a given sample of occasions is

$$\overline{PS}(c,d) = \bar{d}(1 - \bar{d}) + (c - \bar{d})^2 \qquad (3.2)$$

Thus, if Sherry had also made judgments for your counselees listed in Table 3.2, she would have earned the following score:

$$\overline{PS} = (0.6)(1 - 0.6) + (0.75 - 0.6)^2 = 0.2625$$

which is worse than the score achieved by the uniform judge, and certainly much worse than your own.

Back to the historical judge. Since the historical judge is simply a constant judge for whom $c = h$, Equation 3.2 implies that the mean probability score earned by the historical judge is

$$\overline{PS}(h,d) = \bar{d}\,(1 - \bar{d}) + (h - \bar{d})^2$$

For your fellow counselor Catherine, we thus see that if she too had made judgments for your ten counselees, her score would have been

$$\overline{PS} = (0.6)(1 - 0.6) + (0.55 - 0.6)^2 = 0.2425$$

It should be clear from Equation 3.2 that the best possible constant judge is the one who always reports the sample base rate as his or her probability judgment, that is, $c = \bar{d}$. This judge is called simply the **base rate judge**. For your ten counselees, the base rate judge would have achieved a score of

$$\overline{PS} = (0.6)(1 - 0.6) = 0.24$$

Accordingly, as illustrated in Figure 3.1, your $\overline{PS} = 0.18$ was superior to any achievable by a constant judge.

Experts Experts provide a final class of standards for interpreting probability scores. A "real" expert is a human judge who consistently performs a judgment task as well as or better than almost anyone else. You might imagine that the director of your counseling office, since she is far more experienced than all the other staff members, could make more accurate grade predictions than all of them, too. Thus, as suggested in Figure 3.1, we might expect her $\overline{PS}$ accuracy score for your sample of ten counselees to be even lower than your 0.18.

Suppose someone in your office compiled past statistics about students' grades in college courses as well as aspects of their backgrounds, for example, test scores and previous high school and college course performance. In principle, it should be possible to program a computer to use that information to make probabilistic predictions of how well students would do in future courses. Probability scores earned by such "machine" experts yield yet another reference for evaluating how good your own judgments are. Figure 3.1 suggests that real experts should be expected to outperform machine experts. However, as we will see, this does not always happen.

ASPECTS OF EVENT JUDGMENT ACCURACY

Let us return to the medical situation discussed at the beginning of the chapter. Suppose we had records of Dr. Robinson's and Dr. Jefferson's probabilistic predictions for the outcomes of many operations. If we also knew the actual outcomes of those operations, we could then compute their mean probability scores. Imagine that Dr. Jefferson earned the better mark. Then Stuart Prentice might conclude that Dr. Jefferson had superior overall ability to make accurate judgments about surgery outcomes. He should perhaps feel confident in making his own treatment decision according to Dr. Jefferson's opinion. But maybe not. An analogy illustrates a caveat.

Imagine two lawyers, "Denise Fryer" and "Ray Montana." Suppose that Ms. Fryer is a better lawyer overall than is Mr. Montana. This does not necessarily mean that Ms. Fryer is better than Mr. Montana at *all* legal procedures, however. There might be some kinds of cases for which Mr. Montana is clearly the superior legal representative, say, in liability cases. So, if your mother were being sued by a delivery man who slipped on the ice on her front porch, then surely you would recommend Ray Montana, not Denise Fryer. As with legal skill, judgmental skill is not a simple, unidimensional concept. Thus, although Dr. Jefferson's judgments are more accurate than Dr. Robinson's on the whole, there may be aspects of accuracy at which Dr. Robinson is distinctly better. And, for Mr. Prentice's purposes, those aspects could be more important than overall accuracy. In this section we discuss several dimensions of probability judgment accuracy that are particularly important to acknowledge. These elements of judgment ability are most readily appreciated in two different kinds of graphical displays. Our discussion is organized around the points of view provided by these displays.

The calibration graph perspective

To illustrate the ideas, we continue with the counseling problem of anticipating student course performance. Let us say that you convince four of your fellow counselors, Lynn, Terry, Stephanie, and Herman, to try making grade predictions as probability judgments. As an exercise, you provide your friends with all the information they desire about 25 different cases. In each instance, the task is to make a probability judgment of the form $f = P'$(B or better) that the given student will earn a grade of B or better in a specified course. After the term is over, you have all the students' actual grades and then compile the results shown in Table 3.3.

Calibration graph construction In the present approach to analyzing probability judgment accuracy, the first task is to construct **calibration graphs**. [1] Such displays are suitable when the judgments are limited or rounded to a relatively small number of categories, as in the present illustra-

TABLE 3.3 Counselors' Probabilistic Grade Predictions and Actual Grades for 25 Counselees

COUNSELEE	LYNN	TERRY	STEPHANIE	HERMAN	ACTUAL GRADE	OUTCOME INDEX (d)
		COUNSELOR'S PREDICTION (f)				
1	0.6	0.5	0.4	0.8	B or better	1
2	0.4	0.7	0.7	0.3	Less than B	0
3	0.3	0.6	0.2	0.7	B or better	1
4	0.4	0.4	0.4	0.9	B or better	1
5	0.6	0.5	0.6	0.8	Less than B	0
6	0.7	0.5	0.9	0.8	B or better	1
7	0.7	0.7	0.5	0.1	Less than B	0
8	0.7	0.7	0.3	0.3	B or better	1
9	0.3	0.4	0.7	0.7	Less than B	0
10	0.5	0.5	0.6	0.8	B or better	1
11	0.8	0.6	0.4	0.3	Less than B	0
12	0.6	0.6	0.5	0.0	Less than B	0
13	0.3	0.4	0.2	0.8	B or better	1
14	0.6	0.6	0.3	0.7	B or better	1
15	0.7	0.5	0.6	0.3	Less than B	0
16	0.1	0.7	0.3	0.9	B or better	1
17	0.8	0.6	0.7	0.7	B or better	1
18	0.3	0.4	0.6	0.7	Less than B	0
19	0.5	0.6	0.5	0.3	Less than B	0
20	0.8	0.7	0.4	0.8	B or better	1
21	0.4	0.5	0.7	0.2	Less than B	0
22	0.4	0.6	0.2	0.7	B or better	1
23	0.6	0.7	0.9	0.3	B or better	1
24	0.1	0.4	0.6	0.1	Less than B	0
25	0.3	0.6	0.9	0.7	B or better	1

$f = P'$ (B or better). $d = 1$ when actual grade is B or better; $d = 0$ otherwise.

[1] The kinds of analyses discussed in this section are used in several fields, including weather forecasting, medicine, education, business, and statistics, in addition to psychology. However, the terminology differs from field to field.

tion, where all your friends restricted their judgments to the 11 probabilities 0.0, 0.1, 0.2, ..., 1.0. The calibration graphs for your fellow counselors are shown in Figure 3.2. Observe that each point in a calibration graph tells you two things. The first is how often a particular probability judgment category was used. The second is the proportion of times the target event actually happened when that judgment was offered. As an example, consider the highest and rightmost point in Lynn's calibration graph. Notice that that point sits above probability judgment 0.8 and that the number 3 is adjacent to it. This means that there were three counselees who Lynn said had 80% chances of getting grades of B or better. Now notice that the vertical coordinate of that point is 0.67. This says that 67%, that is, 2/3, of these students for whom Lynn made 80% predictions in fact did earn grades of B or better. You might want to verify these claims, as well as the placement of all the other points in Lynn's diagram by referring to Table 3.3.

Perfect and counterperfect judgment How can you interpret your friends' calibration graphs or calibration graphs in general? The graph of a benevolent clairvoyant represents the ideal, the goal that should be sought by any judge. As an example, imagine that Merlin had also participated in your

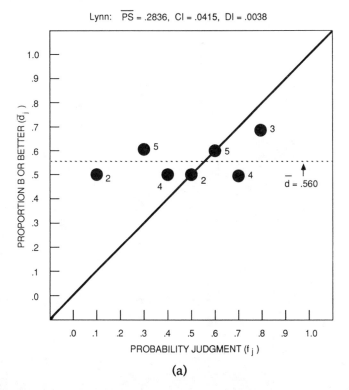

FIGURE 3.2. Calibration graphs for four of your fellow counselors' probability judgments for the event "B grade or better" for 25 students: (a) Lynn, (b) Terry, (c) Stephanie, (d) Herman.

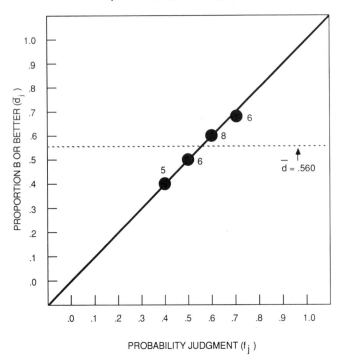

Terry: $\overline{PS}$ = .2368, CI = .0003, DI = .0100

PROPORTION B OR BETTER $(\overline{d}_j)$

PROBABILITY JUDGMENT (f_j)

$\overline{d}$ = .560

(b)

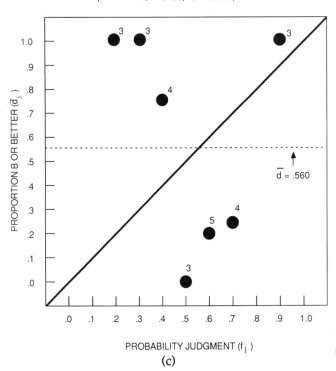

Stephanie: $\overline{PS}$ = .3428, CI = .2508, DI = .1544

PROPORTION B OR BETTER $(\overline{d}_j)$

PROBABILITY JUDGMENT (f_j)

$\overline{d}$ = .560

(c)

Herman: $\overline{PS}$ = .1476, CI = .0037, DI = .1018

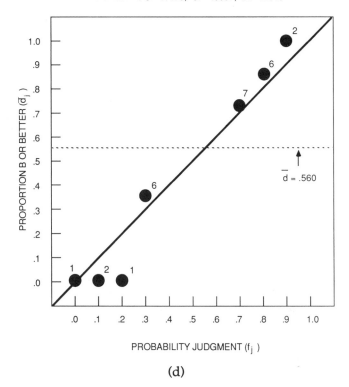

PROPORTION B OR BETTER ($\overline{d}_i$)

PROBABILITY JUDGMENT (f_j)

(d)

exercise. Figure 3.3, including only the filled points, would be Merlin's calibration graph. Notice that there are only two points in such a figure. The point in the lower-left corner represents occasions when the benevolent clairvoyant assigned probability 0% to the target event. Since the target event never occurs when the clairvoyant says that event has probability 0%, the corresponding proportion of occurrences is 0%, too. In your exercise, 11 students failed to get grades of B or better. That is why the number 11 appears adjacent to the lower-left point in Merlin's calibration graph. The point in the upper-right corner of Merlin's graph identifies the 14 cases when he offered a 100% probability judgment that a given student would earn a grade of B or better and when, of course, the student did get such a grade.

At the other extreme from the calibration graph of a benevolent clairvoyant like Merlin is that of a diabolical clairvoyant. Recall that this is the individual who says $P'(A) = 0.0$ whenever the target event A is going to occur and $P'(A) = 1.0$ when it is not. Figure 3.3, including only the open points, would be the resulting calibration graph if a diabolical clairvoyant also participated in your exercise.

The calibration graph for a real person's judgments will have a character somewhere between those for the benevolent and diabolical clairvoyants. Notice that each of the calibration graphs for your fellow counselors shows the corresponding mean probability score $\overline{PS}$. The ordering of the $\overline{PS}$

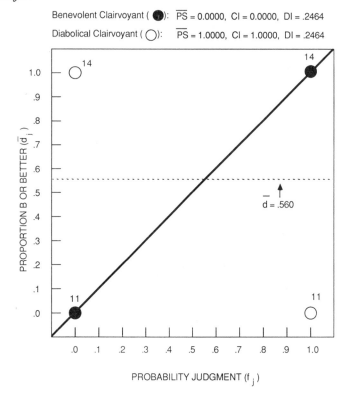

Benevolent Clairvoyant (⬤): $\overline{PS}$ = 0.0000, CI = 0.0000, DI = .2464

Diabolical Clairvoyant (◯): $\overline{PS}$ = 1.0000, CI = 1.0000, DI = .2464

FIGURE 3.3.   Calibration graphs for the probability judgments made by a benevolent clairvoyant (filled points) and a diabolical clairvoyant (open points) for the event "B grade or better" for 25 students.

values may or may not agree with your perception of how closely those individuals' calibration graphs approximate Merlin's perfect graph, going from Stephanie as the least to Lynn, Terry, and Herman as the most accurate overall. But it is obvious that these individuals achieved their respective accuracy levels in very different ways.

Calibration   The first aspect of judgment accuracy we distinguish is **calibration**. Suppose that we group together all the occasions when a person says that the target event has a 70% chance of occurring. We then later discover that, on 70% of those occasions, the target event did indeed occur. We also find that, on 20% of the occasions when this individual said the target event had a 20% probability, it did in fact happen. Based on the evidence available so far, it appears that this person is exhibiting perfect calibration. As this example suggests, in general, we say that an individual's probability judgments are well-calibrated to the extent that those judgments match the proportions of times that the target event actually occurs.

Figure 3.4 illustrates how perfect calibration manifests itself in a calibration graph: All the points lie along the 1:1 diagonal, where the judgment equals the corresponding proportion. You should recognize that a benevolent clairvoyant's judgments, as exemplified in Figure 3.3, also exhibit perfect calibration. Inspecting Figure 3.2, your fellow counselors appear to be ranked as follows with respect to the calibration aspect of judgment accuracy, from best to worst: Terry, Herman, Lynn, and Stephanie.

The "eyeball" test of calibration by visual inspection is sometimes adequate. However, it is often useful to be able to measure calibration numerically. This can be done with the **calibration index (CI)**. It is not essential that you be able to actually compute *CI*. That is why the computational formula is deferred to page 58, an optional section. For interpretational purposes, however, you should know that the calibration index is bounded by 0 and 1, and that smaller values are better; that is,

$$0 \qquad\qquad \le CI \le \qquad\qquad 1$$

(perfect calibration)   (worst possible calibration)

As indicated in Figure 3.3, the benevolent clairvoyant and the diabolical clairvoyant represent the extremes of perfect and worst possible calibration, respectively. The calibration indexes shown in Figure 3.2 rank order your

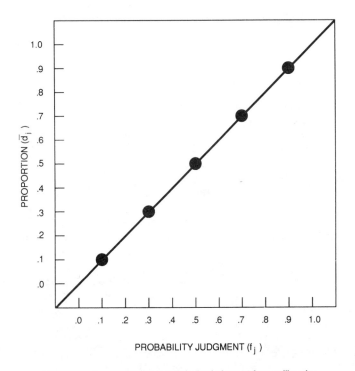

FIGURE 3.4. Calibration graph depicting perfect calibration.

colleagues the way our visual inspection suggested: Terry (CI = 0.0003), Herman (CI = 0.0037), Lynn (CI = 0.0415), Stephanie (CI = 0.2508).

Discrimination   Discrimination is the second aspect of judgment accuracy most readily appreciated in calibration graphs. The discrimination concept is often difficult to understand in the context of probability judgment. So we start by asking you to imagine yourself in another, quite different fictional situation. Here, you are a personnel officer for "Acme Manufacturing, Inc." "Widgets" are a major Acme product. Your primary duty at Acme is evaluating individuals who apply for jobs as widget testers. The essential skill a widget tester needs is the ability to discriminate good widgets from bad ones.

When an applicant comes to the evaluation room, you do the following:

1.   First, you present the applicant with a pile of 250 widgets, 140 (56%) of which are good and the remaining 110 (44%) bad, with good and bad widgets thoroughly mixed.

2.   You then show the applicant a row of 11 colored boxes. From left to right, they are: red, brown, gray, purple, orange, black, green, white, pink, yellow, and blue.

3.   Finally, you read the applicant the following instructions:

> The purpose of this test is to determine your ability to discriminate good widgets from bad ones.
>
> Some of the widgets in the pile are good, the rest bad. I would like you to sort the widgets into the colored boxes. You may use the boxes any way you like, except that you should use *different* boxes for good widgets than for bad ones. In other words, to the extent that you can, you should avoid putting into the same box both good and bad widgets.
>
> You can think of your goal another way, too. Suppose you can perfectly distinguish good from bad widgets. Then, when you are finished, if you have put any widgets at all into a particular box, every one of the widgets in that box should be good, or every one of them should be bad.

Table 3.4 shows the sorting results you obtain for several applicants. For each box, #*T* is the total number of widgets placed into the box. #*G* is the number of those widgets that are good, and %*G* = 100(#*G*/#*T*)% is the corresponding percentage of good widgets contained in the box. Notice that, for every applicant, the percentage of good widgets placed in all the boxes overall has to be 100(140/250)% = 56%.

Consider Applicant BC. Observe that he used only two boxes. He put all 110 bad widgets in the red box and the remaining 140 good ones in the blue box. So the corresponding percentages of good widgets sorted into those boxes were 0% and 100%, respectively. You thus conclude that Applicant BC had perfect ability to discriminate good from bad widgets. Applicant DC performed essentially the same way, except that she used the red and blue boxes in the opposite way from Applicant BC.

Now examine the performance of Applicant PD. This individual used the brown, purple, orange, green, and yellow boxes. Also notice that, within

TABLE 3.4 Widgets Sorted into Various Colored Boxes by Acme Products Job Applicants

APPLICANT		ALL	RED	BROWN	GRAY	PURPLE	ORANGE	BLACK	GREEN	WHITE	PINK	YELLOW	BLUE
								BOX					
BC	#T	250	110	—	—	—	—	—	—	—	—	—	140
	#G	140	0										140
	%G	56%	0%										100%
DC	#T	250	140	—	—	—	—	—	—	—	—	—	110
	#G	140	140										0
	%G	56%	100%										0%
PD	#T	250	—	40	—	50	60	—	60	—	—	40	—
	#G	140		40		0	60		0			40	
	%G	56%		100%		0%	100%		0%			100%	
ND	#T	250	50	—	25	50	—	50	—	—	25	—	50
	#G	140	28		14	28		28			14		28
	%G	56%	56%		56%	56%		56%			56%		56%
L	#T	250	—	20	—	50	40	20	50	40	30	—	—
	#G	140		10		30	20	10	30	20	20		
	%G	56%		50%		60%	50%	50%	60%	50%	67%		
T	#T	250	—	—	—	—	50	60	80	60	—	—	—
	#G	140					20	30	40	40			
	%G	56%					40%	50%	62%	67%			
S	#T	250	—	—	30	30	40	30	50	40	30	—	—
	#G	140			30	30	30	0	10	10	30		
	%G	56%			100%	100%	75%	0%	20%	25%	100%		
H	#T	250	10	20	10	60	—	—	—	70	60	20	—
	#G	140	0	0	0	20				50	50	20	
	%G	56%	0%	0%	0%	33%				71%	83%	100%	

Number Total (#*T*), Number Good (#*G*), Percentage Good (%*G*)

53

any one of these boxes, either all the widgets were good (brown, orange, yellow) or none of them were; that is, all were bad (purple, green). So the corresponding percentages for the groups of boxes were respectively 100% and 0%. Thus, like Applicants BC and DC, Applicant PD exhibited perfect discrimination, too.

Your first three applicants illustrate how to recognize perfect discrimination. That is, the percentage of good widgets in a box containing any widgets at all is either 100% or 0%. But how can we recognize the opposite extreme of nil discrimination ability? Suppose an applicant has absolutely no skill at telling whether a widget is good or bad. The applicant then decides to place good widgets into Box X. When this person selects individual widgets to put into Box X, those widgets are effectively chosen at random from the pile. And since 56% of the widgets in the pile are good, about 56% of the widgets placed into Box X will be good, too. Similarly, suppose our nil discriminator decides to put bad widgets into Box Y. By the same argument, we should expect about 56% of the widgets in Box Y to be good, also. Generalizing, the worst possible discrimination is manifested when the percentage of good widgets in any filled box is the same as the percentage of good widgets overall. Applicant ND provides a good illustration.

Your first four applicants represent ideal cases. The remaining applicants, whose sorting distributions appear below the double line in Table 3.4, are more typical. Observe that the percentages of good widgets in the boxes used by Applicant L deviate only slightly from the overall proportion of 56% good widgets. So it appears that Applicant L's discrimination ability is weak. Applicant T's discrimination is not very strong, either. In contrast, Applicants S and H show quite good discrimination skill.

What does the previous illustration have to do with probability judgment? More than likely, you have already seen through the thinly veiled connection between the situations in your counseling office and on your job at Acme. Applicants BC and DC are the benevolent and diabolical clairvoyants, respectively. And Applicants L, T, S, and H are, correspondingly, your counseling colleagues Lynn, Terry, Stephanie, and Herman. Instead of considering 25 students, they examined 250, that is, ten times as many, widgets. But, in terms of discrimination, they performed exactly the same at Acme as they did as counselors. In the counseling office, instead of discriminating good from bad widgets, they implicitly had the task of discriminating the students who would earn good grades from those who would not.

Discrimination is solely concerned with a person's ability to place different things into different categories; the labels of the categories are irrelevant. In your Acme evaluation room, the categories were eleven boxes "labeled" with distinct colors. In your counseling office, the categories were "labeled" with eleven different probabilities. Following is a correspondence we can establish between the category labels used in the Acme and counseling situations, respectively: red – 0.0, brown – 0.1, gray – 0.2, purple – 0.3, orange – 0.4, black – 0.5, green – 0.6, white – 0.7, pink – 0.8, yellow – 0.9, blue – 1.0.

Reexamine the calibration graphs shown in Figures 3.2 and 3.3. We can now think of the probabilities along the horizontal axis as identifying the different categories into which the counselees might have been classified. The number adjacent to each point is the frequency with which counselees were placed into the given category. The vertical axis indicates the proportion of the counselees in that category who actually got grades of B or better. If you make the above correspondences of probabilities with colors, proportions with percentages, high grades with good widgets, and multiply the frequencies by 10, the calibration graphs pictorially convey the same discrimination information contained in Table 3.4.

More explicitly, ideal discrimination is indicated when each of the points in a calibration graph is at the top of the graph (proportion = 1.0 or 100%) or at the bottom (proportion = 0.0 or 0%). This ideal is exhibited in the calibration graphs for the benevolent and diabolical clairvoyants displayed in Figure 3.3. Imagine that Applicant PD, who demonstrated perfect discrimination, had also participated in your counseling exercise. Then we should expect his calibration graph to provide another illustration of ideal discrimination, as in Figure 3.5a. At the other extreme, nil discrimination would be manifested in a calibration graph in which all the points lie along a horizontal line at an elevation corresponding to the sample base rate for the target event, for example, 56% for your counseling exercise. An example is Figure 3.5b, such as we would expect for Applicant ND if she had taken part in your exercise.

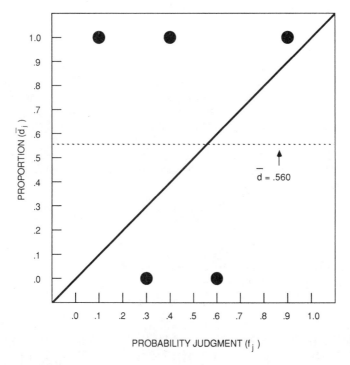

FIGURE 3.5. Calibration graphs illustrating (a) perfect and (b) nil discrimination.

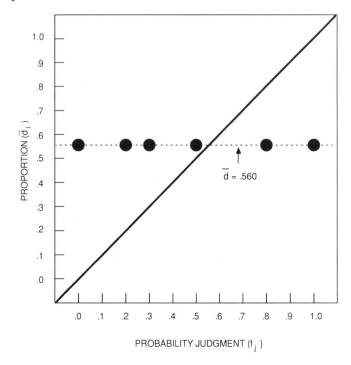

FIGURE 3.5. (Continued)

We can conclude the following: Good discrimination is revealed in a calibration graph to the extent that the vertical locations of the points deviate from the horizontal sample base rate line, and each tends toward either the top or the bottom of the figure. Examining the calibration graphs of your fellow counselors in Figure 3.2, we see varying degrees of discrimination skill being exhibited. Degrees of discrimination are even harder to appreciate visually than are degrees of calibration. Numerical **discrimination indexes (DI)** are thus helpful. Discrimination indexes range from 0, for nil discrimination, to $\bar{d}(1 - \bar{d})$, for perfect discrimination, with larger indexes corresponding to better discrimination; that is,

$$0 \qquad \leq DI \leq \qquad \bar{d}(1 - \bar{d})$$

(nil discrimination)   (perfect discrimination)

Thus, in your counseling exercise, since the base rate was $\bar{d} = 0.56$, discrimination indexes must be such that

$$0 \leq DI \leq 0.2464$$

Figure 3.2 shows that the discrimination indexes order your fellow counselors' discrimination skills as follows, from best to worst: Stephanie ($DI = 0.1544$), Herman ($DI = 0.1018$), Terry ($DI = 0.0100$), and Lynn ($DI = 0.0038$).

Calibration versus discrimination   Calibration and discrimination reflect quite different kinds of judgmental insight. As we have just seen, discrimination concerns the ability of a person to distinguish instances when a target event *is* going to occur from those when it is *not*. The specific labels applied to those instances are immaterial, as long as different labels are used for the cases when the target event happens than those when something else occurs. In contrast, calibration reflects the ability of the person to successfully apply labels that possess the numerical properties we would like probabilities to have.

Calibration is significant because we will often want to use judgments that are appropriately qualified according to how sure the person is that the target event will happen.   We saw in Chapter 2 that this is especially important when the decision maker who uses those judgments wants to trade off the apparent certainty of an event against the seriousness of decision outcomes that depend on that event, for example, in the freeze protection decision facing citrus farmers Keith and Sally Collins (pp.28–29). Thus, suppose we are given a choice between using the judgments of Weather Forecasters A and B, who are equally skilled with respect to discrimination, but are such that Forecaster A has better calibration. We should certainly prefer Forecaster A.

The previous remarks notwithstanding, a case can be made that discrimination skill is a more fundamental ability than calibration skill. Miscalibration sometimes can be corrected rather easily. Refer to Figure 3.2a. Let us suppose that the point in Lynn's calibration curve above probability judgment 0.8 is representative of what would generally happen for her 80% judgments. That is, over all cases in which she indicates 80% certainty that a student will get a grade of B or better, only 67% of the time does that happen. Then we might advise Lynn that, when she feels like reporting an 80% judgment, she should instead report something lower, for example, 70%. This would move the 80% point in her calibration graph closer to the 1:1 diagonal, improving her calibration. Such simple advice would have no effect on discrimination, however, as suggested by the fact that the vertical location of Lynn's 80% point would be unchanged. So how *can* discrimination be improved? The judge must somehow gain access to information that is strongly related to the occurrence of the target event and/or learn how to make better use of such information that is currently available. For instance, Lynn might seek more and better information about her counselees' previous course experience.

Computation of calibration and discrimination indexes (optional)   Table 3.5 illustrates with Lynn's counseling judgments how calibration and discrimination indexes can be calculated. For the most part, the operations used in constructing the table are self-explanatory. However, a couple of clarifying remarks might be helpful. Column 4 indicates the proportions of times (d_j) the target event, that is, B grades or better, actually occurred when the given judgment (f_j) was reported by Lynn. The formula for the entries in column 5 is given at the bottom of the table. These can be thought of as measures of

TABLE 3.5 Computation of Lynn's Calibration (*CI*) and Discrimination (*DI*) Indexes

(1) Category (*j*)	(2) f_j	(3) N_j	(4) $\bar{d_j}$	(5) CI_j	(6) DI_j
1	0.0	0	—	—	—
2	0.1	2	0.50	0.3200	0.0072
3	0.2	0	—	—	—
4	0.3	5	0.60	0.4500	0.0080
5	0.4	4	0.50	0.0400	0.0144
6	0.5	2	0.50	0.0000	0.0072
7	0.6	5	0.60	0.0000	0.0080
8	0.7	4	0.50	0.1600	0.0144
9	0.8	0	—	—	—
10	0.9	3	0.67	0.1587	0.0363
11	1.0	0	—	—	—
Sum (Σ)	—	25	—	1.1287	0.0955
Mean	—	—	—	0.0415	0.0038
Exp'n	—	*N*	—	*CI*	*DI*

$N = \Sigma N_j$

$CI_j = N_j\,(f_j - \bar{d_j})^{\,2} = (3)[(2) - (4)]^2$

$DI_j = N_j\,(\bar{d_j} - \bar{d})^2 = (3)[(4) - (7)]^2,$

where $(7) = \bar{d} = 14/25 = 0.56j.$

calibration for the given categories. As suggested in Table 3.5, the calibration index *CI* is simply the mean of the category calibration measures:

$$CI = \sum \frac{CI_j}{N} \tag{3.3}$$

where the Greek letter Σ is the standard statistical notation for a sum.

The discrimination index, *DI*, is computed in column 6. The formula for the entries in that column is shown at the bottom of the table. Similar to the calibration index, the discrimination index (due to Murphy, 1973) is the mean of the column 6 entries:

$$DI = \sum \frac{DI_j}{N} \tag{3.4}$$

You should convince yourself why this formulation of *DI* reflects the concept of discrimination discussed previously.

The covariance graph perspective

An alternative approach for understanding judgment accuracy is motivated mainly by the following observation: Suppose that someone is very good at making probability judgments. Then the judgments that person assigns to the target event when it actually occurs should tend to be very different from those reported when it does not occur. Covariance graph analysis is mainly a way of visualizing and summarizing *particular* differences between those two sets of judgments.

Covariance graph construction The first step in the present strategy is the assembly of **covariance graphs**. Figure 3.6 shows the graphs for the probabilistic grade predictions made by your colleagues in your counseling exercise.

The basic construction of a covariance graph can be illustrated with Lynn's judgments. To start with, we segregate into two different groups her judgments $f = P'$(B or better) for those 14 counselees who did eventually earn grades of B or better and those 11 who did not. We then place them in order, as you can verify by referring to Table 3.3:

Actual grade B or better ($d = 1$):
  0.1, 0.3, 0.3, 0.3, 0.4, 0.4, 0.5, 0.6, 0.6, 0.6, 0.7, 0.7, 0.8, 0.8
Actual grade less than B ($d = 0$):
  0.1, 0.3, 0.3, 0.4, 0.4, 0.5, 0.6, 0.6, 0.7, 0.7, 0.8

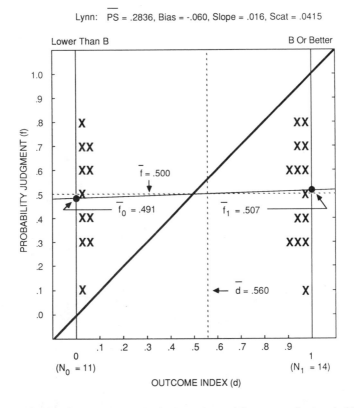

Lynn: PS = .2836, Bias = -.060, Slope = .016, Scat = .0415

FIGURE 3.6. Covariance graphs for four of your fellow counselors' probability judgments for the event "B grade or better" for 25 students: (a) Lynn, (b) Terry, (c) Stephanie, (d) Herman.

Terry: $\overline{PS}$ = .2368, Bias = .000, Slope = .042, Scat = .0108

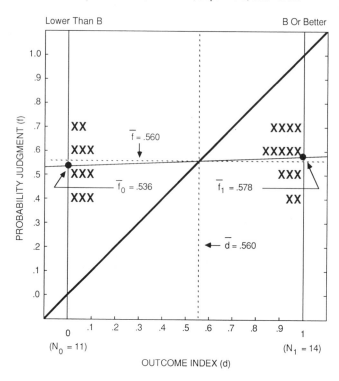

Stephanie: $\overline{PS}$ = .3428, Bias = -.036, Slope = -.103, Scat = .0416

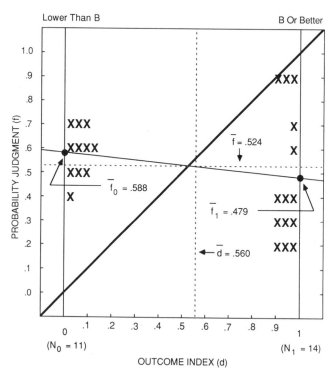

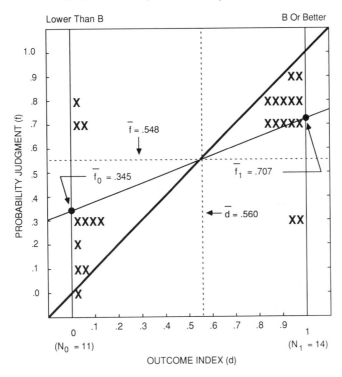

Herman: $\overline{PS}$ = .1476, Bias = -.012, Slope = .362, Scat = .0471

Lower Than B — B Or Better

PROBABILITY JUDGMENT (f)

$\overline{f}$ = .548
$\overline{f_0}$ = .345
$\overline{f_1}$ = .707
$\overline{d}$ = .560

$(N_0 = 11)$

$(N_1 = 14)$

OUTCOME INDEX (d)

Next, we display each distribution as a **histogram**, as shown in Figure 3.6a. The histogram for those cases when grades of B or better were actually received appears on the right, the other on the left. Observe that the vertical axis of the graph is identified with probability judgments. Consider that part of the right-hand histogram associated with probability 0.8. There are two markers (X's) drawn there. These correspond to the two occasions when Lynn reported judgments $f = P'$(B or better) = 0.8 for counselees who eventually did earn high grades. The remaining markers were located similarly.

A reference: the clairvoyant Figure 3.7 is a covariance graph in which the number of judgments at a given level is denoted by a bar instead of X's. It illustrates ideal judgment, for instance, by your clairvoyant friend Merlin. It serves as a reference in evaluating various aspects of real people's judgment accuracy.

Bias The first aspect of probability judgment accuracy easily seen in covariance graphs actually does not make use of the distinction between judgments associated with the occurrence or nonoccurrence of the target event. Observe the horizontal dotted line in each covariance graph. Take the one in Lynn's graph, in particular. That line is drawn through the mean of her judgments over all 25 occasions, denoted $f = 0.50$. Column 2 of Table 3.2 illustrates how such an average is computed. Now observe that the horizontal axis in each graph is marked off in potential values of d, the sample base rate. Recall that, in your counseling exercise, the base rate was 56%. The

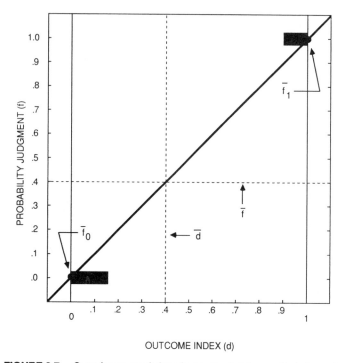

FIGURE 3.7.   Covariance graph for a benevolent clairvoyant's judgments.

vertical dotted line in each of your colleagues' graphs is drawn through that base rate. Finally, you should note in each graph where the horizontal and vertical dotted lines cross each other. That intersection indicates whether and to what extent the person's judgments were biased.

A collection of probability judgments is biased if the average judgment is too high or too low, relative to the base rate for the target event. Formally, the **Bias** statistic is the difference between the average judgment and the sample base rate:

$$\text{Bias} = \overline{f} - \overline{d} \qquad (3.5)$$

For instance, Bias $= 0.50 - 0.56 = -.06$ for Lynn's judgments. A detailed example of how to compute the Bias is contained in Table 3.2.

Suppose a set of judgments is unbiased. This means that $\overline{f} = \overline{d}$. You should realize that, if a person's judgments are unbiased, then the dotted lines for the base rate and mean judgment intersect on the heavy 1:1 diagonal line in the relevant covariance graph. Those judgments are biased to the degree that the intersection is displaced from the diagonal. The bias is positive, that is, the person "overexpects" the target event, if the intersection is above the diagonal; negative bias is indicated by an intersection below the diagonal. We thus see, as indicated in Figure 3.6a, that Lynn's judgments were slightly negatively biased; on average, the students did somewhat better than Lynn anticipated.

The concept of bias is closely related to that of calibration. In fact, bias is an indicator of **calibration-in-the-large**. The terminology is reasonable, since the calibration notion refers to the correspondence between average judgments and proportions of event occurrences. We would thus say that Lynn's judgments exhibited some measure of miscalibration-in-the-large. As suggested in the clairvoyant's covariance graph in Figure 3.7, perfectly accurate judgments contain no miscalibration.

Why might a person's probability judgments be biased? Three possibilities suggest themselves:

1. *Ignorance of historical base rates:* In most situations, the sample base rate will be somewhat close to the historical base rate. So the person can assure a small bias by keeping the historical base rate in mind. But this is impossible if he or she is unaware of that base rate. For example, Lynn's grade judgments might be negatively biased because she is relatively new to your college and because high grades were less common at her old school.

2. *Biased incentives:* Sometimes the judge is subject to incentives to report judgments generally higher or lower than he or she thinks they really are. Take the case of probabilistic medical diagnoses, as discussed in Chapter 2. There it was suggested that physicians' judgments might be subject to value-induced biases because underpredicting serious disease is considered more important than making the opposite error (p. 000).

3. *Biased information:* Opinions also might be biased because the information used to arrive at those judgments is distorted in favor of or against the target event. Students tend to visit counselors mainly to discuss their problems, not their triumphs. Thus, perhaps Lynn's negative bias in predicting high grades is due to her emphasis on counseling file notes, which highlight the students' weaknesses instead of their strengths.

Slope Whenever the target event A is going to occur, a benevolent clairvoyant always says that $f = P'(A) = 1.0$. So if we averaged the judgments over all such occasions, that average would be 1.0, too. The mean of these judgments is a **conditional mean judgment**, specifically, the conditional mean judgment when the target event happens. It is denoted $\bar{f}_1$, where the subscript denotes $d = 1$. Thus, for the clairvoyant,

$$\bar{f}_1 = 1.0$$

There is another conditional mean judgment for occasions when the target event does not occur, denoted by $\bar{f}_0$, since $d = 0$ in those circumstances. For the clairvoyant,

$$\bar{f}_0 = 0.0$$

The difference between the conditional means is called the **slope**:

$$\text{Slope} = \bar{f}_1 - \bar{f}_0 \tag{3.6}$$

For example,

$$\text{Slope} = 1.0$$

when the judge is clairvoyant.

The slope is the second important accuracy dimension readily seen in covariance graphs. Clearly, an individual's judgments are good to the extent that the slope is large. The slope of 1.0 earned by the clairvoyant is the largest possible value. The slopes for real judges generally fall far short of that ideal. As an example, return to your counseling colleague Lynn. Recall that the probability judgments for B grades or better reported by Lynn for the 14 counselees who did earn such grades were 0.1, 0.3, 0.3, 0.3, 0.4, 0.4, 0.5, 0.6, 0.6, 0.6, 0.7, 0.7, 0.8, and 0.8. The sum of these judgments is 7.1. Thus, her conditional mean judgment $\bar{f}_1$ is

$$\bar{f}_1 = \frac{7.1}{14} = 0.507$$

You can similarly show that, for Lynn,

$$\bar{f}_0 = 0.491$$

implying that

$$\text{Slope} = 0.507 - 0.491 = 0.016$$

which is a very modest value indeed.

How are the conditional means and the slope depicted in a covariance graph? On the left side of Lynn's graph (Figure 3.6a) is a filled point located on the probability judgment scale at the conditional mean $\bar{f}_0 = 0.491$. On the opposite side of the figure is another point which identifies the conditional mean $\bar{f}_1 = 0.507$. The line connecting the points is called the **regression line**. What we have called the slope is literally the slope of the regression line, that is, the rate at which the person's probability judgments f increase as a function of the outcome indexes d. The steeper the regression line, the greater the slope is. Figure 3.6a confirms our impression that Lynn's judgments are *very* far from the ideal slope of the clairvoyant, depicted in Figure 3.7. The remaining covariance graphs in Figure 3.6 show that your fellow counselors' judgments varied considerably in slope.

How does a person arrive at judgments that have better or worse slope?:

1. *Discrimination skill:* For the slope to be anything other than 0, the person must be capable of distinguishing occasions when the target event is going to occur from those when it is not. As we saw in our previous discussion of discrimination, this is possible only when the person has access to information that is reliably associated with the target event and understands the nature of that association.

2. *Labeling skill:* An individual whose judgments exhibit good slope must also realize how extreme his or her judgments ought to be, given the current facts. That is, the person must know how to label occasions properly, too. Thus, we see that the slope reflects a particular combination of both discrimination and calibration.

Scatter   Compare the two covariance graphs in Figure 3.8. Imagine that they describe grade judgments $f = P'$(B or better) made by Counselors A and B, respectively. Notice that the biases and slopes in both graphs are the same. But would you consider Counselors A and B to be equally accurate? Probably not. Most people would think that Counselor B is the better judge. This comparison illustrates the final aspect of judgment accuracy highlighted by covariance graphs.

Observe that, when students are destined to earn high grades, the average judgment reported by Counselor A is about 0.70, the same as by Counselor B. However, the variability in those judgments is much greater for Counselor A. A similar situation exists for students who are going to earn lower grades. The extra variability in Counselor A's judgments is useless "noise" or **scatter** that is unrelated to the target event. This random error is measured by the statistic shown in your fellow counselors' covariance graphs as "Scat." The larger the Scat value, the greater the scatter. According to the present measure, your fellow counselors are ordered as follows with respect to the scatter contained in their grade judgments, from most to least: Herman (Scat = 0.0471), Stephanie (Scat = 0.0416), Lynn (Scat = 0.0415), and Terry (Scat = 0.0108). The procedure for computing Scat is illustrated in the next section, which is optional.

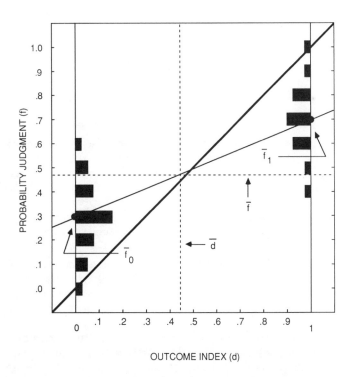

OUTCOME INDEX (d)

FIGURE 3.8a. Covariance graphs depicting different degrees of scatter in judgments for the event "B grade or better": (a) Counselor A, (b) Counselor B.

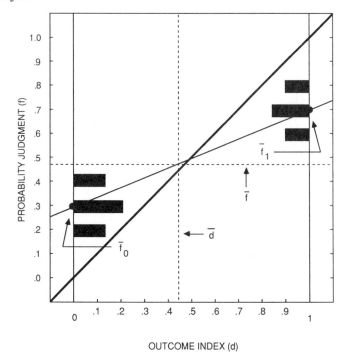

FIGURE 3.8b.   (continued)

Among the leading reasons judgments sometimes contain a lot of scatter are these:

1.   *Reliance on weak cues:*   The judge might base his or her opinions on information that is thought to be strongly related to the target event, but which really is not. For instance, Counselor A might make grade predictions from interview impressions that have little to do with actual course performance, that is, are useless as cues for what might happen in the classroom. Thus, when these cues suggest that the student should do well, in fact, the student is perhaps just as likely to perform either well or poorly.

2.   *Inconsistency:*   Even if a person relies on good information, if that information is used in an inconsistent manner, then average accuracy over many judgments will suffer in a way that manifests itself in scatter. This will happen when, for example, a counselor sometimes interprets low test scores to be a precursor of low grades but at other times ignores such scores.

Computing the scatter measure (optional)   The scatter index Scat is derived from a well-known measure in elementary statistics, the variance. The latter measures the variability of a set of numbers around their mean value. Suppose that Y is an arbitrary variable. The variance of N instances of Y is given by

$$\text{Var}(Y) = \frac{\Sigma (Y - \overline{Y})^2}{N}$$

(3.7)

that is, the sum of the squared deviations between the individual values of Y and their mean.

As a concrete example, let us compute the variance of Lynn's probability judgments for the 11 students in your counseling exercise who earned grades lower than B. Recall that the mean of those values was $f_0 = 0.491$. So the sum of the squared deviations is

$$(0.1 - 0.491)^2 + (0.3 - 0.491)^2 + (0.3 - 0.491)^2$$
$$+ (0.4 - 0.491)^2 + (0.4 - 0.491)^2 + (0.5 - 0.491)^2$$
$$+ (0.6 - 0.491)^2 + (0.6 - 0.491)^2 + (0.7 - 0.491)^2$$
$$+ (0.7 - 0.491)^2 + (0.8 - 0.491)^2$$
$$= 0.4488$$

Thus, the resulting **conditional variance** is

$$\text{Var}(f_0) = \frac{0.4488}{11} = 0.0408$$

In similar fashion, we could compute the conditional variance of the judgments Lynn made when students made high grades: $\text{Var}(f_1) = 0.0421$.

The scatter measure is then defined as follows:

$$\text{Scat} = \frac{N_1 \text{Var}(f_1) + N_0 \text{Var}(f_0)}{N_1 + N_0}$$

(3.8)

That is, Scat is a weighted mean of the conditional variances. In Lynn's case, we see that

$$\text{Scat} = \frac{(14)(0.0421) + (11)(0.0408)}{25} = 0.0415$$

Judgment difficulty

Suppose that Arlene is yet another of your counseling friends. As before, you ask Arlene to make probabilistic predictions of how well each of 25 students will do in a particular course. This time, however, the target event is "Passing grade," not "B or better." Later you are told that the mean probability score for Arlene's judgments is $\overline{PS} = 0.0740$, which is much better than that for any of your other colleagues' judgments. You are astounded and exclaim, "Boy, she's really *good!*" But your astonishment turns to puzzlement when Arlene tells you how she made her judgments:

> I was kind of in a hurry. But I wanted to say *something* that made sense. Now, I remembered reading that about 90% of the grades in this school are passing grades. So, for every student, I just said there was a 90% chance that he or she would pass the course. I'm really sorry I couldn't do a better job. Maybe next time, okay?

What is underneath this peculiar situation is the notion of judgment difficulty.

Judgments are more or less difficult for a host of reasons. However, one element of difficulty is tied to the variability of the target event. An event is easy to predict if it does not vary much, that is, if it almost always happens or almost never happens. Conversely, that event is hard to anticipate if, on any given occasion, it is just as likely to occur as to not occur. This aspect of difficulty is reflected in the base rate for the target event; the more different the base rate is from 0.5, the easier the event is to predict. Your puzzlement now begins to clear up. Arlene looked so much better than your other counseling friends because the judgment task you gave her was so much easier (historical base rate $h = 0.9$ for "Passing grade" versus $h = 0.55$ for "B or better").

One moral of this story is that, in any discussion of judgment accuracy, the difficulty of predicting the target event needs to be taken into account. The probability score reflects both the controllable and the uncontrollable elements of accuracy. The latter include difficulty. The former include such aspects as calibration, discrimination, bias, slope, and scatter. The present observations are another reason why the analysis of judgment accuracy into its parts is so important. We are most interested in those elements of accuracy the judge can control and hence improve.

The predictability of a target event can be represented straightforwardly as the **variability index (VI)**:

$$VI = \bar{d}(1 - \bar{d}) \tag{3.9}$$

The larger is VI, the more difficult is the prediction of the target event. The variability index is maximized when the base rate is 0.5, and minimized when it is 0.0 or 1.0.[2] The effect of judgment difficulty on the probability score is described below.

Interrelationships (Optional)

How do the various aspects of judgment accuracy we have considered relate to one another and to overall accuracy? Within the calibration graph perspective, the connections are summarized in the following **Murphy (1973) decomposition** of the probability score:

$$\overline{PS} = VI + CI - DI \tag{3.10}$$

where, as just indicated, VI is the variability index for the target event, CI is the calibration index, and DI is the discrimination index.

Within the covariance graph point of view, the **covariance decomposition** of the probability score summarizes the relationships (Yates and Curley, 1985):

$$\overline{PS} = VI + \text{Bias}^2 + (VI)(\text{Slope})(\text{Slope} - 2) + \text{Scat} \tag{3.11}$$

---

[2] You might recognize from a previous statistics course that VI is literally the variance of the outcome index d.

A recapitulation

Recall Stuart Prentice's problem: Should he rely on the surgical outcome predictions of Dr. Robinson or Dr. Jefferson? The original suggestion was that he should be guided at least partly by the track record of accuracy exhibited by these physicians' past judgments. We have seen that there are several different aspects of such accuracy. It is often useful to examine them all.[3] The reason is that, although these aspects do indeed tend to be related to one another, they are by no means redundant. Table 3.6 illustrates. It summarizes the rank orderings of your counseling colleagues in your prediction exercise. You should note that in only one comparison does one of the counselors *dominate* one of the others, that is, perform better on every accuracy measure: Terry versus Lynn. There is no counselor who was more accurate than all the others in every way. It is probably doubtful that either Dr. Robinson or Dr. Jefferson dominates the other either.

ASSESSING THE ACCURACY OF PROBABILITY JUDGMENTS FOR QUANTITIES

In Chapter 2, we saw how probability judgments for quantities are commonly elicited. For example, the owners of Copper Star Productions indicated their opinions about how large their music festival crowd would be using credible intervals. Jerry Reed felt there was a 30% chance that the festival would attract between 10,000 and 15,000 people. Steve Houston thought the chance of the crowd being in that range was only 18%. So, for Jerry Reed, (10,000, 15,000] was a 30% credible interval; it was an 18% credible interval for Steve Houston.

Most discussions about the accuracy of probability judgments for quantities focus on the calibration of credible intervals. As indicated in Table

TABLE 3.6 Counselors' Ranks with Respect to Various Aspects of Probabilistic Grade Judgment Accuracy

ACCURACY ASPECT	LYNN	TERRY	STEPHANIE	HERMAN
Overall	3	2	4	1
Calibration	3	1	4	2
Discrimination	4	3	1	2
Bias	4	1	3	2
Slope	3	2	4	1
Scatter	2	1	3	4

Note: 1 = best, 4 = worst.

[3]The specific values taken on by some of the measures we have discussed are affected by the number of cases involved. Thus, comparisons should be made only between judges who consider the same numbers of cases.

3.7, for each of 200 different Copper Star promotions, Jerry Reed made crowd size probability judgments. Suppose we consider one 30% credible interval stated by Mr. Reed on each of those occasions. In some cases, the actual crowd size fell within the reported interval. For example, for Promotion 1, the indicated 30% credible interval was (10,000, 15,000], and the actual crowd size was 12,374. In other instances, for example, for the second promotion, the actual number of people attending the event was not captured by the stated interval. Jerry Reed's 30% credible intervals are perfectly calibrated if exactly 30% of those intervals include the actual crowd sizes, while the remaining 70% do not. In Table 3.7, note that perfect calibration did in fact obtain, since 60 (that is, 30%) of the 200 30% credible intervals contained the actual attendance figures. Thus, we see that the concept of calibration for credible intervals is essentially the same as the one we encountered previously for discrete events.

Ordinarily, probability judgments for a quantity are expressed as credible intervals spanning the entire range of possible values for that quantity. For instance, Steve Houston stated the 0.01, 0.10, 0.25, 0.50, 0.75, 0.90, and 0.99 fractiles of his judged probability distribution for the Copper Star music festival crowd size. Since his 0.01 fractile was 4000 people, (0, 4000] was a 1% credible interval. And since his 0.10 fractile was 12,000 people, (4001, 12,000] was a 9% credible interval, and so on, yielding a total of eight intervals. Suppose Steve Houston reports a similar set of fractiles for each of a large number of Copper Star promotions. We could then determine the calibration for the 1% credible intervals defined by 0 and the 0.01 fractiles. We could do the same for the 9% credible intervals extending from the 0.01 fractiles to the 0.10 fractiles, and for all the other intervals bounded by the successive fractiles. Imagine that *each* of those sets of credible intervals is perfectly calibrated. Then we would say that Steve Houston's probability judgments for crowd size exhibit perfect distribution calibration. More generally, **distribution calibration** holds if the collections of credible intervals of any given level are perfectly calibrated.

Distribution calibration is only one aspect of accuracy for probability judgments for quantities. There exist measures for the overall accuracy of such opinions, although they are used much less often than they should.

TABLE 3.7 Promoter Jerry Reed's 30% Credible Intervals for Crowd Size for 200 Events, with the Actual Attendance at Each Event

PROMOTION	30% CREDIBLE INTERVAL	ACTUAL ATTENDANCE	ACTUAL IN INTERVAL?
1	(10,000, 15,000]	12,374	Yes
2	(3000, 7000]	8,110	No
.	.	.	.
.	.	.	.
.	.	.	.
200	(7,150,–10,500]	9,862	Yes
Summary			60 Yes (30%)
			140 No

Unfortunately, detailed consideration of these measures is beyond our scope (see Matheson and Winkler, 1976; Staël von Holstein, 1972, 1977).

SUMMARY

Accurate judgments are essential for good decision making. It is thus important that we be able to determine just how well a given person's judgments anticipate the events that ultimately occur. Accuracy is most easily characterized when likelihood opinions are expressed as probability judgments.

The probability score is the most common measure of overall probability judgment accuracy. This measure can be conceptualized in terms of discrepancies between a real person's judgments and those of a clairvoyant who knows for sure which events are going to occur.

Likelihood judgment accuracy is not a simple, undifferentiated concept. Although one person's judgments might be superior to another's in an overall sense, the second individual's opinions might be better with respect to some important accuracy components. One such dimension is calibration. An individual's opinions are well calibrated to the extent that his or her probability judgments match the proportions of times the target event actually occurs. If a person tends to report different probability judgments for occasions on which the target event occurs as compared to when it does not, then those opinions are good with respect to a second accuracy dimension, discrimination. Probability judgments are biased to the degree that they are generally higher or lower than the proportions of times the target event occurs. The mean probability judgment given to an event when it actually happens should be greater than the corresponding mean when it does not happen. The judgments have a good slope to the extent that the difference in those means is large. Scatter measures the amount of random error contained in probability judgments.

Probability judgments for quantities can be viewed as statements of how sure the person is that the quantity of interest will fall into various ranges. A form of calibration known as distribution calibration is the most commonly discussed accuracy dimension of probability judgments for quantities.

KEY TERMS

Base rate judge	Covariance decomposition
Bias	Covariance graph
Brier score	Discrimination index
Calibration	Distribution calibration
Calibration graph	Histogram
Calibration index	Historical base rate
Calibration-in-the-large	Historical judge
Conditional mean judgment	Murphy decomposition
Conditional variance	Outcome index
Constant judge	Probability score

Quadratic score
Regression line
Sample base rate
Scatter

Slope
Uniform judge
Variability index

ADDITIONAL READING

Blattenberger and Lad (1985); Habbema, Hilden, and Bjerregaard (1978); Levi (1985); Mason (1982); Murphy and Daan (1985); Sanders (1963); Winkler and Murphy (1968); Yates (1982).

EXERCISES AND STUDY QUESTIONS

1. Bert and Ernie are amateur weather forecasters. Both are asked to make probabilistic forecasts of rain for the next 100 days. Each of these fellows concedes that he knows nothing about weather. So every day Bert reports $f = P'$(Rain) = 0.5. That is, he behaves like a uniform judge. In contrast, on each of 11 poker chips Ernie writes one of 11 percentages: 0%, 10%, 20%, ..., 100%. Every day he randomly picks one of those chips from a hat and reports the selected percentage as his probability judgment for rain for the next day. For example, if he picks 20%, he reports $f = P'$(Rain) = 0.20. At the end of the 100 days, who do you think will have earned the better mean probability score, Bert or Ernie? Explain.

2. (Optional) Two other measures of probability judgment accuracy besides the probability score are the **linear score (Lr)**, defined by

    $$Lr(f, d) = fd + (1 - f)(1 - d)$$

    and the **logarithmic score (Lg)** (see Shapiro, 1977), whose formula is

    $$Lg(f, d) = \log[fd + (1 - f)(1 - d)]$$

    where f is the probability judgment and d the outcome index.

    (a) Provide an intuitive interpretation of the linear score.

    (b) Rewarding a person for accuracy according to the linear score should encourage a special kind of judgment distortion. How so?

    (c) What do you see as a major disadvantage of using the logarithmic score as an accuracy measure?

3. Will a historical judge always outperform a uniform judge? Justify your position.

4. Ziggy Zaden is a movie house bartender who works in the Detroit area. He is reputed to have remarkable judgment powers (Talbert, 1981). Mr. Zaden views every new film that plays in his theater and then makes a prediction about how popular it will be. As the story goes, whenever Mr. Zaden predicts that a film will be a hit, it invariably fails, and conversely. Suppose you were to get Mr. Zaden to make his predictions as probability judgments of the form P'(Hit). What might you expect the calibration graph for Mr. Zaden's judgments to look like?

5. Clarise is a real estate agent. One of her tasks is making predictions of when mortgage rates will decline. Over a fairly large number of occasions, she has made her predictions as probability judgments of the form P'(Rate will decline in two weeks). Chauncey, in analyzing the accuracy of her judgments, has noticed that Clarise's judgments have poor discrimination. To help improve her discrimination, he advises her to stop using so many intermediate probabilities. He says that, instead, she should try to use more probabilities near 0 and 1. This is bad advice. Why?

6. You are looking for a new stock broker. You have reduced your candidates to two, "Connie Kerr" and "Mark Cowen." Both of these brokers have been making probabilistic forecasts of stock price activity for years. Thus, for scores of stocks they have predicted whether or not their prices would increase by 10% or more over the course of a year, that is, of the form P'(Increase $\geq 10\%$). Surprisingly, they gave you access to their records. Following are the coordinates of the points in Ms. Kerr's calibration graph, where the probability judgment category is listed first and then the corresponding proportion of times the stock prices actually rose by at least 10%: (0.4, 0.41), (0.5, 0.48), (0.7, 0.69), (0.8, 0.82). The coordinates for the points in Mr. Cowen's graph are these: (0.3, 0.97), (0.5, 0.02), (0.6, 0.04), (0.8, 0.98), (0.9, 0.03). Which broker should you choose, and why?

7. (Optional) Recall that, when you asked Arlene to make grade predictions for 25 students, she always reported P'(Pass) = 0.9 (p. 67). Twenty-three of the students did pass their courses.

    (a) Show how Arlene's mean probability score of 0.0740 can be derived simply.

    (b) Suppose that Arlene had expressed absolute certainty that each of those students would pass. What mean probability score would she have achieved?

    (c) What score would Arlene have gotten if she had expressed absolute certainty that each would fail?

8. Sports Fan 17 was asked to forecast the outcomes of 20 college basketball games. Following are the results of the exercise, where in each ordered pair (f, d), f is the fan's probability judgment that the home team would win, and d is the corresponding outcome index value, 1 when the home team won, 0 when it lost:

    (0.90, 1), (0.62, 1), (0.77, 1), (0.29, 0), (0.53, 0), (0.60, 0), (0.50, 1), (0.42, 1), (0.80, 1), (0.44, 1), (0.56, 0), (0.50, 1), (0.70, 1), (0.36, 1), (0.46, 0), (0.51, 1), (0.46, 1), (0.53, 1), (0.50, 0), (0.24, 0)

    On the basis of their performance at the halfway point during the term, Instructor B was asked to make probability judgments that each of the 65 students in her course would eventually earn a grade of B. The following ordered pairs (f, d) are the results, where f is the probability judgment, and d is the corresponding outcome index value, 1 when a B was earned, and 0 when some other grade was earned:

    (0.00, 0), (0.70 ,1), (0.60 ,0), (0.10 ,0), (0.40 ,0), (0.00 ,0), (0.70 ,0), (0.00 ,0), (0.90 ,1), (0.00 ,0), (0.30 ,0), (0.30 ,1),

(0.30 ,1), (0.20 ,1), (0.50 ,0), (0.10 ,1), (0.30 ,1), (0.40 ,0),
(0.50 ,1), (0.20 ,0), (0.30 ,0), (0.20 ,0), (0.20 ,0), (0.10 ,0),
(0.20 ,1), (0.20 ,1), (0.60 ,1), (0.30 ,1), (0.60 ,0), (0.20 ,1),
(0.40 ,1), (0.60 ,0), (0.60 ,0), (0.30 ,1), (0.70 ,1), (0.40 ,0),
(0.70 ,1), (0.10 ,1), (0.50 ,0), (0.00 ,0), (0.70 ,1), (0.40 ,1),
(0.70 ,0), (0.30 ,0), (0.20 ,0), (0.60 ,1), (0.00 ,0), (0.00 ,0),
(0.20 ,0), (0.70 ,1), (0.70 ,1), (0.80 ,0), (0.70 ,0), (0.70 ,0),
(0.40 ,0), (0.80 ,1), (0.40 ,0), (0.30 ,1), (0.40 ,0), (0.80 ,0),
(0.80 ,1), (0.40 ,1), (0.30 ,1), (0.00 ,0), (0.80 ,0)

Incidentally, the data for Sports Fan 17 and Instructor B are real.

(a) For Sports Fan 17's data: (i) construct the covariance graph; (ii) calculate $\overline{PS}$; and (iii) (optional) compute the components of the covariance decomposition of $\overline{PS}$.

(b) For Instructor B's data: (i) construct the covariance graph; (ii) calculate $\overline{PS}$; and (iii) (optional) compute the components of the covariance decomposition of $\overline{PS}$.

(c) Discuss the relative strengths and weaknesses of the judgment accuracy dimensions of Sports Fan 17 and Instructor B (ignoring, as you would not do so normally, the fact that the judgments concern different events and were made for different numbers of occasions).

9. Use the data from Problem 8 for this problem.

(a) For Sports Fan 17's data: (i) round the judgments to the nearest tenth; (ii) construct the calibration graph; and (iii) calculate $\overline{PS}$ and (optional) the components of the Murphy decomposition of $\overline{PS}$.

(b) As in part (a), using judgment categories of tenths, for Instructor B's data: (i) construct the calibration graph; and (ii) calculate $\overline{PS}$ and (optional) the components of the Murphy decomposition of $\overline{PS}$.

(c) Are the judgments of Sports Fan 17 or Instructor B uniformly better than those of the other in all respects? Explain.

10. (Optional) Suppose you want a means of indexing the overall accuracy of probability judgments for quantities. Construct such a measure, building on the probability score discussed in this chapter. *Hint:* Break each judged distribution into a set of credible intervals and characterize the accuracy of judgments for each interval (Staël von Holstein, 1972).

Accuracy

The average man's judgment is so poor, he runs a risk every time he uses it.

—Edgar W. Howe

In Chapter 3, we discussed the dilemma of medical patient Stuart Prentice. Mr. Prentice was trying to decide whether or not to have surgery. A major consideration was the possibility of complications that result in his death. The two physicians he consulted gave differing opinions, with Dr. Robinson being more optimistic than Dr. Jefferson about the success of the treatment. It was suggested that Mr. Prentice abide by the assessments of the physician whose judgments are usually more accurate, overall or along the particular dimensions distinguished in Chapter 3. Stuart Prentice's problem was very specific: evaluating the quality of judgment exhibited by two individuals. In this chapter, we consider a more general issue: How accurate can we expect the likelihood judgments of the typical person to be, for example, the average physician?

The first and second sections of this chapter, respectively, examine the accuracy of professionals' and laypersons' judgments for discrete events, for example, whether a patient will survive surgery. The third section discusses the hypothesis that people's likelihood judgments exhibit a special type of inaccuracy characterized as overconfidence. Numerous studies indicate that our memories for our own likelihood judgments are distorted in a particular way, displaying what is known as a hindsight bias. The fourth section reviews the evidence and significance of this phenomenon. The following section addresses the accuracy of likelihood judgments for quantities, for instance, the length of Stuart Prentice's stay in the hospital. The sixth and final major section of the chapter is devoted to the practical problem of improving likelihood judgment accuracy.

EVENT JUDGMENTS BY PROFESSIONALS

Likelihood judgment plays a central role in numerous professions. How accurate can we expect such judgment to be, overall and in terms of various aspects such as calibration? Here we emphasize mainly weather forecasting, medicine, and business.

Weather forecasting

For many years, the U.S. National Weather Service (NWS) reported only categorical forecasts. For instance, forecasters would simply say, "We should see light rain early tomorrow morning" or "There'll be no snow before the weekend." Then, starting in 1965, NWS meteorologists were required to announce probability judgments in addition to their categorical forecasts of precipitation (Murphy and Winkler, 1974). Today it is common to hear broadcasts of statements like, "There's a 70% chance of rain for the metro area this evening, folks!" And when hurricanes are brewing off the southern coast, NWS spokespersons make public pronouncements of probability judgments about where those storms will touch shore. Just how *good* are such judgments?

For a while after 1965, NWS forecasters' probability judgments were not especially impressive. Since then, however, the accuracy of those assessments has improved noticeably (Murphy and Brown, 1984). Consider an illustration. Murphy and Winkler (1977) studied the precipitation probability judgments of weather forecasters in Chicago. Figure 4.1a shows the calibration graph for a typical individual, Forecaster A. The graph is enhanced in that the areas of the points are in proportion to the numbers of cases represented. As the figure suggests, the calibration of Forecaster A's 2916 judgments was outstanding. Over all the occasions when he said there was a 60% chance of precipitation in Chicago, precipitation occurred on almost exactly 60% of those occasions. The same statement could be made about virtually any category of judgments made by Forecaster A.

Figure 4.1b shows the covariance graph for Forecaster A's forecasts. There it is easier to see that his judgments were slightly biased. Precipitation occurred on 25.1% of the occasions Forecaster A considered. However, his

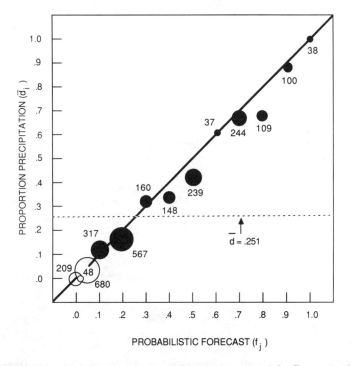

FIGURE 4.1. (a) Calibration graph and (b) covariance graph for Forecaster A's probabilistic forecasts of precipitation for the Chicago area. Numbers adjacent to bars are case frequencies. Source: Murphy and Winkler (1977), Figure 2, adapted with permission from the Royal Statistical Society. Also adapted from Yates and Curley (1985), Exhibits 1(b) and 2(b), by permission of John Wiley and Sons Limited.

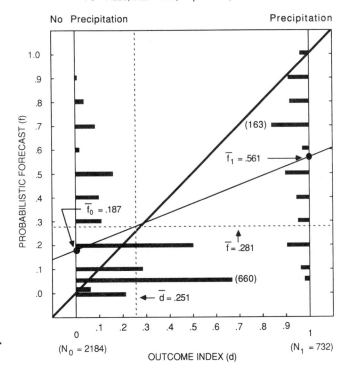

$\overline{PS}$ = .1223, Bias = .030, Slope = .374, Scat = .0483

FIGURE 4.1.
(continued)

average probability judgment was 28.1%, implying a positive bias of 3%. Such biases are common for precipitation forecasts. It is conceivable that they arise from incentive effects. Imagine what would happen if a forecaster's judgments were negatively biased. This would mean that rain occurs more often than the average probability judgment for rain. If people acted on those judgments, they would leave home without umbrellas and get soaked more frequently than "necessary." On the other hand, if probability judgments for rain were positively biased—as they are—this would lead people to carry around their umbrellas more often than they need to. Most of us would prefer to make the latter error than the former. Consciously or otherwise, perhaps weather forecasters are responsive to these feelings.

We thus see that, except for their small positive bias, NWS forecasters' precipitation probability judgments are almost perfectly calibrated, for individual probability categories as well as averaged over all categories. There is practically no room for improvement in that respect. Even in terms of probability scores, reflecting overall accuracy, the judgments of weather forecasters are very good. Recall that, if Forecaster A had behaved like a uniform judge and always said P'(Precipitation) = 0.50, he would have achieved a mean probability score of 0.25. His actual $\overline{PS}$ value of 0.1223 was far superior to that standard. Forecaster A was also considerably more accurate than a base rate judge, who on every occasion would have reported

P'(Precipitation) = $\bar{d}$ = 25.1%, thereby earning a mean probability score of $(0.251)(1 - 0.251) = 0.1880$ (Chapter 3). It seems safe to assume that the historical base rate for precipitation in Chicago is in the vicinity of 25%. If so, Forecaster A's performance surpassed that of the historical judge, too, who in meteorology is known as a "climatological forecaster."

National Weather Service forecasters are real experts themselves. But how do they compare to machine experts (see Chapter 3)? The NWS compiles massive amounts of data. These data come from human observers as well as electronic sensors, for example, in weather balloons and satellites. Coupled with information about current conditions are the records from many previous years. Statistical formulas are applied to these data by computer. The results are considered "objective" probability forecasts. Before they formulate the forecasts that are announced to the public, NWS meteorologists are provided with these objective forecasts. It is left to the discretion of the meteorologist what he or she does from that point on in the forecasting process, and it is unknown exactly what *is* done. Nevertheless, on average, the subjective probabilistic forecasts reported by NWS meteorologists indeed do improve on the objective forecasts (Murphy and Brown, 1984).

So should meteorologists be content that their judgments have gotten as good as they realistically can be expected to become? Probably not. Reexamine Forecaster A's calibration graph, Figure 4.1a. Notice the density of points with vertical coordinates in ranges close to the overall base rate for precipitation, 25.1%. This indicates that Forecaster A's assessments are far from perfect in terms of discrimination, or **resolution,** as it is commonly described in meteorology. That is, there is considerable room for improvement in Forecaster A's ability to discriminate the occasions when precipitation is going to occur from those when it is not. An inspection of Forecaster A's covariance graph (Figure 4.1b) tells a similar story, but from a different point of view. The most striking feature of the graph is how much noise or scatter is contained in the forecasts.

Medicine

Physicians make two major kinds of judgments, *diagnoses* and *prognoses*. The former are opinions about what a patient's current medical condition is, for example, whether a given individual has cancer. The latter are predictions of a patient's future condition, for instance, whether a patient will recover from surgery or whether a heart disease victim will live another six months. There are several reasons we might expect prognostic and diagnostic judgments to differ in accuracy. One is that feedback about prognostic judgments is typically slower, if it arrives at all. For example, a physician can gain a good idea of whether a patient really does have pneumonia by awaiting X-ray results and observing the patient for a few days. On the other hand, it might take a year to evaluate a prognosis of complete recovery from cancer treatment within a year. Another reason differences might be anticipated is that the stakes are seen to be more serious in diagnostic judgment. Often, diagnoses are made in order to aid a person who is in immediate danger. Not so for prognoses.

Probably for the same reasons cited above, prognostic judgments have been studied much less than diagnostic judgments. Nevertheless, the few prognosis studies that do exist have arrived at conclusions surprisingly similar to those from diagnosis studies (see, for example, Dannenberg, Shapiro, and Fries, 1979; Lee and others, 1986; Shapiro, 1977). Thus, it is not entirely inappropriate for us to concentrate our attention on diagnostic judgment. So we first examine the overall accuracy of physicians' diagnoses and then consider various aspects of that accuracy.

Overall diagnostic accuracy In practice, physicians seldom announce their diagnoses as quantified likelihood judgments. More often, it seems, they state their opinions deterministically (see Chapter 1), for example, "I'm afraid you have pneumonia." Or they express their uncertainty in words: "We're pretty sure you don't have heart disease, but we'd like to do more tests to be sure." Nevertheless, numerous investigators have succeeded in getting physicians to report their diagnoses as probability judgments for research purposes. Several studies in which this was done provide some sense of the accuracy of typical diagnoses. Table 4.1 summarizes what was found.

The first column of the table identifies each study. The second indicates whether the study was performed in the participating physician's actual practice or in a laboratory setting. In the latter, each participant was presented with information about former patients and asked to make diagnoses *as if* he or she were the original diagnosing physician. The distinction is an important one. First, in laboratory studies, the information available to the physician is limited, whereas, in actual practice, the physician can ask as

TABLE 4.1   Overall Accuracy of Physicians' Probabilistic Diagnoses

Study[a]	Context[b] Pract	Context[b] Lab	Problem(s)	Better Than Standard? Uniform	Better Than Standard? Base Rate	Better Than Standard? Machine
Centor	x		Streptococcal throat infection	Yes	Yes	No
Christensen-Szalanski	x		Pneumonia	No	No	—
Dolan		x	Heart disease, coronary artery disease, Cushing's syndrome	No	No	No
Hlatky		x	Coronary artery disease	Yes	—	Yes/No[c]
Levi		x	Coronary artery disease	Yes	Yes	No
Tierney	x		Heart attack	Yes	Yes	—

Standards discussed in Chapter 3. Dashes indicate information unreported or machine expert not constructed.

[a]Actual citations: Centor, Dalton, and Yates (1984); Christensen-Szalanski and Bushyhead (1981), with data reanalyzed by Yates and Curley (1985); Dolan, Bordley, and Mushlin (1986); Hlatky, Botvinick, and Brundage (1982); Levi (1986); Tierney and others (1986).

[b]Study done in actual practice setting (Pract) or in a research laboratory (Lab).

[c]Two machine experts were constructed.

many questions and request as many tests as seem reasonable. Second, it is difficult to make the base rate for the relevant disease in the laboratory comparable to the base rate in the physician's customary real world. Finally, the physician in a laboratory study does not have to worry about what will actually happen to each patient, since he or she realizes that the cases have already been resolved, perhaps years ago. The third column in Table 4.1 lists the problems for which probabilistic diagnoses were requested, for example, pneumonia. The fourth through sixth columns indicate whether the overall accuracy level exhibited by the typical physician surpassed various of the standards we discussed in Chapter 3. The specific standards are those set by (1) a uniform judge, for example, a physician who always reports P'(Pneumonia) = 0.5; (2) a base rate judge, for example, one who consistently says P'(Pneumonia) = 0.10 when 10% of the patients under consideration actually had pneumonia; and (3) a machine expert, for example, a computer program that makes judgments on the basis of various patient characteristics that have been associated with the focal problem in the past.

Table 4.1 suggests that there is considerable diversity in how accurate we can expect physicians' diagnoses to be. However, two generalizations seem worth hazarding. First, physicians' judgments usually are more accurate than those of either uniform judges or even base rate judges. However, this is not always the case for individual physicians, even within the studies where the typical physician surpassed these standards. Second, more often than not, well-designed machine experts outperform the average physician in terms of overall accuracy. This latter conclusion might surprise you. Analyses of accuracy components, to which we turn next, shed light on how and why the machine experts sometimes do so well.

Aspects of diagnostic accuracy Calibration is the dimension of diagnostic judgment accuracy that has received the most attention. Figure 4.2 suggests why. That figure shows the calibration graph for probabilistic pneumonia diagnoses reported by physicians in the study by Christensen-Szalanski and Bushyhead (1981) referred to in Table 4.1. Notice that the **calibration curve** connecting the various points in the figure is displaced far to the right of the 1:1 diagonal. This indicates that, on the whole, the physicians' judgments grossly overpredicted the incidence of pneumonia.

The pattern of miscalibration found by Christensen-Szalanski and Bushyhead (1981) is mainly a form of bias, which is more easily appreciated in covariance graphs. Figure 4.3a shows the covariance graph for the probabilistic diagnoses of streptococcal throat infection (strep throat), made by the physicians studied by Centor, Dalton, and Yates (1984). Consistent with the previous pneumonia findings, the physicians markedly overdiagnosed the target disease. Poses and others (1985) observed the same bias in streptococcal infection judgments. Fryback and Thornbury (1976), whose data were closely examined by Wallsten (1981), found similar evidence of overdiagnosis of highly threatening problems when radiologists examined X-ray records and reported probabilistic judgments for malignant (cancerous) tumors versus nonharmful cysts or normal tissue.

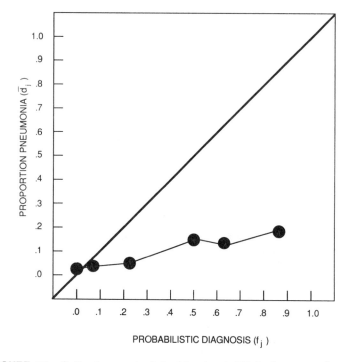

FIGURE 4.2. Calibration graph of physicians' probabilistic diagnoses of pneumonia. Source: Christensen-Szalanski and Bushyhead (1981), Figure 1. Copyright 1981 by the American Psychological Association. Adapted by permission from the publisher and authors.

The above findings suggest the generalization that physicians really do exhibit value-induced biases, whereby they tend to give too-high probability judgments for serious disorders (see Chapter 2). However, not all the available evidence supports that conclusion. Figure 4.4 shows the covariance graph for probabilistic diagnoses of myocardial infarction (heart attack) made by emergency room physicians for patients arriving with complaints of chest pain (Tierney and others, 1986). The positive bias in those judgments was minuscule. Levi (1986) also found little evidence of bias in coronary artery disease diagnoses, although it should be recognized that his study was done in a laboratory setting where the base rate might have differed from that found in normal practice.

The conflicting results indicate that there is no general consensus about calibration and bias in diagnostic judgments. A clearer picture will have to await further study. Nevertheless, large biases are common enough such that we should not expect unbiasedness to be the inviolate norm.

How about discrimination and slope? These closely related aspects of judgment accuracy are most meaningfully evaluated in comparisons with experts. Figures 4.3a and 4.3b, respectively, show the covariance graphs of streptococcal infection judgments made by physicians and by the machine

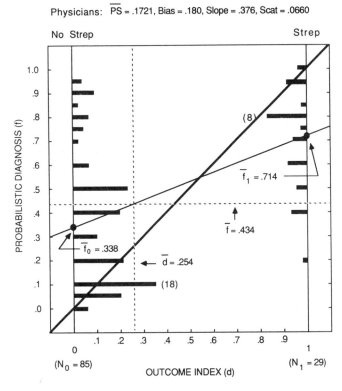

FIGURE 4.3. Covariance graphs of probabilistic diagnoses of streptococcal throat infection: (a) by physicians, (b) by a statistical model. Source: Centor, Dalton, and Yates (1984).

expert constructed by Centor, Dalton, and Yates (1984). Observe that the slope for the physicians' judgments was distinctly greater than that for the machine's judgments. Given that difference, it should not be surprising that the physicians' judgment had better discrimination, too.

Why would a human expert have better discrimination and slope than a machine expert? Recall from Chapter 3 what is necessary in order for a person's judgments to achieve good discrimination or slope: That individual must have access to good information. In all comparisons of real judges with machine experts—"models," as they are called—the human judge has access to at least as much information as that provided to the model, and typically more. For instance, Centor, Dalton, and Yates's physicians actually saw patients face-to-face and could seek any information they desired. In contrast, the machine expert relies on a fixed set of information for every patient, for example, presence of a cough and history of fever. Such an information advantage ought to permit the real expert to discriminate better, as was the case here. However, as found by Levi (1986), when human and machine experts have access to *indentical* information, the machine expert can be expected to often exhibit better discrimination.

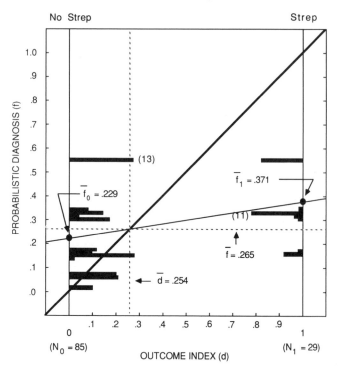

Figure 4.3   (continued)

Let us now consider what happens when we compare the scatter in the judgments of real diagnosticians and models. Again contrast the two covariance graphs in Figure 4.3. Notice that there was much greater scatter in the physicians' diagnoses of streptococcal infection. The same type of physician versus model difference was found by Levi (1986). Why do such differences occur? As indicated in Chapter 3, one possible basis for excessive scatter is reliance on information that is *believed* to be associated with the event of interest, but that actually is not. There is indirect evidence that this contributed to the scatter in the judgments by Centor, Dalton, and Yates's physicians. Poses and others (1985) carefully studied the information physicians actually used in making probabilistic diagnoses of streptococcal infection. Clinical studies have found no more than five patient characteristics to be associated with the infection. However, the physicians consistently relied on eight distinct features, some of which are necessarily unrelated to the disorder. The second potential basis for excessive scatter is the judge's unreliability. This is an inherent disadvantage of people versus machines. No real person can consistently do the same thing the same way, day in and day out. Machines can (see Goldberg, 1970). A human physician's inconsistency manifests itself as scatter, as we see in Figure 4.3a.

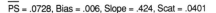

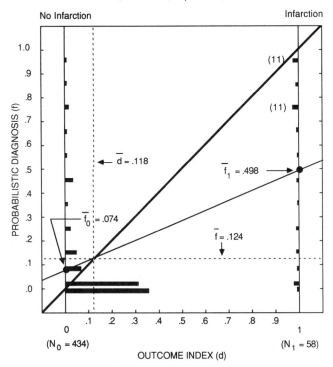

FIGURE 4.4. Covariance graph of probabilistic diagnoses of myocardial infarction (heart attack) by emergency room physicians. Constructed from data reported by Tierney and others (1986), Table 1, with permission from the Society for Medical Decision Making.

Business

Stock prices Imagine yourself as a new parent. You want to build a financially secure future for your daughter. So if anything happens to you or your spouse, she will have the resources needed to pay for her education. Your financial advisor recommends establishing a stock portfolio in trust for your daughter. The stocks comprising the portfolio should be ones with good growth potential and security; current income is relatively unimportant. "Tom Warner" is a local stockbroker. Mr. Warner suggests that you include "Granite Construction" stock in your daughter's portfolio. He says there is a good chance that the price of Granite stock will increase modestly but steadily. How good is Mr. Warner's judgment likely to be? Should you follow his advice?

There have been only a few published studies of business people's probability judgments for events similar to those implicit in the above scenario. A study by Staël von Holstein (1972) is representative of what has been done, however. Staël von Holstein asked his subjects to consider the prices of 12 stocks on the Stockholm Stock Exchange. Each individual gave probability judgments for changes in the price of every stock. For example, the subject was asked to state a probability that the buying price for the stock would increase by more than 3% over the following two weeks, that is, P'(Price increase > 3%). The procedure was repeated over ten sessions, spaced by two-week intervals. Staël von Holstein's group of 72 subjects included investment bankers, stock market experts, statisticians, university business teachers, and business administration students.

Unfortunately, Staël von Holstein's results were not reported in sufficient detail to permit the construction of calibration or covariance graphs. So we cannot analyze various aspects of judgment quality as carefully as we might like. Nevertheless, conclusions can be reached about overall accuracy. Recall that a uniform judge behaves as if all the events that are possible in a given situation are equally likely to occur. In Staël von Holstein's study, only 3 of the 72 subjects achieved PS values better than would have been earned by a uniform judge. In terms of overall accuracy, the various groups of subjects were ranked as follows: stock market experts > statisticians > business administration students > university business teachers > investment bankers. The general inaccuracy of the judgments is remarkable. The ordering of the groups according to accuracy is surprising, too. The low ranking of the investment bankers is particularly puzzling.

So should you follow Tom Warner's recommendation to include Granite Construction in your daughter's stock portfolio? It is quite possible that Mr. Warner, as an individual stock broker, has exceptionally good judgment. Moreover, we might suspect that the results obtained by Staël von Holstein give an unfairly harsh characterization of people's abilities to predict stock price activity. Staël von Holstein acknowledged that there were aspects of his experiment that were different from the conditions under which stock market specialists normally operate. One is the two-week time horizon imposed on the subjects. Ordinarily, market analysts do not make forecasts for such short periods of time.

Yates, McDaniel, and Brown (in press) tested the generality of Staël von Holstein's conclusions under more conventional forecasting conditions. For example, their subjects were asked to make probabilistic stock price change predictions over a financial quarter, that is, three months, rather than two weeks. Although there were fewer participants than in Staël von Holstein's study, 31 versus 72, each individual considered many more stocks, 31 rather than 10. The subjects had up to ten days to make their forecasts, and were allowed to use any sources of information or techniques desired, other than other subjects. In this study, *none* of the participants outperformed the uniform judge. The subjects were all students in university finance courses, although most had previous work experience in the finance world. Despite the fact that they were not (yet) practicing stock forecasters, in view of Staël von Holstein's previous group comparisons, the results provide additional reason to believe that judgments about stock price movement generally are not very good.

There are market theories, as well as some evidence, indicating that stock price changes are largely random (for example, Fama, 1965; Godfrey, Granger, and Morgenstern, 1964).[1] That is why many financial experts believe it is naive to expect any one individual to consistently predict price movement with a high degree of accuracy. Yates, McDaniel, and Brown (in press) hypothesized that this might account for surprising group differences in the accuracy of price activity judgments. Suppose that price changes in fact are inherently highly unpredictable. Then a person who uses various—necessarily worthless—financial indicators to try to foresee price changes will do worse than if he or she ignored those cues, for example, made predictions like a uniform judge. Yates, McDaniel, and Brown anticipated that undergraduate finance students would assume they were too inexperienced to know what indicators should be used to predict price movements. So they would resign themselves to judgments similar to those of a uniform judge. In contrast, master's- and Ph.D.-level business students were expected to believe they *could* make accurate judgments. Accordingly, it was anticipated that undergraduate students would make more uniform and more accurate price-change predictions than their graduate student counterparts. And they did.

Stock earnings Now imagine that you are 65 years old and have just retired from your job. As an investor, you are interested in the security of your funds. However, you are less concerned about growth than when you were younger and trying to provide for your family's future needs. Instead, you want a modest, steady income for your remaining years. Thus, you would like to include in your portfolio stocks that will pay high dividends consistently. So firms that make good earnings, that is, revenues relative to assets, would be attractive to you. Again, we could ask how good Tom Warner, your local stock broker, is likely to be at predicting the earnings for a given company.

The main reason stock prices are so hard to predict is that they are directly determined by the vagaries of millions of competing, equally knowledgeable investors' buying and selling behavior. In principle, earnings should be and often are thought to be more predictable than prices, since they are subject to fewer and more transparent influences. Yates, McDaniel, and Brown (in press) sought to determine if probability judgments about earnings actually are more accurate than judgments about prices. So, in addition to predictions about price changes for 31 stocks on the New York Stock Exchange, their subjects were also asked to report judgments about the prospective earnings of the relevant firms. As expected, the subjects' probability scores were significantly better for the earnings judgments.

---

[1]Prices cannot be entirely random, since they can be anticipated by individuals who are highly knowledgeable about specific firms, for example, inside traders, in the extreme.

Bond defaults   In Chapter 2, we discussed how businesses and governments sometimes borrow money through the mechanism of selling bonds. We also saw how several agencies provide ratings of bond quality. At least indirectly, these ratings reflect the agencies' judgments of how likely it is that the sellers will default on the bonds, that is, be unable to repay them. For example, suppose Standard & Poor's gives its highest rating of AAA to a bond issued by the XYZ Corporation, but assigns only a B rating to an issue offered by QRS, Inc. Then, all other considerations being equal, this almost certainly means that Standard & Poor's considers the chances of default to be greater for QRS than for XYZ.

Suppose you were pondering whether to purchase QRS or XYZ bonds. The decision would not be a simple one. Since the QRS bonds have a lower rating, they may very well promise a higher interest rate to compensate for their implicit greater riskiness. So it would be helpful if you knew just *how much* riskier the QRS bonds were. Put another way, it would be useful if you knew to what extent bond ratings really are associated with default rates.

A well-known study by Hickman (1957) provides some sense of the relationship between bond ratings and default rates. Several agencies besides Standard & Poor's publish bond ratings. However, the ratings of all the agencies are usually quite similar to one another. Hickman formed a composite rating from the different systems. According to this integrated scheme, the highest-quality bonds were assigned the rating I. For example, a bond rated AAA by Standard & Poor's would have a composite rating of I. Bonds assigned the second-highest rating by a particular agency, for instance, AA by Standard & Poor's, would be given a II in the composite system, and so forth. Hickman then compared the default rates of corporate bonds with composite ratings in various ranges over the period 1900–1943. Figure 4.5 shows his findings.

Hickman's results indicate that bond ratings are not a perfect indicator of default rates. Nevertheless, there is clearly a consistent relationship between bond raters' opinions and the actual incidence of default.[2] Thus, at least tentatively, it appears that experts' judgments about bond issues might be better than their judgments about stock price activity.

LAYPERSONS' EVENT LIKELIHOOD JUDGMENTS

Every event is unique in the sense that nothing ever repeats itself literally. Nevertheless, certain classes of events are essentially the same with respect to particular features. For example, the rainstorm we experienced last Thursday was harder and shorter than the one we had yesterday. But on each of those days we experienced rain. So we say that the event "precipitation" was "repeated" on both occasions. In other circumstances, the

---

[2]Bond ratings might actually exert some influence on default rates. Government regulations prevent certain financial institutions, for example, banks, from purchasing bonds with ratings below a certain level. This could mean that some potentially viable firms are unable to acquire the funds they need to stave off bankruptcy; so they fail.

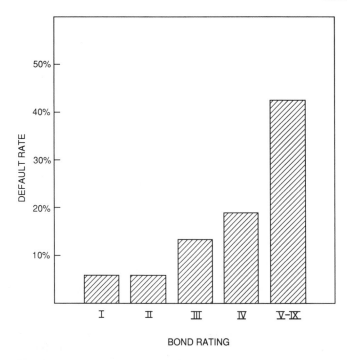

FIGURE 4.5. Default rates as a function of bond ratings. Constructed from data reported by Hickman (1957), Table 1, with permission from the National Bureau of Economic Research, Inc.

similarities between individual occasions are weaker, and we are inclined to consider the specific events to be relatively unique. For instance, a presidential primary election in Alabama is quite different from one in New York. So if Candidate A wins in both states, we are not disposed to saying that the identical event occurred in each place. Conceptually, there is little quarrel with trying to draw inferences about people's judgment tendencies using such measures as probability scores and calibration indexes derived from judgments about repetitive events, for example, "precipitation." There is more uneasiness about such inferences when the judgments concern many different relatively unique events, for example, "Candidate A wins." Nevertheless, most researchers believe that these inferences have some value, as long as the pertinent events have at least some degree of commonality; for example, they all concern presidential primaries instead of some being about elections, some about sports, some about business, and so on.

Most studies of professional judgment have dealt with repeated events. A "layperson" is an individual who makes judgments in an area outside the domain of his or her professional responsibility. In contrast to the situation with professionals, most studies of lay judgment have emphasized unique events. Nevertheless, recent work has encompassed lay opinions about repeated events, too. The distinctions between repeated and unique events are sufficiently great to warrant separate discussions of how people judge their chances.

Repeated events

Studies of laypersons' likelihood judgments about repeated events have been in two areas mainly, sports and parlor games. We consider them in turn.

Sports Yates (1982) examined students' and professors' predictions of college basketball game outcomes (see also Ronis and Yates, 1987). The mean value of PS earned by Yates's subjects was 0.2527, which is worse than the value that would have been earned by a uniform judge who always indicated P'(Home team wins) = 0.50. Almost 40% of the individual subjects failed to surpass this standard. The subjects' judgments were heavily biased, too. The average stated probability for the home team winning was lower by 13.8% than the percentage of times the home team actually won. The average slope in the judgments was 0.074. Yates and Curley (1985) examined similar probabilistic predictions about major league baseball games reported by professional oddsmaker "Jimmy the Greek" Snyder. The basketball judgments reported by Yates's subjects had much worse calibration, but better slopes. Clearly, there must be additional studies of laypersons' sporting event probability judgments before firm conclusions can be established. Tentatively, however, it appears that the predictions of laypersons and professional oddsmakers have different strengths and weaknesses. In terms of overall accuracy, it is not obvious that the oddsmakers' opinions would be better.

Bridge In the card game of bridge, each team makes bids. Essentially, a bid is a team's bet that it will win at least a stated number of tricks during a particular game. Players make such bids on the basis of how good the cards are that have been dealt to them. Obviously, success at bridge hinges on a player's ability to bid well, that is, to accurately judge whether a given number of tricks indeed can be won.

Keren (1987) asked expert bridge players to play a series of games with one another. He did the same for groups of nonexpert players. After the bidding phase during each game, but before actual play began, every player wrote down a probability judgment that the number of games that had been bid actually would be won by the team stating the bid, that is, whether the stated contract would be made. Figure 4.6 shows calibration curves for the two classes of players. The calibration of the expert players was certainly not as good as that of, say, weather forecasters. But it was better than that observed in many other contexts. And it was clearly superior to the calibration of the nonexpert players. The latter individuals exhibited a form of miscalibration that, as we will see, is quite common among laypersons in other settings, too. Unfortunately, insufficient detail was provided to evaluate accuracy at the level of individual players or to do a complete analysis of other aspects of the players' judgment quality, including overall accuracy.

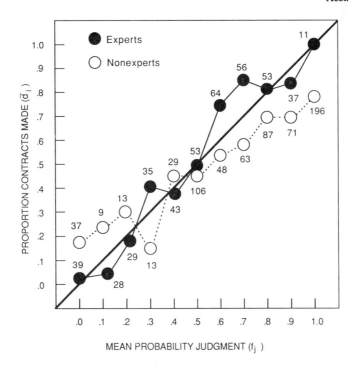

FIGURE 4.6. Calibration curves for expert and nonexpert players' probability judgments that stated contracts in bridge games would be made. Adapted from Keren (1987), Figure 1, with permission from Academic Press and the author.

Unique events

Fischhoff and Beyth (1975) reported a representative study of laypersons' judgments for unique events. In 1972, U.S. President Richard Nixon made two historic diplomatic visits. One was to China, the other to the USSR. Prior to those visits, Fischhoff and Beyth asked subjects to consider several possible outcomes of the visits. Among the outcomes were: "President Nixon will meet Mao at least once," "President Nixon will announce that his trip was successful," and "The USA and USSR will agree to a joint space program." The subjects were required to state probability judgments for each of the events, for example, P'(President Nixon will meet Mao at least once).

Figure 4.7 shows the calibration graph for the subjects' judgments, accumulated over all questions. The calibration depicted in the figure appears quite good. Regrettably, the numbers of cases represented by each point were not reported. So we cannot gain a sense of how good the subjects' judgments were in terms of other aspects of accuracy, for example, discrimination.

Most studies of laypersons' likelihood judgments have required subjects to make judgments in two stages. First, the subject is presented with

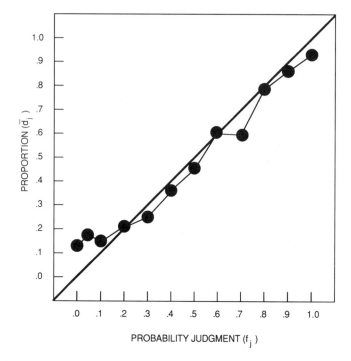

FIGURE 4.7.   Calibration graph of subjects' probabilistic predictions of events that might occur during President Nixon's 1972 diplomatic visits to China and the Soviet Union. Adapted from Fischhoff and Beyth (1975), Figure 2, with permission from Academic Press and the authors.

two alternatives, one of which he or she selects as the correct one, that is, the one more likely to happen. In the second stage of the task, the subject indicates his or her certainty that the chosen alternative is indeed correct. This response is in the form of a probability judgment, constrained to lie between 50% and 100%. The task used by Fischhoff and MacGregor (1982) illustrates the technique.

Each item presented to Fischhoff and MacGregor's subjects concerned an occurrence that might take place within 30 days of the experiment. For example, one item asked the subject about the outcome of an upcoming local election for mayor. The subject was asked to indicate whether he or she expected Candidate A or Candidate B to win. Then the subject reported how sure he or she was that the indicated candidate in fact would win. The items spanned a broad range of topics. Figure 4.8 shows the calibration curve over all items and subjects. In contrast to the results obtained by Fischhoff and Beyth, the judgments of Fischhoff and MacGregor's subjects were very poorly calibrated. The direction of the miscalibration indicates that the judgments were positively biased. Again, nothing can be said about such accuracy dimensions as discrimination, slope, and scatter.

By far, the majority of studies about laypersons' likelihood judgments have involved general knowledge questions. Such items are sometimes

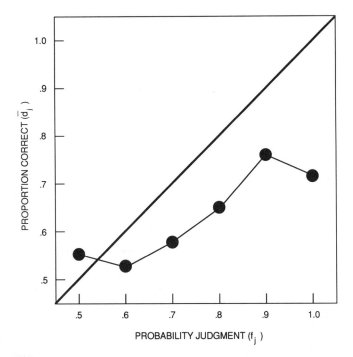

FIGURE 4.8. Calibration graph of probabilistic predictions of various events, for example, election outcomes. Adapted from Fischhoff and MacGregor (1982), Exhibit 5, by permission of John Wiley and Sons Limited and the authors.

called *almanac questions,* because their answers often can be found in almanacs. In this kind of study, the subject might be asked a question like the following: "Which city has more people: (a) London or (b) Paris?" The subject then picks either London or Paris and notes his or her degree of certainty in that response. Figure 4.9 (from Lichtenstein, Fischhoff, and Phillips, 1982) shows calibration curves typical of those found in studies of judgments based on general knowledge questions. Observe that the curves are displaced to the right of the 1:1 diagonal, indicating positive bias.

What general conclusions can we draw about the accuracy of likelihood judgments made by people in their everyday lives? Unfortunately, there have been comparatively few studies of the issue. Moreover, investigators who *have* examined the questions have not reported their results in great detail. What is evident nevertheless is that, as in the case of professionals, there is considerable room for improvement. Tentatively, we can expect to find many instances in which lay judgments are no more accurate overall than the judgments of a uniform judge who believes all possibilities are equally likely. Almost nothing is known about the discrimination of laypersons' likelihood judgments or their slope and scatter. The most thoroughly studied aspect of lay judgments is calibration. Most of the evidence suggests that lay calibration is often quite poor.

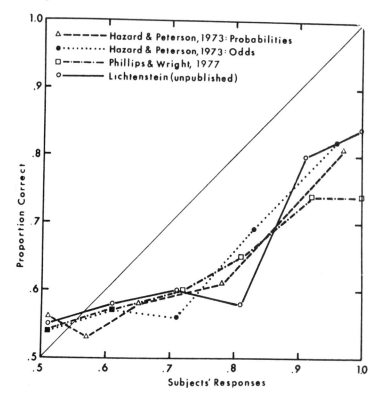

FIGURE 4.9. Typical calibration curves for probabilistic responses to general knowledge (almanac) questions. Reproduced from Lichtenstein, Fischhoff, and Phillips (1982), Figure 2, with permission from Cambridge University Press.

OVERCONFIDENCE IN ONE'S JUDGMENT

Return to the two-stage judgment procedure described above. Recall that, in the first stage, the person states deterministically that one particular alternative is the one that is most likely to occur, for example, "Candidate A will win." The person then reports a probability judgment that the selected event indeed will occur. Literally, the target event for this latter judgment is the event "My previous deterministic judgment was correct," for instance, "I picked the candidate who will actually win." Imagine an individual who makes many such two-stage judgments. Suppose that for this person the average judgment P'(My previous deterministic judgment was correct) is larger than the proportion of times those deterministic judgments *were* correct. Then, as is customary, it seems reasonable to say that this individual is **overconfident** in his or her opinions.

It is often believed that people's judgments are routinely overconfident. If this is true, it poses several practical problems. First, it implies that our decisions will suffer from the inaccuracy of our judgments. More insidiously, we will fail to even recognize the *need* to improve our judgments (and thereby our decisions). A commonly uttered American folk expression is apt: "If it ain't broke, don't fix it!" So what is the extent and magnitude of the overconfidence problem as manifested in likelihood judgments? Are our judgments really "broke," when we think they are just fine? Let us examine the evidence.

The Oskamp study

The best-known study demonstrating overconfidence in judgment was reported by Oskamp (1965). Oskamp's subjects included practicing clinical psychologists and also graduate and undergraduate psychology students. Each was asked to read the clinical case history summary of a 29-year-old man called "Joseph Kidd." The history was described in stages. Stage 1 presented basic information about Mr. Kidd, for example, that he was a World War II veteran, and what his current job was. Stage 2 dealt with his childhood years. Stage 3 discussed his high school and college experiences. The fourth and final stage covered the period from Mr. Kidd's stint in the Army to the present.

The subject was required to complete a 25-item, multiple-choice test four times, after reading each stage of Joseph Kidd's case history. The items were about Mr. Kidd's behavior patterns, attitudes, interests, and typical reactions. The case history did not contain the explicit answer to any of the test items. Subjects were supposed to respond to the items according to standard clinical procedures. That is, they were to form a "personality picture" of Joseph Kidd and make judgments on that basis. Nevertheless, Oskamp (1965, p. 262) indicates that items "were constructed only where there was fairly objective criterion information presented in the case."

After answering each item, the subject indicated his or her confidence that the chosen answer was actually correct. Every item had five alternatives. So the allowable confidence responses extended from 20% to 100%. In this form, the confidence ratings could be interpreted as probability judgments of the form P'(My chosen answer is correct). Figure 4.10 displays the relevant results by stages.

Surprisingly, there were no reliable differences between the various subject groups, that is, clinical psychologists versus graduate students versus undergraduates. The open circles in Figure 4.10 indicate the mean confidence ratings for test items completed after subjects read each stage of Joseph Kidd's case history. The filled circles show the corresponding proportions of correct responses. The stage-by-stage differences between the points are the biases in the subjects' judgments. Notice that the biases were always positive, indicating overconfidence. In addition, the degree of overconfidence got progressively worse as the subjects learned more about Mr. Kidd. It is as if the subjects said to themselves, "Since I am reading more and more about this case, I *must* be getting better at answering these questions." But they were not.

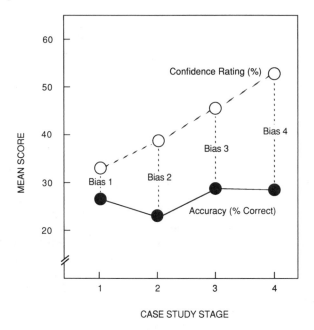

FIGURE 4.10. Mean confidence ratings (open circles) and percentages of correct responses (filled circles) as a function of stage of reading in Joseph Kidd's case history. Constructed from data reported by Oskamp (1965), Table 2. Copyright 1965 by the American Psychological Association. Adapted with permission from the publisher and author.

Professional judgment

The Oskamp study suggests that professional clinical psychologists are just as prone to making overconfident judgments as are less-experienced psychology students. We previously discussed the likelihood judgments of various other groups of professionals. Let us reexamine those judgments to see if they too indicate overconfidence.

The issue can be approached only indirectly. This is because most studies of professional judgment have not used two-stage procedures. Instead, individuals have been asked to state probability judgments for objectively defined events, such as "Rain," "Coronary artery disease," and "Price increase." Think of the problem as follows. Suppose there is only a single target event and, implicitly, its complement, for example, "Precipitation" and "No precipitation." When the person states a target-event probability judgment greater than 0.50, we assume that, in a two-stage procedure, the designated target event would have been selected as a deterministic prediction. Conversely, a probability judgment lower than 0.50 would imply a deterministic prediction of the complementary event. Thus, for example, if a weather forecaster says P'(Precipitation) = 0.60, we would expect "Precipitation" to be chosen as a deterministic forecast. Moreover, we would infer that the forecaster would state P'(My chosen alternative will be correct) = 0.60. On the other hand, if the forecaster says P'(Precipitation) = 0.30, we would anticipate a choice of "No precipitation" and P'(My chosen alternative will be correct) = 0.70. Suppose such a forecaster were overconfident. You should be able to convince yourself that his or her calibration graph will have the following characteristics: (1) points corresponding to judgments above 50% for the target event lie below the 1:1 diagonal, and (2) points associated with judgments less than 50% appear above the diagonal.

Now reexamine the calibration graphs shown in Figures 4.1 and 4.2, which are for professional judgments in weather forecasting and medical diagnosis. Observe that neither of them exhibits the overconfidence pattern described above. Such is the case in other areas, too. So overconfidence is certainly not universal among professional judges. If anything, Oskamp's results seem the exception rather than the rule.

Lay judgment

The case for overconfidence The most consistent evidence of lay overconfidence has emerged in almanac question studies, for example, in which the subject indicates that either London or Paris is bigger and then reports a probability judgment that the chosen alternative is correct. Recall that, as shown in Figure 4.9, the calibration curves found in such studies are heavily positively biased. It makes sense to interpret the results as indicating overconfidence, since subjects' effective judgments of the form P'(My chosen answer is correct) are generally too high.

Perhaps you wonder whether, although individuals *say* they have great confidence in their chosen alternatives, their true beliefs are more modest. The implicit hypothesis is that the people expressing such extreme beliefs would not make decisions as if they actually held those opinions. Fischhoff, Slovic, and Lichtenstein (1977) tested this possibility by giving subjects the opportunity to play certain monetary gambles. The outcome of each gamble depended on whether the subject's chosen answer to a general knowledge question was correct. If the subject really believed the extreme probability judgments he or she stated previously, accepting the gambles should have been seen by the subject as financially advantageous. Otherwise, it should not. The subjects overwhelmingly agreed to play the gambles. So there is little reason to doubt the candor of people's stated probability judgments about their answers to general knowledge questions.

Most almanac question studies have been performed in Western countries. However, recent studies in Asia have yielded results that are similar in some ways to those found in the West, but are surprisingly different, too. Wright, Phillips, and their colleagues (for example, Wright and Phillips, 1980) have discovered that general knowledge calibration curves for several Asian groups tend to be displaced even farther to the right of the main diagonal than those for European and American subjects, suggesting greater overconfidence.

Yates and others (1989) examined Asian–Western judgmental accuracy differences in more detail. Figure 4.11 shows calibration curves for Chinese and American university students' responses to a common set of almanac questions. The proportions of correct answers selected were virtually identical. Confirming the results of Wright and his colleagues, the Chinese students' probability judgments were markedly more biased. Interestingly, however, those judgments were significantly more discriminative. In fact, the complementary differences in calibration and discrimination compensated for each other perfectly. The average values of $\overline{PS}$ were indistinguishable between the Chinese and American subject groups; overall judgment accuracy was equivalent. Yates and others (1989) also found that the mean probability scores of Japanese subjects were essentially the same as those of their Chinese and American subjects. Moreover, the calibration–discrimination pattern for the Japanese subjects more closely matched that of the

PRC (○): PS = .2258, CI = .0289, DI = .0205

USA (●): PS = .2204, CI = .0141, DI = .0126

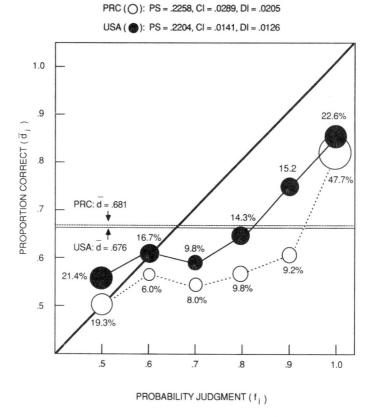

PROBABILITY JUDGMENT (f$_j$)

FIGURE 4.11.   Calibration curves for Chinese and American subjects' probabilistic responses to almanac questions. The sizes of the points are in proportion to the percentages with which given judgment categories were used, which are also reported as the adjacent percentages. Adapted from Yates and others (1989), with permission from Academic Press.

Americans than that of the Chinese. These cross–national comparisons suggest that cultural and sociotechnological circumstances can have marked and complex effects on probability judgment tendencies.

Although most studies indicating lay overconfidence have involved almanac questions, not all of them have. For example, reconsider the calibration curve for Keren's (1987) nonexpert bridge players shown in Figure 4.6. Notice that it is essentially rotated clockwise from the 1:1 diagonal, an indication of overconfidence. Overconfidence is also suggested in the calibration curve of Fischhoff and MacGregor (1982), shown in Figure 4.8. Recall that these investigators' subjects first stated which of two alternative events they expected to occur, for example, Candidate A or Candidate B will be elected, and then reported probability judgments between 50% and 100% that the indicated event would actually occur.

The case against overconfidence Overconfidence in lay judgment is not universal. In contrast to the previous Fischhoff and MacGregor (1982) results, most studies in which laypersons were asked to make judgments concerning future events have not found overconfidence (for example, Wright, 1982; Wright and Ayton, 1986; Wright and Wisudha, 1982). As a concrete example, reexamine the calibration curve shown in Figure 4.7 for Fischhoff and Beyth's (1975) subjects' predictions about various events surrounding President Nixon's trips to China and the Soviet Union. At the far reaches of the calibration curve, there appears to be some evidence of overconfidence. In general, however, there is little. Also recall that the calibration curve for Keren's (1987) expert bridge players (Figure 4.6) showed little consistent miscalibration of any form.

Overconfidence is not uniform even for almanac questions. Two related factors moderate the phenomenon (Lichtenstein and Fischhoff, 1977). First, when questions are relatively easy, in the sense that most people can answer them correctly, people's judgments tend to be *underconfident* rather than overconfident. Second, individuals who answer more items correctly exhibit less overconfidence than others do.

A synthesis So we are left with a muddied but interesting story. There are circumstances in which overconfidence in lay judgment reliably occurs. On the other hand, there are also situations where overconfidence is almost never observed. It will be a while before the picture clears. However, the pattern of existing findings is suggestive of explanations. It seems plausible that feedback about the accuracy of our judgments is a critical determinant of whether overconfidence will or will not occur (see Arkes and others, 1987). Recall that overconfidence is much less common among professionals than among laypersons. Also, as suggested in Keren's bridge study, it seems that expert laypersons are less overconfident than novices. A common difference between laypersons and professionals and between experts and nonexperts is experience. And a major lesson of experience is the limits of our abilities. Perhaps overconfident individuals have had insufficient experience with the specific judgment domain to learn how little they actually know. (Ignorance is bliss?)

HINDSIGHT BIAS

The phenomenon of **hindsight bias** in likelihood judgments is closely related to overconfidence. The previously mentioned study by Fischhoff and Beyth (1975) about President Nixon's diplomatic visits illustrates the bias nicely. To refresh your memory, subjects were asked to make probability judgments about various possible outcomes of the visits to China and the USSR before those trips actually took place. After the visits had been completed, the subjects were asked to recall the probabilities they had stated originally.

Some of the outcomes considered by the subjects actually occurred, whereas others did not. Moreover, subjects sometimes perceived events to have happened when they really did not happen, and conversely. Figure 4.12 shows recalled probabilities as functions of the originally reported probabilities. If the subjects' memories were perfect, all the circles would appear along the dotted diagonal line. The filled circles represent probabilities for outcomes the subjects believed to have actually taken place. The open circles are for events thought to have not occurred. Note that the filled circles cluster near the top of the figure, the open circles much lower. That

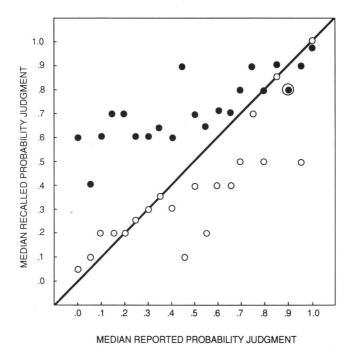

MEDIAN REPORTED PROBABILITY JUDGMENT

FIGURE 4.12.   Recalled probability judgments as a function of originally-reported probability judgments.   Filled circles: Events believed by the subject to have actually occurred.   Open circles: Events thought to have not occurred.   Adapted from Fischhoff and Beyth (1975), Figure 1, with permission from Academic Press and the authors.

is, there was a clear tendency for the subjects to distort their recollections. The subjects felt they had originally offered much higher probabilities for events that eventually occurred and much lower ones for events that did not happen.

Hindsight bias has considerable significance. Like overconfidence (to which it may very well contribute), hindsight bias lulls us into believing that our opinions are more accurate than they really are. We thus fail to recognize the need to try to improve our judgments. Hindsight bias should also cause us to be overly harsh critics of others' judgments (see Arkes and others, 1981; Fischhoff, 1975). When we discover inaccuracies in other people's predictions, we underestimate the difficulty of their task: "They should have *known* that was going to happen! Even *I* could have foreseen it!" For example, picture yourself as a manager who delegates hiring decisions to a personnel director. Inevitably, some of the employees appointed by your personnel director fail. Hindsight bias suggests that you might inappropriately accuse your personnel director of poor foresight. You might even needlessly fire one personnel director after another, not realizing that all of them are exercising judgment as accurate as you should expect.

Why does hindsight bias occur? What can be done about it? We discuss several possibilities in Chapter 7.

JUDGMENTS FOR QUANTITIES

In Chapter 2, we considered the problem faced by Jerry Reed and Steve Houston, the owners of Copper Star Productions. They were trying to anticipate the size of the crowd that would attend a music festival they were managing. Figure 2.2 (p. 22) depicts their judged probability distributions for prospective crowd size, the *random variable C*. For example, it is shown that, in Jerry Reed's view, $P'(10,000 \leq IC \leq 15,000) = 30\%$. That is, 10,000, 15,000] was a 30% credible interval for the number of people who would come to the music festival. How accurate are people's likelihood judgments for quantities? In Chapter 3, we saw that the most commonly discussed aspect of accuracy for such judgments is distribution calibration. For instance, suppose Jerry Reed's calibration were perfect. Then the actual crowd sizes for a large number of concerts will fall within the 30% credible intervals Jerry Reed specifies for 30% of those concerts. We now consider the distribution calibration of real judges, both laypersons and professionals.

Laypersons' distribution calibration

Laypersons' judged probability distributions often exhibit a form of miscalibration characterized as overconfidence. Alpert and Raiffa (1982), in a study initially reported in 1969, were apparently the first to document the phenomenon. Alpert and Raiffa's subjects were mainly business students at Harvard University. Each was asked to consider a variety of quantities. For example, one quantity was the number of foreign automobiles imported into the United States in 1967. Another was the percentage of opinion poll respondents who felt that public school teachers should be permitted to join unions. A quantity of local interest at Harvard was the percentage of first-year MBA students who preferred drinking bourbon rather than Scotch whiskey.

For each quantity, Alpert and Raiffa had their subjects specify the 0.01, 0.25, 0.50, 0.75, and 0.99 fractiles of their judged probability distributions. This defined credible intervals covering all potential values of the quantities. Suppose the smallest possible value of a quantity is specified by LB, for "lower bound," for example, 0 for car imports. Similarly, the largest possible value is denoted by UB, for "upper bound." Also, let us represent the p fractile for the quantity Q by q_p. For example, the 0.50 fractile would be denoted $q_{0.50}$. So the credible intervals obtained by Alpert and Raiffa can be characterized as [LB, $q_{0.01}$], ($q_{0.01}$, $q_{0.25}$], ($q_{0.25}$, $q_{0.50}$], ($q_{0.50}$, $q_{0.75}$], ($q_{0.75}$, $q_{0.99}$], and ($q_{0.99}$, UB]. In each instance, the parenthesis indicates that the value to its right is not included in the specified interval. The square bracket indicates that the adjacent value *is* included in the interval. The listed intervals are, respectively, 1%, 24%, 25%, 25%, 24%, and 1% credible intervals. Suppose a respondent said that the 1st percentile of her judged distribution for car imports was 3000 cars and the 25th percentile was 40,000 cars. Then ($q_{0.01}$, $q_{0.25}$] = (3000, 40,000] would be a 24% credible interval. In effect, the respondent says there is a 24% chance that the actual number of imports was more than 3000, but no greater than 40,000.

Imagine that the judged distributions of Alpert and Raiffa's subjects were perfectly calibrated. Then the proportion of actual values for the various quantities would fall within the credible intervals with frequencies corresponding to the percentages associated with those intervals. For example, 1% of the observed values would fall within the ($q_{0.99}$, UB] interval. The left side of Figure 4.13 displays the probabilities associated with the various credible intervals. The right side shows the proportions of times the quantity values actually fell within the intervals as defined by Alpert and Raiffa's subjects.

There are marked differences between the observed proportions and what those proportions would have been had the subjects' judgments been perfectly calibrated. The pattern of miscalibration was distinctive. There were too few values for the quantities in the middle credible intervals and too many in the extreme intervals. A **surprise** is the observation of a quantity value in an interval that was thought to have a low probability of containing that value. More specifically, "2% surprises" are defined as values of a quantity that fall below the 0.01 fractile or above the 0.99 fractile, that is, within either [LB, $q_{0.01}$] or ($q_{0.99}$, UB]. The **2% surprise index** is the proportion of 2% surprises actually observed. Under perfect distribution calibration, the 2% surprise index would be 2%, of course. Alpert and Raiffa's subjects must have been astonished. Their 2% surprise index was an enormous 42.6%.

It makes some sense to say that Alpert and Raiffa's subjects were overconfident. A confident individual believes there is a high probability that the actual value of a quantity will be within a narrow range of possibilities. If that person is *overly* confident, the true value will fall outside that

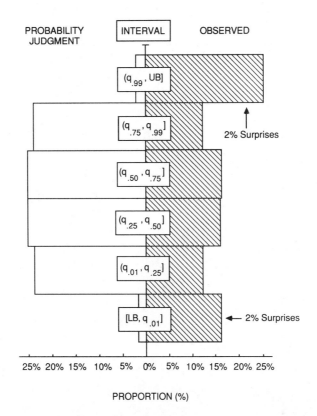

PROPORTION (%)

FIGURE 4.13. Proportions of actual quantity values observed falling within various credible intervals (right side), along with what those proportions would have been under perfect distribution calibration, the implied probability judgments (left side). Based on results reported by Alpert and Raiffa (1982), Table 2, with permission from Cambridge University Press.

range; the person will be "surprised" that the true value is not within the specified range.

Overly confident persons are often said to have judged probability distributions that are too tight. The following example illustrates why. Suppose that two farm experts predict yields for 1000 corn fields. To make things simple, further suppose that all the fields are virtually identical. So each expert can use the same judged probability distribution for the yield of every field. The distribution reported by Expert 1 is shown in Figure 4.14a, that by Expert 2 in Figure 4.14c. Figure 4.14b displays the frequency distribution of the actual yields produced by the 1000 plots. Thus, for example, it is shown that 10 of the fields produced fewer than 300 units of corn; 780 of the fields had output between 600 and 1400 units.

(a) <u>Judged Probability Distribution of Yields: Expert 1</u>

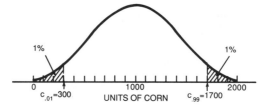

(b) <u>Frequency Distribution of Actual Yields</u>

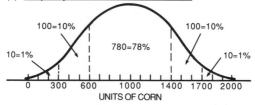

(c) <u>Judged Probability Distribution of Yields: Expert 2</u>

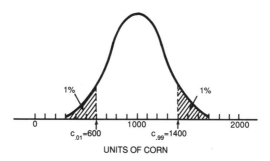

FIGURE 4.14. Illustration of the interpretation of overconfidence in terms of too-tight judged probability distributions. See text for details.

Expert 1's judged probability distribution was perfectly calibrated. Note, for instance, that the 1st percentile of his distribution is 300 units. Exactly 10, or 1%, of the actual yields fell below Expert 1's 1st percentile. Similarly, exactly 1% of the actual yields were higher than 1700 units, the 99th percentile of his distribution. So the 2% surprise index was what it was supposed to be under perfect calibration: 2%.

Now consider Expert 2's judged distribution. She seemed very sure that the actual production for each field would be in the vicinity of 1000 units. The 1st percentile of her distribution was 600 units. Accordingly, she would have expected 10 of the 1000 fields to produce fewer than 600 units. In fact, 110 of the fields had less than 600 units of output, 11% rather than the 1% she anticipated. A similar situation held at the opposite end of the distribution. So, overall, her 2% surprise index was 22%. Her overly narrow or tight distribution was overconfident.

Professionals' distribution calibration

Judged probability distributions for professionals appear to be miscalibrated, too. However, they do not exhibit the marked degree of overconfidence found in laypersons' judgments. Consider two illustrative studies.

Weather forecasting A **central credible interval** is one for which the probability that the quantity will fall below the interval is the same as the probability of its falling above the interval. Suppose a weather forecaster reports that her 70% central credible interval for tomorrow's high temperature is [5° C, 9° C]. This means that the forecaster believes there is a 70% chance that the high temperature will be somewhere between 5° and 9° Celsius. It also means that she thinks there is a 15% chance the high temperature will be below 5° and a 15% chance it will be above 9°.

The high temperature on a given day is the maximum temperature recorded that day; the low temperature is the minimum. Murphy and Winkler (1974) studied the high and low temperature credible intervals of weather forecasters in Denver over about eight months. Figure 4.15 de-

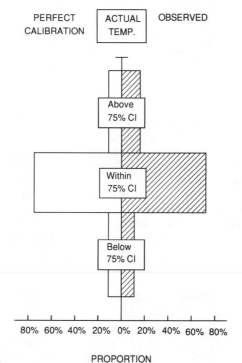

FIGURE 4.15. Actual high and low temperatures falling within and outside professional weather forecasters' 75% central credible intervals (CI): Left side—perfectly calibrated proportions; right side—observed proportions. Source: Murphy and Winkler (1974).

scribes the accuracy of the forecasters' 75% central credible intervals. The left half of the graph shows the proportion of high or low temperatures that would have fallen above, within, and below those intervals if the forecasters' judgments were perfectly calibrated. The right half shows the observed proportions. There was a mild tendency toward overconfidence, in that the proportion of actual temperatures falling within the central intervals was slightly smaller than it should have been. On the whole, however, the calibration of the judgments was remarkably good.

Accounting Corporations are required to have their financial records audited periodically by public accountants. One chore an auditor must perform is estimating the actual balance that exists in each account. ("Based on what the books show and the kinds of errors I have found in examining a sample of cases, what really *were* the sales of 'Massive Industries' last year?") One way such estimates can be expressed is in terms of judged probability distributions.

Tomassini and others (1982) examined the calibration of auditors' distribution judgments. The auditors were presented with actual auditing case studies. Their task was to report their judged probability distributions for the clients' account balances represented in each of the cases. The auditors' 2% surprise index was 7.3%. So, although the auditors' judgments were not perfectly calibrated, they did not exhibit the gross overconfidence found in laypersons' judgments.

IMPROVING ACCURACY

We have seen that, in some instances and in some respects, likelihood judgments by professionals and laypersons are reasonably accurate. On the other hand, we have also learned that there are circumstances in which observed levels of accuracy leave much to be desired. In the latter cases, an important implication is that many of the decisions predicated on the relevant judgments are bound to fail. In Chapters 6 and 7, we will examine the psychological processes by which people arrive at their likelihood judgments. It will then become clearer how some judgments can be improved by directly affecting those psychological mechanisms. What we have learned so far should be helpful, too, as suggested presently.

Judgment improvement through feedback

Phenomena such as overconfidence and hindsight bias suggest that we are often unaware of how inaccurate our likelihood judgments are. If we think our judgments are just fine, then very naturally we will not even *attempt* to improve them. Why should we? And if we did make such efforts, how could we build on them, since we cannot tell whether they succeed or fail? Implicit in these observations are the assumptions underlying **feedback strategies** to improving likelihood judgment.

Simple feedback In the simple feedback approach, a person is given measures of the accuracy of his or her judgments. Previous results suggest that many individuals, particularly laypersons and novices, will be unpleasantly surprised by how poor their judgments are. Hence, they will be motivated to try to improve those judgments. Exactly *how* the person attempts to do this is left to his or her ingenuity. However, further feedback will be beneficial because it will indicate which efforts are effective and which are not.

Staël von Holstein (1971, 1972) conducted two tests of the simple feedback approach. In one experiment, the subjects, including professional weather forecasters, made probability judgments about precipitation. In the other experiment, which was mentioned previously, the subjects predicted stock price movements on the Stockholm Exchange. Both experiments extended over several weeks. Periodically, each participant was told the cumulative accuracy of his or her judgments up to that point in the experiment, as well as most recently, in the form of a score equivalent to PS. The experiments failed; in neither was there consistent improvement in accuracy scores.

Why was Staël von Holstein's feedback ineffective? Consider an analogy: Joe is a tennis player who is having trouble hitting the ball where he wants it to go. It would be ludicrous for his coach to merely tell him, "You aren't hitting the ball very well, Joe." Instead, the coach points out that Joe tends to lift his head to see where the ball is going before he completes the shot. Joe is genuinely surprised, since he thoroughly understands the theory of hitting tennis balls. But, like many athletes, he is not fully conscious of the details of his own behavior. (For an enlightening and possibly depressing experience, videotape yourself engaging in something you do all the time, for example, playing golf or speaking.) Joe now consciously tries to keep his head down. In virtually no time, he is winning matches. The moral of this story is that overall accuracy feedback, such as Staël von Holstein's, might often fail because it is too general. Perhaps detailed feedback about the various accuracy *components*, for example, calibration, discrimination, and slope, would be more promising.

There are indications that detailed simple feedback does indeed improve judgment quality. It has been suggested (for example, by Lichtenstein, Fischhoff, and Phillips, 1982) that a major reason U.S. weather forecasters have achieved such good calibration in their judgments is that they receive constant feedback about calibration. Lichtenstein and Fischhoff's (1980) subjects made likelihood judgments about their answers to general knowledge questions. After each block of items, the subjects were provided with measures of the calibration and discrimination of their judgments. This treatment improved calibration substantially, although it had no effect on discrimination. Hunt and others (1983) found similar improvement in the calibration of physicians' judgments about medical conditions in response to feedback in the form of calibration graphs.

Feedback plus treatment Now consider the feedback-plus-treatment approach to improving accuracy. In this strategy, the person is again provided with accuracy measures. But a deliberate attempt is made to change the way the person makes judgments, too. As anticipated in Chapter 3, this is apparently unnecessary for improving calibration. It is easy to see why. Most miscalibration is actually a manifestation of bias. That is, individuals' likelihood judgments are generally too high or too low. If they are made aware of that fact, they can solve the problem by simply lowering or raising their judgments.

Improving other important accuracy dimensions, such as discrimination and scatter, seems to be more difficult. And it should be. Recall that, for a person to do well with regard to these aspects of accuracy, he or she must have access to good indicators of the future and know how to use them. So to improve distribution, slope, and scatter, the judge must actively experiment with new indicators and also, perhaps, new ways of predicting from indicators that have been available all along. This is such a difficult task that judges probably must be assisted in performing it. The problem would be similar to Joe's tennis coach not only having to point out Joe's errors, but also needing to help him correct those errors.

Consider the example of Centor, Dalton, and Yates's physicians (see Figure 4.3a). The judgments of those physicians about streptococcal throat infection were very widely scattered. We saw that this is probably due in large part to the physicians basing their judgments on patient characteristics they *think* are related to the presence of the streptococcus bacterium, but which really are not. One seemingly reasonable strategy for attacking the problem would be to make the physicians aware of the worthless cues they are using.

Selecting better judges

Not everybody is equally skilled at making likelihood judgments. As private individuals, we often consult others for advice about what is likely to occur in the future. How should we choose our consultants? For example, imagine you are trying to decide whether to buy a house now or to wait until next year when the mortgage interest rates might be lower. Which real estate agents' and bankers' opinions should you seek? Or suppose that you are the manager of an organization that relies on individuals who have good judgment, for instance, a real estate agency or a bank. How can you pick staff members who have superior insight?

A cardinal principle followed by people who evaluate personnel is that the best predictor of future performance is past performance. So one way to select good judges is to examine how accurate individuals' judgments have been in similar situations in the past. In the U.S. National Weather Service, weather forecasters make probability judgments about various kinds of weather events. As we saw in Chapter 3, the accuracy of different individuals' judgments can be compared by examining such measures as PS, bias, and calibration and discrimination indexes. So, in principle at least, anyone who wanted to hire weather forecasters (for example, television stations) could make their decisions on the basis of these skill indicators. Eventually, the same could be done in other fields, including real estate and banking. Earlier in this chapter we saw numerous instances in which machine experts outperformed real experts. So the possibility of turning over certain judgment tasks to more accurate machine experts should not be ruled out either. A less radical strategy is to provide human judges with the opinions of the machine experts as aids. There is evidence that this is sometimes helpful in medicine, for example (see Dannenberg, Shapiro, and Fries, 1979).

Rewarding accuracy

Simply making judges aware of their judgment accuracy will probably encourage improvement in those judgments. Rewarding such improvement might stimulate even greater progress. For instance, suppose that a counseling office adopts a policy whereby counselors make probabilistic predictions of students' grades. Perhaps those counselors could receive bonuses in direct relation to the goodness of their mean probability scores.

SUMMARY

Various professions require their members to make likelihood judgments. In some respects, for example, calibration, these professional judgments sometimes are outstanding. However, there is also considerable room for improvement. A few studies suggest that on occasion professional judgments are systematically and seriously flawed.

Likelihood judgments by ordinary people about matters outside their areas of trained expertise sometimes exhibit persistent biases. One such deficiency is overconfidence in one's own opinions. Another is hindsight bias, distorted recall of previous judgments.

Likelihood judgment accuracy measures can be used in several ways to improve such judgments: (1) as feedback about inaccuracies that would go undetected otherwise; (2) as means for evaluating the judgment skills of experts we might hire; and (3) as bases for rewarding (and hence encouraging) good judgment.

KEY TERMS

Calibration curve	Overconfidence
Central credible interval	Resolution
Feedback strategy	Surprise
Hindsight bias	Surprise index

ADDITIONAL READING

Dowie (1976); Murphy and others (1985); Newman (1984); Pickhardt and Wallace (1974); Seaver, von Winterfeldt, and Edwards (1978); Slovic and Fischhoff (1977); W. Wright (1979).

EXERCISES AND STUDY QUESTIONS

1. This chapter seems to suggest that, in many instances, the accuracy of people's likelihood judgments is deficient. Myra, upon reading the chapter, is very skeptical. She says, "There must be something wrong with the work the author has cited. If people's judgment were *really* that bad, we would all be dead!" Offer arguments in agreement and disagreement with Myra's position.

2. Reexamine the calibration curve shown in Figure 4.2, which is adapted from the article by Christensen-Szalanski and Bushyhead (1981). The task of the physicians in the pertinent study was to state a probability judgment that each of the patients they considered had pneumonia. Some observers say that these results indicate that the physicians were overconfident in their diagnoses. Explain why this is not so.

3. You randomly sample a group of beginning finance students and also a group of beginning stock brokers. You ask the individuals in each group to make probabilistic predictions of the following form for each of 100 stocks: P'(Price will increase at least 10% over the next 3 months). Based on what you have learned, sketch two different covariance graphs, one for the students and one for the brokers, such that the graphs highlight one difference between the judgments of the two groups that it is reasonable to expect. Defend your expectation.

4. Percy has very little confidence in his own opinions. Percy states his judged probability distributions for a large number of quantities, for example, the price of tuition next year, tomorrow's high temperature. What would you expect the 2% surprise index to be like for those distributions? Explain.

5. Reexamine Figure 4.13. It characterizes the distribution calibration of subjects in the study by Alpert and Raiffa (1982). The responses of those subjects display another bias besides overconfidence. Describe it.

6. Oskamp (1965) found a significant amount of overconfidence in clinical psychologists' judgments. This seems atypical of professionals as a whole. What might be the difference between clinical psychology and other professions that would account for this difference?

7. Suggest and defend a reasonable potential explanation for the finding whereby many groups of Asian subjects give especially high probability judgments in response to general knowledge questions. Design an experiment that would test this hypothesis.

8. The other day you had a conversation with your best friend, in which you told him about hindsight bias. He responded, "Big deal! I grant you that that's sort of interesting, but it has no practical significance. After all, people make decisions on the basis of their judgments for what is going to happen in the *future*, not what they said would happen in the past." What argument can you give to your friend to persuade him of the practical importance of hindsight bias?

9. Imagine yourself as the supervising physician in a clinic. Drs. Cass and Kulick are two physicians who have recently joined your staff. Each makes pneumonia probability judgments for a large number of patients who come to the clinic, that is, judgments of the form P'(Patient has pneumonia). Dr. Cass's judgments have a bias of 15.2%, while Dr. Kulick's bias is only 1.3%. What is a good initial

hypothesis for why the biases exhibited by Drs. Cass and Kulick differ as they do? How would you try to assist Dr. Cass in reducing his bias?

10. Use a sports forecasting task to hone your skills in applying simple feedback and feedback plus treatment strategies for improving likelihood judgment accuracy. Specifically, find a friend who is a serious football (or basketball or baseball fan, depending on the season.) Present your friend with a random sample of 50 upcoming games. For each game, ask your friend to make a judgment of the form P'(Home team wins), using whatever methods he or she desires. After examining various aspects of your friend's accuracy, for example, discrimination and scatter, offer concrete advice for improvement. Evaluate the effectiveness of your intervention using another sample of 50 games to be played later. (*Note:* More than 50 cases should be used ideally.)

Coherence

Consistency is the last refuge of the unimaginative.

—Oscar Wilde

Suppose you have a friend, Paula, who makes the following statements:

Statement 1: All lawyers are shysters.
Statement 2: John is a shyster.
Statement 3: So John must be a lawyer.

You immediately point out to Paula that what she said makes no sense, regardless of whether John really *is* a lawyer, a shyster, or both. You say that, if all A's (lawyers) are B's (shysters), and C (John) is an A, we can conclude that C is a B, too. However, if all A's are B's, and C is a B, it is not necessarily the case that C is also an A.

Paula violated an elementary rule of conventional logic. As you indicate in your explanation, principles of logic apply to relationships among statements, for example, that a statement of one form follows from two statements of certain other forms. From a formal perspective, the substantive truth or falsity of the statements is irrelevant. Nevertheless, we generally care a great deal whether our reasoning about real issues adheres to accepted principles of logic. First, we feel uncomfortable whenever we violate those maxims. Moreover, we expect that people who routinely reason in illogical ways will suffer from that failing, that their errors will cost them dearly. Suppose, for example, that Statements 1 and 2 really *were* true (and at least Statement 1 surely is not), and that, according to her previous argument, Paula concludes that Statement 3 is true. George asks Paula if she knows any lawyers he might consult about a legal problem. She sends him to see John. She is more than a little embarrassed when George reports back that John is a plumber, not a lawyer.

In the last chapter, we discussed the quality of likelihood judgments in terms of their accuracy, that is, how well they anticipate events that actually happen. In this chapter, we will consider judgment quality from another perspective, the perspective of coherence. In the previous example, your friend Paula made several statements. The statements may or may not be factually true; for example, John may or may not be a shyster. The degree to which a person's likelihood judgments are accurate is analogous to the extent to which statements such as Paula's are indeed true. It is commonly believed that likelihood judgments ought to relate to one another according to certain rules, regardless of their accuracy. If the relationships among those judgments *are* consistent with those principles, the judgments are said to be coherent. Whether likelihood judgments are coherent is similar to the question of whether statements such as Paula's satisfy standard rules of logic.

What are the coherence principles likelihood judgments should follow? A variety of rules have been proposed. By far, however, the most widely accepted ones are those implicit in probability theory. So our treatment of coherence begins in the first section with a discussion of probability theory and its relevance to human likelihood judgment. Probability theory imposes several requirements on how likelihood judgments should relate to one another. In the second section of the chapter, we examine evidence of how well people's real likelihood judgments conform to some of the most prominent requirements. The following three sections address the importance of people's coherence, or incoherence, as the case may be. The third section, in particular, discusses the conceptual significance of coherence phenomena. The fourth considers the practical consequences of incoherence. Those consequences provide strong motivation for various procedures for improving coherence, which are the subject of the fifth section. Probability theory is not the only collection of coherence principles one might adopt. The closing section of the chapter is a brief discussion of some competing viewpoints.

COHERENCE AND PROBABILITY THEORY

Probability theory: What it is and is not

We have all used the term "probability" in everyday conversation. By the probability of something we mean its likelihood or chance of occurrence. Mathematicians have appropriated the term probability, too. The mathematical meaning of probability is, of course, related to the natural language meaning of the word. There are some noteworthy distinctions, however.

The similarities and differences between the mathematical and ordinary meanings of probability are much like those characterizing the meanings of the word "line" in geometry and in everyday usage. Line has a special definition in geometry. Similarly, probability has a precise interpretation in the branch of mathematics called probability theory, a more restrictive interpretation than our ordinary understanding of the expression. From a mathematical point of view, geometry is a body of reasoning about abstractions, such as lines and angles. Nevertheless, its real-world correspondences can be both enlightening and useful. (How long would our bridges and buildings remain standing if we had no understanding of geometric principles?) So, too, with probability theory. In this section we will review (in largely nonmathematical terms) some of the basic ideas of probability theory. In the next section we will consider the relevance of the theory for human likelihood judgment—its provision of standards for coherence.

Events Imagine a situation in which several different things are possible. An **event** is a collection of some number of those potential occurrences. The **universal event** or **universe** is the special event that contains all possible occurrences. The **family of events** consists of all the events in the given situation. Within probability theory, events are abstractions. However, there *are* real-world instances of events. Suppose the situation of interest is tomorrow's weather at noon. "Rain" is one of the events within the event family. So are "Snow," "Rain or Snow," and "Rain & Snow." The universe for this situation would include *all* potential weather conditions.

It is often convenient to represent events with **Venn diagrams**. By convention, the universe is characterized by a rectangle. All other events are symbolized by closed figures, typically ovals, within the rectangle. Figure 5.1 shows the Venn diagram representation of events in the weather situation.

Probabilities Suppose that, for a given situation, there is a family of events, including events A, B, C, and so on. Suppose further that each of these events is assigned a number, denoted $P(A)$, $P(B)$, $P(C)$, and so forth. Within probability theory, these numbers are called **probabilities** (for example, $P(A)$ is the "probability of event A") if they satisfy the following properties, which are sometimes called **axioms** or **postulates**:

P1: Bounds $0 \leq P(E) \leq 1$, for any event E in the family.

P2: Universe $P(U) = 1$, where U is the universal event in the family.

P3: Additivity $P(A \text{ or } B) = P(A) + P(B)$, when events A and B in the family cannot co-occur, that is, are **mutually exclusive** or **disjoint**. [Note that, if A and B are events in the family, $(A \text{ or } B)$ must be an event in the family, too.]

The bounds and universe properties are easy to understand and accept as compatible with everyday notions about probability. The bounds property simply establishes the convention that probabilities must be numbers between 0 and 1, inclusive. The universe property says that the event that is guaranteed to happen, since it contains all potential occurrences, has the highest possible probability. The additivity property is straightforward, too. Continuing the noontime weather example, consider the events "Rain" and "Fair." Suppose we accept that we cannot simultaneously have both rainy and fair weather. If there is a 30% chance of rain and a 40% chance of fair weather, most of us would agree that there is a 70% chance that it will either

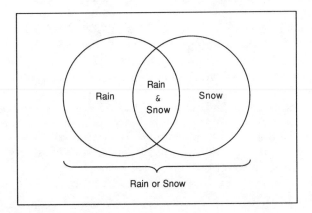

FIGURE 5.1. Venn diagram representation of weather events "Rain," "Snow," "Rain or Snow," and "Rain & Snow."

rain or be fair. Note that the additivity property can be generalized to more than two disjoint events, too. So, for instance, if in our example there is a 10% chance of snow, then there should be an 80% chance of rainy, snowy, or fair weather.

Some observations   There are several important things to realize about probabilities, as they are understood within probability theory. These observations might surprise you.

Multiple sets of acceptable probabilities. Consider a family of events for a given situation. There are literally an infinite variety of ways numbers could be assigned to the events in that family such that the numbers in each of those sets are legitimately considered probabilities. The only thing that must be assured is that the numbers satisfy properties P1 to P3 above. An example illustrates the point.

Again let the relevant event family be weather conditions at noon tomorrow: {Rain, Snow, Fair, (Rain or Snow), (Snow & Fair), Sleet, ...}. Suppose that one collection of numerical assignments to the events is denoted by C_1, another by C_2, and yet a third by C_3. Let us examine the assignments for three events, "Rain," "Fair," and "Rain or Fair":

	Assignments		
Event	C_1	C_2	C_3
Rain	0.20	0.70	0.30
Fair	0.40	0.00	0.10
Rain or Fair	0.60	0.70	0.50
.	.	.	.
.	.	.	.
.	.	.	.

Notice that the C_3 numbers assigned to "Rain," "Fair," and "Rain or Fair" do not satisfy the additivity property. So we immediately know that the numbers in the C_3 collection would not qualify as probabilities, in the probability theory sense. On the other hand, the C_1 and C_2 numbers for the three events under consideration do not violate any of the probability properties. So there is no indication that those collections are not probabilities. To be completely sure, we would have to check the assignments in each collection for *all* the events in the family. The important thing to recognize is that both the C_1 *and* C_2 collections can satisfy all the probability properties. Thus, despite the fact that the numerical values themselves are radically different from each other, both sets of numbers could be appropriately regarded as probabilities.

Lack of accuracy requirements. Nothing in the probability properties demands that numbers called probabilities bear any relationship to what actually happens in the real world. That is, probabilities need not be accurate indicators of whether the given events will or will not occur. Since all that probabilities *must* do is be consistent with one another within the framework of properties P1 to P3, it can easily happen that the accuracy of legitimate probabilities is simply awful. Look again at the weather probabilities C_1 and C_2 in the previous illustration. Suppose it actually rains tomorrow. Then the accuracy of the C_2 probabilities will be pretty good; that of the C_1 probabilities will be terrible.

The essence of probability theory: relations. The emphasis of probability theory is not on the actual values of the probabilities assigned to specific events. Instead, the concern is with the relations that must exist among the probabilities for different *kinds* of events. For instance, the additivity property specifies how $P(A)$, $P(B)$, and $P(A$ or $B)$ must relate to one another when events A and B are disjoint. It is remarkable how many other relations can be derived from properties P1 to P3, along with a few definitions and assumptions. Probability theory itself consists of the relations that can be shown to follow from those properties, definitions, and assumptions.

In view of the previous remarks, the following question has undoubtedly occurred to you: What practical value can probability theory possibly have in real life? In conventional applications of probability theory, for instance, in engineering, business, or empirical research, the answer is this: The person applying the theory *interprets* probabilities to indicate the chances of real events occurring, in the same way we have previously interpreted probability judgments, for example, higher probabilities correspond to greater chances of occurrence. The person next makes assumptions about the probabilities of particular events, usually simple ones. Probability theory is then used to derive what the probabilities of other, typically more complicated, events ought to be. A simple example is illustrative.

Suppose an engineer has established that the chance of a machine failing for Reason 1 is 1%, and the chance of it failing for Reason 2 is 3%. Moreover, she knows that the machine cannot fail for both reasons. Then, applying the additivity property, she concludes that the chance of the machine failing for either of the reasons must be 4%. In actual practice, of course, the events and problems of interest are much more complex. The underlying principles are not, however. You should recognize that, in probability theory applications, the accuracy of the probabilities that are derived is limited by the assumptions that are made at the outset, for example, that there is a 1% chance of a failure due to Reason 1.

Coherence as consistency with probability theory

Likelihood judgments are said to be coherent if they relate to one another such that certain acceptable rules are not violated. The concept of likelihood judgment coherence is quite general. It becomes specific only when we define what we mean by "acceptable rules." Rules regarded as acceptable by one person may not be acceptable to another. Nevertheless, what is *usually* meant when likelihood judgments are described as coherent is that they do not violate probability theory. And unless specified otherwise, that is how the term **coherence** will be used here.

Return once again to the example of tomorrow's weather. Suppose that the three sets of numerical assignments to the various weather conditions were actually probability judgments made by Forecasters 1 to 3, respectively. Recall that the C_3 assignments did not satisfy additivity. So we can conclude that Forecaster 3's probability judgments are incoherent. On the other hand, we have no evidence that the judgments of Forecasters 1 and 2 violate probability theory. That is, on the basis of what we have seen, it appears that those assessments *are* coherent.

Coherence is generally regarded as consistency with probability theory because most people in fact do accept the theory's principles. For instance, if you are like most of us, you consider the bounds, universe, and additivity properties of probabilities to be quite reasonable rules for how measures of likelihood should behave. You would likely feel the same way about the various definitions that are introduced in probability theory, too.

COHERENCE OF HUMAN JUDGMENTS

It is natural to ask the following question: Are human likelihood judgments coherent? A moment's reflection might convince you that the answer surely cannot be "Yes." Research on probability theory consists of discovering the implications of probability properties P1 to P3. Many of the theorems in probability theory are anything but intuitively obvious; there are people who spend their entire lives doing research on the topic. Accordingly, the focus of this section is on more specific issues: (1) What are some of the basic principles of probability theory that are reliably violated by human likelihood judgments? And (2), what is the nature of those violations? As you proceed through the section, you may often ask yourself, "Why do people think this way?" Be patient. Chapters 6 and 7 offer at least partial explanations.

Unity summation

Consider events *A*, *B*, and *C*. Suppose that these events are disjoint, that is, cannot co-occur. Also suppose that, taken together, these events include all the potential occurrences in the given situation, that is, are **exhaustive**. Thus, (*A* or *B* or *C*) = *U*, the universe. A collection of events with these two characteristics is said to constitute a **partition** of the universe. A concrete example of a partition would be "Rain," "Fair," and "Other," when the relevant situation is tomorrow's noontime weather. Another partition for the same situation would include the events "Rain" and "No Rain."

A fundamental result in probability theory is that the probabilities for events comprising a partition should sum to 1. In the three-event case described above, the **unity summation principle** would require that

$$P(A) + P(B) + P(C) = 1 \tag{5.1}$$

Venn diagrams illustrate the partition concept and the unity summation principle very well. Consider Figure 5.2, which shows Venn diagrams for the two weather partitions mentioned above. Metaphorically, you might think of the universe as a large room. A partition divides that room into smaller ones. You could also think of the areas of the rooms as analogous to the probabilities of the events. Subdividing a room will not change the room's area; the sum of the areas of the small rooms must be the same as the area of the original large room (ignoring the thickness of the walls, of course). The probability of the universe is 1. Since the events in a partition do not overlap and they include everything in the universe, their probabilities must sum to 1, too. So if a person's probability judgments for tomorrow's noon weather are coherent, then the following relations must hold:

$$P'(\text{Rain}) + P'(\text{Fair}) + P'(\text{Other}) = 1$$

and

$$P'(\text{Rain}) + P'(\text{No rain}) = 1$$

The numbers in parentheses in the Venn diagrams in Figure 5.2 show probability judgments that *would* be consistent with the unity summation principle.

(a)

(b)

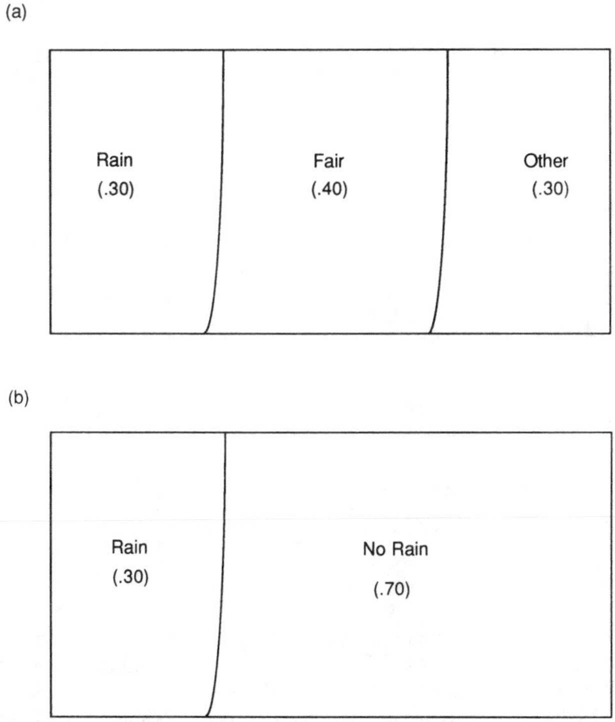

FIGURE 5.2. Venn diagram representations of two partitions of a weather universe.

To test unity summation in actual judgments, Wright and Whalley (1983) required their subjects to consider partitions of various sizes. For example, one group undertook the prodigious task of assessing "the probability that at exactly 6 pm next Wednesday you will be doing one of a set of 16 mutually exclusive and exhaustive acts, e.g.: washing yourself, driving a car, buying something in a shop, sitting down watching television at home and a catch-all of neither of these acts" (p. 235). With such multiple-event partitions containing more than two events, the sums of the average probability judgments typically were much larger than 1, suggesting a general expectation of **superadditivity**, which says that, for events $A_1, A_2, ..., A_K$ comprising a partition,

$$P'(A_1) + P'(A_2) + ... + P'(A_K) > 1 \qquad (5.2)$$

There was a trend in the results, too: The more events there were in the partition, the larger was the sum of the probability judgments for the events. Figure 5.3 illustrates the results. It is remarkable that the sums of individual subjects' probability judgments for all 16 of the "Wednesday evening" events, "Washing myself," "Watching television," and so on, averaged over 300%.

When partitions contained only two events, Wright and Whalley (1983) found that unity summation was almost always satisfied. Interestingly, in studies with children around ages 9 to 10 years, judgments tend to be **subadditive**; that is,

$$P'(A) + P'(A^c) < 1 \qquad (5.3)$$

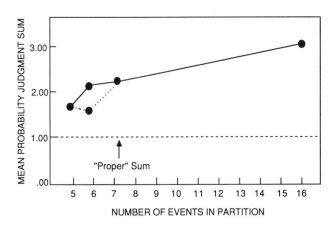

FIGURE 5.3. Probability judgment sums for everyday events in partitions of various sizes. There are two points above 6 because subjects considered two different six-event partitions. Based on data reported by Wright and Whalley (1983), Table 2, with permission from Kluwer Academic Publishers and the authors.

where A is an arbitrary event and A^c is its complement (see, for example, Cohen, Dearnaley, and Hansel, 1956).

Additivity for disjunctions

The **disjunction** of two events is the event that includes all occurrences that are contained in either or both of those events. Events such as A and B are sometimes referred to as **marginal** events. Thus, we say that event (A or B) is the disjunction of marginal events A and B. Suppose events A and B are disjoint or mutually exclusive, that is, cannot both occur. Recall that, according to the additivity property of probability theory, coherence would require that probability judgments for events A, B, and (A or B) satisfy the following relation:

$$P'(A \text{ or } B) = P'(A) + P'(B)$$

The additivity property is easy to visualize with Venn diagrams. Figure 5.4 shows such a diagram for weather conditions. Since marginal events "Rain" and "Fair" are disjoint, the ovals representing them do not overlap. The representation for the disjunction "Rain or Fair" consists of the ovals for "Rain" and "Fair" taken together. Again think of the oval areas as corresponding to probability judgments for the events. Clearly, the area (probability) for "Rain or Fair" must be the sum of the areas (probabilities) for "Rain" and "Fair."

Barclay and Beach (1972) tested the additivity of human probability judgments. Subjects were asked questions like the following (p. 178): "Imagine someone that you know will get a car for graduation. What is the probability that it will be a Chevrolet? That it will be a Ford? That it will be either a Chevrolet or a Ford?" On average, subjects responded such that

$$P'(\text{Chevrolet or Ford}) < P'(\text{Chevrolet}) + P'(\text{Ford})$$

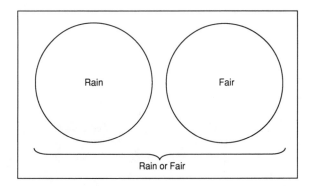

FIGURE 5.4. Venn diagram depicting two disjoint events, "Rain" and "Fair," along with their disjunction, "Rain or Fair."

This finding suggests the following generalization, which can be described as **underjudgment** of the chances of the disjunction:

$$P'(A) < P'(A_1) + P'(A_2) + \ldots + P'(A_K) \tag{5.4}$$

when event A is the disjunction of events $A_1, A_2, \ldots, A_K$, that is, when

$$A = A_1 \text{ or } A_2 \text{ or } \ldots \text{ or } A_K$$

In the above case, $K = 2$, A = "Chevrolet or Ford," A_1 = "Chevrolet," and A_2 = "Ford."

An especially interesting case of underjudgment is observed in results reported by Fischhoff, Slovic, and Lichtenstein (1978). Imagine that your car fails to start one morning. Figure 5.5a is a **fault tree** that might be used in trying to determine the cause of the problem. It contains the seven main branches of the full tree presented to subjects by Fischhoff, Slovic, and Lichtenstein. Each branch identifies a particular class of potential causes of the starting failure. More detail was provided within each of the specified categories. For example, underneath the "Battery Charge Insufficient" box, other more specific battery problems were listed, for instance, "Faulty ground connections" and "Battery weak." The instructions to the subjects were as follows (p. 334):

(a) Full Tree

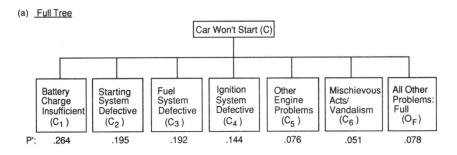

(b) Pruned Tree

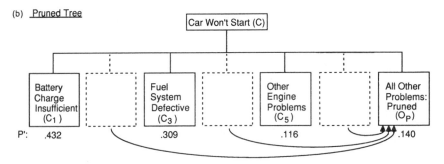

FIGURE 5.5. Full and pruned fault trees for diagnosing why a car fails to start. Source: Fischhoff, Slovic, and Lichtenstein (1978), Figure 1. Copyright 1978 by the American Psychological Association. Adapted by permission from the publisher and authors. See text for details.

For every 100 times that a trip is delayed due to "starting failure," estimate, on the average, how many of those delays are caused by each of the seven factors.

So, in effect, the subjects were asked to state probability judgments that a starting failure was due to each of the categories of problems. The mean probabilities reported by the subjects are listed under the respective boxes. Thus, for instance, it is shown that the mean probability judgment that a starting failure will be due to a defective ignition system was 14.4%.

Now examine Figure 5.5b, which shows a pruned version of the original fault tree. It differs from the full tree in that the starting system, ignition system, and mischievous acts branches were omitted. This pruned tree was presented to a second group of subjects. As before, the subjects were asked to state probability judgments for starting failures due to the factors that were listed. The mean reported judgments are shown under the boxes.

What should be the connection between the judgments made for the two trees? Consider the last branch in each tree, which was labeled for the subjects as simply "All other problems." These are actually different events in the two trees, hence the distinction between "All Other Problems: Full" and "All Other Problems: Pruned," denoted O_F and O_P respectively. "All Other Problems: Pruned" includes more than the causes encompassed by "All Other Problems: Full." As suggested by the arcs underneath the pruned tree, it also contains the causes that had been pruned from the full tree, those related to the starting system (C_2), the ignition system (C_4), and mischievous acts (C_6). In other words, "All Other Problems: Pruned" is the disjunction of the previous "All Other Problems" and the causes in the latter categories. So coherence would require that

$$P'(O_P) = p'(O_F) + P'(C_2) + P'(C_4) + P'(C_6)$$

However, we observe that, on average, $P'(O_P) = 0.140$, which is much less than the sum of the probability judgments for the causes comprising O_P, which is $0.195 + 0.144 + 0.051 + 0.078 = 0.468$.

The generalized disjunction principle

The **conjunction** of events A and B includes all occurrences that are contained both in A and in B. It is denoted $(A \& B)$. For instance, "Rain & Snow" is the conjunction of the marginal weather events "Rain" and "Snow." It would occur on a dreary, slushy day when both rain and snow were observed.

Saying that two events are disjoint or mutually exclusive is equivalent to saying that their conjunction is empty. Of course, not every pair of events is disjoint; many events can and do co-occur. So the additivity principle does not always apply as a description of the relationship between probabilities for marginal events, on the one hand, and their disjunctions, on the other. However, what we will call here the generalized disjunction principle does.

Figure 5.1 is a Venn diagram that illustrates the basic idea of the principle. If two events are not disjoint, then the ovals in a Venn diagram representing those events are shown to overlap. Thus we see that the weather on a given day can include both rain and snow. Let us continue to use the analogy between area and probability. The disjunction "Rain or Snow" is represented by the "Rain" and "Snow" ovals taken together. So the probability of "Rain or Snow" corresponds to the total area covered by those ovals. That area is less than the sum of the areas of the "Rain" and "Snow" ovals taken separately. That is because each of those areas includes the area of overlap, which represents the conjunction "Rain & Snow." Summing the marginal event areas would double count the conjunction area. Therefore, it is easy to see that the area of "Rain or Snow" must be the area of "Rain" plus the area of "Snow" minus the area of "Rain & Snow." The **generalized disjunction principle** for probabilities derives from the same type of reasoning and can be expressed as follows:

$$P(A \text{ or } B) = P(A) + P(B) - P(A \& B) \tag{5.5}$$

for arbitrary events A and B. If an event cannot happen, it has probability 0. If events A and B are disjoint, then by definition their conjunction cannot occur. Therefore, the **joint probability** of the events, $P(A \& B)$, must be 0. This would imply that $P(A \text{ or } B) = P(A) + P(B) - P(A \& B) = P(A) + P(B)$. In other words, the additivity property can be viewed as a special case of the generalized disjunction principle.

There have been only a few studies of the extent to which human likelihood judgments conform to the disjunction–conjunction principle (for example, Barclay and Beach, 1972). The tentative conclusion suggested by those studies is that for nondisjoint events A and B, generally it will be the case that

$$P'(A \text{ or } B) > P'(A) + P'(B) - P'(A \& B)$$

for example,

$$P'(\text{Rain or Snow}) > P'(\text{Rain}) + P'(\text{Snow}) - P'(\text{Rain \& Snow})$$

The extension principle

Whenever we observe the event "Snow falls," we also observe the event "Precipitation occurs," since snow is a special type of precipitation. On the other hand, snow is not the only form precipitation takes. So knowing that precipitation has occurred is no assurance that a snowfall has taken place. These observations imply that we should never consider the chance of snow to be greater than the chance of precipitation.

Probability theory—as well as common sense—agrees with the above conclusion. What can be called the **extension principle** says the following: Suppose event A is contained in event B; that is, all the occurrences in A are also in B. Then it follows that

$$P(A) \leq P(B) \tag{5.6}$$

Venn diagrams convincingly illustrate the extension principle. For example, the diagram shown in Figure 5.6 reassures us that the probability of snow should be no greater than the probability of precipitation.

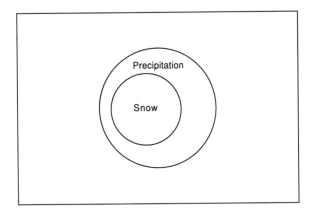

FIGURE 5.6.   Venn diagram representation of events "Snow" and "Precipitation" illustrating the extension principle.

The extension principle as stated here is so intuitively obvious that we cannot imagine it ever being violated by anyone's actual likelihood judgments. That is undoubtedly why adherence to the principle in this form has never been studied. However, there are special cases of the extension principle that apparently are not so obvious.

The conjunction rule   Consider the conjunction of events A and B. By definition, any occurrence in $(A \& B)$ must be contained in both A and B. So $(A \& B)$ is included in A as well as in B. We thus have the following **conjunction rule:**

$$P(A \& B) \leq P(A) \tag{5.7}$$

and

$$P(A \& B) \leq P(B) \tag{5.8}$$

That is, the **joint probability** of two events A and B cannot exceed the **marginal probability** of either of the events comprising their conjunction.

During the late 1970s and the beginning of the 1980s, Bjorn Borg was the preeminent male tennis player in the world. A measure of his dominance is that he won Wimbledon, the most prestigious tournament, several times in a row during that period. In December 1980, Tversky and Kahneman (1982) presented the following problem to their subjects:

> Suppose Bjorn Borg reaches the Wimbledon finals in 1981. Please rank order the following outcomes from the most to least likely:
> - Borg will win the match.
> - Borg will lose the first set.
> - Borg will win the first set but lose the match.
> - Borg will lose the first set but win the match.

A preponderance of the subjects judged it more likely that Borg would lose the first set but win the match than that he would simply lose the first set. The Venn diagram in Figure 5.7 shows why this response violates the conjunction rule and, indirectly, the extension principle. The area of overlap between the two ovals representing the marginal events identifies the conjunction. Clearly, it has to be contained in both of those ovals. Instances in which a conjunction is considered more likely than one of the marginal events comprising that conjunction are called **conjunction errors**, for example,

$$(A \, \& \, B) >_L A \tag{5.9}$$

where, as you will recall, the notation $>_L$ means "is judged more likely than." A person who commits a conjunction error is said to have succumbed to the **conjunction fallacy**. Tversky and Kahneman (1982, 1983) and others (for example, Locksley and Stangor, 1984; Morier and Borgida, 1984) have found occurrences of the conjunction fallacy in a variety of circumstances.

The disjunction rule   The disjunction of events A and B consists of all occurrences that are in either A, B, or both. Thus, event A is contained in event $(A \text{ or } B)$, as is event B. These relations imply the special case of the extension principle called the **disjunction rule**:

$$P(A) \leq P(A \text{ or } B) \tag{5.10}$$

and

$$P(B) \leq P(A \text{ or } B) \tag{5.11}$$

Again, the Venn diagram contained in Figure 5.7 illustrates why the disjunction rule holds.

Carlson and Yates (in press) asked subjects to consider whether the following four events might happen within the coming year: "U.S. auto

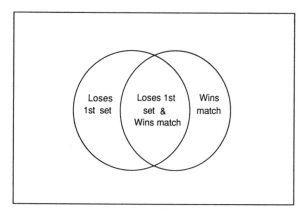

FIGURE 5.7.   Venn diagram depiction of Tversky and Kahneman's (1982) conjunction versus marginal event problem concerning Bjorn Borg's Wimbledon final match.

companies will raise their average car prices by at least $25," "The Detroit Tigers will end the season with a better record than the Cleveland Indians," the conjunction of these marginal events, and their disjunction. The subjects' task was to rank order the events by their probability of actually occurring. Seventy percent of the subjects made **disjunction errors**, considering the disjunction to be less likely than one of the marginal events or both of them. More generally, such errors take a form such as

$$A >_L (A \text{ or } B) \tag{5.12}$$

Conditional probabilities and probability judgments

Consider Table 5.1. It describes a hypothetical population of 10,000 medical patients. The table shows that 4000 of the patients have cancer. It also indicates that positive results were obtained for 4800 of the patients on a certain cancer test, Test X. The cells within the table contain the numbers of patients with various combinations of actual medical conditions and test results. So, for example, it is seen that 1200 of the patients both tested positively and were cancer free.

Suppose a patient is selected at random from the population. What is the chance that that patient will have various characteristics, for example, suffer from cancer or test positively on the test? A good case can be made for the accuracy of proportions as the relevant probabilities. Imagine, for example, that we are interested in the chance of a randomly selected patient being a cancer victim. If this selection were repeated many times, the percentage of the chosen patients who actually have cancer would be very close to the *marginal proportion* of cancer patients in the population:

$$Prop(\text{Cancer}) = \frac{4000}{10,000} = 0.40.$$

It is easy to show that proportions satisfy the principles of probability theory. We will thus find them useful for illustrating some important probability concepts, the first of which is the notion of conditional probability.

It seems that, if a test for cancer is a good one, then patients who have cancer should tend to have positive test results. That is, a high proportion of the individuals who have cancer should test positively. Let us examine Test X from that perspective. Since we are only interested in true cancer

TABLE 5.1 A Population of Medical Patients Tested for Cancer

TEST X RESULTS	ACTUAL CONDITION		
	CANCER	NO CANCER	TOTAL
Positive	3600	1200	4800
Negative	400	4800	5200
Total	4000	6000	10,000

This table depicts dependence between test results and actual medical condition.

victims, we restrict our attention to the 4000 people represented in the first column of Table 5.1. We see that 3600 of those individuals obtained positive test results. Thus, the desired proportion is 3600/4000 = 0.90. It is called the "conditional proportion of positive test results, given cancer," and is denoted as follows:

$$Prop(\text{Test positive} \mid \text{Cancer}) = \frac{3600}{4000} = 0.90$$

That is, 90% of the patients who actually *have* cancer are indicated by the *test* to have cancer. This seems pretty good, although, as we will see, such a high proportion is not foolproof evidence that a test is useful.

The concept of a **conditional probability** is completely analogous to that of a conditional proportion. $P(A \mid B)$, read as "the conditional probability of event A, given event B," is the probability of event A occurring, assuming it is known that event B has occurred. As a concrete example, we can speak of the conditional probability that a patient gets positive test results, given that the patient has cancer. If we were randomly sampling individuals from the population represented in Table 5.1, that probability is reasonably taken as $P(\text{Test positive} \mid \text{Cancer}) = 0.90$.

Since 90% of actual cancer victims tested positively on the test implied in Table 5.1, why is this not sufficient for us to conclude that Test X is a good one? Suppose we asked the cancer victims whether they have breakfast on a regular basis. Perhaps 80% of them would say they do. Should we then think that the "breakfast question" would be a good test for cancer? Probably not. The reason is that about 80% of the noncancer victims would say they have regular breakfasts, too. This example highlights the logic behind conventional ways of evaluating diagnostic procedures.

For a cancer test to be useful, it must differentiate cancer victims from noncancer victims. In particular, two conditional proportions must be very different from each other, *Prop*(Test positive | Cancer) and *Prop*(Test positive | No cancer). Our "breakfast question" test was useless because *Prop*(Regular breakfast | Cancer) = *Prop*(Regular breakfast | No cancer) = 0.80. On the other hand, for Test X, *Prop*(Test positive | Cancer) = 0.90, and *Prop*(Test positive | No cancer) = 1200/6000 = 0.20. So it is indeed a useful test. Physicians have standard terminology for test proportions such as these. The **sensitivity** of a test is defined as

$$\text{Sensitivity} = Prop(\text{Test positive} \mid \text{Disease})$$

The test's **specificity** is

$$\text{Specificity} = Prop(\text{Test negative} \mid \text{No disease})$$

$$= 1 - Prop(\text{Test positive} \mid \text{No disease})$$

Thus, the sensitivity of the cancer test is 90%, while its specificity is 80%. Clearly, the higher a test's sensitivity and specificity are, the better is the test.

If you feel a little confused for the moment, take heart. You are not alone; lots of people sometimes have difficulty with conditional probability concepts (but see Pollatsek 1987). Eddy (1982) reviewed the medical literature on the X-ray diagnosis of breast cancer. He concluded that many physicians think that it must always be true that *Prop*(Test positive I Cancer) = *Prop*(Cancer I Test positive), or that *Prop*(Test negative I Cancer) = *Prop*(Cancer I Test negative). Eddy (1982, pp. 254–255) cites the following passage from an article in a medical journal:

> In women with proved carcinoma of the breast, in whom mammograms are performed, there is no X-ray evidence of malignant disease in approximately one out of five patients examined. If then on the basis of a negative mammogram, we are to defer biopsy of a solid lesion of the breast, then there is a one in five chance that we are deferring biopsy of a malignant lesion.

The reported evidence says that *Prop*(Test negative I Cancer) = 20%. The article erroneously concludes that this also means that *Prop*(Cancer I Test negative) = 20%. In fact, *Prop*(Test negative I Cancer) = *Prop*(Cancer I Test negative) only if *Prop*(Cancer) = *Prop*(Test negative). Situations where the marginal chances of cancer and negative test results are identical have never been reported.

The general product rule

Return to Table 5.1. The conditional proportion *Prop*(Test positive I Cancer) can be expressed in terms of marginal and joint proportions, too. The relevant marginal proportion is the overall proportion of cancer victims in the population, *Prop*(Cancer) = 0.40. In the present situation, the joint proportion of interest is

$$Prop(\text{Test positive \& Cancer}) = \frac{3600}{10,000} = 0.36$$

Notice the following:

$$\frac{Prop(\text{Test positive \& Cancer})}{Prop(\text{Cancer})} = \frac{3600 / 10,000}{4000 / 10,000}$$

$$= \frac{3600}{4000}$$

$$= 0.90$$

$$= Prop(\text{Test positive I Cancer})$$

The observed relationships are not coincidental. It is always true that, for arbitrary events *A* and *B*,

$$Prop(A \mid B) = \frac{Prop(A \,\&\, B)}{Prop(B)}$$

or, equivalently,

$$Prop(A \,\&\, B) = Prop(A \mid B)Prop(B)$$

as long as $Prop(B) \neq 0$. The same relations hold for probabilities, according to what is defined as the **general product rule** for conjunctions:

$$P(A \& B) = P(A \mid B)P(B), \text{ when } P(B) \neq 0 \qquad (5.13)$$

It is helpful—and correct—to think of conditioning as equivalent to restricting the relevant universe. In the unconditioned case, the pertinent universe is the entire collection of possibilities, for example, all 10,000 patients in the medical example of Table 5.1. On the other hand, in the conditioned case, the relevant universe consists of only those possibilities satisfying the property specified in the conditioning event, for instance, only the 4000 cancer patients when we are interested in P(Test positive | Cancer).

How well do people's probability judgments conform to the general product rule? In various conditions, Wyer (1976) gave subjects initial instructions that can be paraphrased as follows: "Suppose that persons *usually* have gene x and that persons with gene x *sometimes* possess attribute X." Across conditions, a total of three different qualifiers were applied to the relevant events, "usually," "sometimes," and "rarely." The subject was then asked, "Estimate the likelihood that Jane has both gene x and attribute X; that she has attribute X, given that she has gene x; and that she has gene x." Subjects' likelihood ratings were expressed in a form that was converted to probability judgments. In the present example, the subjects reported essentially P'(Attribute X & Gene x), P'(Attribute X | Gene x), and P'(Gene x). On average, the probability judgments were such that

$$P'(\text{Attribute X \& Gene x}) > P'(\text{Attribute X} \mid \text{Gene x})P'(\text{Gene x})$$

Results like Wyer's are commonly found. That is, it often happens that joint probabilities are **overjudged**:

$$P'(A \& B) > P'(A \mid B)P'(B) \qquad (5.14)$$

for arbitrary events A and B. Wyer (1976, p. 9) reports that in only a minority of the cases he observed was $P'(A \& B)$ less than both $P'(A)$ and $P'(B)$. Thus, in many instances $P'(A \& B) > P'(A)$ or $P'(A \& B) > P'(B)$. Put another way, subjects' joint probability judgments were so high that they resulted in conjunction errors.

The independence product rule

In everyday conversation, we often say things like, "I think age and wisdom are independent of each other." When we make such statements, we mean that knowing one of the factors does not allow us to better anticipate the other. For instance, if the above claim were true, then knowing that a given individual is old would be no clue that the person is especially likely to be either wise or unwise. As we will see, the concept of independence in probability theory is similar to the everyday meaning of the term.

Suppose that A is an arbitrary marginal event. Recall that the complement of A, event A^c, is the event containing all the occurrences not contained in A. Thus, if A = "Old," then its complement is A^c = "Not old" or "Young."

And if B = "Wise," then B^c = "Unwise." Events A and B are said to be independent of each other if the probability of event A is unaffected by the occurrence or nonoccurrence of event B. More precisely, **independence** holds if

$$P(A \mid B) = P(A \mid B^c) = P(A) \tag{5.15}$$

which is also equivalent to saying that

$$P(B \mid A) = P(B \mid A^c) = P(B) \tag{5.16}$$

So, if the previous assertion about age and wisdom were expressed in probability terms, it would say that

$$P(\text{Wise} \mid \text{Old}) = P(\text{Wise} \mid \text{Young}) = P(\text{Wise})$$

That is, the probability of a person being wise is the same, whether that individual is old or young—simply the overall probability of being wise.

The definition of independence can be viewed in terms of joint probabilities, too. Recall that the general multiplication rule for conjunctions says that $P(A \& B) = P(A \mid B)P(B)$. If independence holds, then $P(A \mid B) = P(A)$. We thus have the **independence product rule** for conjunctions:

$$P(A \& B) = P(A)P(B) \tag{5.17}$$

The product rule can be illustrated conveniently with proportions, which, you will recall, behave like probabilities. Consider Table 5.2, which is similar to Table 5.1. This time, however, the patients in the population have been subjected to a second test, Test Y. We now see that

$$Prop(\text{Test positive} \mid \text{Cancer}) = \frac{3000}{4000} = 0.75$$

which is the same as

$$Prop(\text{Test positive} \mid \text{No cancer}) = \frac{4500}{6000} = 0.75$$

That is, "Test positive" and "Cancer" are independent events.

TABLE 5.2 Another Population of Medical Patients Tested for Cancer

	ACTUAL CONDITION		
TEST Y RESULTS	CANCER	NO CANCER	TOTAL
Positive	3000	4500	7500
Negative	1000	1500	2500
Total	4000	6000	10,000

This table depicts independence between test results and actual medical condition.

Now consider the product rule. Observe that

$$Prop \text{ (Test positive) } Prop \text{ (Cancer)} = \frac{7500}{10,000} \times \frac{4000}{10,000}$$
$$= 0.30$$
$$= \frac{3000}{10,000}$$
$$= Prop \text{ (Test positive \& Cancer)}$$

So the product rule for independent events is indeed satisfied; test results and patient condition are unrelated to each other. Test Y is worthless. If you were to examine corresponding proportions in Table 5.1, you would discover that the events "Test positive" and "Cancer" were not independent, but rather were **dependent**.

Several experiments have tested whether people's likelihood judgments for independent events are consistent with the product rule. The experiment by Cohen and Hansel (1958) was performed with adolescents. However, the method was similar to that used with adults, and so were the results (see Bar-Hillel, 1973, for example).

Figure 5.8a depicts a game considered by Cohen and Hansel's subjects. The subject was shown a row of three boxes and asked to select one of them. If the correct box in this first stage of Game G1 was selected, the game continued to the second stage. If either of the other boxes was chosen, the game ended and no prize was received. If the game went to the second stage and the correct one of three more boxes was selected, the player won a piece of candy; otherwise there was no prize. Cohen and Hansel implicitly assumed that all the subjects would consider the chance of selecting the "continue box" in the first stage to be P'(Continue box) = ⅓. Similarly, it was assumed that the probability judgment for picking the prize box in the second stage was P'(Prize box) = ⅓. Winning candy in the overall game, the event "Candy-G1," is the conjunction of selecting the continue box in the first

(a)

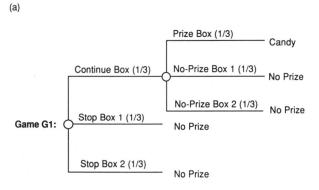

FIGURE 5.8. Structures of Games G1 and G2 presented to subjects by Cohen and Hansel (1958).

stage and the prize box in the second stage. Thus, if the subjects' intuitions agreed with probability theory, their judgments would have satisfied the following relations:

$$P'(\text{Candy–G1}) = P'(\text{Continue box \& Prize box})$$
$$= P'(\text{Continue box})P'(\text{Prize box})$$
$$= \frac{1}{9}$$

which is approximately 11%.

Now consider the single-stage game shown in Figure 5.8b, Game G2. There the player draws a ticket at random from one of several containers. Various of the containers are represented at the bottom of the figure. Each container held only one prize ticket, which, if selected, yielded the same candy prize offered in Game G1. The containers differed from one another in the total number of tickets they held. Thus, the container on the left held only one ticket, a prize ticket. The second held two tickets, the third held five tickets, and so on. Accordingly, the probability of winning the prize when drawing from a container with N tickets was $\frac{1}{N}$. The task of the subject was to indicate which version of Game G2, that is, which container, was such that the chance of winning the prize was closest to that in Game G1. Let us suppose that one particular subject, "Sam Meyer," said that the container with seven tickets provided the same chance of winning in Game G2 as in Game G1. For Sam, the judged probability of winning candy in Game G2 clearly was

$$P'(\text{Candy–G2}) = \frac{1}{7} \approx 14\%$$

(b)

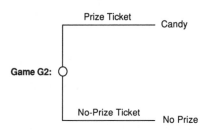

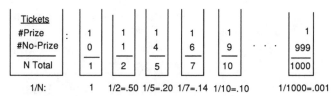

FIGURE 5.8. (continued)

Thus, for Sam,

$$P'(\text{Candy-G1}) = P'(\text{Candy-G2})$$

But this implies that

$$P'(\text{Continue box \& Prize box}) > P'(\text{Continue box})P'(\text{Prize box})$$

since

$$14\% = P'(\text{Candy-G1}) = P'(\text{Continue box \& Prize box})$$

and

$$P'(\text{Continue box})P'(\text{Prize box}) \approx 11\%$$

Cohen and Hansel found that the typical subject behaved much like Sam Meyer. In particular, the median inferred probability judgment for P'(Continue box & Prize box) was about 15%. This suggests the general conclusion of **overjudgment**, that is, for arbitrary independent events A and B,

$$P'(A \& B) > P'(A)P'(B) \qquad (5.18)$$

Bayes's Theorem

Imagine that you are a physician, and that "Eugene Thomas" is one of your patients. Based on your preliminary observations, you think there is about a 5% chance that Mr. Thomas has cancer. To assist you in your diagnosis, you consider using Test X, whose accuracy was demonstrated in Table 5.1. Since you feel that those statistics are reliable and applicable to patients like Mr. Thomas, you accept the relevant proportions as your own probability judgments. Thus, for example, you feel that P'(Test positive | Cancer) = 0.90 and P'(Test positive | No cancer) = 0.20. Mr. Thomas gets positive test results. *Now* what is your probability judgment that Mr. Thomas has cancer?

Problems like this one are common in many practical situations. Symbolically, these problems can be described as follows: There is a hypothesis H at issue, "Cancer" in the present instance. Before any (new) evidence is considered, there is a **prior probability** for the hypothesis, $P(H)$. In Mr. Thomas's case, you had a prior probability judgment P'(Cancer) = 0.05. The prospective relevant evidence is typically denoted by D, for "data," for example, "Test positive" in medical diagnosis. Conditional probabilities of the form $P(D \mid H)$ and $P(D \mid H^c)$ are known, where H^c is the complement of H. $P(D \mid H)$ is called the **(statistical) likelihood** of the data, given the hypothesis; $P(D \mid H^c)$ is the likelihood of the data, given the alternative hypothesis. In the current situation, the former is P'(Test positive | Cancer) = 0.90, while the latter is P'(Test positive | No cancer) = 0.20. The object of the problem is to determine the probability of the hypothesis *after* the evidence is observed, $P(H \mid D)$. This probability is known as the **posterior probability** for the hypothesis; it is "posterior" to the revelation of the data. For example, the judgment you must make for Mr. Thomas is the posterior probability judgment P'(Cancer | Test positive).

Over 200 years ago, an English clergyman, Reverend Thomas Bayes (1763/1958), derived the probability theory solution to this type of problem. That solution is now known as **Bayes's Theorem:**

$$P(H \mid D) = \frac{P(D \mid H)P(H)}{P(D \mid H)P(H) + P(D \mid H^c)P(H^c)}$$ (5.19)

This formula looks more formidable than it is. It follows directly from principles you have already seen. Recall the general product rule for conjunctions, which in this instance can be written as follows:

$$P(H \mid D) = \frac{P(H \,\&\, D)}{P(D)}$$

Focus separately on the numerator and denominator of this expression. First the numerator: The product rule says that

$$P(H \,\&\, D) = P(D \,\&\, H) = P(D \mid H)P(H)$$

Now the denominator: Consider Figure 5.9. The Venn diagram there shows that event D can be partitioned into the conjunction of events D and H, denoted $(D \,\&\, H)$ and represented by the clear space, and the conjunction $(D \,\&\, H^c)$, represented by the region containing horizontal stripes. So, according to the additivity property,

$$P(D) = P(D \,\&\, H) + P(D \,\&\, H^c)$$

We have just seen that $P(D \,\&\, H) = P(D \mid H)P(H)$. By similar reasoning, $P(D \,\&\, H^c) = P(D \mid H^c)P(H^c)$. We thus have

$$P(D) = P(D \mid H)P(H) + P(D \mid H^c)P(H^c)$$

and the story is complete.

How would Reverend Bayes solve your problem of diagnosing Mr. Thomas's condition? His solution would proceed as follows:

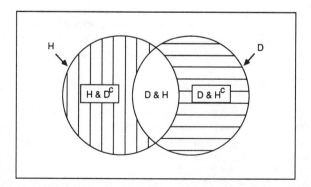

FIGURE 5.9. Venn diagram depicting the partitioning of the event H into $(H \,\&\, D^c)$ and $(D \,\&\, H)$ and event D into $(D \,\&\, H)$ and $(D \,\&\, H^c)$.

$$P'(\text{Cancer} \mid \text{Test positive}) = \frac{P'(\text{Test positive} \mid \text{Cancer})P'(\text{Cancer})}{P'(\text{Test positive} \mid \text{Cancer})P'(\text{Cancer}) + P'(\text{Test positive} \mid \text{No cancer})P'(\text{No cancer})}$$

$$= \frac{(0.90)(0.05)}{(0.90)(0.05) + (0.20)(0.95)}$$

$$= 0.191$$

How does the Bayesian solution compare with your own intuitive probability judgment that Mr. Thomas has cancer? Most people report judgments substantially higher than 19.1%. For instance, when one group of subjects solved the problem, their average response was 47.3%.

Examples such as the present one illustrate the fact that people's actual probability judgments often deviate substantially from the requirements of Bayes's Theorem. The nature of the deviation depends on the situation (see Fischhoff and Beyth-Marom, 1983). In problems suited to the Bayesian framework, we start with an initial opinion $P'(H)$. We are then presented with evidence D, which induces a revised opinion $P'(H \mid D)$. The magnitude of the **probability revision** is

$$R = P'(H \mid D) - P'(H) \tag{5.20}$$

In our cancer diagnosis problem, the proper revision according to Bayes's Theorem was

$$R = P'(\text{Cancer} \mid \text{Test positive}) - P'(\text{Cancer})$$

$$= 0.191 - 0.050$$

$$= 0.141$$

As indicated, people's actual posterior judgments of $P'(\text{Cancer} \mid \text{Test positive})$ in the problem are commonly much greater than 0.191. That is, their revisions are too large, 0.423 on average for the subjects mentioned above. Revisions are not always excessive, however. There are many instances in which revisions are much too *conservative* (for example, Phillips and Edwards, 1966; Phillips, Edwards, and Hays, 1966).

CONCEPTUAL SIGNIFICANCE OF COHERENCE

Do people care whether their likelihood judgments are coherent? Should they? From a conceptual point of view, there are two reasons people often care about coherence: logical esthetics and theoretical elegance.

Coherence and logical esthetics

Many people commit the conjunction fallacy. For example, in the Bjorn Borg problem, almost everybody says it seems more likely that Borg would lose the first set but win the match than that he would lose the first set. However, when it is pointed out to them that this opinion violates the rule that $P'(A \ \& \ B)$ cannot be greater than either $P'(A)$ or $P'(B)$, they are surprised—and sometimes chagrined. They feel they have made a mistake (see Tversky and Kahneman, 1982); they rarely question the legitimacy of the conjunction rule.

The principles of probability theory are very reasonable to most people, once they are understood. Conversely, violations of those principles are repugnant. Such violations appear to offend our sense of **logical esthetics**. In music, certain sound patterns seem naturally pleasing, while others grate on our nerves. Just as certain music offends our musical tastes, many people find that incoherence in likelihood judgments violates their *logical* tastes.

Probability theory as psychological theory

The goal of judgment psychology is to arrive at a simple but sufficient explanation of how people make judgments. Psychologists have taken probability theory as a starting point in their quest for an adequate theory of human likelihood judgment. Suppose that our likelihood judgments *were* coherent. Then probability theory would constitute an elegant psychological as well as mathematical theory.

We have seen that people's likelihood judgments generally do *not* submit to the dictates of probability theory. So probability theory in itself is clearly wanting as a model of human opinion. This does not mean that the theory has been useless in our search for understanding, however. First, probability theory has provided a powerful frame of reference for studies of human judgment. For example, it has afforded precision for such concepts as independence. So when we study people's judgments about independent events, there is little confusion about what is being investigated. Second, probability theory has served as a point of departure for new theories of human judgment. Thus, we know the kinds of phenomena these new theories must explain. For instance, we know that a really good theory of human likelihood judgment must account for people believing that Bjorn Borg is more likely to lose the first set but win the match than that he will simply lose the first set.

PRACTICAL SIGNIFICANCE OF COHERENCE

Suppose that a person's likelihood judgments are incoherent. Will there be material consequences of that fact? There is good reason to suspect that there might.

Accuracy implications

As noted in Chapter 4, if a person's likelihood judgments are inaccurate indicators of the events that actually happen, that individual should make many decisions that turn out badly. At the beginning of this chapter, we also found that coherence is no guarantee that likelihood judgments will be accurate. Nevertheless, in some circumstances, if a person's likelihood judgments are *not* coherent, at least some of those judgments ought to be *inaccurate*, with potentially detrimental consequences. An example is illustrative.

Refer to Table 5.2, which contains frequencies of patients in a population who either have cancer or do not, and who obtain either positive or negative results on Test Y. Suppose "Millie Johnson" makes probability judgments for events in that population. Ms. Johnson's judgments for marginal events agree with the marginal proportions. For example, when she is asked to judge the probability that a randomly selected patient has cancer, she reports P'(Cancer) ≈ *Prop*(Cancer) = 4000/10,000 = 0.40. When asked for the probability that a patient tests positively, she responds P'(Test positive) ≈ *Prop*(Test positive) = 7500/10,000 = 0.75. However, Ms. Johnson's judgments for conjunctions and marginal events do not relate to one another the way probability theory says they should. Instead, as is commonly the case, her probability judgments for conjunctions are too high. For instance, she indicates that P'(Cancer & Test positive) > P'(Cancer)P'(Test positive) = 0.30. So Ms. Johnson's probability judgments for conjunctions cannot be the same as the joint proportions that really exist in the population. Over the long run, those joint proportions would very accurately anticipate which patients had particular combinations of test results and medical conditions. The accuracy of Ms. Johnson's opinions about conjunctions necessarily would be worse.

Susceptibility to material traps

In any business transaction, each party accepts one alternative over all the others that happen to be available. For example, when you buy something in a store, you accept the thing you purchase instead of keeping your money in your pocket. When you trade your bicycle for someone else's typewriter, you choose to acquire the typewriter rather than keep the bicycle. A **material trap** is a transaction (or series of transactions) in which one party is guaranteed to be made no better off than he or she would have been choosing a rejected alternative.[1] People whose likelihood judgments violate at least some of the principles of probability theory are susceptible to being victimized by material traps (see Winkler, 1972). That is, such individuals are prone to accepting propositions that are sure to leave them in as poor a position (if not worse) as any other available option—*regardless of which relevant events ultimately occur.*

Recall Tversky and Kahneman's (1982) Bjorn Borg problem just once more. Try to imagine the following scenario taking place prior to the Wimbledon tournament mentioned in the problem. Jim and Mike are friends as well as tennis fans. Jim asks Mike to choose between the friendly wagers depicted in Figure 5.10a. In Bet 1, if Borg loses the first set of the Wimbledon final, Jim treats Mike to lunch; otherwise, Mike buys lunch for Jim. In Bet 2, Jim takes Mike to lunch if Borg loses the first set but wins the match; otherwise Mike takes Jim. Consistent with the conjunction fallacy, Mike thinks it is more likely that Borg will lose the first set but win the match than that he will lose the first set. So he chooses Bet 2.

[1]Traditionally material traps have been known as **Dutch books.** Because the latter expression might be interpreted as an ethnic pejorative, the former is preferred.

The tree diagrams in Figure 5.10b summarize the potential outcomes of Borg's first set and match, as well as the payoffs of Bets 1 and 2, contingent on those outcomes. We see that, from Mike's point of view, every payoff resulting from Bet 1 is at least as favorable as the corresponding payoff yielded by Bet 2. And for one of the sequences of outcomes, the heavily outlined path through each tree for which the payoffs are circled, the Bet 1 payoff is definitely better. The conjunction fallacy has led Mike into the clutches of a material trap.

Since Mike and Jim are friends, Mike's victimization was surely unintended by Jim. Nevertheless, an unscrupulous individual who is aware of people's violations of probability theory *could* take advantage of others by subjecting them to material traps. Such traps in fact have been sprung for the purposes of demonstration in experiments (for example, Tversky and Kahneman, 1983). There is no reason to think that real-life material traps typically are constructed purposefully. However, even when they occur by accident, as in the case of Jim and Mike, they are no less painful for their victims.

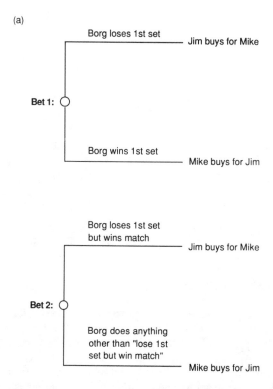

FIGURE 5.10. (a) Bets 1 and 2 for Bjorn Borg's Wimbledon final match offered to Mike by his friend Jim. (b) Potential set and match results and payoffs, contingent on Mike's choice between Bets 1 and 2.

(b)

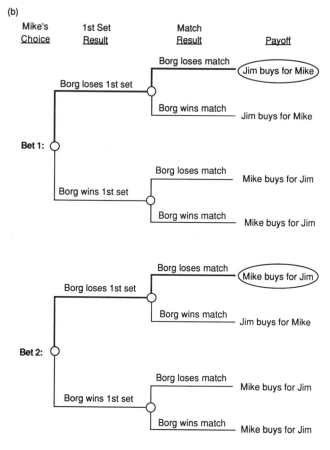

FIGURE 5.10. (continued)

PROCEDURES FOR PRODUCING COHERENT LIKELIHOOD JUDGMENTS

Unfortunately, there is no way of knowing just how serious the consequences of incoherence usually are. So it is unclear how hard we should work to make sure that our everyday judgments are coherent. But consider practical situations in which the stakes are very high, for example, building a nuclear power plant, diagnosing illnesses, or monitoring enemy troop activity in wartime. Under those circumstances, we would want to have every possible advantage in making good judgments. With these types of high-stakes situations in mind, decision theorists have proposed techniques which assure that likelihood judgments are coherent.

Most of these methods involve a strategy known as **decomposition–recomposition**. The essence of the approach is this: The judgment problem is broken down or decomposed into small elements. People are then asked to make likelihood judgments about the individual components of the problem rather than the problem taken as a whole. In the final stage of the strategy, the individual component judgments are recomposed according to probability theory into a judgment for the original, large problem.

The previous description of the decomposition–recomposition strategy is sketchy and abstract. An example should make the ideas more concrete. Let us examine an extremely simple illustration of the fault tree version of the approach, which extends one mentioned previously:

"Jenny Fox" is an engineer whose task is to determine the chance that a complicated machine will fail within two years. She has identified three specific potential faults, or causes of failure, Faults 1 to 3. Ms. Fox has reason to believe that those faults, and all other nonspecific ones, are mutually exclusive. That is, there is essentially no chance that any two of those faults would occur simultaneously. So, effectively, the event "Failure" is partitioned by the events "Fault 1 occurs," "Fault 2 occurs," "Fault 3 occurs," and "Some other fault occurs." The fault tree in Figure 5.11 shows how Ms. Fox has decomposed the overall event of interest into the smaller events.

Fault 1 involves a part of the machine designed by another engineer, "Don Bishop." So Ms. Fox asks Mr. Bishop for his probability judgment that Fault 1 will occur. He reports

$$P'(\text{Fault 1}) = 0.01$$

Fault 2 rests on a part bought from an outside supplier. The records indicate that the part has a 3% failure rate. So Ms. Fox assigns

$$P'(\text{Fault 2}) = 0.03$$

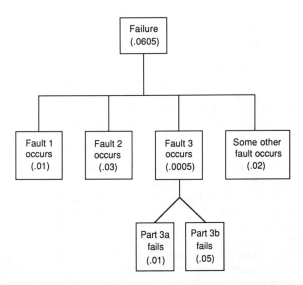

FIGURE 5.11. Fault tree analysis of potential machine failure. See text for details.

Fault 3 occurs only if two other parts fail, Parts 3a and 3b. That is, Ms. Fox has recognized that

Fault 3 = (Part 3a fails & Part 3b fails)

(The fact that Fault 3 is the conjunction of Parts 3a and 3b failing is indicated by the lines from those events converging at Fault 3.) She also considers the failures of those parts to be independent. Since Parts 3a and 3b are produced by Ms. Fox's own division of the firm, she readily judges herself that

$$P'(\text{Part 3a fails}) = 0.01$$

and

$$P'(\text{Part 3b fails}) = 0.05$$

Because the event "Some other fault occurs" involves a host of things, she holds a meeting of several engineers to arrive at a consensus judgment that

$$P'(\text{Other fault}) = 0.02$$

In the recomposition stage of her fault tree analysis, Ms. Fox starts at the bottom of the tree. She notes that the product rule for conjunctions of independent events would require that

$$P'(\text{Fault 3}) = P'(\text{Part 3a fails})P'(\text{Part 3b fails})$$

So she sets

$$P'(\text{Fault 3}) = (0.01)(0.05) = 0.0005$$

The additivity property demands that

$$P'(\text{Failure}) = P'(\text{Fault 1}) + P'(\text{Fault 2}) + P'(\text{Fault 3}) + P'(\text{Other fault})$$
$$= 0.01 + 0.03 + 0.0005 + 0.02$$
$$= 0.0605$$

There are other versions of the decomposition–recomposition strategy. Edwards's (1962) "probabilistic information processing" or PIP system was the prototype for some important examples. It was intended for situations in which Bayes's Theorem applies. That is, suitable judgments of the form $P'(H)$, $P'(D \mid H)$, and $P'(D \mid H^c)$ are available to the judge. Bayes's Theorem is then applied by the computerized system to arrive at $P'(H \mid D)$.

All decomposition–recomposition procedures share several characteristics. First, by design, they force judgments to be coherent. So those judgments should enjoy whatever advantages coherence awards, for example, protection against material traps. As indicated previously, this coherence does not ensure that the resulting judgments will be more accurate than unaided judgments would. Nevertheless, there is at least one compelling argument for the accuracy of judgments derived from decomposition–recomposition procedures: Judgments for the component events rather than the overall events should be easier for people to make with authority. As in Jenny Fox's problem, it is often hard to find anyone who is an expert on an entire situation; individuals knowledgeable about small elements of that situation should be more readily available.

In life we seldom get something for nothing. That is the case here, too; the decomposition–recomposition strategy has costs and risks as well as advantages. Obtaining all the elementary judgments demanded by decomposition–recomposition can be both difficult and time consuming. Moreover, we should recognize that every judgment has a certain amount of random error in it. Because decomposition–recomposition procedures involve so *many* judgments, the compounded unreliability of final judgments derived from those procedures can be considerable. It is also worth noting that the usefulness of a decomposition–recomposition analysis depends on the degree to which the decomposition corresponds to reality, for example, the extent to which the fault possibilities for Ms. Fox's machine are accurately modeled by Figure 5.11 and the assumptions she makes.

ALTERNATIVE COHERENCE PERSPECTIVES

Probability theory is not the only standard for likelihood judgment coherence we might adopt. There is one particular principle of probability theory that is especially troubling to some observers, for example, Shafer (1976) and L. J. Cohen (1977). An event A and its complement A^c form a partition of the relevant universe. Probability theory thus requires that probability judgments satisfy the following **complementarity relation**:

$$P'(A^c) = 1 - P'(A) \qquad (5.21)$$

For example, suppose you are an experienced surgeon who has performed a certain operation hundreds of times. You now consider the case of "Mr. DuPont." You feel secure in judging that there is a 15% chance the operation will fail. Coherence would demand that you believe there is an 85% chance that the operation will succeed.

In cases such as Mr. DuPont's, we are quite comfortable accepting the complementarity relation. But now imagine that, in your capacity as a surgeon, you are considering a completely new operation for "Mr. Naverson." No one has ever tried the procedure you have in mind, although on theoretical grounds you think it ought to work. Mr. Naverson asks you what are the chances the operation will fail. You respond, "15%." He then asks, "So there's an 85% chance it will be successful, right?" Although you know you *should* say, "Of course," you feel uneasy about doing so. If you are like many of us in such situations, you will feel that the chances of the operation succeeding are something less than 85%.

When we know little about a situation, often we might be inclined to have low probability judgments for both an event *and* its complement, thus violating the complementary relation. Authors such as Shafer (1976) argue that this is quite reasonable. They see it as a failing of probability theory that a strong belief in one event demands a weak belief in its complement, and vice versa, regardless of the circumstances. Instead, it seems intuitively appealing to permit the reservation of part of one's belief to an "undecided" event. Investigators have proceeded to try and develop alternative theoretical frameworks that do not make such demands. That work is in progress (see, for example, Shafer, 1987; Shortliffe and Buchanan, 1975).

SUMMARY

Likelihood judgments are said to be coherent to the extent that relationships among those judgments are consistent with accepted principles. The most widely accepted principles of coherence are those underlying probability theory.

Human likelihood judgments systematically violate several implications of probability theory. For example: (1) Probability judgments for the events comprising a partition of a universe often sum to more than 1; (2) similar judgments for disjunctions of mutually exclusive events typically are less than the sums of their probability judgments for the events constituting those disjunctions; and (3) people sometimes reliably judge a conjunction of two events to be more probable than one of them.

Likelihood judgment coherence is an important issue on both conceptual and practical grounds. If a person's judgments are incoherent, then there is a limit to how accurately those judgments can anticipate the events that actually occur in the real world. It can be shown that a person whose judgments are incoherent sometimes can be exploited by material traps.

KEY TERMS

Axiom	Independence
Bayes's Theorem	Independence product rule
Coherence	Joint probability
Complementarity relation	Logical esthetics
Conditional probability	Marginal event
Conjunction	Material trap
Conjunction error	Mutually exclusive
Conjunction fallacy	Overjudgment
Conjunction rule	Partition
Decomposition–recomposition	Posterior probability
Dependence	Postulate
Disjoint	Prior probability
Disjunction	Probability
Disjunction error	Probability revision
Disjunction rule	Sensitivity
Dutch book	Specificity
Event	Statistical likelihood
Exhaustive	Subadditive
Extension principle	Superadditive
Family of events	Underjudgment
Fault tree	Unity summation principle
General product rule	Universe
Generalized disjunction principle	Venn diagram

ADDITIONAL READING

Bandler and Kohout (1985); Fishburn (1986); Freedman and Purves (1969); Fryback and Thornbury (1976); Hacking (1975); Halmos (1944); Lindley, Tversky, and Brown (1979); Moskowitz and Sarin (1983); Peterson and Beach (1967); Pitz (1975); Politser (1984); Schum (1980).

EXERCISES AND STUDY QUESTIONS

1. Shirley reports, among others, the following probability judgments concerning the outcome of a Democratic primary election for governor: P'(Stovall wins) = 18%, P'(Moss or Stovall wins) = 42%, P'(Parks wins) = 22%, P'(McGee or Parks wins) = 57%, P'(Moss wins) = 24%.

   (a) Garrett examines these judgments and then declares, "Shirley's probability judgments for election outcomes are coherent." Garrett's declaration is premature. What more would you need to know before you agreed with Garrett's claim?

   (b) Based on what is known about the coherence of people's probability judgments, identify a particular aspect of the above judgments that should be seen as surprising. Instead of what is actually observed, what *should* we have expected to see?

2. (a) It is known that the diseases "arprosy" and "blemia" are mutually exclusive. It is also known that the probability that a certain type of person will contract arprosy is 5%, while the chance that he or she will develop blemia is 10%. Jane was asked what the probability was that a person would get both arprosy and blemia. Being aware of the previous facts, she says that the desired probability is 0.5%. She is wrong. How so? Why do you think she made the error she did?

   (b) Suppose you randomly sample three groups of physicians and present each with all the facts about the patient implied in part (a). The first group judges the probability that the patient has arprosy, the second that he has blemia, and the third that he has either arprosy or blemia. Describe the relationship you would expect to observe among the average judgments made by the three groups. Justify your expectation.

3. Trent just finished reading this chapter. Based on the chapter, he says that we should expect that people's probability judgments for conjunctions usually will be positively biased, in the sense defined in Chapter 3. For instance, suppose a stock broker is asked to state P'(Gain & Dividend) for lots of different companies, where the event "Gain" means that a share of the company's stock will gain in price over the next year, and the event "Dividend" means that the company will pay a dividend that year, too. So Trent expects that the average value of P'(Gain & Dividend) will be substantially higher than the proportion of companies whose stocks gain in value and who pay dividends. Trent has misinterpreted the results described in the chapter. How so?

4. One task auditors perform is identifying "material weaknesses" in the financial controls of the firms whose records they audit. Andrew is an auditor. Ewart,

another auditor, tells him that 2% of all firms that have Weakness *W* in their accounting systems have records indicating Transaction Error *E*. Andrew dismisses Ewart's comment: "Big deal. That error probability is so tiny it can't possibly help me in my audits."

(a) Do you agree with Andrew's position? Why or why not, in intuitive terms?

(b) (Optional) Argue your position on the basis of Bayes's Theorem.

5. Illustrate how to construct a material trap that victimizes a person whose judgments violate the disjunction rule of probability, that is, the rule which says that $P(A \text{ or } B) \geq P(A)$ and $P(A \text{ or } B) \geq P(B)$.

6. You hear the following news item on the radio: "Scientists at Humongous State University announced today that they have developed a remarkably good test for 'Jackson's Disease!' A full *92%* of confirmed Jackson's patients were found to score positively on the HSU test! For no other test do more than 80% of true Jackson's patients score positively." Based on this report alone, you are unsure that the excitement over the HSU test is justified. Why?

7. Recruit the assistance of a friend who has a paper or other assignment due. First ask your friend for a probability judgment that he or she will complete the assignment at least one day before it is due. Next, derive a probability judgment for that event using a fault tree analysis. Finally, compare the results. Is the difference in results consistent with what you would expect, according to common findings concerning the coherence of people's likelihood judgments? Explain.

8. Observers disagree about the importance of the practical consequences of probability judgment incoherence. Offer at least one argument on each side of the issue.

6

Formal Procedures

*Believe what you have Proved. They most deceive
Themselves who try to Prove what they Believe.*

—Arthur Guiterman

"David Ross" owns a small accounting firm. In the course of his working day, he makes many likelihood judgments—implicitly and explicitly. In an audit of "Pinnacle Enterprises," he estimates what the correct balance was in each of their accounts at the end of the last fiscal year. In preparing the "Pulaskis's" tax return, he judges how likely it is that the Internal Revenue Service will allow all the deductions the Pulaskis want to claim. In deciding whether to expand his staff by two accountants, he must judge whether the recent increasing trend in his business will continue.

David Ross's role as a judge does not end when he leaves the office. For example, he and his wife Marilyn are building a new and larger house for their growing family. But they have the problem of deciding when to put their old house on the market. They know when the new house is *scheduled* to be completed. However, they are unsure that the contractor will actually finish the work by that time. So they must make judgments: What is the chance they will be able to move into the new house on the scheduled date? Moreover, what is the chance that, if they put the old house up for sale two months in advance, they would find a buyer willing to close the sale around the time they want to move?

In previous chapters, we have gained some sense of how accurate people's likelihood judgments usually are. So we can anticipate the extent to which David and Marilyn Ross's opinions will faithfully correspond to what ultimately occurs. We have also learned how well—and sometimes how poorly—people's judgments conform to the requirements of probability theory. In this chapter and the next, we will probe more deeply: *How* do people, such as the Rosses, arrive at their assessments of how certain it is that various events will occur? That is, what are the processes underlying human likelihood judgment?

People judge likelihood according to many procedures. These processes fall into two broad categories. The first consists of **formal** procedures. To say that something is formal means that it emphasizes form or structure, rather than nature or content. The application of probability theory is a convenient example. Suppose we seek the probability of a die showing a single pip on each of two consecutive tosses. We assume that there is a $\frac{1}{6}$ probability of a single pip on each toss. We also assume that observations of single pips on both tosses are independent events. We recognize that getting single pips on both tosses is the conjunction of obtaining single pips on the individual tosses. Using the multiplication rule, we therefore conclude that the probability of consecutive single pips is $(\frac{1}{6})(\frac{1}{6}) = \frac{1}{36}$.

Notice the following about how we solved the above problem. From past experience or from arguments about the symmetry of the die, we accepted the assumption that every side of the die has an equal chance of appearing on top. We then specialized the rule which has the form

$$P(A \ \& \ B) = P(A)P(B)$$

to the particular case where A = "Single pip on Toss 1" and B = "Single Pip on Toss 2." These features of our method highlight the hallmark of formal procedures: They do not require an analysis of the natural processes by which the events of interest happen, for example, how one's fingers turn the faces of the die, the angles at which the die hits the table, and the like. Moreover, the rules we used, that is, generalizing from past experience and the multiplication rule, are completely indifferent to the content of the problem. As far as they are concerned, the problem could as easily have been about the chances of being admitted to both Stanford and Oxford as about dice. What *did* matter, however, was that the form or structure of the situation corresponded to the form assumed by the rules that were used.

The second category of judgment procedures that can be distinguished is **substantive** techniques. In various ways, these procedures *do* entail consideration of how events actually take place, or at least how people *think* those events are determined. The present chapter addresses some of the most well-documented formal procedures. The next chapter is devoted to substantive processes. Our discussion of formal methods starts in the first section with procedures that amount to deferring to experts. The second section considers opinions based on the application of probability theory concepts. The following section reviews evidence that people sometimes make likelihood judgments in a fashion very similar to applying probability theory, but according to rules quite different from those of probability theory. The last two sections of the chapter examine indications that people use various proportions as their probability judgments.

The procedures we will consider in this chapter and the next are responsible for several of the human judgment inaccuracies and incoherencies we have seen previously, as well as others. Nevertheless, as we will see, they are thought to have advantages, too. There is documentation that every one of the techniques we will discuss is used at some time or other by many people. A most important question, however, is *when* we can expect the various processes to come into play in real life. That is, what determines that event A's likelihood will be judged according to Process 1, whereas opinions about event B's occurrence will be derived from Process 2? Arguments and evidence on this issue will be offered throughout our consideration of the individual procedures. In the last section of Chapter 7, we will address this procedure assignment problem more pointedly.

DEFERENCE TO EXPERTISE

> *Red sky at night, sailor's delight.*
> *Red sky in the morning, sailor take warning.*

You have probably heard this old saying often. At one time, it was a major means of forecasting. Note two things about it. First, predicting weather via the "red sky" principle was easy. Second, the typical sailor of old respected the saying because it was assumed to be based on the wisdom of the ages—or an even greater authority. For instance, in the Bible, Matthew (xvi,2) wrote,

"When it is evening, ye say, It will be fair weather: for the sky is red." So perhaps some sailors followed the rule as being divinely inspired.

Things have changed. But in some ways they have also remained the same. If we had to think through every judgment problem personally, we would be swamped. Not only would we be incredibly busy, but we would not do a very good job either. Each of us cannot be knowledgeable about everything. So perhaps more often than not, we rely on others' judgments, assuming that they are more expert than we. For instance, we do not try to judge what is wrong with our bodies when we are sick; we defer to the physician. But it is impossible for even any single physician to have had extensive personal experience with every disorder. He or she does not have the time to analyze in detail every case that comes along. Instead, the physician typically makes judgments according to protocols taught in medical school: "If the patient has Symptom A, Symptom B, ..., then there's a good chance the disorder is X." Other examples of deferring to expertise abound. For instance, we take the National Weather Service's probability judgments for rain as our own. Or when the Nuclear Regulatory Commission says that the chance of a major accident in a power plant is 1 in 3 million, what can we say other than, "Well, they ought to know"?

It is hard to say how often our personal opinions about events' chances of occurrence are really judgments we have appropriated from those we consider to be more expert than ourselves. However, perhaps we do not defer to expertise as often as we should. We saw previously that laypersons' likelihood judgments are frequently overconfident. A logical extension of such overconfidence would be a failure to recognize the *need* to seek expert opinion. But also recall the conditions that seem to affect overconfidence. The phenomenon is especially pronounced when the person thinks he or she possesses relevant knowledge about the given area, for example, almanac questions versus stock prices. This suggests that we should be especially prone to defer to experts in domains where technical knowledge is clearly required, for example, automobile or electronics repairs and medicine. We also know that overconfidence is lessened by abundant and clear-cut feedback about our own judgment accuracy. Thus, although sometimes we are unimpressed by meteorologists' predictions, we are even less impressed by how good our own weather forecasts are; so we defer to the professionals. It would not be surprising if, *when* we defer to experts' judgments, we are overly confident in their opinions. This is because we are rarely told how accurate the experts' opinions actually are. Indeed, in many cases the experts do not know themselves; weather forecasters are the exception rather than the rule.

APPLICATION OF PROBABILITY THEORY PRINCIPLES

There is evidence that, at least sometimes, people arrive at their likelihood judgments by invoking probability theory concepts. An example was described in Yates and Carlson's (1986) study of the conjunction fallacy. In each of several situations, subjects were asked to rank order by their probability two marginal events, *A* and *B*, their conjunction, (*A* & *B*), and the conjunction of their complements, (A^c & B^c). For instance, in one problem, the events were:

A: Syria and Israel will sign a peace treaty with each other this year.

and

B: The University of Michigan will win at least 4 of its 11 games during the 1984 football season.

Subjects were not only required to make judgments about the relative chances of the events, but also to "think out loud" as they considered their judgments. That is, they gave their reasoning about how and why they ranked the probabilities of the events the way they did.

Most subjects made conjunction errors, that is, judged event (*A* & *B*) to be more likely than one of either event *A* or event *B*. However, there was an identifiable minority who almost never made such mistakes. These individuals said it was impossible for event (*A* & *B*) to be more likely than event *A* or event *B*. For the events described above, a common argument can be paraphrased as follows:

> In order for event D^1 to occur, "Syria and Israel sign a treaty and UM wins at least 4 of its games," two things have to happen. On the other hand, for event *A* to occur, only one thing has to happen. The same for event *B*. So I know that event *D* can't have a higher probability than either event *A* or event *B*.

Subjects who reasoned this way made implicit use of probability theory concepts, even though they did not describe them as such. It just seemed to be a part of their natural judgment apparatus to think in a way that is consistent with probability theory. Nisbett and others (1983) argue that everyday human thinking has evolved to the point where many people have a fundamental appreciation for basic ideas in statistical (and probability) theory. They cite several examples from common experience.

We would expect people formally trained in probability and statistics to be especially prone to making likelihood judgments according to probability theory principles. It is unclear that they are. Nisbett and others (1983) offer evidence that training generalizes to some judgment situations. Nevertheless, Tversky and Kahneman (for example, 1971, 1974, 1983) have documented many instances in which people's likelihood judgments routinely violate probability theory's demands. Almost invariably, they have found that individuals well trained in probability and statistics violate those requirements just as often as laypersons. Surely these individuals know the principles of probability theory and how they can be applied. So why do they not use these potentially valuable rules more often than they do?

---

[1] This is how event (*A* & *B*) was labeled.

Again, studies of the conjunction fallacy suggest a reason. One of Yates and Carlson's (1986) judgment problems was based on one from Tversky and Kahneman's (1982) article. Event A was "President Reagan will provide for increased defense spending." Event B was "Reagan will provide federal support for unwed mothers." Of course, the conjunction of these events, (A & B), was "Reagan will provide for increased defense spending and federal support for unwed mothers." Subjects sometimes argued that event (A & B) was more likely than either event A or event B because it represented a political compromise, that is, increased defense spending would be more acceptable to a liberal Congress if coupled with support for unwed mothers. On the other hand, support for unwed mothers would be better regarded by a conservative president if Congress also granted him a larger defense budget.

Implicit in the above argument is the subject's assumption that event A really means event (A & B^c), and that event B is equivalent to event (A^c & B). That is, "increased defense spending" precludes "federal support for unwed mothers," and vice versa. Markus and Zajonc (1985) have hypothesized this as an explanation for at least some individuals' conjunction errors. You should note that, if a person does view the events as suggested, there is nothing fallacious about the judgment that is typically reported. That is, probability theory does not prohibit our believing it is more probable that "Reagan will provide for increased defense spending and federal support for unwed mothers" than that "Reagan will provide for increased defense spending but not increased federal support for unwed mothers."

An alternative interpretation of the previous hypothesis is that the person's reasoning does not involve probability-theory-like concepts at all. Instead, it rests on substantive—in this case political—considerations. This example suggests a general phenomenon. If a judgment problem is couched in compelling substantive terms, the person will be so caught up in that way of viewing things that it will simply not occur to him or her to apply probability theory principles, and hence the errors. As one subject put it in debriefing after one of the Yates and Carlson (1986) studies, "Oh, I didn't *realize* this was a math problem! Otherwise I would have gotten it!" Nisbett and others (1983) have proposed a similar explanation for why people sometimes do not apply their more general statistical knowledge.

JUDGMENT VIA NONPROBABILITY THEORY RULES

In the last section, we saw that people sometimes infer probability judgments for a target event from their judgments for more elementary events, using rules equivalent to those in probability theory. For example, consider the case when subjects were asked to judge the relative likelihood of the events

A = There will be a Mideast treaty

B = Michigan will win at least 4 games

and

C = There will be a Mideast treaty and Michigan will
win at least 4 games

We saw that some subjects acknowledged that

$$C = (A \ \& \ B)$$

and then recognized that, on "logical grounds," their probability judgment
for event C should be such that

$$P'(C) \leq P'(A)$$

and

$$P'(C) \leq P'(B)$$

no matter what the judgments for events A and B happen to be. There are
also indications that we sometimes arrive at likelihood judgments for compound events from elementary event judgments via rules that are fundamentally different from those contained in probability theory.

Averaging

Imagine yourself in the following situation: After first thinking that a
certain business proposition had a 50–50 chance of succeeding, you look
closer and conclude that there is a 65% chance the venture will "fly."
Nevertheless, you hire two independent consultants to give you *their* opinions. The consultants are equally and highly regarded. After making an
investigation of the proposition, Consultant 1 concludes that there is a
probability of 75% that the business would succeed. After *his* study, Consultant 2 arrives at a more pessimistic position. He is only 25% sure that the
venture would be profitable. Would your consultants' statements affect
your opinion? Should they?

The reasoning implicit in one interpretation of Bayes's Theorem says
that your consultants' judgments ought to have no influence on your belief
that the proposed business project has a 65% chance of success. In effect,
according to probability theory, their judgments ought to "cancel each other
out." However, if you made judgments according to an **averaging procedure**, your opinion indeed would be affected by the consultants' impressions. In particular, your initial, favorable assessment of the chances of the
business succeeding would become more lukewarm. For instance, suppose
that you equally weight your initial opinion and those of your consultants.
Then the average of all three success probabilities would be

$$\frac{65\% + 75\% + 25\%}{3} = 55\%$$

which is less than your original probability judgment of 65% that the venture
would do well.

Do people in fact sometimes reliably make judgments via averaging?
Several experiments have indicated that they do, under a variety of circumstances. For instance, Troutman and Shanteau (1977) found evidence of

(weighted) averaging in an experiment that, conceptually, at least, was essentially similar to your consulting situation. Carlson and Yates (in press) found that averaging provides a good account for the disjunction errors discussed in Chapter 5 (pp. 126–27). Recall that, for instance, subjects considered the marginal events A = "U.S. auto companies will raise their average car prices by at least \$25" and B = "The Detroit Tigers will end the season with a better record than the Cleveland Indians." A distinct majority of subjects considered the disjunctive event (A or B) to be less likely than either event A, event B, or both. This is just what we would expect if the judgment $P'(A \text{ or } B)$ is an average of the judgments $P'(A)$ and $P'(B)$.

Why do people make judgments according to averaging? The rationale for this behavior is unclear and is thus the subject of current study. One hypothesis is that, in the case of disjunction errors, the basis lies in the connotations of the connective "or." In everyday language, the word **or** suggests compromise, for example, "I would be willing to accept either Apartment 1 or Apartment 5." Thus, when asked to evaluate the likelihood of "event A *or* event B," perhaps the terminology disposes us to make a compromise between the judged chances of events A and B separately. Another hypothesis is that people follow conventional wisdom, which says that, when confronted with conflicting evidence about any issue, the safest course is the middle road. This is plausibly what occurs in situations such as when you have three different opinions about whether your business proposition will succeed.

Signed summation

Yates and Carlson (1986) asked subjects to consider several events. Among them were "Congress will raise taxes in this election year" and "Bo Derek will not be nominated for an Academy Award for her performance in her latest film." Subjects were asked to rank order events in judged likelihood and to write down the underlying reasoning for their rankings. Following is an excerpt from one individual's protocol:

> These two separate events (Congress [raising] taxes, & no Bo nomination) are almost guaranteed locks I believe. Putting them both in the same statement then *must* be rated w/ the highest prob.

This passage illustrates the spirit as well as a possible rationale for a non-probability theory formal procedure for judging the likelihood of a conjunction, **signed summation**. The more complete judgment routine of which signed summation is a part is embodied in the **signed sum model**, described as follows (Yates and Carlson, 1986).

There are three key features of the signed sum model. The first is that it concerns qualitative or relative likelihood judgments, that is, judgments that one event is simply more, less, or equally likely as some other event. It is not about "quantitative" judgments, opinions about *how* likely an event is in absolute terms. Let us say that the model applies to yourself. The model says that you make judgments *as if* according to a scale in your head called a *qualitative likelihood scale,* as depicted in Figure 6.1. Every event you might consider has a value along that scale, called its *qualitative likelihood index,* denoted by the Greek letter λ. The higher the value of λ, the more likely you consider the corresponding event to be. In effect, when you are required to compare the chances of two events occurring, you do this by "looking up" their qualitative likelihood indexes on the scale. The event with the higher λ is the one considered more likely to occur. Thus, suppose you are asked to judge the relative chances of Candidates Grey and Brown being elected to the city council. As indicated in Figure 6.1, λ(Grey) = 3 and λ(Brown) = –3. Thus, you would say that Grey has the better chance of winning.

The second key feature of the signed sum model is the claim that people make a sharp distinction between likely and unlikely events. A *likely* event is one that is thought to have a greater chance of occurring than not occurring. For instance, suppose you are asked whether Candidate Green has a better chance of being elected or defeated, and that you say, "Elected." Then this means that you consider Green's election to be a likely event. If you had made the opposite response, then the event "Green is elected" would be an unlikely event, from your point of view. If you think Green's election and defeat are equally likely, we say that "Green is elected" is a *neutral* event. Likely and unlikely events are represented by positive and negative qualita-

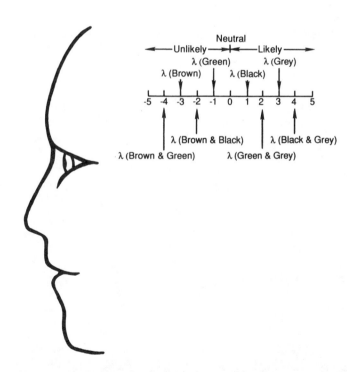

FIGURE 6.1. A qualitative likelihood scale showing the qualitative likelihood indexes for the chances of various candidates being elected to the city council.

tive likelihood indexes, respectively. Neutral events have λ's of 0. Thus, Figure 6.1 indicates that you in fact consider Green's election unlikely, although not as remote a possibility as Brown's election. On the other hand, you think that the elections of Grey and Black are likely occurrences.

The third feature of the signed sum model is an assertion about how the likelihoods of conjunctions are determined. Specifically, the *signed sum rule* of the model says that the qualitative likelihood index of a conjunction of two events is simply the sum of the indexes for the events themselves. Thus, the qualitative likelihood index for the election of both Candidates Brown and Black to the city council (several seats are available) would be, as shown in Figure 6.1,

$$\lambda(\text{Brown \& Black}) = \lambda(\text{Brown}) + \lambda(\text{Black})$$
$$= -3 + 1$$
$$= -2$$

Now suppose you are asked, "Which is more likely to happen, that Brown and Black will be elected, or that Green will be elected?" Recall that $\lambda(\text{Green}) = -1$. Thus, since

$$\lambda(\text{Green}) > \lambda(\text{Brown \& Black})$$

you respond, "Green should win."

What does the signed sum model have to say about conjunction errors? It should be easy for you to convince yourself (perhaps aided by the examples implicit in Figure 6.1), that the model predicts the following for marginal events A and B:

Case 1: A and B both likely:

$$(A \,\&\, B) >_L A$$

and

$$(A \,\&\, B) >_L B$$

that is, double conjunction errors. Example: (Black & Grey) versus Grey.

Case 2: A likely and B unlikely:

$$A >_L (A \,\&\, B) >_L B$$

that is, a single conjunction error. (The opposite should occur if A is unlikely and B likely.) Example: (Brown & Black) versus Brown and (Brown & Black) versus Black.

Case 3: A and B both unlikely:

$$A >_L (A \,\&\, B)$$

and

$$B >_L (A \,\&\, B)$$

that is, no conjunction errors. Example: (Brown & Green) versus Brown and (Brown & Green) versus Green.

To test the signed sum model, Yates and Carlson (1986) constructed special ensembles of marginal event pairs. Table 6.1 shows one such ensemble. In the likely–likely (LL) pair, both event A and event B were expected to be seen by most people as highly likely at the time. In the likely–unlikely (LU) pair, event A was expected to be viewed as likely, event B as unlikely. In the unlikely–unlikely (UU) pair, it was anticipated that both events would be considered unlikely.

As Figure 6.2 indicates, subjects' judgments were consistent with the predictions of the signed sum model. Note that double conjunction errors were common only when both marginal events were likely. Single conjunction errors predominated when one marginal event was likely, the other unlikely. And, finally, errorless judgment was most frequent when both marginal events were unlikely.

What might induce a person to make judgments according to signed summation? Once again, the reason this judgment strategy is used is unclear and is under study presently. However, as in the case of averaging, linguistic connotation might be implicated, as suggested in the protocol concerning the Congress–Bo Derek problem (p. 154). The connective "and" suggests the amplification of a property that two similar things have in common. Thus, if event A is likely, as is event B, then the event (A and B) must be *really* likely.

PROPORTION ESTIMATES AS PROBABILITY JUDGMENTS

Imagine yourself starting an insurance company from scratch. You have little formal knowledge about actuarial procedures and the like, just normal good sense and some capital. "John Strong" inquires about a life insurance

TABLE 6.1 An Ensemble of Events Used by Yates and Carlson (1986) to Test the Signed Sum Model

EVENT PAIR TYPE		EVENT
Likely—Likely (LL)	A:	The University of Michigan will win at least 4 of its 11 games during the 1984 football season.
	B:	Syria and Israel will not sign a peace treaty with each other this year.
Likely—Unlikely (LU)	A:	The University of Michigan will win at least 4 of its 11 games during the 1984 football season.
	B:	Syria and Israel will sign a peace treaty with each other this year.
Unlikely—Unlikely (UU)	A:	The University of Michigan will win fewer than 4 of its 11 games during the 1984 football season.
	B:	Syria and Israel will sign a peace treaty with each other this year.

Source: Yates and Carlson (1986), Table 3, with permission from Academic Press and the authors.

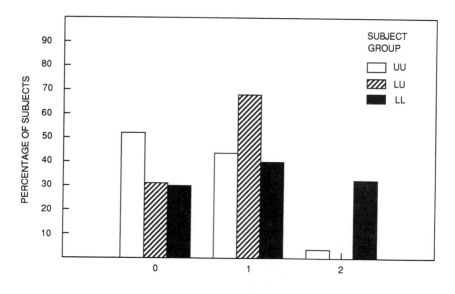

FIGURE 6.2. Percentages of subjects committing either zero, one, or two conjunction errors on various versions of the judgment problem described in Table 6.1. UU indicates that both marginal events were unlikely; LU indicates that one marginal event was likely, the other unlikely; and LL indicates that both marginal events were likely. Adapted from Yates and Carlson (1986), Figure 2b, with permission from Academic Press.

policy. To set a sensible premium rate for Mr. Strong's policy, there is one important judgment you need to make: How long is Mr. Strong likely to live? If you charge only a small amount for his coverage and he dies within a year or so, you will lose a pile of money. On the other hand, if you charge plenty (but for some strange reason Mr. Strong still buys your policy) and he lives until he is 70 years old, you will make a tidy sum. As an insurance provider, you will have to set premiums for a lot of "Mr. Strongs." The more accurately you are able to anticipate how long those individuals will live, the more successful your business will be.

One approach to your judgment task would be to use proportion estimates as your probability judgments. Concretely, suppose you estimate that, in the past, 40% of the population has lived to at least 70 years. Then for Mr. Strong, you judge

$$P' \text{ (Mr. Strong lives to 70)} = Prop' \text{ (Previous person lived to 70)}$$
$$= 0.40$$

Using judgments such as this, you then determine the premiums you must charge to assure the expectation that you will make money.

The way you have operated your "scratch" insurance business is primitive and contrived. Real insurance companies are much more sophisticated. Nevertheless, they normally set life insurance premiums using the same basic ideas you did. Implicitly, they judge the probability that a given customer will live to a certain age by means of actuarial tables. These tables indicate the proportions of relevant populations who actually have lived to various ages.

In effect, the strategy of using proportion estimates as probability judgments is this: The person considers a specific event A. He or she then thinks of past situations that are essentially similar to the current one. The proportion of times events like event A occurred in those situations is estimated, $Prop'(A)$. That proportion is taken as $P'(A)$. Mr. Strong's life and death only happen once. However, the lives and deaths of everyone else in the population are considered by your insurance company and others to be essentially similar to Mr. Strong's. In your insurance business, your proportion estimates were based on your own recollections. In contemporary real-life insurance companies, such proportion estimates are much more accurate, being based on official death records.

Probability judgments as proportions can be found in many settings. For instance, when patients ask about the chances of their treatments succeeding, their physicians often quote past success rates. Another example is from baseball. Take the case of "Plug Jones," a so-called "percentage" manager, pulling "Billy Basher" from the lineup because the opposition switches from a right-handed to a left-handed pitcher. He does this because he knows that, in the past, for Basher,

$Prop$(Hit | Left-handed pitcher) < $Prop$ (Hit | Right-handed pitcher)

and thus in the present situation, he feels that

P'(Hit | Left-handed pitcher) < P'(Hit | Right-handed pitcher)

In many judgment situations, unlike baseball managers, we do not have access to good records. So we must generate proportion estimates from our own memories or by some other psychological means. How good are those estimates? In laboratory situations, the subject's attention is pointedly directed to the events of interest. In such special environments, people are remarkably accurate at estimating event proportions (for example, Neimark and Shuford, 1959). We are not nearly as good at estimating proportions in naturalistic situations. Although we make sizable estimation errors in natural settings, our mistakes are not haphazard. Results reported by Christensen-Szalanski and others (1983) are illustrative. Both physicians and regular college students were asked to estimate the mortality rates for various diseases in the U.S. population. The mortality rate for a given disease is the number of deaths that occur each year due to that disease, per 100,000 people, that is, a proportion. Figure 6.3 displays the findings for the ten diseases with the highest mortality rates among those considered. If the subjects' estimates were perfectly accurate, the points representing corresponding estimated and actual mortality rates would lie along the 1:1 diagonal line shown in each panel. There are two distinctive features of the judgments that you should note; similar patterns have been observed in other contexts (for example, Lichtenstein and others, 1978).

160   *Formal Procedures*

(a) <u>Physicians</u>

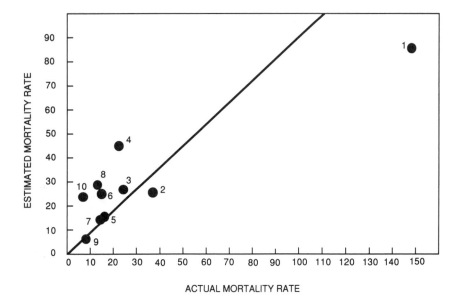

FIGURE 6.3. Estimated mortality rates as a function of actual mortality rates: (a) physician subjects, (b) student subjects. Disease code: 1 - myocardial infarction (heart attack), 2 - lung cancer, 3 - pneumonia, 4 - cerebral embolism and thrombosis, 5 - diabetes, 6 - breast cancer, 7 - cirrhosis of the liver, 8 - arteriosclerosis, 9 - pancreatic cancer, 10 - emphysema. Based on results reported by Christensen-Szalanski and others (1983), Table 1. Copyright 1983 by the American Psychological Association. Adapted by permission from the publisher and authors.

The first thing that stands out is that the subjects' estimates generally increased with actual mortality rates, as they should have. On the other hand, there were marked differences in the absolute values of the estimated and actual rates. Although it is not evident for the ten diseases represented in Figure 6.3a, on average, the physicians slightly overestimated the mortality rates for the various diseases they considered. As shown in Figure 6.3b, the students' estimated mortality rates were obviously and dramatically *much* too high. The vertical and horizontal axes of Figure 6.3b had to be scaled differently simply to get all the points in the figure. The United States would be a terrifying place to live in if the actual mortality rates were the same as the students' estimates.

How do people arrive at proportion estimates? A leading hypothesis says that such estimates rely on our memories of observing repeated prior occurrences of the relevant events (Howell, 1973; Jonides and Naveh-Benjamin, 1987). One of several versions of this hypothesis is that there is a special frequency counter in memory that registers each occurrence of an event, for example, every time we hear of someone dying from cancer. Other versions say that frequency encoding is more indirect. For instance, one suggestion

(b) Students

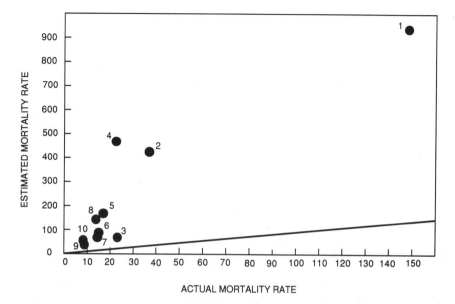

ACTUAL MORTALITY RATE

FIGURE 6.3 (continued)

is that each event repetition modifies, for example, strengthens or elaborates, the memory trace for the event. Thus, the frequency with which we have heard of cancer deaths can be inferred, even if imperfectly, from the character of the memory trace for such deaths.

It seems that frequency and proportion estimation ought to be equivalent to each other. For instance, suppose Chuck estimates that he has seen more Chevrolets than Ford cars, that is,

$$Freq'(\text{Chevrolet}) > Freq'(\text{Ford})$$

where *Freq'* denotes a frequency estimate. Then we might expect that, if he is asked to estimate the proportion of cars he has seen that were Chevrolets and also the proportion that were Fords, he will indicate

$$Prop'(\text{Chevrolet}) > Prop'(\text{Ford})$$

However, Estes (1976) and Arkes and Rothbart (1985) have found evidence that things might not be so simple. That is, Chuck might report proportion estimates that have the opposite order. How might this happen? One possibility is the following.

When Chuck was asked to say whether he has seen more Chevrolets or Fords, he certainly could not literally recall how many cars of each type he has encountered; there were far too many. As has been suggested, he might have inferred the comparative frequencies from the strengths (*Str*) of the respective memory traces, for example,

$$Str(\text{Chevrolet}) = 3 > Str(\text{Ford}) = 2$$

for the sake of concreteness. When he was later asked to estimate the proportions of Chevrolets and Fords he has seen, perhaps he "derived" his estimates from memory trace strengths in a manner crudely represented like so:

$$Prop'(\text{Chevrolet}) = \frac{Str(\text{Chevrolet})}{Str(\text{Chevrolet}) + Str(\text{Non–Chevrolet})}$$

Suppose that $Str(\text{Non-Chevrolet}) = 12$ and $Str(\text{Non-Ford}) = 7$. These strengths would imply that

$$Prop'(\text{Chevrolet}) = 3/15 = 0.20 < Prop'(\text{Ford}) = 2/9 = 0.22$$

And there is nothing in the human memory system to prevent such an occurrence.

Reliance on memory for previous observations cannot be the whole story behind proportion estimation. Take the study by Christensen-Szalanski and others (1983) on estimated mortality rates. It would not be surprising if many of the student subjects in that study never knew of *any* individual person dying from some of the causes of death cited, for instance, pancreatic cancer. So other mechanisms must be involved. For example, perhaps because of extensive news or medical literature coverage, some diseases rather than others are more easily brought to mind and hence are thought to be more pervasive (see also Lichtenstein and others, 1978). Maybe simply being asked about the mortality rate for one specific disease encourages us to think about *deaths* from that disease, but not *non*-deaths from that cause. This would be consistent with the tendency observed by Christensen-Szalanski and others for individuals to overestimate mortality rates generally.

CONDITIONAL PROPORTION ESTIMATES AS PROBABILITY JUDGMENTS

Let us return to your insurance company. You estimated that, in the past, 40% of the general population lived to age 70. Let us assume that your estimate is accurate. In addition, however, suppose that there is a regional difference in longevity. Specifically, 50% of the people in the eastern part of your service area live to 70, while only 30% of those in the western part do. Nevertheless, you still consider each of your potential clients to have a 40% chance of living to age 70, no matter where he or she resides. "Mona Perez" lives in the east, John Strong in the west. Regardless, you set premiums as if

$$P'(\text{Ms. Perez lives to 70}) = P'(\text{Mr. Strong lives to 70}) = 0.40$$

Assuming that survival patterns remain the same, you will eventually observe the following: Overall, your probability judgments will be unbiased; all your judgments—and hence their average—will be 40%, the same as the proportion of your clients who live to 70 years of age. Considered separately, however, your judgments for eastern clients' survival to age 70 will be negatively biased by about 10%. That is, although the survival probability judgment assigned to every easterner is 40%, the actual proportion of easterners living to 70 years will be around 50%. On the other hand, by the same reasoning, your probability judgments for the survival of western clients should be *positively* biased by approximately 10%.

Suppose you choose to make different judgments for your eastern and western clients. In particular, suppose that for any easterner, such as Ms. Perez, you judge

P'(Ms. Perez lives to 70) = *Prop'* (Previous eastern person lived to 70)
= 0.50

Similarly, for every westerner, like Mr. Strong, you indicate

P' (Mr. Strong lives to 70) = *Prop'* (Previous western person lived to 70)
= 0.30

Then your probability judgments for your eastern and western clienteles essentially will be unbiased; your judgments will be more accurate.

Terminology and rationale

In standard parlance, we would say that survival and residence in the present example are **associated, correlated,** or **contingent** variables. It might also be said that residence is *diagnostic* for survival. More generally, event B (and necessarily its complement) is diagnostic for event A if those events are dependent, that is, not independent. In terms of proportions, event B is **diagnostic** for event A if

$$Prop\ (A \mid B) \neq Prop\ (A \mid B^c) \tag{6.1}$$

as in the present case

Prop'(Lived to 70 | Eastern residence) ≠ *Prop'* (Lived to 70 | Western residence)

We can speak of *degrees* of diagnosticity (or association, correlation, contingency), too. The difference in the relevant conditional proportions, the **diagnosticity statistic,** measures the degree of diagnosticity:

$$\Delta = Prop(A \mid B) - Prop(A \mid B^c) \tag{6.2}$$

The larger the difference, in absolute terms, the greater is the diagnosticity. In the present example,

Δ = *Prop'*(Lived to 70 | Eastern residence) − *Prop'*(Lived to 70 | Western residence)
= 0.50 − 0.30
= 0.20

Suppose that all the easterners live beyond 70 years, while all westerners die before they get that old. Then the contingency between residence and survival would be perfect, yielding

$\Delta = Prop'$(Lived to 70 | Eastern residence)$- Prop'$(Lived to 70 | Western residence)
$= 1.00 - 0.00$
$= 1.00$

As the example of your insurance company suggests, the existence of a contingency between the event of interest and other events is fortuitous. It means that estimates of conditional proportions would be more accurate probability judgments than simple unconditioned proportion estimates. Two questions are suggested by this insight. The first is, "Do we in fact ever adopt estimates of conditional proportions as our likelihood judgments?" The answer to this question is unequivocally "Yes." The example of percentage baseball managers is again illustrative. Other examples are equally easy to bring to mind.

The second question suggested by the previous insight is, "How good are we at recognizing when some events indeed are diagnostic of others?" If we fail to acknowledge real contingencies, then we miss the opportunity to improve our judgments. On the other hand, if we perceive contingencies where none exist, then our judgments will be worse than they would have been had we simply ignored those imagined contingencies. Let us review what is known about the issue.

Contingency detection with explicitly presented data

Suppose we are directly confronted with data sufficient to establish that a contingency between two events does or does not exist. How likely are we to draw the correct conclusion? A classic study by Smedslund (1963) suggests that our chances of making an error are surprisingly high.

Student nurses were told they were participating in an experiment on the ability "to form an opinion about the practical usefulness of a symptom in diagnosis" (p. 166). Every subject was presented with a deck of 100 cards. Each card represented an excerpt from a patient's file. The card indicated whether symptom A was present or absent, and whether illness F was or was not found in that patient. The subject was told (p. 166):

> Your task is to look through the pack of cards once, and form an impression of the extent to which A is a useful symptom in the diagnosis of F. In other words, do you think A is a symptom one should pay attention to in trying to determine whether or not the patient is likely to be diagnosed as F?

The distribution of symptom–diagnosis combinations in one of the decks was as follows: $(A \,\&\, F) - 25$, $(A \,\&\, F^c) - 25$, $(A^c \,\&\, F) - 25$, and $(A^c \,\&\, F^c) - 25$. Thus,

$Prop$(Diagnosis F | Symptom A) $= Prop$(Diagnosis F | Symptom A^c)
$= 25/50$
$= 0.50$

That is, there was no contingency at all between symptoms and diagnoses. Nevertheless, only one subject out of 19 said that symptom A and diagnosis F were unrelated.

In another procedure, subjects were shown summaries of 100 cases in which the presence and absence of symptom A and diagnosis F were recorded. Table 6.2 shows three of the distributions the subjects examined. The subjects were instructed to "decide whether A and F are related (correlated)" (p. 167). Table 6.2 also shows the numbers of subjects who felt that symptom A and diagnosis F were and were not related in the respective distributions, as well as the diagnosticity statistics for those distributions. Observe, for instance, that in Distribution 1,

$$Prop(\text{Diagnosis } F \mid \text{Symptom } A) = 50/50 = 1.00$$

and also that

$$Prop(\text{Diagnosis } F \mid \text{Symptom } A^c) = 50/50 = 1.00$$

yielding

$$\Delta = 0$$

which implies that symptom A was completely nondiagnostic for disease F. Nevertheless, 31 of the 35 nursing students felt that the symptom and diagnosis in fact were related. In Distribution 2, there was a perfect symptom–disease contingency, but only 4 of the subjects concluded that A and F were correlated. The actual relationship was perfect in Distribution 3, too, although opposite in direction. In this instance, almost all the subjects acknowledged the relationship. Puzzling?

Other investigators have found results similar to Smedslund's. However, a number of factors have been shown to affect contingency perceptions. One is how the pertinent evidence is presented. In real life, information

TABLE 6.2 Summaries of Symptom A versus Disease F Distributions Shown to Nursing Student Subjects by Smedslund (1963)

DISTRIBUTION	SYMPTOM–DISEASE COMBINATION FREQUENCY			
	$A \& F$	$A \& F^c$	$A^c \& F$	$A^c \& F^c$
1 $\Delta = 50/50 - 50/50 = 1 - 1 = 0$ Perceived relationship?: Yes, 31; No, 4	50	0	50	0
2 $\Delta = 0/50 - 50/50 = 0 - 1 = -1$ Perceived relationship?: Yes, 4; No, 31	0	50	50	0
3 $\Delta = 50/50 - 0/50 = 1 - 0 = 1$ Perceived Relationship?: Yes, 34; No, 1	50	0	0	50

Source: Smedslund (1963), Table 3, with permission from Almqvist & Wiksell Periodical Company.

typically comes along one case at a time and in the midst of various distractions. For instance, a nurse might see only a handful of suspected pneumonia cases over the course of an entire year, during which she sees hundreds of patients suffering from a multitude of other maladies. As you might imagine, people have a harder time judging whether two events are related to each other when cases are presented sequentially rather than in summary form (Shaklee and Mims, 1982; Ward and Jenkins, 1965).

Part of the reason people make errors in evaluating whether or not events are dependent is that they sometimes rely on only part of the information needed to make such a determination. Consider Table 6.3. It shows the symptom–diagnosis distributions from the Smedslund (1963) study, but now organized into **contingency tables**. By tradition, the cells of such tables are labeled A to D, as shown. The frequencies in contingency tables are often denoted by corresponding lowercase letters *a* to *d*. The "proper" way to tell if there is a contingency is to compare the conditional proportions. In the present case, for example, we would compare

$$Prop(\text{Diagnosis } F \mid \text{Symptom } A) = \frac{a}{a + c}$$

to

$$Prop(\text{Diagnosis } F \mid \text{Symptom } A^c) = \frac{b}{b + d}$$

Smedslund (1963) proposed that, instead, people tend to judge contingencies by how often the two focal events co-occur, that is, on the basis of frequency *a*. As Table 6.3 indicates, Smedslund's results are certainly consistent with the conclusion that subjects employed the hypothesized **Cell A strategy**.

Subsequent to Smedslund's pioneering work, more strenuous tests have shown that people do not always judge contingency by the above Cell A strategy. Other approaches, including the proper one, are sometimes employed. Shaklee and Tucker's (1980) subjects, for instance, often went about the task by comparing $(a + d)$ to $(b + c)$, employing the technique known as the **sum-of-diagonals method**. In the Smedslund medical diagnosis problem, note that $(a + d)$ is the number of cases compatible with symptom A being associated with diagnosis F and symptom A^c with diagnosis F^c; $(b + c)$ is the number of cases conflicting with those associations. There is evidence, however, that the Cell A method of contingency judgment is especially likely to be used when observations are presented one case at a time (Arkes and Harkness, 1983; Shaklee and Mims, 1982). Conversely, under those conditions people are less prone to judge contingency according to the correct method. Typically, these effects are explained in terms of the relative ease with which the Cell A technique can be applied. After all, the Cell A approach requires keeping track of the cases that go into only one of the four cells of the contingency table.

There is also evidence that, although contingency judgment is often flawed, it is not universally as poor as Smedslund's results imply. Consider this: In order for a person to employ the Cell A strategy, how does he or she know what Cell A is? Somehow, two of the events must be designated as

TABLE 6.3 Smedslund's (1963) Symptom *A* versus Disease *F* Distributions Displayed in Contingency Table Form

Distribution 1

SYMPTOM

DIAGNOSIS	A	A^c
F	Cell A $a = 50$	Cell B $b = 50$
F^c	Cell C $c = 0$	Cell D $d = 0$

$\Delta = {}^{50}\!/_{50} - {}^{50}\!/_{50} = 1 - 1 = 0.$
Perceived relationship?: Yes, 31; No, 4

Distribution 2

SYMPTOM

DIAGNOSIS	A	A^c
F	Cell A $a = 0$	Cell B $b = 50$
F^c	Cell C $c = 50$	Cell D $d = 0$

$\Delta = {}^{0}\!/_{50} - {}^{50}\!/_{50} = 0 - 1 = -1.$
Perceived relationship?: Yes, 4; No, 31

Distribution 3

SYMPTOM

DIAGNOSIS	A	A^c
F	Cell A $a = 50$	Cell B $b = 0$
F^c	Cell C $c = 0$	Cell D $d = 50$

$\Delta = {}^{50}\!/_{50} - {}^{0}\!/_{50} = 1 - 0 = 1.$
Perceived relationship?: Yes, 34; No, 1

Source: Smedslund (1963), Table 3, with permission from Almqvist & Wiksell Periodical Company.

focal or target events so that the person can concentrate on their co-occurrence. In Smedslund's (1963) study, this was enhanced by various aspects of the procedure, including telling the subjects, "You are to concentrate entirely on symptom A and diagnosis F" (p. 166). More generally, such focusing of attention on two of the events can be heightened by how the relevant variables are represented. Take the variable "Pigmentation." It could be described *asymmetrically* as either "Present" or "Absent." Or it could be characterized *symmetrically* as either "Dark" or "Light." In a symmetric description, each level of the variable is of equal status. But in an asymmetric description, one level is implied to be of greater status. Beyth-Marom's (1982) analysis suggests that the Cell A strategy is less likely to be employed when variables are characterized symmetrically rather than asymmetrically, as they were by Smedslund.

There are several other indications that people are better able to recognize contingencies than their responses would lead us to believe. For example, when subjects are explicitly asked to compare the relative chances of event *A*, given event *B*, to those of event *A*, given event B^c, their implied acknowledgement of contingencies is better than when they are asked about contingencies in other ways (Beyth-Marom, 1982; Shaklee and Tucker, 1980). Another way that contingency recognition can be inferred is from a person's decisions. Seggie and Endersby (1972) asked subjects to make hospitalization decisions about hypothetical patients on the basis of past records of the possible contingency between hospitalization and recovery. If, for instance, the records indicated that relatively more patients recovered when they were not hospitalized, subjects should have recommended treatments other than hospitalization. The contingencies represented in the various collections of records presented to subjects were identical to ones used by Smedslund (1963). In contrast to Smedslund's subjects' inaccurate verbally expressed contingency perceptions, the decisions of Seggie and Endersby's subjects were just what they should have been.

It appears that some of the difficulties associated with contingency detection are due to semantics. Beyth-Marom (1982) has found that people's everyday notions of whether categorical variables are related rarely agree with the accepted statistical conception, which rests on a difference in conditional proportions. Instead, people seem especially inclined to *say* that two variables are related when they satisfy other criteria. Results such as these suggest that perhaps as serious a problem as *recognizing* contingencies is the problem of *communicating* contingency perceptions. Even if, as in the Seggie and Endersby (1972) study, people really do know the extent to which two factors are related to each other, unless they are asked in a certain way, we might never discover that fact.

Primacy effects in contingency detection

Yates and Curley (1986) asked subjects to consider a fictitious plant called the "Rhododipsia." Rhododipsia were described as being of two types, distinguished by their color, light versus dark. Rhododipsia also were reported to be found in two regions, A and B. The task of the subjects was to judge whether there was a relationship between Rhododipsia color and region and the nature of that relationship if it existed. To do this, subjects were asked to view successive slides depicting randomly selected Rhododipsia plants from the two regions.

Altogether, there were 28 plants. Table 6.4a shows the colors and regions of origin of those plants. Thus, it is apparent that Rhododipsia color and region were completely independent of each other. The actual slide

TABLE 6.4 Distributions of Rhododipsia by Color and Region in Yates and Curley's (1986) Contingency Judgment Study

(a) Overall

	REGION	
COLOR	A	B
Light	7	7
Dark	7	7

(b) Block 1: Light–to–A Contingency

	REGION	
COLOR	A	B
Light	5	2
Dark	2	5

(c) Block 2: Light–to–B Contingency

	REGION	
COLOR	A	B
Light	2	5
Dark	5	2

Source: Yates and Curley (1986), Figure 1, with permission from Elsevier Science Publishers and the authors.

presentations of the plants were not completely random, however. The slides were divided into two blocks of 14 slides each. The color–region distribution of the slides in Block 1 is shown in Table 6.4b, that for Block 2 slides in Table 6.4c. Notice that, in Block 1, color and region were related such that light plants were more likely to be found in Region A and dark plants in Region B. That is, Block 1 exhibited a "Light–to–A" contingency. The opposite dependency existed in Block 2. Subjects in the "Light–to–A first" group saw the Block 1 slides first, then the Block 2 slides; subjects in the "Light–to–A second" group saw the slides in the reverse order. Within each block, the slides indeed were shown in random sequence. And, of course, the subject was not told that the slides were partitioned into blocks.

There was a secondary task, too. After he or she had seen all 28 slides, every subject was asked to recall the numbers of slides of each type that had been shown, for example, the number of slides of dark Rhododipsia from Region A. However, only some of the subjects, those in "Warning" conditions, were told in advance that eventually they would have to recall slide frequencies. The recall test came as a surprise for subjects in "No warning" conditions.

Each subject was asked (Yates and Curley, 1986, pp. 298-299): "Suppose a Rhododipsia plant is from Region A. What is the chance that it is Light in color rather than Dark?" The response to this question was taken as a probability judgment P' (Light I Region A). A parallel question yielded the judgment P' (Light I Region B). Figure 6.4 shows the means of the implied judged diagnosticity statistic

$$\Delta' = P' \text{ (Light I Region A)} - P' \text{ (Light I Region B)}$$

for various groups of subjects. Notice that subjects who received no warning that they would have to recall slide frequencies felt rather strongly that Rhododipsia region and color were related to each other. This misperception was significantly weaker for the forewarned subjects. Also observe that, when subjects were exposed first to the block of slides in which light-colored Rhododipsia tended to be found in Region A rather than in Region B, they thought that this was the form of the contingency throughout the slide sequence. Subjects who saw the opposite contingency in the first block of slides had the opposing perception.

The subjects exhibited what is known as a **primacy effect**; information presented early had a greater effect than information presented later. The difference in judgments made by individuals warned and not warned of the recall test suggests that the primacy effect is at least partly due to attentional factors. Since they did not think they would have to remember all the slides, the subjects who were not warned apparently paid attention to only the first

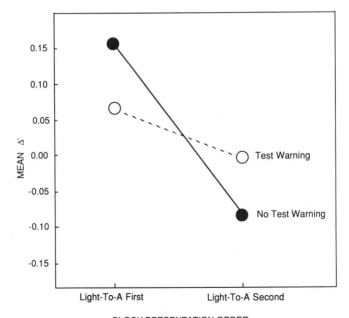

FIGURE 6.4. Mean inferred diagnosticity statistics $\Delta' = P'$(Light|Region A) $-P'$(Light|Region B), as functions of presentation order and warning of the impending frequency recall test. Adapted from Yates and Curley (1986), Figure 2, with permission from Elsevier Science Publishers and the authors.

several slides and ignored the rest. Thus, their contingency judgments were based on only a small part of the available information—that which had been presented early. Similar instances of what Anderson (1981) has called **attention decrement** during impression formation have been observed in many contexts. If the Yates and Curley results can be generalized, they imply that our judgments of whether or not two events are independent of each other will be unduly influenced by the first few cases we happen to observe. And those first few cases *can* be misleading.

Illusory correlations: "Don't bother me with the facts!"

The Draw-a-Person Test (DAP) is a projective instrument used for diagnosing psychological disorders. The patient draws a picture of a person. The clinician then examines the drawing for the presence or absence of various features. Certain characteristics are considered to be indicators that the patient possesses particular clinical symptoms. Chapman and Chapman (1967) wondered whether practicing clinicians and laypersons differ in how they perceive contingencies between DAP characteristics and clinical symptoms. Previous research had suggested that the contingencies clinicians reported do not really exist.

A group of experienced clinicians who used the DAP in their practices considered a list of patient symptoms, for example, "He is worried about how intelligent he is," "He is suspicious of other people," and "He is concerned with being fed and taken care of by other people." Each clinician was asked to indicate how such symptoms would be manifested in the DAP. For example, for male patients suspicious of other people, the clinician was asked to complete the following statement with two items: "The pictures drawn by such men would more often be characterized by ...." For this particular symptom, suspiciousness, 91% of the clinicians indicated that the pictures would contain atypical eyes, for example, large or elaborated.

Undergraduates unfamiliar with the DAP were then asked to examine a series of drawings, most of which actually were produced by psychotic patients. Each drawing was accompanied by statements of two symptoms the patient who drew the figure was alleged to possess. In reality, statements were assigned to drawings such that there was no association at all between symptoms and characteristics of the drawings. Thus, for instance, the statement, "The man who drew this is suspicious of other people," appeared equally often with drawings that did and did not have atypical eyes; that is, *Prop* (Suspicious I Atypical eyes) = *Prop* (Suspicious I Typical eyes). After the students had examined the pictures and statements, they were asked to perform essentially the same task as the clinicians. They indicated which symptoms they perceived to have been associated with which features in the drawings they had seen.

There was a remarkable similarity between the responses of the clinicians and the naive students. Table 6.5 lists several of the symptoms the subjects considered. It also shows the drawing characteristics mentioned first and second most often as being associated with the symptoms. Notice, for example, that "atypical eyes" was the clinicians' most commonly re-

TABLE 6.5   Patient Symptoms and First and Second Most Frequently Mentioned Associated Drawing Characteristics

SYMPTOM	FEATURES	
Worry over manliness	Clinicians:	(1) Broad shoulders, muscular, manly
		(2) Feminine, childlike
		(2) Hair distinctive
	Students:	(1) Broad shoulders, muscular, manly
		(2) Feminine, childlike
Suspiciousness	Clinicians:	(1) Eyes atypical
		(2) Ears atypical
	Students:	(1) Eyes atypical
		(2) Facial expression atypical
Worry over intelligence	Clinicians:	(1) Head enlarged or emphasized
		(2) Detailed drawing
	Students:	(1) Head enlarged or emphasized
		(2) Facial expression atypical
Concern with being fed and cared for	Clinicians:	(1) Mouth emphasis
		(2) Passive posture, outstretched arms
	Students:	(1) Feminine, childlike
		(2) Passive posture, outstretched arms

Source: Chapman and Chapman (1967), Table 1. Copyright 1967 by the American Psychological Association. Adapted with permission from the publisher and authors.

ported characteristic of drawings made by suspicious patients. The students "saw" the same thing. These perceptions occurred despite the fact that none of the drawing characteristics was actually related to any of the symptoms. That is, the subjects saw contingencies where none existed—**illusory correlations**. Chapman and Chapman found these illusory correlations to persist even when subjects were given extensive exposure over three days to paired drawings and symptoms in which no relationships existed.

In another experiment, Chapman and Chapman paired the drawings and symptom statements such that there *was* an association between symptoms and drawing characteristics. However, the associations were such that they contradicted the direction of the previously perceived relationships. For example, statements that the patient was suspicious appeared more often with drawings having *typical* eyes than with those containing *atypical* eyes. Subjects indeed were less prone to seeing the usual associations. Nevertheless, some degree of illusory correlation persisted. Subjects tended to see favored contingencies even in data that directly contradicted those contingencies.

Chapman and Chapman argued that illusory correlations often rest on cognitive associations; for example, the word "suspiciousness" tends to bring to mind the word "eyes." For these and other potentially valid reasons, people come to expect certain associations, too. The Chapmans's experiments have shown, for example, that laypersons would anticipate essentially the same connections between DAP characteristics and psychopathology symptoms as clinicians and experimental subjects report they actually perceive to occur. The Chapmans and others have demonstrated that the kinds of effects described are not limited to the Draw-a-Person Test. They occur with numerous other diagnostic procedures as well (see Shweder, 1977).

In various practical situations, the events of interest to us are frequently psychologically associated with one another, perhaps by nothing more than having been encountered in close proximity in the past. In addition, we often can convince ourselves why some events ought to depend on others. Thus, when we are required to evaluate whether those events are correlated, we do not start with a clean slate. Instead, we have expectations about what the contingencies might be. Results on illusory correlations suggest that these preconceptions will be surprisingly resistant to evidence contradicting them. In the extreme, this is prejudice (see Hamilton and Rose, 1980).

Illusory correlations plausibly could account for some of the known peculiarities of human judgment. They imply, for instance, that people can easily maintain beliefs in and make judgments on the basis of dependencies between events that are assumed to exist but actually do not. The effect would be to introduce "noise" into the person's opinions. That is, the person will tend to raise and lower his or her likelihood judgments in a way that has no bearing on the actual occurrence or nonoccurrence of the events in question. (See, for example, Chapter 4, pp. 84–85.) The mechanisms underlying illusory correlations might also contribute to the previously noted general difficulty people have recognizing contingencies. Alloy and Tabachnik (1984) examined a large number of contingency judgment studies. They concluded that, when people do not have prior expectations about possible dependencies, their contingency perceptions are rather accurate. It is when such expectations are strong that serious problems arise. (But also see Wright and Murphy, 1984.)

Limited and misinterpreted contingency information

One type of contingency has special significance, that between our *predictions* of what is going to occur and what actually *does* occur. The typical hiring situation provides a good example. An employer's ultimate interest is in how well an applicant might carry out his or her assigned duties. Often the evaluation of the applicant can be viewed as an attempt to predict what that eventual performance level would be if the applicant were hired. The situation can be conceptualized as shown in Table 6.6a, where, for simplicity, only two levels of performance are distinguished, "good" and "poor." The employer, call her "Amanda Ward," hopes that there is a strong contingency between predicted and actual job performance, specifically, that

Prop(Actual–Good | Predicted–Good) > *Prop*(Actual–Good | Predicted–Poor)

On the assumption that the desired contingency really does exist, Ms. Ward hires individuals who are predicted to do well; all others are rejected.

The present situation is representative of a general approach to making decisions: The decision maker predicts how things would turn out if a particular alternative were chosen. If a favorable outcome is anticipated, that

TABLE 6.6 Contingency Tables between Predicted and Actual Job Performance Levels

(a) The General Case

	PREDICTED PERFORMANCE	
ACTUAL PERFORMANCE	GOOD	POOR
Good	a	b
Poor	c	d

(b) An Expected or Hoped-for Distribution

	PREDICTED PERFORMANCE	
ACTUAL PERFORMANCE	GOOD	POOR
Good	70	20
Poor	30	80

(c) A Possible Real Distribution

	PREDICTED PERFORMANCE	
ACTUAL PERFORMANCE	GOOD	POOR
Good	70	70
Poor	30	30

alternative is selected; otherwise, not. (Makes eminent sense, does it not?) People seem to be extremely confident of their predictive abilities. Some investigators believe that we might be *overly* optimistic about the strength of the contingencies between our predictions and the events of interest. Einhorn and Hogarth (1978) suggest two reasons why such overoptimism or **illusions of validity** might persist.

Partial information access Einhorn and Hogarth's first observation is that people ordinarily have access to only half the information needed to verify (or contradict) the existence and strength of a contingency. Let us continue with the hiring situation, as characterized in Table 6.6a. To evaluate the contingency between predicted and actual performance, Amanda Ward would have to compare the conditional proportion

$$Prop \text{ (Actual–Good | Predicted–Good)} = \frac{a}{a+c}$$

to the proportion

$$Prop \text{ (Actual–Good | Predicted–Poor)} = \frac{b}{b+d}$$

Usually, however, employers will only have available frequencies a and c. That is because they will only hire applicants predicted to perform well.

Imagine that 200 people applied for jobs and that all were hired. Eventually, half of them perform well and half do not. The typical employer (Amanda Ward) will assume (hope?) that the complete contingency table casting predicted and actual performance against each other would resemble Table 6.6b. There we see that 70% of the employees Ms. Ward predicted to perform well in fact did so, whereas only 20% of those predicted to do poorly achieved that high level of performance. On the other hand, the situation might be more like that shown in Table 6.6c, where the chance of good performance was 70%, regardless of Ms. Ward's predictions. However, Ms. Ward will never know for sure whether Table 6.6b or 6.6c is more descriptive of her own company. Of course, Amanda Ward might say, "I don't mind if my predictions are worthless, as long as 70% of my employees are good ones. I can't afford to take the chance of hiring people I think will do poorly just to find how accurate my judgment really is." The wisdom of this stance depends on the risks and costs of potential "bad hires" compared to the risks and costs of maintaining a worthless applicant review system (see Klayman and Ha, 1987).

Treatment effects According to Einhorn and Hogarth (1978), treatment effects can be expected in many situations, too. A hypothetical example inspired by Einhorn and Hogarth's illustrates what this means. Imagine a fictitious government agency called the "Scientific Research Institute (SRI)," whose responsibility is to provide funding for scientific research. The SRI review board examines applicants' proposals and then makes predictions of their future research productivity. It recommends funding for those applicants who are expected to have high productivity, but not for those expected to do otherwise. During Year X, 200 applications were reviewed. As the bottom row of Table 6.7a shows, 100 of the applicants were predicted to have high research productivity, the remaining ones low productivity. Moreover, the former applicants' proposals were funded, those of the latter were not. SRI was interested in learning about the accuracy of the board's predictions. So it did a follow-up study of the actual productivity of the researchers who were predicted to do well and poorly. As Table 6.7a indicates, 60% of those predicted to have high productivity lived up to that expectation, whereas only 30% of those expected to do poorly achieved such high standards.

On the face of it, Table 6.7a perhaps suggests that the SRI review committee has good insight about research potential. But let us examine what happened in follow-ups of two other review cycles. During Year Y, there was a budget crisis, and so SRI was unable to fund the research of *any* of its applicants. Table 6.7b shows how well the researchers did. As indicated, only 30% of them achieved high productivity. During Year Z, the government had a surplus of funds that it wanted to devote to scientific research. So it asked SRI to fund all its applicants, regardless of the review board's predictions. As Table 6.7c shows, 60% of all the investigators had high productivity, whether they had been predicted to do so or not. Very clearly, in Years Y and Z, the SRI review board's predictions had no validity. Why the discrepancy, as compared to Year X?

TABLE 6.7 Contingency Tables between Predicted and Actual
Research Productivity Levels

(a) Year X: Funding to Those Predicted to be Productive

	PREDICTED PRODUCTIVITY	
ACTUAL PRODUCTIVITY	HIGH (FUNDED)	LOW (NOT FUNDED)
High	60	30
Low	40	70
Total	100	100

(b) Year Y: Funding to No Applicants

	PREDICTED PRODUCTIVITY	
ACTUAL PRODUCTIVITY	HIGH	LOW
High	30	30
Low	70	70
Total	100	100

(c) Year Z: Funding to All Applicants

	PREDICTED PRODUCTIVITY	
ACTUAL PRODUCTIVITY	HIGH	LOW
High	60	60
Low	40	40
Total	100	100

Actually, there *is* no discrepancy. Table 6.7a is not a true contingency table of predicted against actual research productivity. The problem is that there is a **confounding** between the board's predictions and SRI's funding decisions; applicants predicted to have high productivity are funded, whereas those not so predicted get no funding. As suggested by Tables 6.7b and 6.7c, the only thing that discriminates those who eventually do achieve high productivity from those who do not is whether they have SRI's financial assistance. So the real contingency implicit in Table 6.7a is between funding and actual productivity. Since the SRI board's predictions determine funding decisions, which in turn affect the outcome the board was trying to predict, we say that the predictions have a **treatment effect**.

The previous illustration obviously was contrived to emphasize a point; the validity of real research review boards undoubtedly is much better than nil. However, Einhorn and Hogarth (1978) suggest that similar situations are quite common. Thus, when people observe results analogous to Table 6.7a, they are inclined to misinterpret treatment effects as strong evidence of good judgment.

Positive testing and pseudodiagnosticity

The previous arguments suggest that often not all the information necessary to determine whether or not events are independent will be available. But suppose the individual has the opportunity to request any information. Would he or she seek out all the required facts? There is evidence suggesting otherwise.

Assume the role of one of the physicians who participated in the study by Wolf, Gruppen, and Billi (1985). As implied by Figure 6.5a, in trying to diagnose what is wrong with a certain patient, whom we can call "Virginia Whipple," you have narrowed the possibilities down to either Disease A or Disease B. You know that half the patients like Ms. Whipple suffer from

(a)

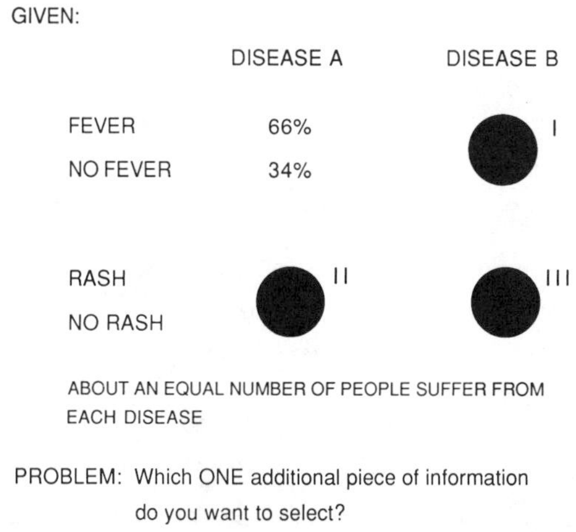

GIVEN:

	DISEASE A	DISEASE B
FEVER	66%	● I
NO FEVER	34%	

RASH	● II	● III
NO RASH		

ABOUT AN EQUAL NUMBER OF PEOPLE SUFFER FROM EACH DISEASE

PROBLEM: Which ONE additional piece of information do you want to select?

(b)

NUMBER OF CORRECT SELECTIONS (IN 3 PROBLEMS)	0	1	2	3
PERCENTAGE OF PHYSICIANS	14%	33%	29%	24%

FIGURE 6.5. (a) Hypothetical diagnostic situation for medical patient Virginia Whipple. (b) Percentages of physicians who correctly solved none, one, two, or all of three problems similar to the Virginia Whipple problem. Part (a) adapted from page 2860, *Journal of the American Medical Association*, Volume 253, 1985, by F. M. Wolf, L. D. Gruppen, and J. E. Billi. Copyright 1985, American Medical Association.

Disease A, the rest from Disease B. Ms. Whipple has two prominent medical signs, a fever and a rash. As indicated in the upper-left cell of the display in Figure 6.5a, you can recall that 66% of patients with Disease A have fever, while only 34% do not. Unfortunately, you cannot remember (but you know where to find) the items of information represented by the remaining three cells, which are blocked out by the disks and are labeled I, II, and III. Cell I indicates the percentages of Disease B sufferers with and without fever. Cells II and III indicate the percentages of Disease A and Disease B victims, respectively, who do and do not have rashes. Because this is a crisis situation, you have enough time to look up the information in only one of the cells. Which cell's information should you seek out in order to make a defensible diagnosis for Ms. Whipple?

Let us see how you would approach this problem from the perspective of probability theory. Since you know that Virginia Whipple has fever and rash, ideally your goal is to arrive at a reasonable judgment P'(Disease A I Fever & Rash). You might consider using Bayes's Theorem (pp. 134–36), as specialized to the present situation:

$$P' \text{ (Disease A I Fever \& Rash)}$$
$$= \frac{Prop(\text{Fever \& Rash I Disease A})Prop(\text{Disease A})}{Prop(\text{Fever \& Rash I Disease A})Prop(\text{Disease A}) + Prop(\text{Fever \& Rash I Disease B})Prop(\text{Disease B})}$$

You already know that the two diseases are equally common. That is, you know that the base rates for the diseases are

$$Prop(\text{Disease A}) = Prop(\text{Disease B}) = 0.50$$

So, to complete your solution, you need $Prop$(Fever & Rash I Disease A) and $Prop$(Fever & Rash I Disease B), the proportions of people with Diseases A and B who have both fever and rash. Unfortunately, the only information you have on hand is the percentage of people with Disease A who have fever, that is,

$$Prop(\text{Fever I Disease A}) = 0.66$$

You do not even have the potential to learn $Prop$(Fever & Rash I Disease A) and $Prop$(Fever & Rash I Disease B); you have no idea where to find such information.

As a good Bayesian diagnostician, you conclude that your next best course of action is to take advantage of the fever–Disease A information you can recall. So you again note the form Bayes's Theorem would take:

P' (Disease A I Fever)

$$= \frac{Prop(\text{Fever I Disease A})Prop(\text{Disease A})}{Prop(\text{Fever I Disease A})Prop(\text{Disease A}) + Prop(\text{Fever I Disease B})Prop(\text{Disease B})}$$

$$= \frac{(0.66)(0.50)}{(0.66)(0.50) + Prop(\text{Fever I Disease B})(0.50)}$$

inserting all the proportions you already know. Thus, it is clear that the information you should seek out is in Cell I in Figure 6.5a, *Prop*(Fever I Disease B), the proportion of patients with Disease B who have fever.

Of course, no real person, physician or otherwise, can be expected to apply Bayes's Theorem directly to cases like Virginia Whipple's. However, the basic principle implicit in the theorem agrees with everyone's intuitions. It says that you should seek information that would allow you to establish whether the signs possessed by Ms. Whipple are more, less, or equally common among Disease A as compared to Disease B sufferers. Since you know how often Disease A victims have fever, that is, 66% of the time, you should find out the corresponding incidence of fever among people with Disease B. If that percentage is less than 66%, then Ms. Whipple's fever should push you toward diagnosing Disease A. If the percentage is greater than 66%, for example, 90%, you should favor a Disease B diagnosis.

Each physician in the Wolf, Gruppen, and Billi (1985) study considered three problems like your Virginia Whipple case. Figure 6.5b presents the percentages of physicians who made various numbers of correct information requests, for example, for *Prop*(Fever I Disease B). Notice that fewer than a quarter of the physicians never made a mistake. An especially popular request was for the proportion of Disease A sufferers who had rash, Cell II in Figure 6.5a. Most people, when they see that Virginia Whipple has fever and that 66% of patients with Disease A have fever, hypothesize that Ms. Whipple has Disease A, too. Given that hypothesis, they expect that Cell II would reveal that a high percentage of Disease A victims have rash. Thus, the request for Cell II information represents an instance of **positive testing,** whereby a person seeks information that is expected to be consistent with one's current hypothesis (Klayman and Ha, 1987).

Positive testing is sometimes useful. In the Virginia Whipple case it is not, however. Suppose that you request Cell II information and discover that, say, 75% of Disease A victims have rashes. Would this affect how sure you are that you were correct to hypothesize that Ms. Whipple has Disease A? If you are like many people, you will become even more convinced that you were right. However, since you know nothing about the commonness of either fever or rash among Disease B victims, your newly acquired information about rash is statistically nondiagnostic; it does not differentiate the diseases. The fact that you responded to the information as if it were diagnostic is termed a **pseudodiagnosticity effect** (Beyth-Marom and Fischhoff, 1983; Doherty and others, 1979).

SUMMARY

Formal procedures for judging likelihood are similar to the tools a statistician uses. They rely, directly or indirectly, on principles the person believes to govern the relationships among the chances of various events.

The simplest of all judgment procedures is that in which the person does not directly make judgments at all. Instead, the opinions of a presumed expert are appropriated as one's own.

People sometimes make likelihood judgments in a fashion equivalent to applying the rules of probability theory. Some people possess personal rules for deriving desired likelihood judgments from other judgments they have already made or assumed. However, these personal rules, for example, averaging, differ in form from analogous rules contained in probability theory.

Individuals often take the probability of a future event to be the relative frequency or proportion of times essentially similar events have occurred in the past.   The accuracy of such likelihood judgments is improved significantly if the person is able to appropriately restrict the previous cases considered to be essentially similar to the current one. This can be done effectively if the person can recognize when certain aspects of a situation are associated with the occurrence of the event in question. However, this recognition ability seems to be limited or compromised by several aspects of the procedures by which contingencies are typically judged.   For instance, people often and erroneously base their contingency judgments on the frequency with which relevant events co-occur.

KEY TERMS

Associated	Illusion of validity
Attention decrement	Illusory correlation
Averaging	Positive testing
Cell A strategy	Primacy effect
Confounding	Pseudodiagnosticity effect
Contingency table	Signed sum model
Contingent	Signed summation
Correlated	Substantive procedure
Diagnostic	Sum-of-diagonals method
Diagnosticity statistic	Treatment effect
Formal procedure	

ADDITIONAL READING

Crocker (1981); Fong, Krantz, and Nisbett (1986); Nisbett, Zukier, and Lemley (1981); Pitz and others (1981); Wyer (1976).

EXERCISES AND STUDY QUESTIONS

1. Stacey considers the following events: "The winner of the next state gubernatorial (governor's) election will be a Democrat," "The winner of the next U.S. presidential election will be a Democrat," and "The winners of both the next state gubernatorial and the next U.S. presidential elections will be Democrats." Suppose Stacey were asked to rank order these events in terms of their likelihood of occurrence.

    (a) What would her ordering be if she made judgments according to averaging? Explain.

    (b) Describe her ordering if she judged according to signed summation. Again, give your rationale, making explicit what your assumptions are.

2. It is sometimes claimed that people tend to overestimate small proportions and underestimate high ones. Are the mortality rate estimates reported by the subjects of Christensen-Szalanski and others (1983) consistent or inconsistent with that hypothesis (pp. 159–60)? Explain.

3. In this chapter, we considered the case of your insurance company (pp. 162–63). Initially, you reported for everyone P'(Live to 70) = $Prop'$(Previous person lived to 70) = 0.40. Let us call that the *marginal proportion method*. Later, you made a distinction between people from the eastern and western parts of your service area. For every individual from the east, you reported P'(Live to 70|Eastern residence) = $Prop'$(Previous eastern person lived to 70) = 0.50 and P'(Live to 70|Western residence) = $Prop'$(Previous western person lived to 70) = 0.30. We can call this approach the *conditional proportion method*.

    (a) Suppose that your proportion estimates are essentially accurate; for example, $Prop'$(Previous person lived to 70) $\approx$ $Prop$(Previous person lived to 70), the actual proportion of people who have lived to at least age 70. Sketch how calibration graphs for your judgments would most likely appear for your alternative ways of making judgments.

    (b) According to which judgment method would you expect your mean probability score $\overline{PS}$ to be better? Justify your expectation.

4. Many patients, as well as their physicians, avoid making likelihood judgments according to proportion estimates based on past cases. Their reasoning is that their situations are so unique that it is inappropriate to consider them essentially similar to those of the previous patients. What would you expect to be the consequences of this practice? Explain.

5. Consider the standard layout for a contingency table, for example, Table 6.3. The proper way to judge whether events E and F are contingent is to compare the proportion $a/(a + c)$ to the proportion $b/(b + d)$. It has been found that people sometimes try to make this assessment according to the sum-of-diagonals method, comparing the frequency $(a + d)$ to the frequency $(b + c)$.

   (a) Construct a table in which the proper and the sum-of-diagonals strategies lead to different conclusions about whether the events are dependent on each other.

   (b) What is a real-world example of a situation in which you might expect to observe tables where the sum-of-diagonals strategy would result in erroneous contingency judgments?

6. Mercedes and Charles are elementary school teachers. Over the period of a year, each of them is exposed to evidence relevant to the question of whether Computer Math, that is, instruction via certain computer programs, is more effective than traditional or Old Math in developing pupils' calculation skills. The frequencies of various combinations of methods and high versus low calculation test scores were as follows: Computer & High, 10; Computer & Low, 40; Old & High, 40; Old & Low, 10. (You might want to construct a contingency table of these results.) After being shown this evidence, Mercedes concludes that there is only a weak contingency between method and test scores. Charles feels that the relationship is very strong.

   Some observers contend that perceptions of contingency are strongly affected by people's prior expectations. How might such expectations rationally account for the different conclusions of Mercedes and Charles, *even if at the beginning of the year both believe that there is no contingency between method and scores*? Do you see any connection between this issue and the illusory correlation phenomenon? Explain.

7. Keith learns that 80% of the students who are admitted to "Oak College" were on the honor roll in high school. Keith then concludes that being on the honor roll is predictive of admission to Oak. In effect, he infers that admission and honor roll membership are contingent variables.

   (a) Keith's conclusion is hasty. Explain why.

   (b) This example suggests another general strategy that people sometimes use for judging contingency. Characterize that strategy.

8. Describe a possible practical implication of primacy effects in contingency judgment.

9. Geneva is a petroleum engineer. She thinks there is a 50–50 chance that the area in which she is working contains significant amounts of oil. She observes a certain pattern of readings on her instruments; call it Pattern Q. Since she is unfamiliar with Pattern Q, she has to look it up in her reference books. There she finds that $P(\text{Pattern Q}|\text{Oil}) = 70\%$.

(a) Should Geneva's opinion change from her initial 50–50 belief that oil is present in the area? Explain.

(b) Would you *expect* Geneva's opinion to change? Again, justify your expectation.

Substantive Procedures

Most people reason dramatically, not quantitatively.

—Oliver Wendell Holmes, Jr.

At the start of the last chapter, we considered the case of "David and Marilyn Ross." One task facing the Rosses was to judge how likely it was that their builder would complete their new house on schedule. It is plausible that they would make such a judgment according to the formal procedures discussed in Chapter 6. For instance, they might check around with other people who have used their contractor in the past. Suppose they discover that the contractor completed 65% of those jobs on time. The Rosses will be tempted to consider the chance of *their* house being finished on schedule to be around 65%, too. On his job as an accountant, David Ross had to reach an opinion about the Internal Revenue Service disallowing the tax deductions the Pulaskis wished to claim. It is possible that Mr. Ross would arrive at these judgments using some other formal approaches. However, there are other ways such judgments might be made, too.

Formal judgment procedures resemble the methods statisticians use in their work. These techniques sometimes rely on records of past occurrences, assuming that the future will be much the same as the past. Or they involve applying rules that derive the likelihood of one event from the already-determined likelihoods of other events. When people use formal methods, they do not consider the natural mechanisms by which events are actually brought about. The present chapter addresses substantive approaches to likelihood judgment. These are procedures that *do* involve analyzing the details of how events literally happen.

Our study of substantive procedures starts with intuitive judgment processes known as heuristics. In the first section, we consider metacognitive heuristics. These strategies rely on the person's conceptions about the relationship between how people think about events and the real-world processes that actually give rise to those events. The second section examines more general heuristics that rest on a variety of intuitions about how we can fathom what will occur in the world. In the third section, we review procedures that involve reasoning about how nature determines what does and does not happen. This chapter and the previous one describe a long list of procedures people have been documented to use at one time or another. This poses a dilemma: How is it determined which of these procedures will be applied to any *specific* judgment task? The fourth section is devoted to this most important procedure assignment problem. The last major section brings attention to a theme that unifies the numerous effects discussed in this and previous chapters, including procedure assignment.

METACOGNITIVE HEURISTICS

For as long as people have been building things, carpenters have occasionally measured lengths with their thumbs. So, for example, a table leg might be two thumbs wide. Or a support beam might be five thumbs across. Hence the origin of the term "rule of thumb" for any method of accomplishing tasks that is practical even if crude. Rules of thumb are developed and determined to be generally sufficient through experience and practice rather than careful, scientific analysis. Thus, generations of carpenters have found that, although measuring lengths by their thumbs is less precise than using rulers, for many purposes the achieved level of precision is quite adequate. It is also much faster.

People sometimes use rules of thumb to arrive at likelihood judgments, too. These rules are commonly known as **judgmental heuristics**. In this section we examine heuristics that rest on people's metacognitions. A **metacognition** is a cognition or thought about thought. Underlying each metacognitive heuristic is an assumption. Specifically, the person assumes that there is a reliable relationship between the way he or she *thinks* about an event and the natural processes by which that event occurs.

Recall availability

Answer the following question: In an arbitrary English word, is it more likely that you will observe the letter R in the first position or in the third position? If you are like most of us, you will respond, "The first position, of course!" Tversky and Kahneman (1973) posed just that question. And indeed they found that subjects typically thought there were more English words with R in the first position than in the third. In fact, the reverse is true. This exercise illustrates the **availability heuristic** for likelihood judgment. According to Tversky and Kahneman (1973, p. 208):

> A person is said to employ the availability heuristic whenever he estimates frequency or probability by the ease with which instances or associations could be brought to mind.

Two versions of the availability heuristic can be distinguished. We will call the one involved in the previous R problem the **recall availability heuristic**. The other will be discussed later.

Figure 7.1 describes the sequence of occurrences that are asserted to take place, according to one interpretation of the recall availability heuristic: (1) a single instance of the target event *A* is recalled; (2) the person judges how easily that recollection was made; and (3) the likelihood of event *A* is judged to be proportionate to the ease with which the recollection took place. For example, in the R problem, the person attempts to bring to mind a word

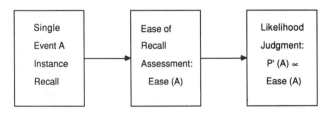

FIGURE 7.1. Schematic characterization of the recall availability heuristic.

that starts with an R, say, "rabbit." He or she then evaluates how easy it was to think of that word. Call the resulting assessment *Ease*(Rabbit). The person also tries to bring to mind a word that has R in the third position, for example, "carbon." Again, a determination is made of how easy it was to come up with the target word, say, *Ease*(Carbon). So in each instance, the person forms a metacognition, specifically, a judgment of how easy it was to think of a particular kind of word. A critical assumption is then invoked: The easier it is to bring an event to mind, the more often that event must have been observed to occur in the past. It is easier to think of words beginning with R than words with R in the third position:

$$Ease(\text{Rabbit}) > Ease(\text{Carbon})$$

Hence, in the R problem, people conclude that it is more likely that an English word will have R in the first than in the third position; that is,

$$P'(\text{R in 1st position}) > P'(\text{R in 3rd position})$$

Note that, in an alternative interpretation of the recall availability heuristic, the person does not bring to mind a single past instance of the target event. Instead, he or she might do something like try to recall as many instances as possible in a fixed amount of time. The number that can be successfully remembered is taken as an indicator of the ease of recall.

The pivotal assumption underlying the recall availability heuristic seems reasonable and probably is often valid. However, it can easily fail. That is, more frequently observed events may sometimes *not* be more easily recalled. For example, there is reason to believe that words are more often stored and retrieved from memory according to their first letters than their third letters. (How many dictionaries list words by their third letters?) So, for virtually any letter, it should be easier to bring to mind words *starting* with that letter than words with that letter in the third position.

The recall availability heuristic seems highly plausible. But what is the evidence for it? Scores of studies have yielded results that have been taken as support for the hypothesis. One is the R problem demonstration of Tversky and Kahneman. Another is a study of death rates by Lichtenstein and others (1978). On each trial in this study, the subject was presented with a pair of potential causes of death, for example, asthma versus tornadoes. The subject was asked to consider an arbitrarily chosen American resident. The task was to indicate which cause was more likely to bring about the demise of that individual within the next year. The subject was also requested to judge how many times more likely it was that the person would die from the more probable killer. Subjects' judgments were only weakly related to the actual relative proportions of deaths in the United States due to the various causes. For instance, subjects felt that death by tornado was more likely than death by asthma. In reality, more than 20 times more people die from asthma than from tornadoes. However, deaths due to tornadoes are publicized far more than asthma deaths. To wit, our evening television viewing is never interrupted by announcements like the following: "Asthma kills 25 in Kansas! Details at 11!" Closely related to the publicity difference is that tornadoes are much more dramatic than asthma. Lichtenstein and others (1978) thus proposed that certain causes of death are more available in memory than others due to their publicity and their vividness. Those highly publicized and vivid causes will be seen as more probable killers.

Interestingly, as it was described by Tversky and Kahneman (1973), the recall availability hypothesis is largely untested. Almost all the studies considered to implicate recall availability have been correlational (see also Beyth-Marom and Fischhoff, 1977). That is, they have documented cases where likelihood judgments tended to rise and fall in correspondence with factors that affect our ability to recall instances of the relevant events. But they have not clearly shown, as implied by the availability heuristic and depicted in Figure 7.1, that people infer likelihood from an availability metacognition (one exception is a study by Hoch, 1984). Those experiments have not sharply distinguished judgment according to recall availability from more general likelihood judgment via proportion estimation, as suggested in Chapter 6 (pp. 157–62). Consider the R problem, for instance. How do we know that subjects did not respond on the basis of the comparative strengths of memory traces for words with R in the first and third positions rather than the ease of instance recall? The mechanisms implicit in these alternative explanations ought to be related to each other, for example, the ease of bringing instances to mind should be affected by memory trace strength. However, the explanations are not identical.

Scenario availability

Imagine having a paper due in your literature course two weeks from now. To be on the safe side, you set a target date for completing the paper two days before it must be turned in. What is the chance that you will actually finish the assignment by the target date? Suppose you cannot envision a single set of circumstances whereby the paper will not get done. Then you will probably say you are absolutely sure you will turn in the paper on time. Now let us consider another assignment, a project in your experimental psychology course. This time, you can immediately think of "a million reasons" why you could miss the target date: Your other classes have tests around the same time. Your brother says he is thinking of visiting you. You suspect that you will get stuck at a critical point in the project and cannot make an appointment to see your professor. And on and on. Tversky and Kahneman (1973) would expect you to believe there is a very good chance your assignment will be late.

The second sense of Tversky and Kahneman's availability heuristic applies to relatively unique situations, such as those involving your literature and psychology assignments. A "scenario" is a sequence of actions leading to an event. According to the **scenario availability heuristic**, an event is judged likely to the extent that it is easy to bring to mind scenarios resulting in that event's occurrence. Since you were unable to imagine a scenario in which you did not complete your literature paper on time, you concluded that it was impossible for you to miss the target date. Because it was so easy to think of circumstances in which you failed to finish your psychology project, you judged that there was an excellent chance you would in fact not meet the deadline.

One variation of the scenario availability heuristic is depicted in Figure 7.2. The person tries to conjure up a single chain of occurrences that leads to the event of interest, for example, missing your literature deadline. To the extent that this task is easy to do, the person assumes that the target event is likely to actually occur. In a second variation, the person tries to exhaustively bring to mind *every* circumstance whereby the focal event would happen (perhaps as in the case of your psychology project). That event is judged probable in direct relation to the number of such scenarios that are actually constructed. The rationality of judgment via scenario availability seems compelling: "I'm a reasonably smart person. So, if it's hard for me to think of a way that I might miss my literature deadline, that must be because there *is* virtually no way that can happen."

As in the case of recall availability, the assumptions underlying the use of scenario availability can be in error. Tversky and Kahneman speculate that people tend to think of only the simplest scenarios. In many practical fields these days, computer models are built to simulate the relevant contexts. For example, engineers sometimes construct computer simulations of new manufacturing processes before the factories that execute those processes are assembled. Such a computer model is then operated under various conditions that ultimately might be experienced by the factory itself. If the model behaves unsatisfactorily, the engineers can redesign relevant aspects of the manufacturing process until the model's performance is acceptable. The behaviors of computer simulations are often counterintuitive—and hence valuable—because they create complex scenarios that indeed can occur, but would never be envisioned by humans.

One of the more convincing demonstrations of scenario availability was reported by Levi and Pryor (1987). In the fall of 1984, subjects were asked to think about the debate between U.S. presidential candidates Ronald Reagan and Walter Mondale, which was scheduled for a few days hence. Their primary task was to state a probability judgment for the winner of the debate, according to the consensus of commentators and analysts. Before they made their judgments, each subject was presented with one of six different potential scenarios for what might happen, as suggested by the design shown in Table 7.1. Thus, half of the scenarios indicated or implied that Reagan won, the others that Mondale did. The scenarios differed in the

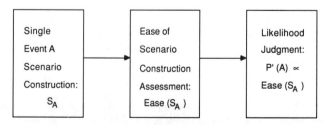

FIGURE 7.2. Schematic characterization of the scenario availability heuristic.

TABLE 7.1   Scenario Design in the Levi and Pryor (1987) Study

| | DEBATE DETAIL | | |
DEBATE WINNER	OUTCOME	REASONS	OUTCOME + REASONS
Reagan	×	×	×
Mondale	×	×	×

detail provided, too. In the minimal situation, the scenario did little more than state who the winner was, the outcome. In a second level of detail, the pronounced winner was not explicitly reported. However, the scenario provided a specific account of things that occurred during the debate that could clearly serve as reasons why one candidate or the other should be expected to win. For instance, in Mondale-wins scenarios, it was reported that "Mondale successfully points out the unfairness and long-term costs of Reaganomics," and that "throughout the debate, Mondale remains composed, assertive, and articulate, whereas Reagan appears evasive and hazy on specifics" (p. 223). In the final level of detail, scenarios explicitly stated the outcomes as well as presented the reasons supporting those outcomes.

Figure 7.3 summarizes the results. As indicated, the distinction that really made a difference in subjects' judgments was whether scenarios

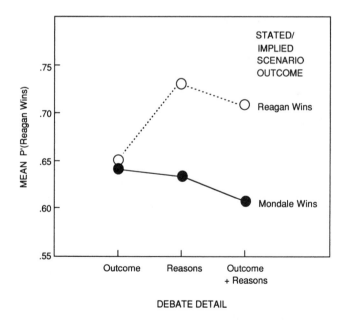

FIGURE 7.3. Mean probability judgment for Ronald Reagan winning his debate with Walter Mondale, as a function of the outcome and level of detail in alternative hypothetical scenarios. Adapted from Levi and Pryor (1987), Figure 1, with permission from Academic Press and the authors.

contained specific incidents that would lead to one candidate or the other actually winning; explicitly stating the outcome in the scenario had no influence. Reagan was generally expected to win, as indicated by the fact that P'(Reagan wins) > 50% in all conditions. However, the judged probability of this outcome was diminished when subjects had read a scenario in which Mondale was depicted as having done concrete things contributing to his victory.

There is evidence that, under normal circumstances, a person is likely to construct only a small number of scenarios, for example, one, for a given judgment situation. Indeed, it seems that the construction of any particular scenario diminishes the person's ability to generate alternative scenarios (Gregory, Cialdini, and Carpenter, 1982). So, for instance, we should expect that, if a person went to the trouble of assembling a scenario wherein one candidate won an election, it would be relatively unlikely for that individual to build a competing scenario in which the previously indicated winner *lost* the election. Lord, Lepper, and Preston (1984) have directly shown that judgment can be improved by getting people to explicitly consider the opposite conclusion from the one held initially. This result is consistent with the principle that the existence of a scenario favoring one event ordinarily **inhibits** the generation of scenarios favoring other outcomes.

Despite its appeal, you should realize that not all the existing evidence favors judgment by scenario availability. Recall the study about fault tree analyses of car-starting failures, by Fischhoff, Slovic, and Lichtenstein (1978), which was discussed in Chapter 5 (pp. 122–23). Besides being asked to state probability judgments that starting failures were due to various causes, subjects were also requested to estimate the rate of automobile starting failures per 1000 attempts in the United States. Table 7.2 shows the results when professional mechanics were asked to make such estimates after being presented with either a full fault tree explicitly displaying the possible starting failures shown in the first column, or after being shown a pruned

TABLE 7.2 Explicitly Displayed Potential Causes of Starting Failures and Median Failure Rate Judgments by Professional Mechanics

	DISPLAYED CAUSES	
	FULL TREE	PRUNED TREE
	Battery	Battery
	Starting system	—
	Fuel system	Fuel system
	Ignition system	—
	Engine	Engine
	Mischief	—
	Other	Other
Median failure rate per 1000 attempts	20	100

Source: Fischhoff, Slovic, and Lichtenstein (1978), Table 5. Copyright 1978 by the American Psychological Association. Adapted with the permission of the publisher and authors.

tree, in which three of those causes were omitted. As indicated, estimated failure rates were *lower* with the full tree display; judgment via scenario availability would have yielded the opposite result.

The memory trace library assumption

In Chapter 4, we discussed the accuracy of people's likelihood judgments concerning their answers to factual questions. In such almanac question tasks, the subject is asked to indicate which of two answers to a question is correct. The subject then reports how sure he or she is that the chosen answer really is correct. For example, an item might ask: "Is Khartoum the capital of Zaire?" It then lists "(a) Yes" and "(b) No" as the alternatives. The subject picks either (a) or (b) and states a probability judgment between 50% and 100% that the correct alternative has been selected. Recall that almanac question judgments are commonly overconfident; people's average probability judgments are much higher than the proportions of their answers that are actually correct.

Fischhoff, Slovic, and Lichtenstein (1977) offer an interesting hypothesis for how such overconfidence arises. They suggest that, for some almanac questions, people assume that they answer the questions directly from memory. In effect, people seem to believe that in our heads we have a *memory trace library*. To answer a question, we look in the "card catalogue" under the appropriate headings. If we find an answer, we assume that it is true. After all, how could one find a "book," that is, a memory trace for something, if it did not really exist? For instance, if I *remember* seeing someplace that Khartoum is the capital of Zaire, then it must *be* the capital of Zaire. The fact of the matter is that memory is often reconstructive (see, for example, Loftus and Palmer, 1974). This means that we do not keep "copies" of all our experiences in memory. Instead, sometimes when we attempt to recall something, we use memory fragments to try and reconstruct what the experience was. So, I might have heard of Khartoum and I might have heard of Zaire, both in the context of discussions about Africa. Realizing that they are in Africa, I might have "put 2 and 2 together" and concluded that Khartoum is the capital of Zaire.

We seem to have difficulty discriminating reconstructed memories, including erroneously reconstructed memories, from memories of direct experiences. Since a direct experience cannot be in error, we are overly confident in our recollections. A classic study by Bransford and Franks (1971) illustrates the difficulties. The top section of Table 7.3 shows several sentences presented to subjects during the acquisition phase of the Bransford and Franks experiment. Collectively, the sentences conveyed the idea contained in the "complete idea sentence," which was not included in the list of acquisition sentences.

Later in the experiment, subjects were given a recognition memory test. Each subject was presented with test sentences. Some of the test sentences were OLD, having been presented previously in the acquisition stage. The remaining sentences were NEW. The subject was asked to indicate whether each sentence was OLD or NEW, that is, whether or not it had been presented

TABLE 7.3   Acquisition and Test Sentences, along with Confidence Ratings That Test Sentences Were Either New or Old

EXPERIMENT PHASE	SENTENCE
Acquisition	"The ants ate the sweet jelly which was on the table." "The ants were in the kitchen." "The jelly was on the table." "The ants ate the sweet jelly." Complete idea (not presented): "The ants in the kitchen ate the sweet jelly which was on the table."
Test	Actually NEW: "The ants in the kitchen ate the sweet jelly which was on the table." Mean confidence rating: 4.26 Actually NEW: "The ants in the kitchen ate the sweet jelly." Mean confidence rating: 3.63 Actually OLD: "The ants ate the sweet jelly." Mean confidence rating: 2.93

Ratings: −5: Highly confident NEW → +5: Highly confident OLD.

Source: Bransford and Franks (1971), Table 1 and Figure 1, with permission from Academic Press and the authors.

earlier. Care was taken that the subject understood that OLD meant that the sentence had been presented literally, not that simply its meaning had been communicated. The subject also rated his or her confidence that each sentence was in fact OLD or NEW. The bottom section of Table 7.3 shows three illustrative test sentences, along with their average confidence ratings. Observe that subjects were very confident they had heard the complete idea sentence before. In fact, they were more confident that the complete idea sentence was OLD than they were sure that many *actual* OLD sentences were OLD. That is, the subjects' likelihood judgments were dictated by what they *inferred* they had heard, not what they had *actually* heard.

GENERAL HEURISTICS

There is evidence for several other judgmental heuristics. These more general heuristics do not depend on the person's metacognitions. Instead, their rationales seem to be as diverse as the heuristics themselves.

Representativeness

Imagine going on a trip to a farming area where large families are common. Your friends plan to take you to visit their neighbors, "Floyd and Sarah Richards." They tell you that the Richardses have six children. Out of curiosity, you wonder what the sequence of births of male and female children in the family was. Let B denote boy and G denote girl. The sequence

$$S_1 = \text{G-B-B-G-B-G}$$

is one potential birth order;

$$S_2 = \text{B-B-B-G-G-G}$$

is another. Is the actual sequence in the Richards family more likely to be S_1 or S_2? Most people choose sequence S_1, hands down. According to probability theory, one order should be just as likely as the other.

Kahneman and Tversky (1972) propose that people respond the way they do in the above birth-order problem because of the **representativeness heuristic**. As articulated by Kahneman and Tversky (p. 431):

> A person who follows this heuristic evaluates the probability of an uncertain event, or a sample, by the degree to which it is: (i) similar in essential properties to its parent population; and (ii) reflects the salient features of the process by which it is generated.

The operations comprising the representativeness heuristic are shown schematically in Figure 7.4. Thus, it is proposed that, when the person thinks about the process by which the focal event is generated, certain features stand out. In the determination of a child's sex, it is assumed that one essential property is F_1 = *randomness*. Also, when the person considers the target event itself, again certain characteristics tend to be noted, for example, the randomness of the sequence of male and female births in a family, feature

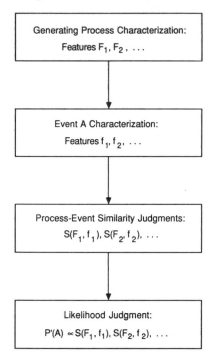

FIGURE 7.4.   Schematic characterization of the representativeness heuristic.

f_1. Next, according to the representativeness heuristic, the person makes a judgment of the similarity between the presumed event generator and the target event with respect to corresponding essential features, for instance, F_1 versus f_1. Finally, the target event is considered probable to the extent that the similarity is judged to be high. People consider birth order S_1 to be more random than order S_2 because it contains more alternations. That is why it would be considered more representative of the birth process and hence more probable. Numerous other demonstrations have provided additional support for the representativeness heuristic, as will be further illustrated in later sections.

It is easy to appreciate the rationale for using the various metacognitive heuristics discussed previously. For instance, if an alert individual cannot easily think of ways that an event might occur, perhaps that is because none exists, and hence the likelihood of the event is indeed remote. Although metacognitive heuristics will sometimes lead to serious judgmental errors, it seems that often they will yield reasonable opinions. However, it is not immediately obvious why the representativeness heuristic is so compelling. Judgment by representativeness might be a carryover of overgeneralized thinking patterns from ages past, when superficial similarity was assumed to have deep significance. According to Hacking (1975), during the sixteenth century, Paracelsus was known as the "Luther of the Physicians" (p. 39). He popularized the **doctrine of signatures**. Everything in nature was presumed to have an inherent signature, which was the key to its essence. Thus, Paracelsus asserted that nature made the herb liverwort in the shape of a liver as a sign that it would cure ailments of that organ. In the same way, perhaps, we might follow the representativeness heuristic because events originating in some process ought to share the signature of that process. Given the weakness of its rationale, it is not surprising that the representativeness heuristic can produce judgments markedly at variance with more carefully reasoned assessments. Such was the case in the birth-order problem.

Concrete thinking

In the Canadian province of Quebec, French is the dominant language; most people are Francophones. However, Quebec does have a significant number of Anglophones, that is, English speakers. Consider the following problem about two Quebec towns:

> Anglophones comprise all (100%) of the voters in Town A but are a minority (40%) in Town B. A random sample of voters is selected from one of the towns. 70% of the sample is Anglophone. Is the sample more likely to have been drawn from Town A or Town B?

"Obviously," a town that has only Anglophone voters can yield samples containing only Anglophones. That is, *every* sample from Town A must be 100% Anglophone. So the 70% Anglophone sample *must* have been taken from Town B. Olson (1976, p. 603) posed essentially this same problem to 30 subjects. Seventeen of them said the sample was more likely to have been drawn from Town A. If you responded the same way, you have plenty of company. Many people, when first confronted with this problem, feel it is so obvious that the correct answer is Town A that they cannot understand why the problem is a "problem." After hearing the argument for why the answer must be Town B, however, they feel that their initial judgment was an embarrassing mistake.

Olson proposes that people err in the previous sampling problem because they make their judgments according to **concrete thinking**, a form of reasoning considered especially characteristic of middle childhood (Piaget and Inhelder, 1975). Concrete thinking implies that likelihood judgments are made so as to be consistent with the surface properties of the numbers involved in the situation, as if those numbers represented physical objects rather than proportions. In the above problem, a concrete thinker would reason that 70 Anglophones can be selected from 100 Anglophones, but not from 40 of them. Hence it is concluded that a 70% Anglophone sample can come from a 100% Anglophone town, but it cannot be drawn from a 40% Anglophone town.

Another of Olson's (1976, p. 602) problems was the following:

> Consider two Quebec towns. Anglophones are a majority (65%) of the voters in Town A, but are a minority (45%) in Town B. There is an equal number of electoral ridings[1] in each town. You have the voters' lists from all ridings in both towns. You randomly select a list from one riding, and observe that exactly 55% of the voters are Anglophones. What is your best guess—is the riding in Town A? or in Town B?

According to probability theory, the correct answer should be Town B. (This is straightforward but tedious to show.) As Olson found, people typically consider Town A to be the more likely origin of the sample. By Kahneman and Tversky's (1972) reasoning, this response is due to the representativeness heuristic. This interpretation rests on the assumption by Kahneman and Tversky that majority–minority relations are an essential feature of event-generating processes in situations like the present one, and therefore are used in applying the representativeness heuristic. Here the two towns are distinguished by whether Anglophones are in the majority (Town A) or the minority (Town B). Since Anglophones are in the majority in the sample, the representativeness heuristic leads to the conclusion that the sample is more likely to have come from Town A. Notice, however, that concrete thinking would imply the same conclusion, since 55 Anglophones can be selected from 65 of them, but not 45.

Suppose the problem is changed so that the percentages of Anglophones in the towns and the sample are as follows:

Town A: 55% (majority Anglophone)
Town B: 35% (minority Anglophone)
Sample: 45% (minority Anglophone)

[1] A riding is a political unit similar to a precinct in an American city.

By the previous reasoning, the representativeness heuristic would yield the conclusion that the sample was more likely to have been drawn from Town B. Concrete thinking would produce the opposite judgment. Olson found that subjects generally do indeed consider it more probable that the sample was taken from Town A. They clearly did not make judgments via the representativeness heuristic, at least the version resting on the majority–minority feature.

Anchoring and adjustment

Suppose you randomly pick the name of one of the countries in the United Nations. What is the probability that the country you select will be an African country? This was essentially the question Tversky and Kahneman (1974, p. 1128) posed to their subjects. They did it in a highly structured way, however, in three stages that can be paraphrased as follows:

Stage 1: A wheel-of-fortune was spun, which stopped on some number between 0 and 100.
Stage 2: The subject was then asked whether the actual percentage of United Nations countries that are in Africa is higher or lower than the number indicated in Stage 1.
Stage 3: The subject was then asked to arrive at a final estimate of the actual percentage of African nations in the United Nations by moving upward or downward from the Stage 1 number.

When the Stage 1 starting number was 65, the median estimated percentage of African nations in the United Nations was

$$Prop'(\text{African nations}) = 45\%$$

On the other hand, when the starting number was 10, the median response was only

$$Prop'(\text{African nations}) = 25\%$$

Paying subjects for accuracy did not reduce the starting point effect.

Tversky and Kahneman attribute the observed phenomenon to the **anchoring and adjustment heuristic.** According to this procedure, when a person must make a judgment, he or she starts with an initial, approximate judgment—an "anchor." This judgment gets the individual "in the ball-park," so to speak. Then, in view of other considerations, the person arrives at a final judgment by adjusting away from that initial assessment. The problem is that such adjustments often are inadequate; final judgments are too close to the anchor. (There are notable exceptions to this rule, however; see Anderson, 1986, for examples.)

The basic idea behind judgment via anchoring and adjustment is appealing, and people seem to apply it in many circumstances (see Hogarth, 1981). For instance, suppose you are presented with great masses of information about an issue, for example, the wisdom of buying a certain house.

A seemingly reasonable way to keep from being overwhelmed is to make a tentative appraisal on the basis of the first few facts you learn about the house and to simply alter that assessment as you learn more and more. In some situations, it is sensible to expect that information which is presented early is more important and hence ought to be given greater weight. But this is not always the case. In some circumstances, for instance, the African countries problem, it is obvious that presentation order should have no significance. Nevertheless, it does. In others, the presentation order does have importance, but a tendency to emphasize early information works against the judge's interests. For example, the seller of a house can be expected to present the strengths of the house right away; the weaknesses will be revealed later, when they have little effect on the seller.

EVENT PROCESS REASONING

Sometimes our likelihood judgments for events rest on our conceptions of how nature literally creates those events. We now consider some specific ways in which this is done.

General causality principles

When we hear a claim that one thing causes another, we expect certain general conditions to be satisfied. Perhaps the most well-recognized causality principle is that purported causes must precede their effects in time. We also expect causes and effects to be close to each other in both time and space. For instance, defendant "Jack Turner" could not be responsible for the disappearance of "Phil Johnson's" car if, at the time of the theft, Jack was 200 miles away and did not return to the city until a day later.

There is evidence that causality principles directly affect people's likelihood judgments—and sometimes inappropriately so. How would you respond to this problem, originally posed by Tversky and Kahneman (1980)?:

Which of the following events is more probable?
(a) That a girl has blue eyes if her mother has blue eyes;
(b) That the mother has blue eyes, if her daughter has blue eyes; or
(c) The two events are equally probable.

Before considering how people *usually* answer this question, let us see how probability theory says it *ought* to be approached. Let B denote the event that the mother has blue eyes, and let b stand for the event that the daughter has blue eyes. Then the problem reduces to whether $P(b \mid B)$ is larger than, smaller than, or equal to $P(B \mid b)$. Going back to the definition of conditional probability, we conclude that the following must describe the relationship between $P(b \mid B)$ and $P(B \mid b)$:

$$P(b \mid B) = \frac{P(B \mid b)P(b)}{P(B)}$$

Now $P(B)$ is the marginal probability that a given mother will have blue eyes; $P(b)$ is the marginal probability that a given daughter will be blue-eyed. Most people agree that these probabilities must be the same. After all, why should the commonness of blue-eyed females differ by generation? Hence, canceling $P(b)$ and $P(B)$ from the numerator and denominator of the above expression, we conclude that

$$P(b \mid B) = P(B \mid b).$$

That is, the correct answer to the question should be alternative (c).

About 45% of Tversky and Kahneman's subjects agreed that it was equally likely that a mother or daughter would have blue eyes, given that the other does. However, nearly 42% felt it was more likely that the daughter would be blue-eyed, given that the mother was blue-eyed. Only about 13% held the opposite view. (How did you respond?) Tversky and Kahneman argue that causal reasoning is implicated in these results: Mothers exist before their daughters. *They* "cause" their daughters to have certain features, not the other way around. So their possession of blue eyes should have greater effect on the probability that their daughters will have blue eyes than conversely.

Event process models

How likely is it that the Democratic candidate will win the next United States presidential election? How did you arrive at your judgment? If you are like many people, you based your opinion at least partly on your conception of how the American electorate behaves. We might say that you have in your head a personal **mental model** of the process by which American presidential elections are determined (see Kahneman and Tversky, 1982b; Thuring and Jungermann, 1986). In general, such models consist of various essential elements of the relevant domain and the relationships that hold among those elements. The way these models are applied is suggested in Figure 7.5a. The person examines the current conditions of the situation. These conditions then serve as input to the person's model of such situations. The model is "run" on those conditions, resulting in a judgment of what will happen.

To be explicit, suppose, as indicated in the middle section of Figure 7.5b, that your mental model says that among the major election determinants are foreign trade policies, campaign funding, and the charisma of the candidates. In your view, such factors not only directly affect the outcome of an election, but also affect one another, hence the "influence arrows" as shown. To use your model, you seek out the information it demands. So you note, for instance, that the public favors protection of American industries, that the Democratic candidate also espouses protectionism, but that the Republican candidate is antiprotectionist. These observations support the Democrat's chances of election, as does his charisma advantage. On the other hand, the Republican Party has much more money than the Democrats for such things as advertising. Implicit in your model are your beliefs as to how such relative strengths and

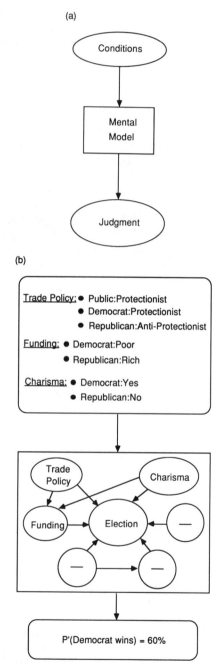

FIGURE 7.5. Judgment via personal event process models: (a) the generic case; (b) anticipating the outcome of the next U.S. presidential election. See text for details.

weaknesses affect the election outcome. Eventually, the model leads you to conclude that the Democratic candidate has a 60% chance of winning.

Abelson (1976) has argued that judgment by concrete, situation-specific procedures, for example, by **event process models,** is the rule rather than the exception. It is unclear exactly *how* extensively people use such procedures. But it is apparent that judgment via these procedures is not rare. Consider an example. In Chapter 2, we discussed bond ratings. Recall that these are ratings that various services assign to the bonds businesses and governments sell to the public as a means of borrowing money. At least indirectly, the ratings reflect the rating service's opinions about the chances that bond sellers will repay the principal and interest on the bonds. Table 7.4 contains an excerpt from the rationale the Standard & Poor's service gave for the relatively low ratings it assigned to a set of bonds offered by the Phillips Petroleum Company and its affiliates. This rationale provides a good example of judgment according to event process modeling. Implicit in the rationale is a reasoned, coherent conception of how the oil business in general operates, as well as Phillips's particular financial situation.

Mental models in likelihood judgment have not been studied extensively. However, similar modes of thinking in other domains, for example, physics, have received much more attention (see Johnson-Laird, 1983). To the extent that we can generalize from those other contexts, we should expect the following (Norman, 1983): First, the models should be incomplete and

TABLE 7.4 Bond Rating Rationale Illustrating Judgment via Event Process Modeling

A 'BBB' rating is assigned to the senior notes and a 'BBB–' to the subordinated debentures.... Long-term debt leverage will increase significantly to approximately 80% from an estimated 36% at year-end 1984 as a result of the $4.5 billion of additional debt and equal reduction in equity arising from the transaction. Flexibility will be severely impaired as the company concentrates on generating cash to reduce debt. Approximately $2 billion of asset sales are planned over the next year that are expected to aid in the debt reduction program. The company's strained financial structure leaves it vulnerable to significant declines in oil prices. Such an occurrence would lower income and cash flow, forcing Phillips to sharply curtail capital expenditures to meet its desired debt reduction goals. The company undertook a fairly aggressive capital expenditure program in recent years, including the purchase of General American Oil (GAO) and Aminoil, in an effort to strengthen its reserve base. Phillips' own exploratory efforts had been hampered by high finding costs and poor reserve replacement in recent years. Some of the expenditure program's potential benefits will clearly be foregone as a result of Phillips' efforts to rebuild its financial strength.

Source: Schlanger (1985, April, p. 27)

unstable. That is, the person's conception of the world will include relatively few of the factors that are actually capable of affecting the target event's occurrence, for instance, the factors that influence a firm's financial future. Moreover, from one occasion to the next, the person is likely to bring to mind quite different considerations. In addition, the relationships contained in the person's mental model are likely to be simple and often at variance with what actually happens in the world. This expectation agrees with what we have seen about the difficulties people have learning contingencies and constructing elaborate scenarios, for example, recognizing conditions that really are predictive of a firm's welfare. The final expectation is that a person often will have great difficulty deriving the logical consequences of the principles that are embodied in his or her mental model, even if those principles are essentially correct (see Dawes, 1979).

A special problem: Value biasing

There are two candidates for mayor in your town, "Cheryl Frayer" and "Clarence Walls." You prefer Frayer, while your friend likes Walls. Suppose you are both asked to indicate how sure you are that Ms. Frayer will be the next mayor. Would your judgments differ in any particular way? Previous results suggest that they would. A study by Rothbart (1970) indicates what we might expect. In the 1960s and 1970s, there seemed to be a serious possibility that French-speaking Quebec would separate itself from the rest of Canada, which is English-speaking for the most part. Rothbart asked Anglophone subjects in Montreal and Toronto to indicate their personal attitudes toward separation, with alternatives ranging from "strongly opposed" to "strongly in favor." He also asked the subjects to report how likely they thought it was that Quebec in fact would separate within 5 to 10 years, using response categories from "certainty" to "impossible." In both groups, Rothbart found significant correlations between attitudes and likelihood judgments. Specifically, the more strongly opposed to separation individuals happened to be, the less likely they felt it was that separation would actually occur. The general conclusion implied by Rothbart's correlational study has been documented in numerous other investigations, including controlled experiments (for example, Pruitt and Hoge, 1965): All other considerations being equal, people tend to think that positively valued events have a greater chance of occurring than negatively valued events. For instance, we should anticipate that you would be more certain of Cheryl Frayer's victory than would your friend.

As is the case with many people, perhaps the above **value biases** in likelihood judgment do not surprise you. Nevertheless, it is not immediately obvious how and why they occur. One seemingly plausible hypothesis is that value biases reflect what the person *hopes* will happen rather than what he or she actually *believes* will happen. Interestingly, there is no hard evidence that this is so (Pruitt and Hoge, 1965); value biasing seems to be "real." The most well-supported explanation for how the phenomenon comes about entails information processing. When they are reflecting about reasons events may or may not occur, people more readily generate reasons favoring positive rather than negative events (Hoch, 1985). (Why this is so is another, unanswered question.) Relatedly, it is also known that value biasing weakens as the situation becomes less ambiguous, from the judge's point of view. For instance, Rothbart (1970) found that the correlation between attitudes and expectations about Quebec separation was moderated by greater knowledge about the facts of the political situation. The principle makes sense: The more transparent are the realities, the less room there is for value biasing mechanisms to operate.

Another special problem: Overconfidence in one's actions

Consider some interesting statistics: About one out of every two marriages in the United States ends in divorce. In 1973, the U.S. Small Business Administration reported that about one-third of all new businesses are discontinued within a year, one-half within two years, and two-thirds within five years (Metcalf, 1973). It is doubtful that current new business success rates are dramatically different. Despite discouraging statistics like these, millions of people continue to initiate marriages and businesses that are doomed to fail. Why? There are undoubtedly many reasons people make what seem to be such bad decisions. It is quite plausible, however, that a major contributor is a special form of biased judgment—**overconfidence** in one's own actions. For instance, generalizing from known results, we can expect that, if a large sample of fledgling entrepreneurs were asked to judge the probability that they would still be in business five years from now, the average judgment would be much greater than 33%.

The type of implied overconfidence is such that, if a person feels that his or her actions are capable of influencing a situation, then the judged likelihood that the resulting outcome will be positive tends to be unduly high. The overconfidence phenomenon has been observed in a variety of contexts, in both real world and laboratory contexts (for example, Howell, 1971; Svenson, 1981; Zakay, 1984). Interestingly, it is unnecessary that the person *actually* be capable of influencing the event. Langer (1975) provides a good illustration of the influence of "illusory control." Office workers were given the opportunity to purchase lottery tickets for $1. The lottery was such that all the participants' tickets would be placed in a container. One ticket was to be selected at random. The participant whose ticket was drawn would win $50. All other participants would get nothing. The lottery tickets themselves were actually football cards. Each card contained the picture of a famous football player, his name, and the name of his team. Every lottery participant in Langer's "choice" condition was allowed to look through a large collection of cards and select the one that would serve as his or her lottery ticket. Each participant in the "no-choice" condition was simply given as a lottery ticket a football card that had been chosen by a randomly designated participant in the choice condition.

Later, the experimenter, that is, the ticket seller, returned to each participant and said (p. 316): "Someone in the other office wanted to get into the lottery, but since I'm not selling tickets any more, he asked me if I'd find out how much you'd sell your ticket for." The average selling price demanded by subjects in the no-choice condition was $1.91. In contrast, subjects in the choice condition required on the average an enormous $8.97 to part with the tickets they had selected themselves. So it appeared that subjects generally felt that

P'(Win with ticket chosen by self)

was much greater than

P'(Win with ticket chosen by someone else)

This occurred despite the fact that all the tickets, regardless of how they were assigned to the subjects, clearly had the same chance of being picked in the randomized drawing.

How is overconfidence in one's actions generated? One popular hypothesis is that overconfidence reflects an attempt to maintain a positive self-image. This hypothesis has not been directly tested in the specific context of overconfidence. However, it has been explored as an explanation for the closely related phenomenon of hindsight bias (pp. 100–101). Surprisingly, there is virtually no support for the claim (for example, Leary, 1981). Similar to what we saw in the case of value biasing, there *is* evidence for an information-processing basis for overconfidence. When likelihood judgments are based on recall of similar events in the past, the bias might be due to distorted recollections. Holmes (1970) asked subjects to keep daily records of their experiences and ratings of the degree to which those experiences were pleasant or unpleasant. We can assume that the illustrative experience, "Failed important physics test," was in the unpleasant category. One week later, the subjects were asked to freely recall as many of the previously recorded experiences as possible. Figure 7.6 shows the general pattern of the relationship between the proportion of times an experience was recalled and its degree of pleasantness or unpleasantness. So, as Holmes's results suggest, perhaps one reason we think our actions will be so effective in the future is that we misremember them as being inordinately effective in the past.

PROCEDURE ASSIGNMENT

Picture yourself in the following situation: You have worked for "Paradise Industries" for the past three years, but have just gotten an offer of a better job at a major competitor, "New World Manufacturing." You must now

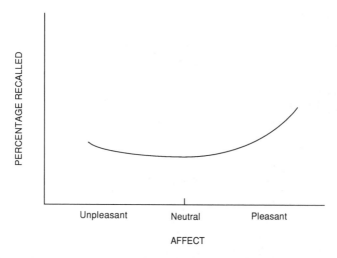

FIGURE 7.6. General pattern of the relationship between the percentage of incidents recalled and the affect associated with those incidents. Based on Holmes (1970).

decide whether to go or stay. You like working at Paradise very much. The only thing that displeases you is the low status of your job. You would seriously consider remaining at Paradise if the prospects of a promotion within the next couple of years were high enough. So, to make a decision, you must, essentially, arrive at a judgment of the form P'(Promotion). If it is above some threshold, for example, 60%, you will stay at Paradise. Otherwise, you will accept the offer at New World. Question: How will you arrive at your judgment?

There is a bewildering array of judgment procedures that might be applied to your problem. Figure 7.7 lists only those we have discussed in this chapter and the previous one; there are more. When researchers report evidence for various judgment procedures, they typically say such things as that people "often" or "sometimes" apply those procedures. They almost never say *when* those approaches will be adopted. Usually, the conditions under which various demonstrations work are poorly understood. Sometimes experiments are purposely structured to induce the use of a particular procedure. Such was the case, for instance, in the Tversky and Kahneman (1974) "African nations" demonstration of the anchoring and adjustment heuristic (pp. 197–98). The judgment task was carefully designed to ensure that subjects employed an anchoring mechanism. It would be a tremendous leap to conclude from that demonstration that in normal, everyday situations people routinely make judgments via anchoring and adjustment. So we are left with a most interesting general issue: Each of us has a large repertoire of procedures at his or her disposal. How is it determined which will be assigned to solve a given specific judgment problem, for example, evaluating how likely it is that you will be promoted within two years?

A perspective

An appreciation for the dimensions of the issue as well as insights into some potential assignment principles can be gained by considering how each of the procedures displayed in Figure 7.7 *might* be applied to judging your chances of promotion at Paradise:

Deference to experts: There is nothing to prevent you from asking your boss or older colleagues to give you their opinions about your promotion prospects.

Probability theory principles and non-probability theory rules: It is not immediately obvious how such formal rules could be applied in situations like yours. This suggests two rudimentary procedure assignment principles. First, to apply formal rules equivalent or alternative to those in probability theory, the judge must perceive the target event to be some combination of other events. Thus, you would have to construe the event "Promotion" as some combination of other events, for example, the conjunction of "Continue to do good work" and "Keep the same boss." The second principle reemphasizes that using formal rules presumes that the person has already made judgments for the elementary events contributing to the target

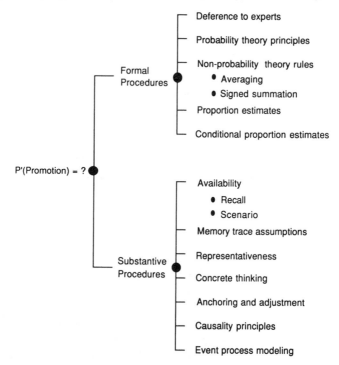

FIGURE 7.7. Tree diagram depicting alternative procedures that might be applied to the task of judging your chances of being promoted at Paradise Industries within the next two years.

event. For instance, given the previous conjunctive construal of "Promotion," to arrive at a final judgment, you would have to already have made judgments such as P'(Continue to do good work) and P'(Keep the same boss). These judgments would have to have been made via other procedures. That is, multiple judgment procedures would be demanded.

Proportion and conditional proportion estimates: Perhaps you could take as P'(Promotion) the proportion of people in the past who have been promoted within two years. You could estimate that proportion in your head or perhaps look in the records. But there is an immediate problem: Which people would you consider to be essentially similar to yourself, so that a generalization seems warranted? It is worth speculating that you would be disinclined to apply the proportion estimation strategy because you see so many differences between yourself and your predecessors that few if any would be regarded as essentially similar.

Recall availability and memory trace assumptions: These judgment mechanisms are, at heart, ways of estimating the proportions of times essentially similar events have occurred in the past. So you would apply them only when you would see such proportions as relevant to your own promotion. Why would you use these devices rather than others to make estimates, for example, examining the records? It has been speculated that effort is one consideration (Tversky and Kahneman, 1973).

Scenario availability, causality principles, and event process modeling: Having been at Paradise for three years, you feel that you understand the company quite well. Each of the present judgment approaches would rely on your conception of how promotions are determined at Paradise, but in different ways. It seems hard to resist taking advantage of what you think are your fundamental insights into how an event such as your promotion literally would be determined. This suggests the general principle that, when a person has had some experience with the inner workings of the pertinent domain, the present devices are likely to be invoked.

Representativeness: To apply the representativeness heuristic, you would have to bring to mind your conception of the promotion process at Paradise. As suggested above, it seems plausible that you would do this, given your experience with the company. You would then evaluate the similarity between your conception of the event "My promotion" and the Paradise promotion process, and judge P'(Promotion) accordingly. This seems highly contrived and thus implausible.

Concrete thinking: This device seems applicable for only a narrow class of judgment problems, those involving sampling. Such is not the case here.

Anchoring and adjustment: It is conceivable that this mechanism might be used in conjunction with some other procedure. For example, you might use the past two-year promotion percentage at Paradise, say 50%, as an anchor. Then, comparing your own abilities to those of the typical past employee, you would adjust downward or (as is more likely) upward to arrive at P'(Promotion) for yourself. This does not seem out of the question.

Several hypotheses about procedure assignment principles were outlined in the previous discussion. A number of others have been the subject of some debate, and there exist actual data that are relevant to them.

Representativeness exclusivity: base rate neglect Imagine yourself as one of Ajzen's (1977, p. 310) subjects, who were told of the following situation:

> In a small liberal arts college students take, as an elective, a general interest course in either history or economics. To obtain student reactions, the history professor recently interviewed 70 students who had taken his general interest course in history. In order to enable comparisons, he also interviewed 30 students who had taken the course in economics.

Subjects were then given a description of a hypothetical student, "Barbara T.," who was among the 100 individuals interviewed (p. 310):

> She is a thoughtful person with a good sense for the dramatic. Having a broad range of interests, she studied more for her own information and education than to fulfill course requirements. She reacted with skepticism to the statements of politicians, *being more concerned with the general trend of events than with immediate and passing issues.* [Italics added.]

Subjects were then asked to indicate the following:

The probability that Barbara T. took the course in history is ____%.

How would you respond? Suppose that you had been in a different group of Ajzen's subjects, who were told that the professor was in economics, and that he interviewed only 30 students who had taken the history course and 70 who had been in his economics class. Would you have answered differently? Should you?
A version of Bayes's Theorem (pp. 134–36) provides the standard probability theory solution to the above history and economics problem. The logic implicit in the solution ought to agree with your intuitions. In the second version of the problem, the base rate or prior probability that Barbara T. took the history course was low, 30%. Barbara T.'s description closely fits most people's stereotype of a student interested in history. Thus, this *individuating information*, which distinguishes Barbara T. from other students who might have been sampled, should have increased subjects' judgments that Barbara T. took the history course upward from 30%. In the first version of the problem, the base rate for history students was high, 70%. Again, Barbara T.'s profile should have pushed judgments even higher, above 70%.
When the history base rate was low, the mean probability judgment was

$$P'(\text{Barbara T. took history}) = 56.9\%$$

When the base rate was high, the average was

$$P'(\text{Barbara T. took history}) = 61.3\%$$

The difference is in the right direction, consistent with the difference in base rates. However, it is very small, much smaller than Bayes's Theorem would prescribe. Kahneman and Tversky (1973) proposed that, in tasks like Ajzen's, people make their judgments via the representativeness heuristic. Specifically, their argument is that the probability judgment that Barbara T. took the history course is dictated by the closeness of her description to the history student stereotype. According to Kahneman and Tversky (1973, p. 238), base rates do not affect representativeness. Hence, when judgments are made with the representativeness heuristic, base rates essentially are ignored, as seemed to be the case in the history and economics problem. This amounts to an assertion of **exclusivity**. That is, when the representativeness heuristic is used to make judgments, this precludes the role of other judgment procedures, for example, the reliance on proportions.

At the time it was proposed, the representativeness exclusivity hypothesis seemed plausible. It is now apparent that it was too strong. Numerous experiments have shown that the **base rate neglect** observed with the history and economics problem does not always occur (Anderson, 1986; Bar-Hillel, 1983). For instance, base rates do have an effect when a given individual sees more than one base rate (Fischhoff, Slovic, and Lichtenstein, 1979; Manis and others, 1980). So we could expect that, if you had responded to *both* versions of the history and economics problem, the difference in your judgments would have been more than the 4.4% (61.3% – 56.9%) difference Ajzen observed for people who saw only one version of the problem. Results such as these, along with our previous observations, indicate that a person's judgment easily can be affected by multiple judgment procedures. But they also suggest another important assignment principle: There are times when one's attention is dominated by only one procedure.

Substantive procedure precedence   Ajzen (1977, p. 310) also had two other versions of the history and economics problem, one of which began with the following story:

> In a small liberal arts college students take, as an elective, a general interest course in either history or economics. A recent analysis of enrollment figures showed that out of every 100 students, 70 students take the general interest course in history, while 30 students take the course in economics.

The second of these new versions described the same situation, except that it was indicated that 70% of the students choose the economics course and only 30% the history course. Once again, subjects were shown the description of Barbara T. and were asked to state a probability judgment that the history course was the general interest course she had actually elected. This time, when the history base rate was 30%, the mean response was

$$P'(\text{Barbara T. took history}) = 47.5\%$$

which rose to

$$P'(\text{Barbara T. took history}) = 75.6\%$$

when the base rate was 70%. Why was there a large base rate effect here but not before?

Ajzen (1977) described the base rates in the present *choice* versions of the problem as "causal," whereas they were "noncausal" in the previous *interview* versions. In the choice versions, the base rate conveyed information that might be indicative of students' general propensity to study history rather than economics—something that would literally "cause" them to do one thing rather than another. Because the professor just happened to pick particular numbers of students who had taken either the history or the economics course, the interview version base rate information could not be taken as evidence of the relative campus-wide popularity of history and economics.

Ajzen's results suggest a generalization that seems consistent with other observations we have made: People tend to see the world as a "stage play" in which people and forces are constantly acting on one another. A fundamental human objective is to understand how the world operates, the "script," as it were. For, if we understand how things work, not only can we predict, but we can also control our destinies. This implies that substantive judgment procedures have precedence. Thus, given a choice, the typical person will make judgments according to substantive rather than formalistic procedures. Moreover, as in the case of Ajzen's experiments, formal procedures are more likely to be adopted if their roles can be integrated with substantive reasoning.

Procedure–situation match   The final procedure assignment hypothesis is one that was forced on us as we considered how you might judge your chances of being promoted on your job at Paradise Industries. We saw that it seemed highly implausible that certain procedures would be employed because the information required by those procedures was not present in the situation, or the procedure is simply inapplicable to tasks like the one at hand, for example, concrete thinking.   Hastie and Park (1986) note, for example, that two classes of judgment situations can be distinguished, those which emphasize past instances, for instance, Tversky and Kahneman's (1974) R problem (pp. 186–88), and those that highlight current information, for example, Olson's (1976) Quebec Anglophone problems (pp. 195–97). The former lend themselves to such procedures as proportion estimation and recall availability, the latter to approaches such as representativeness and concrete thinking.

A RECURRENT THEME: WORKING REGISTER ACCESS PRIORITY

Throughout our discussion of likelihood judgment, we have encountered many phenomena and various explanations for them.   Several of these phenomena and explanations, including ones pertaining to procedure assignment, appear to share a basis in particular features of the human cognitive system, as described presently.

As suggested in Figure 7.8, the cognitive system is often conceptualized as including (among others) two major components (Klatzky, 1980).[2] The first is **long-term memory**, which can be thought of as a storehouse for information encountered by the person in the past. As we have seen, long-term memory does not contain literal copies of that information. Instead, it is populated by the person's own characterizations of various facts, with the constituent items being interconnected by associations, inferences, and meanings (Anderson, 1985).

The second component of the cognitive system on which we focus is the **working register**, sometimes called short-term memory. This is the subsystem that directly supports current cognitive work and is also the path

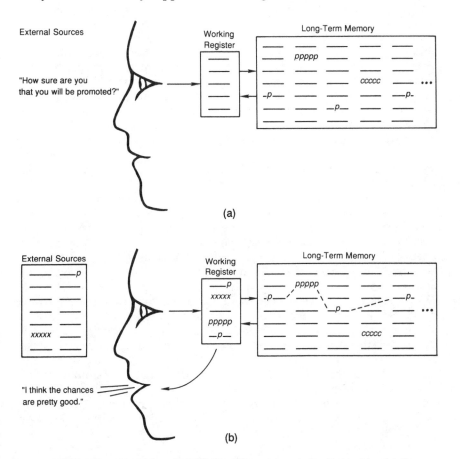

FIGURE 7.8. Illustration of working register access priority. See text for details.

[2] Although there is some controversy about the true distinguishability of such components (for example, Glass and Holyoak, 1986), the present viewpoint frequently proves useful.

through which information is transmitted to long-term memory from external sources. The capacity of long-term memory is thought to be virtually boundless. For instance, there is no reason to think that, as we get older, we either run out of room for storing new facts or that old information must be discarded in order for us to accommodate new entries. On the other hand, there is good evidence that the capacity of the working register has rather strict limits (Miller, 1956). For example, we have great difficulty doing complicated mental arithmetic because the results of early steps in our operations are lost from the register before they can be combined with those from later steps. (You can convince yourself of this by trying to multiply 382.6 by 14.73 without paper and pencil.)

What are the implications of these simple ideas for judgment? An example illustrates. Let us return to the scenario in which you are contemplating your future at Paradise Industries. Figure 7.8a suggests a state of affairs we might expect in your long-term memory when you are asked about the likelihood of being promoted in the near future. Item *ppppp* consists of "pro" information which is indicative that you will be promoted. Items such as _ *p*____ and ____ *p*_ are related to Item *ppppp*. For instance, if Item *ppppp* is an argument emphasizing your good work, then Item _ *p*____ might pertain to cases involving other workers whose records were similar to yours. Item *ccccc* is an instance of "con" information, which supports the conclusion that you will *not* be promoted. Items in long-term memory differ in their probabilities of being called forward into the working register. In Figure 7.8, the closeness of various items to the tops of their respective item stacks are rough indications of their activation probabilities. Thus, consistent with results such as Holmes's (1970), Item *ppppp* has a high probability of being called forward, and hence influencing your judgment; Item *ccccc*'s probability is lower.

Figure 7.8b is a "snapshot" suggesting what happens when you form a judgment about your promotion chances. In view of its high probability of being called into the working register, pro Item *ppppp* is shown as being deposited there. This causes something interesting to happen in long-term memory, as suggested by a comparison of Figures 7.8a and 7.8b (see Rundus, 1973). Because Item *ppppp* is activated, items that are related to it (dashed lines) increase their chances of gaining access to the working register, too. And, necessarily, the activation probabilities of unrelated items decrease. Thus, we see that pro items such as Item _ *p*____ move higher in their stacks, and con items like Item *ccccc* move down. This means that bringing to mind one type of judgment consideration enhances the chances of similar considerations affecting judgments, for example, Item ___ *p*___ , and it effectively inhibits the chances of contradictory considerations influencing those opinions. Analogous **access priority** effects can be expected in the interaction between the working register and external sources, such as when you are perusing Paradise Industries' written promotion policies. The presence of pro Item *ppppp* in the register serves to **prime** or heighten your sensitivity to similar externally presented information (see Meyer and Schvaneveldt, 1976). That is what draws Item _____ *p* into the working register, along with other items like Item *xxxxx*. The net effect of these various mechanisms is that you arrive at a more optimistic promotion forecast than you might have otherwise.

The framework just outlined has been tested most directly by Hoch (1984). Besides overconfidence, as implied in the illustration, it suggests explanations for several other judgment effects we have noted, including value biasing, availability-induced biases, anchoring on initial judgments, and hindsight biases. It also provides accounts for some of the procedure assignment effects that have been documented. An example is the finding by Ginossar and Trope (1987) that, if a person happens to rely on base rates instead of the representativeness heuristic in making Judgment *A*, this increases the chance that he or she will do the same in making Judgment *B* a short time later.

The proposed framework has practical implications, too. There have been several demonstrations that judgment quality can be improved by pointedly forcing individuals to search for reasons why an initial judgment (generated by the person himself or herself, or suggested to them by someone else) might be in error (for example, Arkes and others, 1988; Hoch, 1985; Koriat, Lichtenstein, and Fischhoff, 1980). The present view indicates why such pressure is necessary for so many of us. Interestingly, work by Verplanken and Pieters (1988) implies that there might be substantial individual differences in people's inclinations to free themselves from the binding influences of what happens to get into their working registers first. Aside from individual differences, it is known that these access priority effects dissipate over time. This suggests another remedy for the types of biases indicated above: simply wait. For instance, if you want to make a really good judgment about your promotion chances, one that fairly takes into account the broad panoply of legitimate considerations, make repeated judgments (and record them, along with your reasoning) on several different occasions. In the end, simply weigh them all, one against the other.

SUMMARY

Substantive judgment procedures rely on the person's consideration of how real-world circumstances lead to an event's occurrence or nonoccurrence. Metacognitive judgmental heuristics are one class of such procedures. These methods, such as the availability heuristic, assume that there is a relationship between how a person *thinks* about an event and the natural processes responsible for *producing* that event. Other judgmental heuristics, such as the representativeness heuristic, rest on a miscellany of assumptions. People also make likelihood judgments through detailed reasoning about the processes they surmise to account for the events of interest, for example, through personal theories about the world.

Every individual has at hand many judgment procedures that might be applied to a given judgment task. The principles by which one or more of those procedures might be assigned to that task are not well understood, although some clarification is emerging. For example, there is evidence that substantive procedures have precedence over the formal procedures studied in Chapter 6. Other assignment principles are implied by current conceptions of the nature and role of the working register in the human cognitive system, such as the tendency for a recently used procedure to be employed again. Those conceptions also provide accounts for various judgment phenomena discussed previously.

KEY TERMS

Access priority	Long-term memory
Anchoring and adjustment heuristic	Mental model
Base rate neglect	Metacognition
Concrete thinking	Overconfidence in actions
Doctrine of signatures	Recall availability heuristic
Event process model	Representativeness heuristic
Exclusivity	Scenario availability heuristic
Inhibition	Value bias
Judgmental heuristic	Working register

ADDITIONAL READING

Bar-Hillel (1980); Beach, Barnes, and Christensen-Szalanski (1986); Cohen (1979); Gabrielcik and Fazio (1984); Kahneman, Slovic, and Tversky (1982); Locksley and Stangor (1984); Nisbett and Ross (1980); Wallsten (1983).

EXERCISES AND STUDY QUESTIONS

1. "Medical student's disease" is the syndrome whereby medical students tend to suspect that they have the disease they are currently studying. It is tempting to consider medical student's disease a manifestation of the recall availability heuristic. Argue why we both should and should *not* view it as such.

2. Joyce is a college student who takes courses in which there are lots of multiple-choice "objective" tests on factual material. She has been doing more poorly than she thinks she should. (She protests, "But I *knew* the answers to the questions I missed!") Joyce feels that her problem has been overconfidence. Based on principles discussed in this chapter, suggest at least one idea Joyce might try in order to improve her test performance.

3. Reconsider the birth order problem discussed on pages 193–95. Recall that, when people are asked whether birth order S_1 = G-B-B-G-B-G is more probable than order S_2 = B-B-B-G-G-G, they generally say that it is, and that this response has been attributed to the representativeness heuristic. An alternative explanation that has been proposed is that people interpret the question to be, "Which is more probable, an order *like* S_1 or one *like* S_2?" How would you test this hypothesis?

4. "Acme Party Mix Company" advertises that its "Cashew Mix" contains an average of 55% cashew nuts and only 45% peanuts. A disgruntled former employee claims that Acme operates its mixers such that "Cashew Mix" actually

contains only 35% cashews and 65% peanuts. In a court case, a sample of "Cashew Mix" was found to contain 45% cashews. If a juror made likelihood judgments according to the representativeness heuristic, as originally described by Kahneman and Tversky, who would she conclude is more likely to be telling the truth, Acme or the employee? How likely do you think it is that she *would* apply the representativeness heuristic in this situation? Explain.

5. Tversky and Kahneman (1974) have suggested that judgment according to anchoring and insufficient adjustment provides an explanation for the tendency of people to make judgments for disjunctive events that are "too low," for example, $P'(A$ or $B) < P'(A) + P'(B)$, for disjoint events A and B. Describe how anchoring and adjustment could account for such judgment patterns.

6. You are the head of strategic planning for "Guardian Manufacturing, Inc." A major responsibility of your unit is to evaluate the chances that each of the new products proposed in your company would be profitable. Based on the findings discussed in this chapter, outline at least two precautions you should take in your work.

7. Think about one of the courses you are taking presently. In particular, consider the probability that you will earn an A grade in that course, $P'(A$ grade). Review each of the judgment procedures we have discussed in Chapters 6 and 7. Briefly outline reasons why it seems either plausible or implausible that you would apply each of those procedures to the task of arriving at $P'(A$ grade).

8. Two groups of individuals were asked to make probability distribution judgments for the per-credit-hour law school tuition rate at Wayne State University using the fractile method (p. 22). Thus, each person indicated the 1st percentile of his or her judged probability distribution by completing the following statement: "I am 99% sure that the rate is more than $____/credit." The 10th, 25th, 50th, 75th, 90th, and 99th percentiles were indicated by completions of similar statements, with different percentages substituted for 99%. Group 1 reported their percentiles in the ascending order indicated above. Group 2 described theirs in the reverse order. One might expect that, on average, the percentiles for the two groups would be about the same, but they were not. For instance, for Group 1, the average 1st and 99th percentiles were $55 and $312, respectively, whereas for Group 2 these averages were $70 and $381. What is a plausible detailed explanation of these differences? How would you test the validity of your explanation?

8

Bedrock Principles

216

If you bet on a horse, that's gambling. If you bet you can make three spades, that's entertainment. If you bet cotton will go up three points, that's business. See the difference?

—Blackie Sherrod

"Felicia Pine" wants to go to law school. She has already applied to several schools and has enough money left to apply to only one more. She has narrowed the possibilities to the law schools at "Central University" and "Ivy State University." To which should she apply? A major consideration for Ms. Pine is the chance that she would be admitted to each of the schools. Indeed, the only reason she applied to more than one school in the first place is that she was unsure of being accepted at "Premier University," her top choice.

Probably the majority of the decisions people face every day are similar to Felicia Pine's: The decision maker is uncertain about which of the potential outcomes of each alternative would actually occur if that option were selected. In situations where the ultimate outcomes of at least some options are indeterminate, the alternatives are often called **prospects**, to emphasize the uncertainty. Because of their commonness and importance, decisions under uncertainty have been the subject of serious study for centuries. Scholars in various disciplines have had two aims. The first has been **prescriptive** or **normative**, to understand how uncertain decisions *should* be made. More recently, there has also been a **descriptive** goal, to understand how people *in fact* make such decisions. We are interested in both objectives, although our primary emphasis is on description.

The present chapter begins our study of decision making under uncertainty. Here and in the next chapter we will review certain classic views of the subject. Some of the ideas we will discuss have roots at least 200 years old. It is essential to understand them. They continue to provide a frame of reference for contemporary attempts to comprehend how people decide, even though current understanding of decision behavior has gone far beyond these earlier conceptions. Moreover, the classic ideas form the basis for many present-day decision technologies, such as decision analysis, which we consider in Chapter 9.

This chapter introduces several fundamental, bedrock ideas concerning decision making under uncertainty. In the first section, we become acquainted with standard methods of representing and discussing uncertain decision situations. The second section discusses the dominance principle, a most compelling decision rule which, unfortunately, is not universally applicable. The section after that begins our treatment of decision making according to expectations. In particular, we review more systematically a special case we have applied on several occasions in earlier chapters, expected value decision principles. In Chapter 2 (pp. 28–29), citrus farmers Keith and Sally Collins were trying to decide whether to protect their crop against a possible overnight freeze. Recall that we used the expected value choice principle to derive a recommendation for the Collinses' decision, taking into account their potential losses and the local weather forecaster's probability judgment for a freeze. The dominance principle and expectation principles assume that the decision maker has firm opinions about the chances of various decision outcomes. The fourth section briefly comments on principles that apply in conditions of ignorance, when the decision maker has no idea how likely various possibilities are.

STANDARD REPRESENTATIONS OF DECISION SITUATIONS

It is convenient to characterize uncertain decision situations in ways that highlight the important considerations, which fall into three categories. The first category consists of the **decision alternatives** or prospects themselves, for example, "Apply to Central University" and "Apply to Ivy State" in Felicia Pine's law school problem. The second category includes the **significant outcomes** of the decision. When any decision is made, numerous things might occur as a result of that decision. However, only some of those outcomes are significant, in the sense that the decision maker is not indifferent to experiencing them. In applying to Central University, the significant outcomes are being granted the option to either attend the law school there or go elsewhere. If she were admitted to Central, Ms. Pine would have lots of other opportunities, including an invitation to join the bowling club. But she is largely indifferent to those other outcomes. The third category of decision considerations is comprised of **determining events**. These are events that normally have little intrinsic interest for the decision maker. They matter only because, according to the circumstances of the current situation, they dictate the outcomes that *are* significant. At Central University, a student advisory committee reviews applications. They recommend either "Reject" or "Admit." However, final admission is granted solely by a faculty committee. Thus, the action of the latter group is the determining event when Felicia Pine applies to Central; that of the student committee is not. Schematically, the three categories of decision considerations are related as follows:

Decision alternative → Determining event → Significant outcome

You will find that constructing standard representations often goes a long way toward solving many practical decision problems; in the process of building and looking at the depictions of the situations, the appropriate decision sometimes just "jumps out" at you. These representations help us to think about how people actually decide, too. In previous chapters we have already used some of the representations described here. So some of what we do presently will be a review.

Ordered lists are one method of describing prospects. In this format, Felicia Pine's option of applying to Central University would be represented as

Apply to Central: (Admitted, Can attend Central;
                     Rejected, Cannot attend Central)

The opposing alternative would be

Apply to Ivy State: (Admitted, Can attend Ivy State;
                      Rejected, Cannot attend Ivy State)

So we see that an ordered list is simply a listing of the potential outcomes of a prospect, each preceded by the event that determines whether or not that outcome would be experienced. In a slight variation, an ordered list includes the probabilities of the determining events (or, equivalently, the probabilities of experiencing the significant outcomes) instead of the determining events themselves. Thus, applying to Ivy State might be represented as

Apply to Ivy State: (75%, Can attend Ivy State; 25%, Cannot attend Ivy State)

where it is clear that the probabilities of admission and rejection are 75% and 25%, respectively.

An especially helpful characterization consists of trees. Figure 8.1a shows **prospect trees** describing the alternatives facing Felicia Pine. All the prospect trees that are pertinent in a given choice situation are sometimes combined into a **decision tree**, as exemplified in Figure 8.1b, for Felicia Pine's law school dilemma. Two kinds of nodes are distinguished in decision trees. **Choice nodes** are points where the decision maker must make a choice, for example, between applying to Central University and Ivy State University. By convention, these are represented by squares. There are also circular **chance nodes**, which denote points where the decision maker is uncertain of which events will occur next, for instance, whether Felicia Pine's application will be accepted or rejected.

Sometimes the outcomes of the prospects under consideration all depend on the same uncertain determining events. Then it is convenient and often useful to characterize the situation as a **payoff matrix**. Such was the case with Keith and Sally Collins. Table 8.1 reproduces the payoff matrix we first saw in Chapter 2. One dimension of a payoff matrix represents the

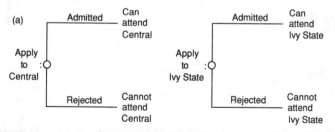

FIGURE 8.1. (a) Prospect trees for Felicia Pine's options of applying to law school at Central University and Ivy State University. (b) Decision tree for Felicia Pine's law school application decision problem.

(b)

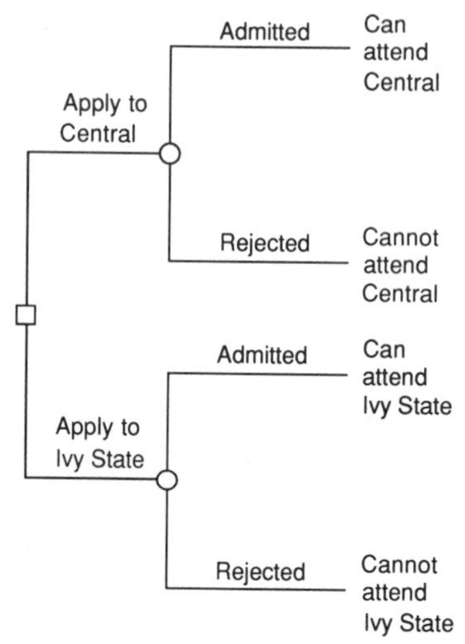

FIGURE 8.1. (continued)

TABLE 8.1   Payoff Matrix (Costs) for Citrus Farmers Keith and Sally Collins

	TEMPERATURE	
ACTION	FREEZING	NOT FREEZING
Protect trees	$5000	$1000
Do nothing	$15,000	$0

pertinent events, for example, "Freezing" versus "Not freezing," the other the decision maker's options, for instance, "Protect trees" versus "Do nothing." The cell entries are the significant outcomes, for example, various potential costs for the Collinses.

THE PROBABILISTIC DOMINANCE PRINCIPLE

Picture yourself shopping for a new car. You have narrowed the possibilities to a pool of alternatives in which only two distinctions matter to you, color and fuel economy. Now consider two members of that pool, the "Whizzer" and the "Zephyr." These cars can be described as follows:

Whizzer: (Red, 25 mpg)
Zephyr: (Blue, 30 mpg)

where mpg stands for miles per gallon, the fuel economy of the given car. You certainly prefer greater fuel economy to less. So the Zephyr is clearly superior on that dimension. But suppose that you prefer red cars to blue ones. Since, for you, the Whizzer has the better color, it is not immediately obvious which car you should choose. On the other hand, suppose you like blue cars more than red ones. Then it *is* apparent which car you ought to pick—the Zephyr.

The latter situation described above is an instance of **dominance**. One alternative is said to dominate another if it is just as good on all the pertinent aspect dimensions and better on at least one. In the case where you like blue more than red, the Zephyr dominates the Whizzer. A fundamental maxim of decision making is the **dominance principle**. It says that, if one alternative dominates another, the decision maker should select the dominating option.

It is hard to imagine anyone disagreeing with the dominance choice principle; it seems almost trivial. One reason it is *not* so trivial is that in real life dominance is sometimes hard to detect. For instance, there might be so many cars on the market with such a bewildering array of features that you cannot easily tell whether there exists one car that dominates all the rest. Indeed, an important first step in practical decision making is eliminating from consideration all the options that are dominated by others. The decision maker should then devote his or her attention to choosing among the undominated alternatives that remain.

A special case of the dominance principle applies to uncertain choice situations. A couple of examples illustrate the idea. In the first, suppose that Felicia Pine's law school application options are characterized as follows:

Apply to Central: (80%, Can attend Central; 20%, Cannot attend Central)
Apply to Ivy State: (75%, Can attend Ivy State; 25%, Cannot attend Ivy State)

Furthermore, suppose that Ms. Pine would rather attend law school at Central University than at Ivy State. So where should she apply? In the present situation, there are two pertinent dimensions of each alternative: having or not having the opportunity to attend the given law school, and the chances associated with those opportunities. We see that applying to Central is better on both dimensions. That option *probabilistically dominates* its competitor. Extending the previous reasoning, it is clear that Felicia Pine should apply to Central.

Our second example: It is winter time. You are considering taking a vacation to a warm location, either "Heaven's Isle" or "Splendor Cove." Only one thing matters to you in choosing between the two, the weather conditions during your one-week stay. You classify these conditions as "great," "okay," and "awful." After consulting a weather expert, the following are the characterizations of your options, where the numbers are your consultant's probability judgments for the associated weather conditions:

Heaven's Isle: (0.10, Awful; 0.25, Okay; 0.65, Great)
Splendor Cove: (0.05, Awful; 0.25, Okay; 0.70, Great)

Again, it seems apparent where you should to go to escape the cold, snow, and slush: Splendor Cove.

The probabilistic dominance concept is implicit in the previous examples. More formally, the notion can be described as follows: Suppose the outcomes in a decision situation can be ordered in their appeal to the decision maker, for example, "great" is better than "okay," which is better than "awful." Furthermore, for any given prospect, the decision maker can say what the likelihood is that the prospect will yield, say, outcome C or "something better." For instance, at Splendor Cove, the probability of weather that is "okay" or better is 25% + 70% = 95%. Now suppose that, for *any* outcome, other than the least attractive, the chance of getting that outcome or something better is greater for Prospect A than for Prospect B. Then we say that Prospect A **probabilistically dominates** Prospect B. The **probabilistic dominance principle** says that, when given the opportunity, we should pick a probabilistically dominating prospect over any prospect it dominates, for example, Central over Ivy State and Splendor Cove over Heaven's Isle.

As in the general case, the probabilistic dominance principle is nontrivial because dominance is sometimes hard to recognize. Sensible decision making under uncertainty ought to proceed in stages. First, dominated options should be eliminated from consideration. Attention should then be devoted to choosing among the remaining, nondominated alternatives. Most of what follows in this book concerns situations in which the dominance principle cannot help us. That is, dominance might not exist between the prospects under consideration. For instance, in real life, it is usually harder, not easier, to get into more desirable law schools. In other situations, the dominance concept might be inapplicable because the outcomes of the available alternatives are qualitatively different from one another, for example, in choosing between taking a vacation and buying a videotape recorder.

EXPECTED VALUE PRINCIPLES

The situations of interest

Suppose you are offered the following gambles, one of which you *must* choose:

G1:   (Heads, $12; Tails, –$5)
G2:   (1–2, $15; 3–5, $2; 6, –$12)
G3: $3.50

In Gamble G1, you toss a fair coin. If the coin lands on heads, you win $12; otherwise, you lose $5. In Gamble G2, you toss a fair die. If the die shows 1 or 2 pips, you win $15; if it shows 3 to 5 pips, you win $2; if the 6 appears, you lose $12. Finally, in "Nongamble" G3, you are simply awarded a gift of $3.50. Which gamble do you select, G1, G2, or G3?

The situation just posed is contrived, but captures essential features of a broad class of practical decision situations. Consider another example from that class. A fast-food chain is trying to decide between two ways of organizing its counter service. Extensive testing has indicated that the following are the approximate probability distributions of waiting times associated with the two methods:

Method A: (0.25, 6 min; 0.30, 4 min; 0.45, 1 min)
Method B: (0.10, 8 min; 0.50, 3 min; 0.40, 1 min)

Assuming that the costs of the methods are the same, which should be used?
    In yet another example, a medical board is attempting to decide which of two alternative heart disease treatments to recommend, surgical or medical. Following are the approximate distributions of survival times for hundreds of former patients who received the treatments:

Surgery: (30%, 0 years; 20%, 2 years; 50%, 10 years)
Medicine: (15%, 0 years; 55%, 2 years; 30%, 10 years)

where the indicated survival times are averages. The main reason the surgical treatment's distribution looks the way it does is that a fair number of patients die during surgery. However, when patients survive the surgery itself, they have a good chance of living a fairly long time. What should the board recommend?
    One common feature of the situations described above is that the outcomes are quantified. Moreover, either more is always preferred to less, for example, money or years of life, or vice versa, for instance, waiting time. Indeed, the amount of the outcome can be taken as a measure of its "objective value." A second common aspect of the situations of interest is that the uncertainty can be expressed in probability form. A third shared feature is that the dominance principle does not offer a solution, since there are no dominating alternatives. However, the present situations are tailor-made for the application of expectation decision principles, to which the remainder of this section is devoted.

The expected value choice principle

The **expectation** or **expected value (EV)** of a quantity is the sum of the potential magnitudes of the quantity, each of which is weighted by its probability. Thus, the EV of a prospect is the sum of the objective values of the outcomes multiplied by their probabilities of being obtained. For example, the expected value of Gamble G1 above would be

$$EV(G1) = P(\text{Heads})(\$12) + P(\text{Tails})(-\$5)$$
$$= (\tfrac{1}{2})\,(\$12) + (\tfrac{1}{2})\,(-\$5)$$
$$= \$3.50$$

We would determine the expected survival time for surgical heart patients as

$$EV(\text{Surgery}) = (0.3)\,(0\text{ years}) + (0.2)\,(2\text{ years}) + (0.5)\,(10\text{ years})$$
$$= 5.4\text{ years}$$

The **expected value (EV) choice principle** applies when a decision maker must choose among two or more prospects. It says that the decision maker should select the prospect that has the best expected value. If more of the quantity is preferred to less, then the best EV is the largest; if the opposite is true, then the decision maker should try to select the alternative with the smallest EV. In the gambling situation, you can easily show that

$$EV(G2) = \$4.00$$

And, of course,

$$EV(G3) = \$3.50$$

So, when given the choice among Gambles G1, G2, and G3, Gamble G2 should be picked. If asked to choose between Gamble G1 and the sure amount $3.50, the decision maker should be indifferent, since the expectations of the alternatives are identical.

In the fast-food restaurant example, short waiting times are preferred to longer ones. Observe that

$$EV(\text{Method A}) = 3.15 \text{ minutes}$$

whereas

$$EV(\text{Method B}) = 2.70 \text{ minutes}$$

Thus, Method B should be chosen.[1]

The expected value evaluation principle

The second expected value principle applies to evaluation decisions. Recall that these involve situations where the decision maker must state (and be willing to act on) the subjective worth of a given alternative, for example, in bidding for a house or car. The **expected value (EV) evaluation principle** says that the evaluation of a prospect should be identical to its expected value. So, if asked how much he or she would pay for the opportunity to play Gamble G2, the person should say, "No more than $4."

Rationales for expected value as a prescription

Why would a person want to make decisions according to expected value? Are there circumstances when optimizing expected value, for example, choosing the alternative with the best EV, is unarguably the wisest course to take? Are there other conditions in which it clearly is not? In other words, are EV decision principles an appropriate prescription for how decisions should be made?

[1] In many decision situations the quantities of interest are best thought of as continuous, assuming all possible values within a given range, rather than a finite number of discrete values as in our examples. There exist ways of computing expectations in such instances. However, they rely on methods of calculus and are thus beyond the scope of the present text (see Winkler, 1972).

The long run Reconsider Gambles G1 and G2 on page 222. Imagine playing each of them many times. What would be your net gain or loss? To provide a sense of what to expect, both gambles were simulated by computer for 300 plays.

Figure 8.2a shows the total payoff for each gamble after the first play and then after every 20 plays. Thus, in the first play, Gamble G1 paid $12.00, Gamble G2 $2.00. After 40 plays, the net winnings were $174.00 for Gamble G1 and $232.00 for Gamble G2. Going out to the ends of the plots, we see that the total amount earned by playing Gamble G1 300 times was $1118.00; Gamble G2 would have yielded $1215.00. Clearly, in hindsight, if given the choice of playing either Gamble G1 or Gamble G2 300 times, it would have been more advantageous to choose Gamble G2.

The present example illustrates an important general principle: Under applicable conditions, the expected value of a prospect is the long-run average value yielded by that alternative. Recall that the expected values of Gambles G1 and G2 were EV(G1) = $3.50 and EV(G2) = $4.00, respectively. If these are indeed the average winnings provided by the gambles, then over 300 plays Gamble G1 should produce approximately 300 × EV(G1) =

(a)

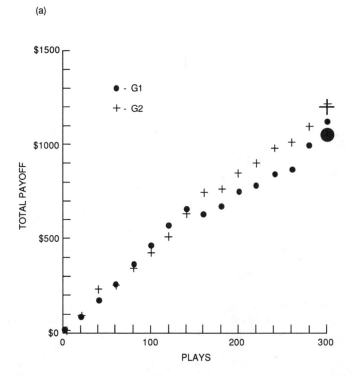

FIGURE 8.2. (a) Total payoffs yielded by Gamble *G*1 = (Heads, $12; Tails, −$5) and Gamble *G*2 = (1–2, $15; 3–5, $2; 6, −$12) after indicated numbers of plays. (b) Mean payoffs yielded by Gambles *G*1 and *G*2 after indicated numbers of plays.

(b)

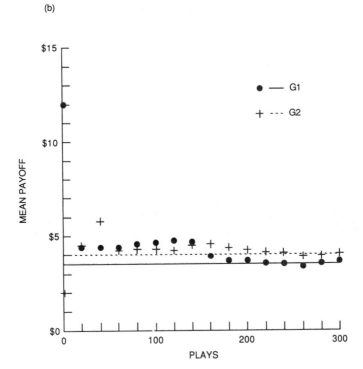

FIGURE 8.2.   (continued)

$1050.00, and Gamble G2 ought to result in about $300 \times$ EV(G2) = $1200.00. These amounts are shown as the oversized symbols in the plots in Figure 8.2a. Thus, we see that Gamble G2 paid off almost exactly what it was "supposed to," $1215.00 versus $1200.00. Gamble G1 was somewhat more generous than expected, $1118.00 versus $1050.00.

The principle we have used is derived from a fundamental idea in probability theory, the **Law of Large Numbers** (Feller, 1968; Woodroofe, 1975). One interpretation of the Law of Large Numbers can be stated as follows:

1. Let Q be some uncertain quantity of interest, for example, the heights of adult American women.
2. Let the expected value of Q be EV(Q), for example, 64 inches or 5 feet, 4 inches.
3. Randomly sample N instances of Q, for example, $N = 100$ women's heights.
4. Compute the mean value of Q for the sample of N cases. Call that mean $\overline{Q}_N$, for example, $\overline{Q}_{100} = 63.4$ inches for our given sample of 100 women.

Then the Law of Large Numbers says that the following will be true: The discrepancy between EV(Q) and $\overline{Q}_N$, that is,

$$|EV(Q) - \overline{Q}_N|$$

will tend to become progressively smaller as the sample size N increases. Thus, in our sample of 100 women, the discrepancy was

$$|EV(Q) - \overline{Q}_{100}| = |64 - 63.4| = |0.6| = 0.6$$

If we were to instead sample $N = 1000$ women, their average height could be almost anything. However, there is a very good chance that the discrepancy will be less than 0.6. For instance, we should not be surprised to observe heights such that $Q_{1000} = 64.3$, which yields

$$|EV(Q) - \overline{Q}_{1000}| = |64 - 64.3| = |-0.3| = 0.3$$

In general, the larger our sample of women happens to be, the more assured we should feel that the mean height of the sample will be close to the mean height of the entire population of American women.

Figure 8.2b provides, literally, a graphic demonstration of the Law of Large Numbers. It contains the same information as in Figure 8.2a, but simply displayed differently. Instead of the total payoffs from Gambles G1 and G2, it presents the mean payoffs after various numbers of plays. The horizontal solid and dashed lines show, respectively, the expected values of Gambles G1 and G2. Observe that, as the number of plays increases, the mean payoffs tend to converge to the expected values.

The short run Suppose that your aim is to be in a favorable material position after repeatedly executing a prospect over the long run. Then the previous arguments and illustrations imply that there is a very good chance that, if you decide according to expected value, you will be better off than if you decide any other way. But suppose that you execute the selected alternative only once, or just a few times. In that case, the force of the Law of Large Numbers is not behind expected value decision principles; there is little assurance that abiding by those principles will result in an advantageous position.

Return once more to Gambles G1, G2, and G3. In particular, note that in Gamble G1 your worst possible outcome would be a loss of $5. In contrast, you could lose as much as $12 in Gamble G2. Suppose you are down to your last $5. So you cannot possibly risk losing $12. Clearly, it is in your interests to choose Gamble G1, despite its lesser expected value. Now, recall that Gamble G3 is an outright gift of $3.50, which is the same as EV(G1). According to the EV evaluation principle, you should be indifferent between that gift and playing Gamble G1. But suppose you have *no* money and thus cannot afford to lose even $5. Obviously, you should take the $3.50. The moral of these stories: There are often very good reasons to reject the guidance of expected value decision principles in short-run decision situations.

A special issue: The "probabilities" It is assumed that the "probabilities" used in computing expected values are just that—numbers that satisfy the rules of coherence that constitute probability theory. We saw in Chapter 5 that there are an infinite variety of numbers that are consistent with those rules. However, for the Law of Large Numbers to apply, the pertinent probabilities are ones that would be perfectly calibrated over large numbers of repetitions of the relevant events. Sometimes these are loosely referred to as the "true" probabilities. This means that the proportion of times each event occurs over the long run approaches the given probability. For instance, if the coin we use is perfectly balanced, then over thousands of tosses, the proportions of heads we observe should be increasingly close to the number we take as the probability of the event "Heads" on any one toss, P(Heads) = $\frac{1}{2}$. But there are two difficulties with the present view of probability.

The first problem is that, in many situations, the concept of the long run is meaningless. This is because the pertinent situations either will not or cannot be repeated. Thus, there is something fundamentally different between tossing a coin, which can yield either heads or tails, and undergoing heart surgery, an operation in which you will either die or survive. The second difficulty is different from but related to the first. Often the probabilities used in expected value computations are probability judgments articulated by people. The resulting expectations are sometimes called **subjective expected values (SEVs)**, to emphasize the distinction. In non-repeatable situations, for example, your prospective heart surgery, the probabilities virtually *must* be probability judgments. Of course, the probabilities you or your surgeon adopt as your own probability judgments could be the proportions of patients in the past who have died from or survived *similar* surgeries. In fact, this is commonly recommended. However, as suggested in Chapter 7, it is tempting for you to resist doing this, proclaiming, "But my situation is unique! It's *different* from those others!" These observations remind us that the quality of our decisions, even if made through subjective expected values, can be no better than the accuracy of the probability judgments on which they rely.

Expected value as a description of how we actually decide

We have seen that expected value at least sometimes is a reasonable guide for how we ought to make decisions. But how good are expected value principles as descriptions of how people *actually* decide? No one ever seriously thought that people routinely follow those principles consciously. However, it is legitimate to ask whether people decide *as if* they adhere to expected value rules.

The evidence We need go no further than everyday experience to convince ourselves that people do not generally decide according to expected values. Take the case of state lotteries, which seem to be everywhere these days. For example, in one of the cheapest games, the player submits a number to the lottery commission, purchasing a ticket for $1. The next day a three-digit number is selected at random on television. If the player's designated number matches the number picked on television, the player wins $500, otherwise nothing. A **fair game** is one whose expected value is $0. State lotteries are unfair games. From the lottery commission's perspective, the expected value of each lottery ticket must be positive. It has to be; if not, the commission would go broke. The commission's gain is the player's loss. Thus, a lottery ticket has a negative expected value from the player's point of view. For instance, from this perspective, the expected value of the above game is

$$EV(\text{Game}) = \frac{1}{1000}\,(\$500) + \frac{999}{1000}\,(-\$1) \approx -\$.50$$

Keeping the price of the ticket in one's pocket is an option with expected value \$0. Since lottery commissions are generally quite prosperous (to say nothing of casinos world-wide), it is apparent that lots of people do not decide according to expected value when they gamble.

It is unnecessary to consider such non-essential activity as gambling to be convinced that expected value principles are not generally descriptive of how people decide. Think about automobile insurance, for instance. From the insurer's perspective, a car insurance policy has positive expected value; it thus has negative expected value from the insured's point of view, for example, yours. Otherwise, insurance companies would be unprofitable, and most of them surely are not.

You might argue that perhaps people *do* decide according to expected values when buying lottery tickets and insurance. However, they only *appear* to violate expected value principles because they are unaware of the objective, long-run probabilities. Instead, they decide according to expectations involving their personal probabilities, that is, through subjective expected values. So maybe a better test of the descriptiveness of expected value principles would be in situations where the probabilities are very clear-cut.

One such test was performed by Lichtenstein, Slovic, and Zink (1969). They presented subjects with gambles whose outcomes depended on the spin of a roulette wheel. One example of the gambles employed was the following:

Gamble 8: ($\frac{8}{18}$, \$3.15; $\frac{10}{18}$, \$0.00)

in which \$3.15 was won if a ball stopped on a specified 8/18 of the slots on the roulette wheel; otherwise, nothing was won. Another was:

Gamble 9: ($\frac{9}{18}$, \$3.00; $\frac{9}{18}$, \$0.00)

which was played similarly. Subjects first chose among the available gambles with no special guidance. The subjects were then carefully instructed in the EV choice principle. After that, they were allowed to choose among the gambles again. In this version of the choice task, the expected value of each gamble was displayed along with the gamble itself, for instance, EV(Gamble 8) = \$1.40 and EV(Gamble 9) = \$1.50 for the alternatives shown above.

Lichtenstein, Slovic, and Zink found that about one-third of their subjects made decisions that were more consistent with the EV choice principle after instruction than before. However, about a quarter of the subjects did the opposite. On the whole, EV instruction had little influence on subjects' decisions. Detailed analyses of the subjects' choices as well as their stated rationales were revealing. Most subjects felt that expected value was irrelevant to their decisions. They gave a variety of reasons for believing this to be so. A few subjects indicated that EV was irrelevant because they would play their chosen gambles only once. More often, however, subjects said such things as "probability was most important" or "money was most important." These responses suggest a limited scope of attention; the subjects were not making the tradeoffs between uncertainty and value that are at the heart of the expectation concept.

One potentially valid criticism of the previous experiment is that Lichtenstein, Slovic, and Zink (1969) examined differences in individual subjects' decisions before and after they were exposed to arguments for expected value optimization. It is known that people are resistant to changing their behavior, if for no other reason than their desire to appear consistent. To test this possibility, Montgomery and Adelbratt (1982) repeated the Lichtenstein, Slovic, and Zink experiment, but with one major difference. One group of subjects made decisions without ever being instructed about expected value. Another entirely different group of individuals decided only after receiving EV coaching and being given the expected values of the gambles among which they chose. Again, EV instruction had minimal effect when subjects were to play their chosen gambles only once. However, Montgomery and Adelbratt found that subjects were more favorably disposed toward deciding according to expected value when the selected gamble would be played many times.

In summary, two conclusions seem warranted by the available evidence. First, since expected value instruction has at least some effect on decision behavior, people appear to be somewhat inclined to accept the wisdom of EV principles. Second, as they should, people are more willing to subscribe to the dictates of expected value in the long run than in the short run. We are left with both a prescriptive problem as well as a descriptive one. The prescriptive problem is, "How should people decide in situations where expected value principles do not apply, for example, in the short run and when the outcomes are not quantified?" The descriptive problem is, "Are people's deviations from expected value principles haphazard or are they systematic? And if they are the latter, what principles *do* govern our behavior?" At least partial answers to these questions will emerge as our study proceeds.

Risk-taking terminology The expected value concept is the basis for a standard way of labeling risk-taking behavior (for example, Keeney and Raiffa, 1976, pp. 149–151). Imagine that you are offered a choice between an uncertain alternative and a **sure thing** that is identical to the expected value of that alternative. To make things concrete, suppose the options are

Gamble G = (Heads, $10; Tails, $0)

which has expected value

$$EV(G) = \frac{1}{2}(\$10) + \frac{1}{2}(\$0) = \$5$$

and an outright gift of $5. Suppose that, when presented with such prospects, you say that the options are equally attractive. Then we would say that your decision is **risk neutral** or **risk indifferent**. But suppose you pick the gift. Then we would describe your behavior as **risk averse**. On the other hand, if you choose the gamble over the sure thing, the behavior is classified as **risk seeking**. The rationales for these terms are not unreasonable. According to their "objective worths," that is, expected values, the previous alternatives are identical. However, Gamble G entails uncertainty or risk, whereas the $5 gift does not. So, if a decision maker expresses a preference one way or the other, the basis for that preference must reside in the person's feelings about facing risk.

Characteristic risk-taking behavior We can now approach one of the questions posed above, whether people's deviations from deciding according to expected value are systematic. The answer seems to be "Yes." In the type of situation described previously, when you were offered the choice between Gamble G and a direct gift of $5, most people take the $5. That is, their behavior is risk averse. Now picture yourself living in a most unusual town, "Chance City." All parking tickets in Chance City must be paid in person at City Hall. When the offending driver presents a ticket to the cashier, an option is offered. One alternative is that the driver simply pays a fine of $5. The other is that the driver plays the "Ticket Gamble." The outcome of the Ticket Gamble depends on the toss of a balanced coin. To convince drivers of the city's fairness, the driver is allowed to specify either heads or tails as the losing side. If, when the coin is tossed, the losing side comes up, the driver pays a fine of $10; otherwise, no payment is required. You have gotten a parking ticket. Would you rather pay the $5 for sure, or would you rather take your chances with the Ticket Gamble? Most people would play the gamble. (This is why Chance City gives violators the option.) The present examples illustrate a generalization that has been observed on many occasions (although not all, as we shall see in later chapters). Specifically, people tend to be risk averse in the domain of prospective gains, but are inclined to be risk seeking in the context of potential losses (see Fishburn and Kochenberger, 1979).

Risk attitudes An attitude is a tendency to react positively or negatively to something. That something could be certain kinds of people (for example, tall folks), or an institution (say, the church), or an object (for instance, Cadillacs). It could also be an abstraction, such as uncertainty or risk. The previous paragraph suggests that, as a group, people have a risk-averse attitude when facing prospects involving gains, and a risk-seeking attitude when dealing with alternatives that entail losses. It is certainly not the case that every person reacts to risk the same as everyone else. It is also unreasonable to expect a given individual to exhibit the same risk-taking behavior in every situation that arises. However, a natural question to ask is whether people have characteristic **risk attitudes** such that, individually, each of us is *usually* either risk averse, risk seeking, or risk neutral. Thus, would it be reasonable for you to seek to characterize your own risk attitude as generally conservative, that is, risk averse, and to perhaps label your brother as reckless, an incurable risk seeker?

The answer to questions like the above depends on how broadly we interpret such phrases as "usually" and "generally." Suppose we limit the context very sharply, say, to monetary prospects involving gains. Under those circumstances, a given individual is likely to be quite consistent (Cohen, Jaffray, and Said, 1987). For instance, suppose that on one occasion "Brent Rockford" is offered the choice between Gamble G and $5, as on page 231, and that Gamble G is chosen. Later, he is asked to choose between

$$\text{Gamble } G^* = (\frac{1}{3}, \$18; \frac{2}{3}, \$3)$$

and a gift of $8, which is the expected value of Gamble G^*. Then there is a fairly good chance that Mr. Rockford would select Gamble G^*. That is, his behavior is likely to be risk seeking on both occasions. But now suppose that Mr. Rockford is faced with the choice between the following two unappealing prospects,

$$\text{Gamble } G^{**} = (\frac{1}{5}, -\$10; \frac{4}{5}, -\$5)$$

and a sure loss of $6, which is the same as EV(G^{**}). There is only a slight chance that Mr. Rockford would pick the gamble in this situation, too. More generally, there is little consistency between individuals' risk-taking behavior for monetary prospects in the context of gains and that in the domain of losses.

Suppose that a person is generally risk averse in money matters. Should we expect that individual to be cautious in other risky situations, too, for example, driving? In view of the inconsistency between risk-taking behavior for prospects entailing monetary gains and losses, it should not surprise you that there is little evidence of general tendencies to take or avoid risks, tendencies that span such widely differing contexts as finances and highway safety (Slovic, 1962, 1964). Thus, the conclusion seems to be that, to the extent that people do have risk attitudes, those attitudes are very context dependent.

Properness: Counteracting probability judgment hedging (Optional)

"Elwood Keeser" manages the local office of the "C. D. Button" brokerage house. When Button's brokers express their opinions to clients about future stock prices, they do so in the form of probability judgments. For instance, they are required to report P'(IBM up), where "IBM up" means that, over the next year, IBM stock will increase in price more than average. Mr. Keeser is concerned about hedging, that is, about his brokers not reporting what they really think. In particular, he suspects that his brokers hedge toward the middle, giving clients judgments that are less extreme than their honest opinions. In this section we examine an application of expected value principles that is thought to provide at least a partial solution to such hedging problems.

In Chapter 3 (pp. 39–41), we became acquainted with the probability score (*PS*). Mr. Keeser decides to use the probability score to evaluate the accuracy of his brokers' price judgments. To encourage their hard work, he also awards bonuses to his brokers in relation to how good their average probability scores are. Thus, for a given broker, the bonus for an entire year's judgments is

$$\text{Bonus} = \$5000\,(1 - \overline{PS})$$

where $\overline{PS}$ is the mean probability score for the judgments. Suppose that a broker behaved like a uniform judge, reporting $P'(\text{Stock X up}) = 50\%$ for every Stock X. Then that individual would earn a bonus of $\$5000(1 - 0.25) = \$3750$. Clearly, the better the judgments, the lower will be PS and the more money the broker will make. This should indeed stimulate the brokers to work hard to improve their judgment skills. The probability score has a special property, called properness, that should also encourage the brokers to report their opinions honestly, that is, not to hedge. This property is illustrated by the following example.

"Ruby Tanaka" is one of Elwood Keeser's brokers. She thinks there is an 80% chance that General Motors stock will be up over the next year. Should she truthfully report this opinion or should she hedge? The decision tree in Figure 8.3 is a good representation of her situation. In the middle we see the option of telling the truth, reporting the judgment $f_T = P'(\text{GM up}) = 0.80$. Above that point we see the options of hedging high; below are options of hedging low. In each case, specific hedges are described in detail. Thus, one high hedge is such that she reports $f_H = 0.9$, and one low hedge yields the report $f_L = 0.6$. Ms. Tanaka's aim is to achieve the lowest possible probability score. She will be making about 1000 judgments similar to the present one. So a good case can be made that she should base her reporting decision on expected value principles. Specifically, she should report the judgment that has the smallest subjective expected value (p. 228), where "subjective" means that the probabilities used in computing expectations are Ms. Tanaka's actual probability judgments, and "value" refers to the probability score. Let us see how this strategy would be carried out.

Consider the high hedge $f_H = 0.9$, described at the top of Figure 8.3. The subjective expected value (SEV) of reporting $f_H = 0.9$ is as follows:

$$\text{SEV(Report } f_H = 0.9) = P'(\text{GM up})PS(\text{Report } f_H = 0.9, \text{GM up})$$

$$+ \ P'(\text{GM down})PS(\text{Report } f_H = 0.9, \text{GM down})$$

As indicated in the figure, Ms. Tanaka's actual opinion is that $P'(\text{GM up}) = 0.8$, and hence $P'(\text{GM down}) = 0.2$. Recall that the probability score is defined by

$$PS = (f - d)^2$$

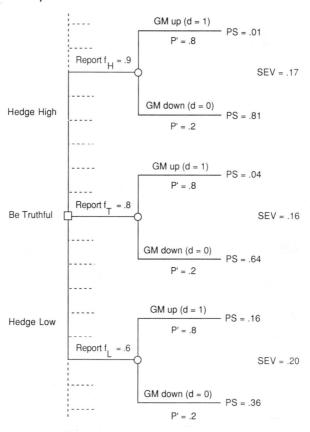

FIGURE 8.3. Tree representation of Ruby Tanaka's decision to either hedge or truthfully report her judgment that P'(GM up) = 80%. See text for details.

where f is the reported probability judgment and d, the outcome index, is 1 if the target event occurs (for example, GM up) and 0 otherwise. This implies that

$$PS(\text{Report } f_H = 0.9, \text{GM up}) = (0.9 - 1)^2 = (-0.1)^2 = 0.01$$

and

$$PS(\text{Report } f_H = 0.9, \text{GM down}) = (0.9 - 0)^2 = (0.9)^2 = 0.81$$

Thus, as also indicated in the figure, the resulting subjective expected value is

$$SEV(\text{Report } f_H = 0.9) = (0.8)(0.01) + (0.2)(0.81) = 0.17$$

You should be able to show similarly that

$$SEV(\text{Report } f_T = 0.8) = 0.16$$

and

$$\text{SEV}(\text{Report } f_L = 0.6) = 0.20$$

We therefore see that, among the three possible reports highlighted in Figure 8.3, the SEV is indeed lowest, or best, when Ruby Tanaka reports the truth. It can be shown that the SEV for a truthful report is better than that for *any* other report. That is what it means to say that the probability score is **proper**.

The probability score's properness implies that, in terms of maximizing her expected bonus, Ruby Tanaka should not hedge. But will Elwood Keeser's bonus system actually have the intended effect of inducing more honest reporting by his brokers? On the face of it, previous experience is discouraging. Most research has indicated that rewarding people by means of *proper scoring rules*, such as the probability score, has minimal influence on their reported judgments (see Echternacht, 1972; Jensen and Peterson, 1973). However, it is unclear that those previous studies have been fair tests of the strategy. In particular, there is little evidence that the participants understood that it really was in their best interests to report their opinions truthfully.

A COMMENT: PRINCIPLES FOR IGNORANCE

In all the situations discussed so far, it has been assumed that the decision maker has firm opinions about the chances that various determining events would actually occur. In actual practice, this might not be the case. In the extreme, the decision maker might not have a clue about such likelihoods. Under such circumstances, the decision maker is said to be in a state of **ignorance**.[2] How should and do people decide when they are ignorant?

Although states of ignorance in principle can exist, they are rare. And even when they do exist, people tend not to recognize them because of such phenomena as overconfidence. Or they tend to avoid altogether situations in which there is little basis for judgment (see Chapter 13, pp. 356–57). This explains why actual behavior under conditions of ignorance is virtually unstudied. Nevertheless, decision theorists have acknowledged several choice principles that might apply in ignorance. One is the **maximin principle**, which says that the decision maker should choose the alternative whose least attractive potential outcome is as good or better than that of any other alternative.[3] A competing **maximax principle** says that one should pick the alternative that has the most attractive possible outcome—again effectively ignoring uncertainty. Yet another rule, the **Principle of Insufficient Reason**, also known as the **Laplace Rule**, recommends that the decision maker should, effectively, assume that all the pertinent events are equally

---

[2]Sometimes the term "uncertainty" is used to describe the state of ignorance. The present usage is adopted to minimize the possibility of confusion with other uses of the word uncertainty.

[3]You should be aware that some authors (for example, Milnor, 1954) describe this principle as the "minimax rule." Confusing, no?

likely and then select the option with the best expected value (Luce and Raiffa, 1957, Chapter 13).

SUMMARY

There are several standard ways of representing uncertain decision situations: ordered lists, prospect and decision trees, and payoff matrices. All serve to highlight the essential features of those situations and how they relate to one another. These are (1) the potential outcomes that are valued by the decision maker and (2) the events that determine whether those outcomes would actually be experienced.

Suppose that two options offer the same or similar outcomes, and that the probabilities of good outcomes are always higher in one option than the other. The probabilistic dominance principle says that, when given the choice, the decision maker should pick the former dominating alternative. Expected value decision principles apply in situations where the potential outcomes of the options have numerical objective values and there is also a probability associated with each of those outcomes. According to the expected value choice principle, the available alternative with the best expected value should be chosen. A closely related expected value evaluation principle implies that the subjective worths of prospects are determined by the expected values of those prospects.

Standard expressions for risk-taking behavior, such as risk aversion and risk seeking, are defined in terms of expected values. People are often risk averse for prospects that promise gains and risk seeking for those that offer potential losses. There is little evidence that a given individual is likely to respond to risk in the same way in contexts that are very different from each other.

In certain rare circumstances, the decision maker has no basis for judging how likely the events are that will dictate the outcomes of the available options. Several principles have been proposed for how decisions should be made under such conditions of ignorance.

KEY TERMS

Chance node	Fair game
Choice node	Ignorance
Decision alternative	Laplace Rule
Decision tree	Law of Large Numbers
Descriptive	Maximax principle
Determining event	Maximin principle
Dominance	Normative
Dominance principle	Ordered list
Expectation	Payoff matrix
Expected value	Prescriptive
Expected value choice principle	Principle of Insufficient Reason
Expected value evaluation principle	Probabilistic dominance principle

Properness
Prospect
Prospect tree
Risk attitude
Risk averse
Risk indifferent

Risk neutral
Risk seeking
Significant outcome
Subjective expected value
Sure thing

ADDITIONAL READING

Hadar and Russell (1969); Lopes (1981); Tversky and Bar-hillel (1983); Winkler and Murphy (1968).

EXERCISES AND STUDY QUESTIONS

1. Is it possible to represent Felicia Pine's law school application decision situation (p. 000) in the form of a payoff matrix? If so, construct such a matrix. If not, explain why.
2. "Michael Martin" is a commercial fisherman. Mr. Martin must decide whether to go out to fish on a day when there is a nonnegligible chance of a serious storm at sea. If he goes out and there is a big storm, he almost certainly will catch no fish and might very well lose his boats and the lives of his crew and himself. On the other hand, he can expect to make about $5000 if he goes out and the storm does not materialize. Characterize Mr. Martin's options in ordered list, tree, and payoff matrix forms.
3. John and Marcia have been seeing each other for a couple of years. John realizes that neither of them is getting any younger, and so he should either propose marriage to Marcia or suggest that they start seeing other people. John is fond of Marcia, but he is unsure that they are perfectly suited for each other.
   (a) Construct a tree representation of John's decision problem, including what seem to you to be major determining events and outcomes that ought to be taken into account.
   (b) What advice do you have for John about how he should arrive at good judgments of the chances of the pertinent events?
4. Describe a situation in which the dominance principle (not the *probabilistic* dominance principle) *cannot* be applied.
5. Following is the description of a gamble played at a church "Mardi Gras Night," an annual fund-raising event for which participants make substantial donations to attend: First, the player draws a card at random from a deck of cards. If the card is a heart, a balanced coin is tossed. If the toss comes up heads, the player loses $16; if tails appears, the player wins $40. If, in the card drawing, a non-heart is drawn, the player then tosses a balanced die. If a single pip shows, the player wins $24; any other outcome yields a loss of $8.
   (a) Construct a tree representation of the gamble.
   (b) Is the game fair?
6. Ask a friend to consider opportunities to invest in either of two restaurant ventures, which are described as follows:

Opportunity A: "Tasty Treats": An application for a license to operate in the city must be obtained. There is a 20% chance that the application would be rejected, in which case the investor would lose $500 in application costs and lawyers' fees. On the other hand, if the application is approved, there is a 50% chance that a profit of $5000 would be realized within a year; otherwise, a net loss of $2000 would be incurred.

Opportunity B: "Dandy Dude Hamburgers": The license has already been obtained. So the only considerations are the potential operating profits or losses. Within a year, there is a 45% chance of a $5000 profit, a 20% chance of a loss of $500, and a 35% chance of a $2000 loss.

(a) Assuming that the concern is with profits and losses over the next year (ignoring discount rates), ask your friend to choose the preferred option and to state a rationale.

(b) Which principle discussed in this chapter seems most applicable to the present case? What option *should* your friend have chosen, according to that principle? *Suggestion:* Construct a tree representation of each alternative and then reduce that representation to an ordered list.

(c) Assuming that the reasoning given in parts (a) and (b) disagree, which do you think is more compelling? Why?

7. Al has just bought an expensive stereo system at "Sound City." The standard warranty on the system is for 60 days. After that, the owner is responsible for all repair costs. The salesman offers Al the "Sound City Safe Buyer Plan," a 5-year extended warranty. There are two versions of the plan. In the deductible version, which costs $\$C_D$, the owner pays the first $100 of any repair bill, but nothing after that. In the no-deductible version, with a price of $\$C_{ND}$, the owner never pays anything for repairs. Before making a decision about an extended warranty, Al does some research to determine the approximate distribution of repair costs that can be expected for his system over a 5-year period after the standard warranty expires. He learns that there is a 95% chance that nothing will go wrong with his system, a 4% chance of a $400 expense, and a 1% chance that there will be a bill of around $1000. The chance that the owner will have to repair the system more than once is negligible. *Note:* For parts (b) and (c), ignore the existence of the no-deductible warranty.

(a) Construct a decision tree representing the situation facing Al.

(b) According to expected value decision principles, what is the most Al should be willing to pay for the deductible extended warranty, that is, the largest value of $\$C_D$ he should accept?

(c) Would you *expect* Al to be willing to pay less, the same, or more than the amount you derived in part (b)? Explain.

8. (Optional) Show that the probability score really *is* proper. That is, suppose a person thinks that the probability of the target event A is $f_T = P'(A)$. She considers reporting judgment f_R, which may or may not be the same as f_T. Show that this individual's expected probability score is best (lowest) when she reports the truth, $f_R = f_T$.

9. (Optional)   Return to C. D. Button's local brokerage office (pp. 232–35). Manager Elwood Keeser considers an alternative bonus scheme. In this new approach, a broker's annual bonus is given by

$$\text{Bonus} = \$5000 \overline{PA}$$

where the score PA is the probability judgment the broker assigns to the stock price event that actually occurs, and $\overline{PA}$ is the mean of such judgments. For instance, if Ruby Tanaka says $P'(\text{GM up}) = 80\%$ and the price of GM stock really does go up, her score is $PA = 0.80$. But if GM stock does not go up, her score is $PA = 0.20$, since, implicitly, she has stated that $P'(\text{GM down}) = 20\%$. The proposed bonus system seems quite reasonable, since it rewards the broker in direct relation to his or her judgment for the event that really happens.

(a) Elwood Keeser hopes that the above system will discourage hedging by his brokers. In fact, however, the system should *encourage* hedging. Explain why, intuitively.

(b) PA is actually the linear scoring rule (Lr), which was discussed in Problem 2 in Chapter 3. Show that the linear score is not proper, which is the reason it should promote hedging. *Suggestion:* Use the same approach used in Problem 8 to show that the probability score is proper.

(c) Exactly what sort of hedging should the linear scoring rule instigate?

(d) Perform an experiment to test whether the probability score and the linear score really *do* lead to different kinds of reports.

9

Expected Utility

In the long run, we'll all be dead.

—John Maynard Keynes

We met Felicia Pine in the introduction to the last chapter. Recall that Ms. Pine was trying to decide where to apply to law school, at Central University or Ivy State University. Expected value was a major focus in Chapter 8. We saw that, in certain circumstances, it makes sense to decide according to expected value decision principles. It does not appear that Felicia Pine's situation fits the conditions for those rules, however, and for several reasons. For one thing, whereas expected value principles apply when the decision maker is interested in a single quantified object of value, for example, money, this is not the case for Felicia Pine; law school is more than a dollars-and-cents proposition for her. We have already seen that people's actual decision behavior often disagrees with expected value principles. The present observations suggest that frequently these rules simply *cannot* be employed.

This chapter discusses decision principles that, in form, are closely related to expected value concepts. However, these expected utility rules have fundamental differences from their expected value counterparts, including their applicability to problems such as Felicia Pine's. The first section of the chapter argues for an improvement on expected value principles. The second section describes expected utility concepts in detail. The third reviews evidence about how well expected utility principles describe people's actual decision behavior. To anticipate the punch line, we will discover consistent differences between how those principles say people should decide and how they in fact decide. In view of this evidence, you will wonder why the expected utility notion continues to attract the attention it does; without question it is *the* dominant concept in the history of scholarship on decision making. A major reason is that, regardless of how people really decide, there are cogent arguments for expected utility principles as guides for proper—some say rational—decision making. The fourth section of the chapter reviews these arguments. The fifth section describes and illustrates basic methods of decision analysis, with emphasis on techniques that apply expected utility ideas to real-life decision problems. You might find some of the material in this chapter more challenging than that in previous chapters. Stick with it, though; the effort should prove worthwhile.

A SPECIAL OFFER

Suppose that your state lottery commission considers adding a new game to those it offers to the public, the "Toss Game". The commission is trying to arrive at a reasonable price to charge for the Toss Game. So they ask you, along with lots of other folks, to indicate how much you would pay for an opportunity to play the game.

This is how the Toss Game works: When the player visits the neighborhood lottery vendor, he or she is presented with a balanced coin. To convince the player that the game is not fixed, the player is allowed to designate either heads or tails as the winning side in a toss of the coin. Suppose that the player designates heads as winning. The player then tosses the coin until heads appears for the first time. Let N denote the number of tosses required. The payoff rule says that the player then wins $(\$2)^N$. Thus, if heads appears on the first toss, the payoff is $(\$2)^1 = \$2$. If the first toss yields tails, but heads appears on the second toss, the prize is $(\$2)^2 = \$4$. If three tosses are needed to get the first heads, the payoff is $(\$2)^3 = \$8$. And so on. So how much *would* you pay for a ticket to play the Toss Game?

Before we discuss how most people react to the Toss Game, let us determine its expected value. Suppose we denote heads by H and tails by T. Then the Toss Game can be represented as follows:

Toss Game = (H, $2; TH, $4; TTH, $8; TTTH, $16; TTTTH, $32; ...)

Bear in mind that the events that determine the player's payoff are actually conjunctions of outcomes from successive coin tosses. Those tosses are independent of one another. Recall from Chapter 5 that the probability of a conjunction of independent events is simply the product of the probabilities of those events taken alone. If you assume that $P(\text{H})$ = $P(\text{T}) = \tfrac{1}{2}$, it should be easy to convince yourself that the probability that the first heads occurs on the Nth toss is simply $(\tfrac{1}{2})(\tfrac{1}{2})(\tfrac{1}{2})$... $(\tfrac{1}{2}) = (\tfrac{1}{2})^N$, in other words, $1/2$ multiplied by itself N times. Thus, we can describe the Toss Game in terms of the probabilities of the potential prizes this way:

Toss Game = ($\tfrac{1}{2}$, $2; $\tfrac{1}{4}$, $4; $\tfrac{1}{8}$, $8; $\tfrac{1}{16}$, $16; $\tfrac{1}{32}$, $32; ...)

The expected value of the Toss Game is now easily seen to be

$$\text{EV(Toss Game)} = (\tfrac{1}{2})\,(\$2) + (\tfrac{1}{4})\,(\$4) + (\tfrac{1}{8})\,(\$8) + (\tfrac{1}{16})\,(\$16) + (\tfrac{1}{32})\,(\$32) + ...$$
$$= \$1 + \$1 + \$1 + \$1 + \$1 + ...$$

Question: Where does the summation end? Answer: It never does. This is because, although the chance of the first heads appearing on toss N becomes progressively smaller as N increases, that probability never becomes 0. And as rapidly as the chance of the first heads appearing on successive tosses diminishes, the size of the player's payoff increases. The implication of all this is that the expected value of the Toss Game is infinite (see also Lee, 1971).

No state lottery commission has ever offered the Toss Game. In view of the game's expected value, they would be foolish to do so; they could not afford it. However, in various forms, the concept of the Toss Game has been presented to prospective ticket buyers for more than 250 years. It is commonly known as the St. Petersburg game and was described for posterity by Daniel Bernoulli (1738/1954). Although the St. Petersburg game has an infinite expected value, people are seldom willing to pay more than a pittance for the opportunity to play it. For instance, individuals rarely offer more than $4 to play the Toss Game. (How about you?) The observed reluctance to pay very much for the St. Petersburg game, despite its objective attractiveness, has been dubbed the **St. Petersburg Paradox.**

EXPECTED UTILITY CONCEPTS

The St. Petersburg Paradox could have been taken as simply another demonstration that people do not decide on the basis of expected value. However, Bernoulli (1738/1954) had a more positive goal. He considered reactions to the St. Petersburg game to be consistent with the proposition that people decide among prospects not according to their expected *objective* values, but rather their expected *subjective* values, which bear a characteristic relationship to the objective ones. We will refer to subjective values in the context of uncertainty as **utilities**. Later we will return to the St. Petersburg game to clarify Bernoulli's proposition.

Expected utility principles

The expected utility viewpoint assumes that the decision situation is represented in a particular way, as was the case with expected value. In particular, the events that determine the significant outcomes are seen as a partition of the possibilities (see Chapter 5, pp. 118–19). That is, no two of those events can both occur, and collectively those events exhaust all the potential occurrences. As a specific example, suppose that "Charlie Y." faces the option of going to trial on two burglary charges, as opposed to pleading guilty to a lesser charge of larceny. The pertinent events for the burglary trial, along with their associated outcomes for Charlie Y., can be represented as follows:

EVENT	OUTCOME
"Guilty" verdicts on both charges	10-year sentence (?)
"Guilty" verdict on one charge, "Not guilty" on other	5-year sentence (?)
"Not guilty" verdicts on both charges	Freedom
Hung jury, no verdict	Retrial later
Other possibilities, for example, mistrial	Retrial later (?)

The events "Guilty–both charges," "Guilty–one charge," "Not guilty," "No verdict," and "Other" would thus be the partition for the trial prospect. The question marks indicate that the specified outcomes are not guaranteed, but are most likely, given the determining event.

Each of the possible outcomes of a prospect has a utility, that is, subjective value, that is represented numerically. We will symbolize these in the form $u(C)$, for arbitrary outcome C. The more appealing an outcome is, the higher its utility. The **expected utility (EU)** of a prospect is simply the sum of the utilities of the potential outcomes, each weighted by its probability. So the expected utility of Charlie Y.'s trial option would be

EU (Trial) = P (Guilty–both charges) u (10–year sentence) + P (Guilty–one charge) u (5–year sentence)
   + P (Not guilty) u (Freedom) + P(No verdict) u (Freedom) + P(Other) u (Retrial)
   + P (No verdict) u (Retrial)+ P(Other) u (Retrial)

To make things even more concrete, the following are list characterizations of the trial prospect:

Trial = (Guilty–both charges, 10-year sentence;
Guilty–one charge, 5-year sentence; Not guilty,
Freedom; No verdict, Retrial; Other, Retrial)

and

Trial = (25%, 0; 40%, 35; 30%, 100; 3%, 50; 2%, 50)

In the latter listing, the representation is in terms of the probabilities and Charlie Y.'s utilities for the corresponding outcomes. Therefore, the expected utility for the trial option would be

$$\text{EU(Trial)} = (0.25)\,(0) + (0.40)\,(35) + (0.30)\,(100) + (0.03)\,(50) + (0.02)\,(50)$$
$$= 46.5$$

According to the **expected utility choice principle**, when choosing among two or more prospects, the decision maker should always select the option with the highest expected utility. Suppose that pleading guilty to the larceny charge carries with it a guaranteed sentence of four years in prison. Then the EU choice principle says that Charlie Y. should make the plea if

$$\text{EU(Plead)} = u(\text{4-Year Sentence}) > \text{EU(Trial)} = 46.5.$$

If the opposite is true, he should take his chances in court. For instance, if for Charlie Y., $u(\text{4-year sentence}) = 40$, he should go to court.

Now imagine that the plea-bargaining situation is a bit different. Instead of offering Charlie Y. a take-it-or-leave-it proposition, suppose the prosecutor is willing to negotiate with him, seeking a larceny sentence for Charlie Y. that would be agreeable to both sides. What is the longest sentence Charlie Y. should accept? The **expected utility evaluation principle** says that the decision maker's evaluation of a prospect should imply a sure thing whose utility is identical to the expected utility of that prospect. In this case, the pertinent prospect is the trial. Its evaluation is to be expressed as the length of sentence Charlie Y. is willing to accept in its place. Suppose that, for Charlie Y., $u(\text{3½-year sentence}) = 46.5$. Based on our previous analysis, we observe that

$$u(\text{3½-year sentence}) = \text{EU(Trial)}$$

Accordingly, Charlie Y. should accept as much as 3½ years behind bars in exchange for dismissal of his two burglary charges.

Risk taking and utility function shape

Suppose that a decision maker is considering prospects whose potential outcomes are quantitative and positively oriented. That is, more is always preferred to less. Money usually satisfies these requirements. So does the longevity of a critical part in a new model being designed by an automobile manufacturer. Yet another example is the number of lives that would be saved by prospective public health regulations. By assumption, a graph of the relationship between such outcomes and their utilities will be (strictly) *monotone increasing*; the greater the outcomes, the higher their utilities. Beyond being monotone, the graph could take on any shape. However, certain particular shapes have special significance.

The curves in Figures 9.1a to 9.1c represent alternative utility functions for money in the range $0 to $10, for Ms. A, Ms. B, and Ms. C. The shapes of the utility functions for these individuals are said to be **concave, linear,** and **convex,** respectively. (The significance of the difference between the solid and dashed curves in Figures 9.1a and 9.1c is discussed below.) Suppose that all three women make decisions according to expected utility. We can show that Ms. A, Ms. B, and Ms. C will make, in turn, risk-averse, risk-neutral, and risk-seeking decisions, in the senses that these terms were defined in Chapter 8.

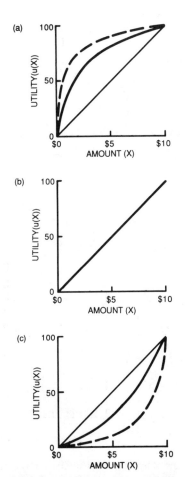

FIGURE 9.1. Monetary utility curves for (a) Ms. A (concave, risk averse), (b) Ms. B (linear, risk neutral), and (c) Ms. C (convex, risk seeking).

Consider a specific case. Imagine that Ms. A is given a choice between an outright gift of $3.50 and a chance to play

Gamble $G^* =$ (Spade, $8; Non-spade, $2)

In the latter, Ms. A selects a card at random from an ordinary deck of playing cards. If the card is a spade, she gets a prize of $8; if the card is from any other suit, she wins only $2. Clearly, the expected value of Gamble G^* is

$$EV(G^*) = (¼)($8) + (¾)($2) = $3.50$$

Figure 9.2a shows an enlargement of the solid utility curve for Ms. A. Notice that, for Ms. A, the utility of $3.50 is

$$u($3.50) = u(EV(G^*)) \approx 75$$

Therefore, Ms. A will take the $3.50 gift instead of Gamble G^* only if the expected utility of the gamble is no greater than 75 **utiles** or utility units. Now, again consulting Figure 9.2a, we see that

$$u($8) \approx 96$$

and

$$u($2) \approx 60$$

Thus, we find that the expected utility of Gamble G^* is

$$EU(G^*) = (¼)(96) + (¾)(60) \approx 69$$

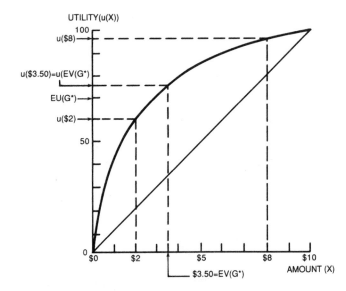

FIGURE 9.2. Close-ups of Ms. A's solid monetary utility curve: (a) Illustration of the relationship between curve shape and risk-taking behavior, assuming decision making according to expected utility. (b) Illustration of risk premium interpretations. Note: Gamble $G^* =$ (Spade, $8; Non-spade, $2).

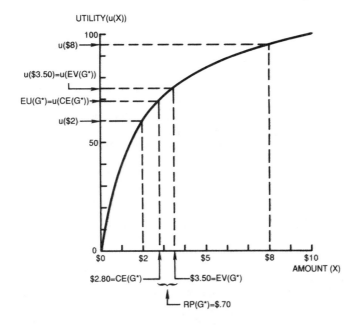

FIGURE 9.2. (continued)

And so, since

$$u(\$3.50) \approx 75 > \mathrm{EU}(G^*) \approx 69$$

Ms. A indeed does choose the gift of $3.50.

There is nothing unique about Gamble G^*. It simply illustrates a general principle: If a utility function is concave, a decision maker who maximizes expected utility will always choose a sure thing over a prospect whose expected value is identical to that sure thing. That is, the decision maker's behavior will be risk aversive. Similarly, if such a decision maker has a linear utility function, for example, Ms. B, that individual's decisions will be risk neutral. Finally, if the relevant utility function is convex, for instance, for Ms. C in Figure 9.1, the decision maker will choose in a risk-seeking manner. It might be useful to convince yourself of the latter two assertions in the case of Gamble G^* for Ms. B and Ms. C.

We can also speak of *degrees* of risk aversion and risk seeking. Suppose that Decision Maker 1's behavior is more risk aversive than that of Decision Maker 2, and that each is asked to state the outright gift such that he or she is indifferent between that gift and the opportunity to play Gamble G^*. Then the amount stated by Decision Maker 1 should be less than that stated by Decision Maker 2; the risk implicit in Gamble G^* makes it *especially* unattractive for Decision Maker 1.

Indifference amounts like those articulated by Decision Makers 1 and 2 are called **certainty equivalents (CE)**; they are to be received for certain and are considered equivalent to the indicated risky prospects. Suppose we denote a certainty equivalent for Gamble G^* by $CE(G^*)$. Then the following is the decision maker's **risk premium (RP)** for that prospect:

$$RP(G^*) = EV(G^*) - CE(G^*)$$

In words, the risk premium is the difference between the expected value of a prospect and the guaranteed outcome that is considered just as attractive as that prospect. Put another way, it is the amount of expected value the decision maker is willing to "give up," perhaps to avoid the risk entailed by the prospect. Thus, the risk premium for risk-shy Decision Maker 1 should be greater than that for Decision Maker 2.

Suppose that a decision maker, for example, Ms. A, not only chooses according to expected utility, but evaluates prospects on that basis, too. Then we can infer that individual's risk premium for a prospect from his or her utility function. Refer to Figure 9.2b, which is the same as Figure 9.2a, with a few additions. Start with the expected utility of Gamble G^*,

$$EU(G^*) = 69$$

If Ms. A were asked to state a certainty equivalent for Gamble G^*, she would report an amount of money $CE(G^*)$ that has the same utility, that is,

$$u(CE(G^*)) = EU(G^*) = 69$$

Observe that the sum of money with utility 69 is $2.80, that is,

$$u(\$2.80) = 69$$

Thus, we know that Ms. A's certainty equivalent for Gamble G^* must be

$$CE(G^*) = \$2.80$$

So her risk premium for the gamble would be

$$RP(G^*) = EV(G^*) - CE(G^*) = \$3.50 - \$2.80 = \$0.70$$

which is positive, indicating risk aversion.

The strength of an expected utility maximizer's risk attitude (Chapter 8) traditionally has been taken to be indicated by the degree of concavity or convexity of the utility function (Pratt, 1964). Thus, the more concave the curve happens to be, the more strongly that individual's decisions exhibit risk aversion. For instance, if Ms. A's utility function were the dashed one shown in Figure 9.1a instead of the solid one, then she would be especially risk averse; for the same prospects, corresponding risk premiums would be larger. Similarly, the dashed utility curve shown in Figure 9.1c would indicate greater risk seeking on the part of Ms. C than the corresponding solid curve. Risk premiums implied by each function would be negative, markedly so for the dashed function.

St. Petersburg revisited

We can now make sense out of Bernoulli's (1738/1954) hypothesized explanation of people's lukewarm reactions to the St. Petersburg game. The argument is that the typical individual decides according to expected utility and that his or her monetary utility function is concave. That is, people's choices are normally risk aversive. Bernoulli proposed a particular form of concave utility function for money. That utility function, along with many others, implies that the expected utility for the St. Petersburg game is finite. Accordingly, the decision maker should *not* be willing to "sell the farm" to make enough money for a ticket to the game.

EXPECTED UTILITY PRINCIPLES AS DESCRIPTIONS

Is it indeed the case, as implied by Bernoulli, that people typically make decisions in agreement with expected utility decision principles? In this section we consider the evidence.

Some preliminary remarks

Before we proceed, it is worth noting that two kinds of expected utility are commonly recognized. The distinction rests on the probabilities that are used in the expectations. In the broad sense, the expression "expected utility" implies that the probabilities might arise from any source. In the narrow sense, the expression is interpreted to mean that the probabilities are "objective" ones. That is, they are the kinds of probabilities that a statistician might compute by probability theory, starting from plausible assumptions about the given situation or from records concerning the relative frequencies of similar events in the past (see Chapter 5). The term **subjective expected utility (SEU)** describes the case when the probabilities are the decision maker's probability judgments (Edwards, 1961; Savage, 1954).

A few more observations before we continue. You may be inclined to reject expectation models out of hand as descriptions of how people decide. For one thing, you might contend, the computations they entail are far too complicated for any normal human being to do. Second, you cannot recall having done similar things yourself. On the first point, as indicated in Chapter 8, no one ever seriously thought that people literally perform the calculations implicit in expectation models. Instead, it was argued that people behave *as if* they make those computations; the details of how they arrive at their decisions almost certainly would be different from the arithmetic of calculating expectations. On the second point: Introspection about one's own thought processes can sometimes be helpful. However, there is plenty of evidence that we often mislead ourselves about how we think (see Ericsson and Simon, 1980; Nisbett and Wilson, 1977). In those cases, carefully constructed experiments provide more trustworthy evidence.

If we can set aside the previous objections, a deceptively optimistic appraisal of expected utility suggests itself: Expected utility principles seem bound to agree with much of our decision behavior. Why? Expected utility theory, or simply **utility theory**, as it is sometimes described, rests on three basic ideas. First, there is the effect of value. Utility theory says that how we value potential outcomes influences our decisions; the more highly valued an outcome is, the more favorably disposed we are toward alternatives that promise to deliver that outcome. Next, there is the effect of uncertainty. Utility theory claims that our opinions about the likelihood of various outcomes affect our decisions; good chances of attractive outcomes move us toward an option; similar likelihoods of unappealing outcomes have the opposite effect. Finally, there is the notion of a **combination rule**, the means of synthesizing the influences of both value and uncertainty. Utility theory says that the combination is interactive. Thus, differences in the likelihoods of various outcomes matter little unless the outcomes themselves are significant to us, that is, have great value. Conversely, differences in significant outcomes are increasingly important as they are accompanied by larger differences in likelihood.

All three of the basic ideas underlying utility theory are uncontroversial. In fact, some would say that they are only common sense: *Of course* Felicia Pine will take into account how much she likes various law schools when she decides where to apply. *Of course* she will consider her chances of being admitted before investing her time and money applying to Ivy State. In deciding whether to apply there, *of course* she weighs her chances of being admitted against her attraction to the school in the first place. How could utility theory possibly be wrong? Is it thus trivial and vacuous?

Despite misgivings such as the above, some investigators have tested utility theory using an essentially correlational approach. That is, they have observed or placed people into fairly naturalistic situations where their values and likelihood judgments have been measured or assumed. They have then examined the extent to which the subjects' decisions are predicted by expectations computed with those utilities and subjective probabilities. In view of the previous observations, you will probably find it unsurprising that the predictions tend to correlate highly with subjects' decisions (for example, in the classic test by Mosteller and Nogee, 1951).

Although the conclusions of correlational studies might seem obvious, those tests were necessary. (Beware of the hindsight biases of Chapter 4.) Even seemingly obvious assumptions need to be tested, since they are sometimes wrong. However, more often either of two alternative tacks has been taken to testing utility theory as an account for decision behavior. Both essentially concede that people's decisions are largely consistent with the theory. The first of these alternative approaches has focussed on the two key factors emphasized by utility theory, that is, decision makers' opinions about uncertainty and their values. Studies within this approach have sought detailed understanding of those contributors, a pursuit that is far from trivial. For instance, all the work described in Chapters 2 to 7 has been about people's likelihood judgments. Analogously, researchers have also tried to understand the specifics of how people value outcomes. Broadly, Bernoulli's assertion that the typical utility function is concave can be seen in this light. That assertion is very specific, falsifiable, and thus nonvacuous. And, as we will discover, its truth is quite limited.

The second of these alternative testing approaches has paid special attention to utility theory's combination rule, the claim that uncertainty and value influence people's decisions interactively, via the probability × utility feature of expectations. It is accepted that perhaps most of the time people do indeed at least "try" to make such tradeoffs. However, investigators have looked for and, as we will see, found circumstances where people systematically and unequivocally do *not* adhere to these rules. Thus, the obvious is not so obvious after all. We now turn to an example.

Uncle Harvey

Imagine that you had a long-lost rich uncle, Harvey, who recently passed away. Uncle Harvey was not only long-lost and rich, but also had a keen sense of humor. In his will, he instructed his executor to offer you a choice between the following alternatives:

Option I: You are awarded $1,000,000 from Uncle Harvey's estate, simple as that.

Option II: You play a lottery. You are to place 1000 bingo balls into a large bin, 100 red balls (10%), 890 white balls (89%), and 10 blue balls (1%). You then pick one ball at random ("No peeking!" Uncle Harvey's will insists). If the selected ball is red, you are awarded $5,000,000; if you pick a white ball, you get $1,000,000; if you draw one of the blue balls, you get nothing, $0.

Which alternative do you take, Option I or Option II?

Now imagine that a revised version of Uncle Harvey's will is discovered. In this new will, you are offered a choice between *these* two alternatives:

Option I*:   You again play a lottery. You place 1000 bingo balls into the large bin, 110 orange balls (11%) and 890 purple ones (89%). You then pick a ball at random. If the selected ball is orange, you are awarded $1,000,000; otherwise, you get nothing, $0.

Option II*: There is yet another lottery. This time you fill the bin with 100 yellow balls (10%) and 900 green ones (90%), for a total of 1000. You are then allowed to select a ball at random. If it is yellow, you get $5,000,000 from the estate, otherwise nothing, $0.

Once more, what is your pleasure, Option I* or Option II*?

Most people, when presented with the situations just described, choose Option I in the first and Option II* in the second. Let us suppose that you did too. (Did you?) We now show that such a choice pattern would be impossible had you made your decisions according to the most straightforward interpretation of expected utility theory (see also Coombs, Dawes, and Tversky, 1970, pp. 126–128).

Let us represent your utility function for money by $u(\$X)$, where $\$X$ is an arbitrary amount of cash. Then your expected utilities for Options I and II would be, respectively,

$$EU(I) = u(\$1,000,000)$$

and

$$EU(II) = (0.10)u(\$5,000,000) + (0.89)u(\$1,000,000) + (0.01)u(\$0).$$

If you preferred Option I to Option II and you chose as if maximizing expected utility, we infer that

$$EU(I) > EU(II)$$

After working through the algebra, you will see that this is equivalent to saying that

$$(0.11)u(\$1,000,000) > (0.10)u(\$5,000,000) + (0.01)u(\$0)$$

Now let us consider Uncle Harvey's revised will. The expected utilities of Options I* and II* are

$$EU(I^*) = (0.11)u(\$1,000,000) + (0.89)u(\$0)$$

and

$$EU(II^*) = (0.10)u(\$5,000,000) + (0.90)u(\$0)$$

Given that you preferred Option II*, we infer that

$$EU(II^*) > EU(I^*)$$

It is easy to show that this is the same as saying that

$$(0.10)u(\$5,000,000) + (0.01)u(\$0) > (0.11)u(\$1,000,000)$$

which is exactly opposite of what was implied by your choice in the first situation. We thus conclude that you could not possibly have decided via expected utility maximization.

The structures of the options in the Uncle Harvey case are due to the economist Allais (1953). The pattern of choices, which appears to violate utility theory, has come to be known as the **Allais Phenomenon** or the **Allais Paradox**. It is representative of strong tests of utility theory in which it is unnecessary to do things like measure individuals' utility functions (see also, for example, Coombs and Huang, 1976). Instead, situations are carefully structured such that the mere preference ordering of the alternatives allows us to infer whether the theory is being violated.

A summary view

So what can we conclude about the adequacy of utility theory as a description of how people decide under conditions of uncertainty? Two conclusions seem warranted. One is that expected utility maximization is a decent first approximation of people's actual decision behavior in many situations. On the other hand, however, there have been many demonstrations of systematic discrepancies between people's decisions and what utility theory would predict; the theory's obviousness is misleading. The Allais Phenomenon is just one such example. We will see several others in later chapters. It seems clear that we do not always decide as if according to expected utility.

Part of the key to this puzzling situation is that the descriptiveness of utility theory depends on how closely we examine people's behavior. In the "big picture," for example, in correlational studies, utility theory frequently does quite well as an account for how people decide; at the level of microscopic detail, the account is often flawed. Another part of the key concerns the character of the decision situation. As implied in later chapters, there are certain circumstances that are especially likely to encourage people to decide in ways that conflict with utility theory's demands.

EXPECTED UTILITY AS A PRESCRIPTION

For the moment, leave aside the question of how we actually decide. In burglary suspect Charlie Y.'s case, we have seen examples of utility theory's prescriptions for people's decisions. But why should we follow such prescriptions? Would doing so really be in our interests?

The long run

Suppose that the relevant prospects all involve quantitative outcomes, for instance, money, time, or lives saved. Suppose further that each prospect will be repeated many times, and that the decision maker's ultimate aim is to be as well off as possible in the long run. One example of the type of situation in mind is that described in Chapter 8 (pp. 225–26). There you were presented with a choice among Gambles G1, G2, and G3, where it was understood that the selected gamble would be played repeatedly. Perhaps a more realistic illustrative situation would be that faced by a large life insurance company. The company is considering two small policies. Suppose that, based on current mortality tables, the expected net profit for the company on each issue of Policy A is $5000, while that for Policy B is $5500. The decision is which policy to offer to the public. The firm can expect to sell thousands of whichever policy is chosen.

We saw in Chapter 8 (pp. 226–27) that the Law of Large Numbers applies in circumstances like that described. In particular, it says that, over many repetitions of a prospect, say N of them, the total outcome should be very close to N times the expected value of the prospect. Thus, if 2000 customers bought Policy A above, the total profit to the insurance company would be about

$$2000 \times \$5000 = \$10,000,000$$

The corresponding profit from selling Policy B would be in the vicinity of $11,000,000. The insurance company, like everyone else, prefers more money to less. So, as was concluded previously, the most sensible strategy for a person faced with decisions like the present ones is to maximize expected value. Expected utility prescriptions do not always agree with expected value prescriptions, for example, when the decision maker's utility function for money is concave or convex. Thus, if the decision maker followed expected utility, he or she could easily choose an alternative that is virtually certain to leave him or her worse off than had a competing option been chosen. For instance, it might have led you to select Gamble G1 (EV = $3.50) over Gamble G2 (EV = $4.00). We therefore conclude that deciding via expected utility is not the appropriate thing to do.

The short run

Let us suppose, as is often the case, that the decision maker's selected prospect will be executed only once or at most a few times. A good example is Felicia Pine's law school application decision. In such unique situations, long-run considerations clearly are irrelevant. Another important difference from the previous situations is that at least some of the significant outcomes of Ms. Pine's decision are nonquantitative, for example, the scholarly atmosphere at Central University versus that at Ivy State. Although expected value principles do not apply under these conditions, a good case can be made for expected *utility* principles.

Strong justifications for expected utility date from watershed mathematical developments by von Neumann and Morgenstern (1947). Similar results and extensions have been proved by several others since then (see Schoemaker, 1982).[1] The distinctions among the analyses involve differing assumptions about the decision situations as well as the decision maker. The developments by Luce and Raiffa (1957) are probably the easiest to understand and are thus chosen for discussion here.

The Luce and Raiffa axioms The following is a useful way to think about what Luce and Raiffa's (1957) results mean:

Principles P1, P2, ..., P7 are seven basic principles of decision making. Such principles are examples of **axioms** or **postulates**. Suppose that the decision maker carefully considers each principle and agrees that it is reasonable. In particular, the decision maker thinks it is important to make decisions that are consistent with all these principles. A crude analogy to these principles might be the "Golden Rule," which says, "Do unto others as you would have them do unto you," and which you might adopt as a guide for your interpersonal relationships. The theorem proved by Luce and Raiffa implies that, if a person decides according to expected utility, then he or she can be assured that the resulting decisions indeed *will* conform to the stated basic principles. In other words, an important advantage provided by expected utility is that it prevents the decision maker from violating fundamental principles considered to be essential. Literally, it forces the decision maker to be true to his or her ideals.

We now examine the Luce and Raiffa axioms, Principles P1 to P7. For concreteness, we do so in the context of Felicia Pine's law school application decision situation.[2] As the discussion proceeds, ask yourself if you would want your *own* decisions to agree with each principle.

Context: Finite outcomes. There is a finite set of outcomes under consideration.

---

[1]Fishburn (1970, Parts II and III) and Roberts (1979, Chapters 7 and 8) present good, systematic treatments of these ideas. However, they presume a fair amount of mathematical experience.

[2]"Felicia Pine" is a real person (different name, of course) who was actually considering applying to law school. The interchange that is described is very similar to that which really occurred.

In our example, Felicia Pine tells us that she is considering only five different law schools, those at "Premier University," "Central University," "Ivy State University," "the University of the West," and "Diamond Institute."

Principle P1: Comparability of outcomes. For any two outcomes, the decision maker either prefers one to the other or is indifferent between them. The decision maker never says, "I just can't compare them."

In the following dialogue, "I" denotes the interviewer, "FP" Felicia Pine:

> I   Suppose we take any two of your five schools, say, Ivy State and Diamond Institute. Can you tell me which you prefer, or, if you can't do that, would it be reasonable to say that you are indifferent?
>
> FP   Absolutely! I've really looked into these places.
>
> I   Do you think that you should always be able to compare outcomes this way?
>
> FP   Well,…I'm not so sure about that. You know, sometimes it's like comparing apples and oranges. I mean, like how can you compare a vacation to getting a new transmission for your car?
>
> I   But don't you still find yourself *eventually* choosing in such situations, or at least saying that you don't care?
>
> FP   Well, I suppose you are right. So I guess I'll go along with your first principle. I'm still a bit uncomfortable with it, though.

Principle P2: Transitivity of outcome preferences. Suppose that A, B, and C are three outcomes such that the decision maker indicates that $A \geq_p B$ and $B \geq_p C$. In such circumstances, the decision maker always indicates that $A \geq_p C$, too. In this notation, $\geq_p$ means "is at least as preferred as" or "is not less preferred than."

The dialogue:

> I   Pick any three schools A, B, and C such that you like A at least as much as B and B at least as much as C.
>
> FP   I prefer Central to West and West to Diamond.
>
> I   Between Central and Diamond, which do you prefer?
>
> FP   Central, of course!
>
> I   Is there any set of schools A, B, and C, with the stated precondition, such that you would in fact prefer C to A?
>
> FP   I can't imagine saying something like that. That's silly.
>
> I   So, in general, you think that your preferences among outcomes should be transitive?
>
> FP   No doubt about it.

At this point, it now makes sense for us to speak of a preference ordering over the entire set of outcomes. For convenience, we suppose that Ms. Pine's preference ordering over her prospective law schools is as follows:

> Premier University $\geq_P$
> Central University $\geq_P$
> Ivy State University $\geq_P$
> University of the West $\geq_P$
> Diamond Institute

In such circumstances, it is meaningful to acknowledge a BEST outcome, which is at least as appealing as any other, for example, Premier University. Similarly, there is a WORST outcome, which is not preferred to any of the other outcomes, for instance, Diamond Institute. To rule out degeneracy, we assume that the BEST outcome is strictly preferred over the WORST.

Principle P3: Reduction of compound prospects. There is no attraction or aversion to gambling. Functionally, the only things that matter when choosing between two prospects are the ultimate outcomes and their probabilities, as calculated via probability theory. In particular, outcomes that are contingent on compound events make a prospect neither more nor less attractive.

The dialogue:

I   Ms. Pine, imagine the following fantasy. Suppose that all the law schools in this country enter a special agreement. Prospective students are first screened to meet minimal standards of acceptability. Admission to the schools a student considers suitable is then decided by lottery. Okay?

FP   Seems bizarre, but I'll go along with it.

I   Thanks. Consider Lottery C, which is displayed in Figure 9.3a. In the first stage of the lottery, you draw a ball at random from an urn containing 1000 balls, 500 of which are red, the remainder white. If a white ball is drawn, you are admitted to the law school at the University of the West. If a red is picked, you go on to the second stage of the gamble. There, you draw from an urn with 500 blue balls and 500 green ones. If you select green, you again are admitted to West; otherwise, you are accepted at Central University. Clear?

FP   Clear.

I   Now examine Lottery S, which is shown in Figure 9.3b. In this lottery, you randomly pick a ball from an urn with 250 yellow balls and 750 black ones. If you select a yellow ball, you are accepted at Central, otherwise at West. Okay?

FP   Fine.

I   Suppose you had to choose between Lotteries C and S. Which would you pick, or would you be indifferent?

(a)

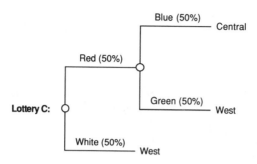

(b)

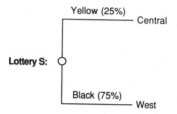

FIGURE 9.3. Lotteries illustrating the Reduction of Compound Prospects Principle. This principle implies that Felicia Pine should be indifferent between compound Lottery C, in (a), and simple Lottery S, in (b).

FP   Oh, Lottery C, for sure. I like Central better than West.

I   You *really* prefer Lottery C? Are you aware that the chances of getting into the schools are the same in both lotteries?

FP   You're kidding, right?

I   Not at all. Does that change your mind?

FP   Yeah, it does. Which law school I get into is serious business. So the only thing I care about is the chance of getting into the better school. *If* what you said is true, that the chances are the same in both lotteries, then I really don't care which lottery I play.

I   So, would you say that, in general in situations like this, you would be indifferent between lotteries in which the ultimate chances of the same outcomes are identical?

FP   Actually, no, I wouldn't. It depends on whether I'm playing for "fun" or for "keeps." If I'm really trying to make money or something, the only thing that matters to me is the actual chance of getting ahead. But if I'm at a party trying to have a good time, the excitement of playing the game is what's important. I'd want to sort of string things out. Know what I mean?

I   Sure, lots of people feel that way.

Principle P4: Continuity. Take any arbitrary outcome, say A. There is a probability p_A such that the decision maker is indifferent between experiencing A for sure and an *indifference lottery* that promises the BEST outcome with probability p_A, and otherwise the WORST outcome.

The dialogue:

I   Think about the situation shown in Figure 9.4. You are given a choice between a flat-out acceptance at Ivy State and a lottery, which we have called "Lottery L_{Ivy}." The lottery is such that you select one ball at random from an urn containing 1000 balls total, some of them red, the others white. If a red ball is selected, you are admitted to your top choice, Premier. Otherwise, you are accepted at Diamond, the law school that is least attractive, among those you would consider attending. Okay so far?

FP   Sure, but how many reds and whites are there in the urn?

I   That's where you come in. My question is this: Is there some composition of the urn such that you would be *indifferent* between the lottery and guaranteed admission to Ivy State? If so, what is it?

FP   That's a toughie. I feel like there *has* to be such a composition, but I'm hard-pressed to tell you what it is. (After a few moments.) Oh, what the heck ..., I'll say about 600 reds.

I   Fine. Am I to understand that, in general, you feel that in situations like this there should be an urn composition such that you would be indifferent between the sure thing and a lottery promising either the BEST or WORST outcome, contingent on drawing from that urn?

FP   Yeah. I feel kind of funny about this one, but I suppose it's reasonable.

We thus conclude that, for Felicia Pine, the *indifference probability* for admission to Ivy State is $p_{Ivy} = 60\%$, and that she accepts the continuity principle, even if a bit reluctantly.

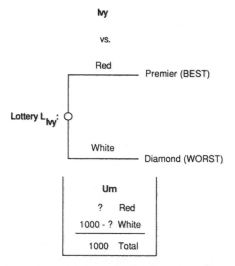

FIGURE 9.4. Illustration of the Continuity Principle. According to that principle, there should be some composition of the urn such that Felicia Pine is indifferent between outright admission to Ivy State and playing Lottery L_{Ivy}. She says that this composition consists of 600 red balls and 400 white ones.

Principle P5: Substitutability. Any outcome and its indifference lottery can substitute for each other in any situation, without affecting the decision maker's decisions.

The dialogue:

I Compare Lotteries 1 and 2 in Figure 9.5. In each lottery, the percentages represent the proportions of balls of various colors in an urn, the selections of which yield the indicated outcomes. Notice that Lottery 2 is the same as Lottery 1, except for one difference. Guaranteed admission to Ivy State is replaced by the lottery you previously indicated to be just as attractive as admission to Ivy State.

FP Sure, I see the difference. What's the question?

I Simple: Which do you prefer, Lottery 1, Lottery 2, or are you indifferent?

FP Gee! I know that I *should* be indifferent. But Lottery 2 sure does look better! I think that what makes it look so good is that it offers

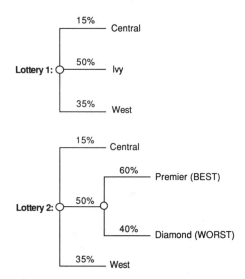

FIGURE 9.5.   Illustration of the Substitutability Principle. This principle says that, given her previous indication of indifference between outright admission to Ivy State and Lottery L_{Ivy}, with the urn composition being 600 red balls and 400 white, Felicia Pine should be indifferent between Lotteries 1 and 2.

at least a *chance* of getting into Premier. Nevertheless, I'll be consistent with what I said before and say I'm indifferent. That's what you wanted to hear, right?

I   Hey, in the decision business, the customer is always right! At any rate, am I to assume that Principle P5 is acceptable to you?

FP   Okay, I'll go along with that.

Principle P6: Transitivity of prospect preferences.   Preferences over prospects, for example, lotteries, are transitive. That is, if Prospect 1 $\geq_P$ Prospect 2 and Prospect 2 $\geq_P$ Prospect 3, then it is always true that Prospect 1 $\geq_P$ Prospect 3.

Felicia Pine readily accepts Principle P6.

Principle P7: Monotonicity.   Suppose that p and q are probabilities such that $p \geq q$. Then Prospect Q is not preferred to Prospect P, where Prospect P = $(p,$ BEST; $1 - p,$ WORST$)$ and Prospect Q = $(q,$ BEST; $1 - q,$ WORST$)$. And, conversely, if we start with alternatives with the forms of Prospects P and Q, with Prospect Q not preferred to Prospect P, it is always the case that $p \geq q$. Essentially, the attractiveness of prospects improves with increasing probabilities of attractive outcomes.

The dialogue with Felicia Pine:

> I   Examine Lotteries 1 and 2 in Figure 9.6. Observe that, in Lottery 1, if you select a red ball from Urn 1, you are admitted to Premier, your most attractive law school. If you pick a white ball, you get into Diamond, your least appealing but acceptable school. Lottery 2 is similar, except that the outcomes are contingent on drawing from Urn 2. The only difference between the compositions of the urns is that there is one more good ball in Urn 2 than in Urn 1. Suppose you had the opportunity to choose between the lotteries. Would you have a preference and, if so, for which lottery?
>
> FP   I don't have *strong* feelings, but of course I'd pick Lottery 2. Who wouldn't, assuming that they like Premier better than Diamond?
>
> I   So you think that Principle P7 is a sensible rule to follow?
>
> FP   Absolutely. It's about the best you've come up with so far.

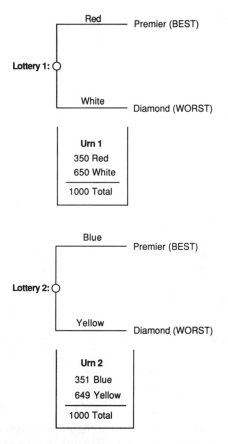

FIGURE 9.6. Illustration of the Monotonicity Principle. If this principle applies, Felicia Pine will prefer Lottery 2 to Lottery 1.

Prescriptive Conclusion. Suppose that a person such as Felicia Pine thinks it is important that his or her decisions never conflict with the ideals represented by Principles P1 to P7. Luce and Raiffa (1957, p. 29) show that this will be assured if that individual always decides according to expected utility. Just how this can be done is illustrated in the case of Felicia Pine's law school application (p. 264).

Descriptive Conclusion. Luce and Raiffa's theorem also has a descriptive interpretation. Suppose that a person's actual behavior is indeed always consistent with Principles P1 to P7. Then that individual can be described as deciding by expected utility. Certain of the basic principles are **necessary**, for example, P7, monotonicity. This means that, if the person decides according to expected utility, that principle *has* to be satisfied. Put another way, if a condition necessary for utility theory is *not* fulfilled, we immediately know that expected utility cannot be followed, either. Looking to see whether people violate necessary conditions is thus an especially powerful way of testing utility theory (see Coombs and Huang, 1976; MacCrimmon, 1968).

The significance of fidelity to basic principles Back to the problem of prescription, how a person *should* decide. Developments like those of Luce and Raiffa indicate that deciding on the basis of expected utility prevents the decision maker from violating various principles he or she sees as desirable. But why is this important?

The situation is completely analogous to that we encountered in Chapter 5, when we discussed the coherence of likelihood judgments. One reason some people care about rules such as Luce and Raiffa's Principles P1 to P7 is that violations of those rules are offensive to their senses of **logical esthetics**. To some folks, an unkempt lawn offends their tastes in how neighborhoods ought to look; it violates people's principles of residential esthetics. Similarly, violations of rules such as monotonicity, Principle P7, are uncomfortable because they conflict with people's ingrained tastes about what is logically reasonable. Deciding according to expected utility would prevent such discomfort.

You might scoff, "That's all well and good, but I can't eat 'logical esthetics.' What will maintaining consistency with Principles P1 to P7 do for me *tangibly*?" It has been shown that, if a decision maker reliably violates certain of the principles underlying utility theory, that individual can be victimized in **material traps**. Recall from Chapter 5 that a material trap is a series of transactions (perhaps one) in which one party, the victim, is guaranteed to be materially no better off after the transactions are completed than he or she was before. Thus, deciding according to expected utility protects one from material traps. An example illustrates the possibilities.

Picture yourself strolling around an art fair. There are three comparably priced art objects that appeal to you: a painting, a glass figurine, and a ceramic pot. It so happens that your preferences among these objects are intransitive; that is, they violate Principle P2. Specifically, you like the painting better than the figurine, the figurine better than the pot, but the pot better than the painting. We follow you around the art fair and watch you engage in several transactions.

Transaction 1: In the pottery section, you come across the pot. Since you like it, you buy it. Your current position: You own the pot.

Transaction 2: You make your way to the glass section and observe that your friend "Tom Thorne" has bought the glass figurine you find so appealing. Tom sort of likes your pot, although he is not "crazy" about it. Nevertheless, he agrees to give you the figurine in exchange for the pot plus $5. Your current position: You own the figurine, less $5.

Transaction 3: You eventually arrive at the painting section and discover the attractive painting, just as your neighbor "Rita Phelan" has bought it. You strike a deal with Rita. She gives you the painting in exchange for the figurine and $5. Your current position: You own the painting, less $10.

Transaction 4: As you are about to go home, you run across Tom Thorne again. Recall that you like Tom's pot more than your painting. Despite your mutual embarrassment, he agrees to give you back the pot, in exchange for the painting and $5. Your current position: You own the pot, less $15.

Note that, after the fourth transaction, you are in the same position you were after the first, but $15 poorer. In principle, this vicious cycle could continue indefinitely, with you playing the role of a **money pump**. The reason the cycle can exist is that your preferences are intransitive. You may or may not realize why things are going so badly for you. But in such a transparent situation, it will be obvious to you that *something* is awry, and you simply stop trading.

Perhaps you protest, "This is really far-fetched. *Nobody* has reliable intransitive preferences." Not true. It is indeed the case that, when people recognize that their preferences are intransitive, they usually consider those preferences to be mistakes and then change them. But they might not notice. Tversky (1969) has shown how one can construct situations in which some people consistently exhibit intransitive preferences; so has Montgomery (1977).

Now you might say, "Well, suppose people *do* sometimes violate principles so that they are vulnerable to material traps. These mythical material traps just might not be 'out there.' Situations like the one you described are so contrived, they are bound to be rare." This may well be true. No one has carefully studied naturally occurring situations to gain a sense of how hostile the world really is. But should you take the chance?

DECISION ANALYSIS

The term **decision analysis** describes a growing collection of techniques for assisting people to make decisions (see von Winterfeldt and Edwards, 1986; Weinstein and Fineberg, 1980). The expression is appropriately beginning to assume a very broad meaning. But it is still most often used to refer to methods that help the decision maker to decide according to expected utility. In this section we briefly illustrate and discuss essential elements of decision analysis as applied expected utility theory.

Felicia Pine's law school application decision

Suppose that Felicia Pine's law school situation has developed further. Recall that her preference ordering over the five schools that are acceptable to her is as follows, from most to least preferred: 1 - Premier University; 2 - Central University; 3 - Ivy State University; 4 - University of the West; and 5 - Diamond Institute. Diamond Institute has a very inexpensive application fee and an early admissions policy. Ms. Pine has already been accepted there. She has also applied to her top two schools, Premier and Central. But she has only enough time and money to apply to one more, either Ivy State or West. The problem is which. Let us see how decision analysis might be used in her situation.

A large part of decision analysis has nothing to do with rules such as expected utility. Instead, it entails arriving at a good understanding of the situation with which the decision maker is faced. This process is sometimes called **structuring** the decision problem (von Winterfeldt, 1980). In effect, the decision analyst and the decision maker build a model of the essential elements of the situation and how those elements relate to one another. Typically, the model includes a decision tree. In Felicia Pine's case, the decision tree happens to be very simple, as depicted in Figure 9.7. Often, the mere structuring exercise itself is helpful. It also assists in the later stages of the decision analysis, when expected utilities are computed.

The first step on the road to obtaining expected utilities is measuring utilities for the potential outcomes. Expected utility theory allows the utilities for two of the outcomes to be assigned arbitrarily. A common convention is to set the utilities for the most and least preferred outcomes as u(BEST) = 100 and u(WORST) = 0, respectively. Thus, in Felicia Pine's case, we have u(Premier) = 100 and u(Diamond) = 0.

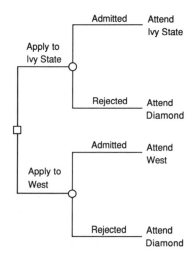

FIGURE 9.7. Decision tree representation of Felicia Pine's law school application decision problem.

The measurement procedure then assumes that, for simple prospects, the decision maker actually does decide according to expected utilities. To obtain the utilities for the remaining, nonextreme outcomes, the decision maker describes the indifference lotteries for each of those outcomes. Recall that the indifference lottery for a given outcome promises either the BEST or the WORST outcome, contingent on a random process for which the canonical probabilities of various outcomes are obvious, for example, selecting balls from an urn. Specifically, it is the lottery of that form such that the decision maker is indifferent between playing the lottery and experiencing the given outcome for sure. Previously, we found that Felicia Pine was indifferent between guaranteed admission to Ivy State and the lottery (60%, Premier (BEST); 40%, Diamond (WORST)). We therefore conclude that

EU(Guaranteed Ivy State admission) = EU(Ivy State indifference lottery)

But

$$EU(\text{Guaranteed Ivy State admission}) = u(\text{Ivy State})$$

and

$$
\begin{aligned}
EU(\text{Ivy State indifference lottery}) &= (0.60) \, u(\text{Premier}) + (0.40) \, u(\text{Diamond}) \\
&= (0.60) \, (100) + (0.40) \, (0) \\
&= 60
\end{aligned}
$$

So we infer that $u(\text{Ivy State}) = 60$.

Similar reasoning from additional responses led to the following complete listing of Felicia Pine's utilities shown in the second column below:

OUTCOME	u(OUTCOME)	r(OUTCOME)
Premier (BEST)	100	100
Central	80	90
Ivy State	60	85
West	50	75
Diamond (WORST)	0	0

To illustrate a point, Felicia Pine was also asked to rate the attractiveness of the various law schools on a 0 to 100 point scale, with the restrictions that 100 should be assigned to the most appealing school and 0 to the least. Her responses are listed in the third column above. Why should the attractiveness ratings differ from the utility measures? It is possible that the differences are nothing more than measurement error. In general, however, such differences are taken to have substantive meaning. For one thing, while the utilities were inferred from actual decisions, Ms. Pine had nothing at stake when she reported the ratings. It is also thought that, whereas utilities reveal a person's feelings about risk, ratings do not.

Let us be more explicit on the latter distinction. Felicia Pine's utilities were derived from her indifferences for lotteries. Those lotteries involved both valued outcomes *and* uncertainty—risk. Thus, Ms. Pine's indifferences should have reflected two things: (1) how she feels about attending each school, and (2) her attitude toward risk. Recall that, when Felicia Pine was asked to rate the attractiveness of the law schools, there was no mention of uncertainty. So, in a sense, the ratings should have provided a purer measure of her feelings about the schools themselves, a measure uncontaminated by her disposition toward uncertainty (see Krzysztofowicz, 1983). (More on such matters in the next section.) So why should Ms. Pine's ratings not be used as the utility measures in the remainder of the decision analysis? The main reason is that the decisions Ms. Pine wishes to make involve risk. Accordingly, the decision analyst *wants* the utility measures to capture both her feelings about the outcomes themselves as well as her feelings about risk.

Back to the analysis. Felicia Pine goes to visit the prelaw counselor at her college, "Leland Wagner." Dr. Wagner is considered an expert at judging students' chances of getting into various law schools, given their credentials. In his opinion, the probabilities of Felicia Pine being admitted at Ivy State University and the University of the West are 40% and 70%, respectively. Felicia Pine would go to either Ivy State or West only if she were rejected at both Premier and Central. So, as implicit in her decision tree (Figure 9.7), applying to each is a prospect in which she will attend the given school if she is admitted, or else she will go to Diamond Institute. Thus, the expected utilities of applying to these schools are

$$\text{EU (Apply to Ivy State)} = (0.40) \, u(\text{Ivy State}) + (0.60) \, u(\text{Diamond})$$
$$= (0.40) \, (60) + (0.60) \, (0)$$
$$= 24$$

and

$$\text{EU (Apply to West)} = (0.70) \, u(\text{West}) + (0.30) \, u(\text{Diamond})$$
$$= (0.70) \, (50) + (0.30) \, (0)$$
$$= 35$$

According to the calculations, the analysis implies that Ms. Pine should apply to the University of the West.

A digression: The concept of utility

The analysis of Felicia Pine's law school problem highlights a question that has probably lurked in the back of your mind since you began reading this chapter: Exactly what does the concept of utility entail? The issue is worth discussing because the everyday meaning of the term differs somewhat from its meaning among contemporary decision theorists. Indeed, the word is not used in a consistent way even by the experts.

Utility as satisfaction   In the dictionary, "utility" is a measure of usefulness. It is commonly recognized that the extent to which a thing is useful depends on the person and the context; a glass of water is indispensable if you are stranded in the Sahara Desert, but of little consequence at Niagara Falls. This usefulness interpretation is closely related to but not identical to the notion of utility as the term was used by Bernoulli (1738/1954) and in present-day economic theory. To Bernoulli, utility was the satisfaction of any sort of "want" (p. 25). Similarly, in modern economics, utility is "the satisfaction that someone receives from consuming commodities" (Lipsey, Steiner, and Purvis, 1987, p. 129; see also Henderson and Quandt, 1971, Chapter 2). This kind of utility-as-satisfaction is sometimes called **Bernoullian utility.**

Recently, a more precisely defined form of Bernoullian utility has been distinguished. It measures the strength or intensity of a person's preferences (Dyer and Sarin, 1982). To understand what this means, let us return to Felicia Pine once again. Recall that Ms. Pine has already been admitted to the law school at Diamond Institute. Presumably, she experiences some satisfaction with that state of affairs. Now we ask her to imagine the following sequence of events: First, Ms. Pine receives a notice that she has been admitted to the University of the West. We then ask her, "About which admission did you feel better, to Diamond or to West?" We know that Ms. Pine would freely choose to attend West rather than Diamond. So it is not surprising when she responds, "West." Next, Ms. Pine gets another letter, indicating that she has been accepted into the law school at Ivy State. Now we ask, "Which admission made you feel better, the one to West or the one to Ivy State?" Ms. Pine thinks she likes Ivy State's law school even better than that at the University of the West, so she says, "Ivy State." Finally, we ask: "Which was greater, the increase in satisfaction you felt when you were admitted to West, or the subsequent increase you experienced upon getting into Ivy State?"

It is possible that Felicia Pine would answer our questions on the basis of a special form of Bernoullian utility function known as a **measurable value function.** Let us denote the value function by v. Thus, it is as if in the decision maker's head there is a number $v(C)$ associated with each outcome C, such that the numbers or "values" for the outcomes are consistent with the decision maker's reported satisfaction differences. To be concrete, Ms. Pine's first answer would have followed from

$$v(\text{West}) > v(\text{Diamond})$$

and her second from

$$v(\text{Ivy State}) > v(\text{West})$$

Suppose that to our last question Ms. Pine had responded, "The increase in satisfaction was much greater when I heard from Ivy State." This would be interpreted as an indication that

$$v(\text{Ivy State}) - v(\text{West}) > v(\text{West}) - v(\text{Diamond})$$

To be even more concrete, a set of specific value assignments agreeing with these relations would be

$$
\begin{aligned}
v \text{ (Ivy State)} &= \quad 10 \\
v \text{ (West)} &= \quad\ 4 \\
v \text{ (Diamond)} &= \quad 0
\end{aligned}
$$

Of course, lots of other assignments would lead Ms. Pine to say the same things.

   Utility and feelings about risk   Notice that, as in the previous case of ratings, there was no mention of uncertainty in our questions to Felicia Pine. Thus, the above value assignments are riskless. There is a growing convention to use different terminology to describe measures of subjective worth that do and do not involve risk. Measures of subjective worth for outcomes themselves are described as **value functions**. Accordingly, Bernoullian utility functions, measurable value functions, and even ratings would be examples of value functions. In contrast, the convention says that worth measures that reflect both outcome worth and feelings about risk, for example, the ones derived in Felicia Pine's decision analysis, should be called **von Neumann–Morgenstern (vN–M) utility functions**, or simply **utility functions**. Unless indicated otherwise, these are the conventions we will follow in the remainder of the book.

   Various shapes of value functions for quantified outcomes have special meaning. Consider the concave value function for monetary gifts shown in Figure 9.8. Start at the amount $5. Observe that the corresponding value assignment is $v(\$5) = 34$. Suppose that, instead of receiving $5, the person gets $10, that is, $5 more. Since $v(\$10) = 52$, the increase in value is

$$\Delta_{\$10-\$5} = v(\$10) - v(\$5) = 52 - 34 = 18$$

Now imagine the person starting with a gift of $30. Once again, this gift is increased by $5, to $35. This time the difference in subjective value is

$$\Delta_{\$35-\$30} = v(\$35) - v(\$30) = 88 - 83 = 5$$

In each of these two scenarios, the person begins at a particular point and then experiences a relatively small or "marginal" improvement in wealth. In both cases, the increase is the same, a gain of $5. However, the increase in subjective worth or value is not; the value increment was smaller when the starting point was $30 rather than $5. This is an instance of the general phenomenon represented by a concave value function, **diminishing marginal value**, or diminishing marginal utility, in the Bernoullian sense of the term. Bernoulli (1738/1954, p. 25) contended that it is a part of the "nature of man" that value functions for wealth exhibit this property, which is sometimes attributed to satiation. That is, to the degree that a need comes close to being fulfilled, objects that satisfy that need lose their intrinsic ability to attract the person. As we will see, Bernoulli's generalization does not always hold.

   The distinction between value and utility functions allows for more refined conceptions and measures of people's reactions to risk. Consider the monetary utility function in Figure 9.9a, derived by, say, the type of indifference lottery procedure we used in Felicia Pine's decision analysis, but applied to sums of cash in the range $0 to $20. Suppose that the person in question decides according to expected utility. Since the utility function is concave, the decision maker's choices and evaluations will be risk averse (Chapter 9, pp. 244–48). But is it reasonable to say that the person is repelled

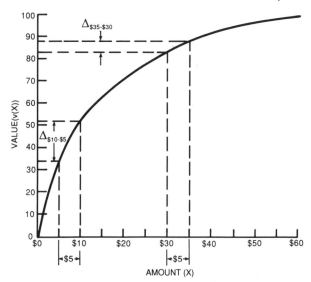

FIGURE 9.8. A concave value function for money illustrating the concept of diminishing marginal value. The significance of constant additions of money diminishes as the base to which the additions are made increases, e.g., $\Delta_{\$35 - \$30} < \Delta_{\$10 - \$5}$.

by risk itself? Perhaps not. Suppose that we also assess the decision maker's measurable value function for money. The result is shown in Figure 9.9b. Observe that the value function has even greater concavity than the utility function. The utility function reflects both the intrinsic subjective worth of money for that person (which is presumably implicated in the value function, too) *and* his or her reactions to risk. Therefore, we should conclude that our decision maker is actually *attracted* by risk. For, if the person were truly indifferent to risk, the utility function would coincide with the value function. Differences in the curvatures of value and utility functions thus provide purified indicators of a person's **true** or **relative risk attitudes**, as they are sometimes known (Dyer and Sarin, 1982; Krzysztofowicz, 1983).

The previous remarks highlight the fact that an individual's risk-taking behavior can be due to either or both of two factors. The first is how that individual feels about risk, the other how he or she feels about getting more of the outcome in question, that is, whether for that person marginal value increases or decreases. Bernoulli (1738/1954) did not explicitly acknowledge feelings about risk. Thus, he appears to have assumed that people's risk-aversive behavior was solely a consequence of diminishing marginal value.

Value and utility assessments as predictions We have been discussing value and utility assignments as if they really do describe the decision maker's feelings about the worth of potential outcomes and the risk entailed in prospects involving those outcomes. For instance, recall that the utility assignments for Felicia Pine's attending law school at Central University and Ivy State University were 80 and 60, respectively. Thus, we would expect

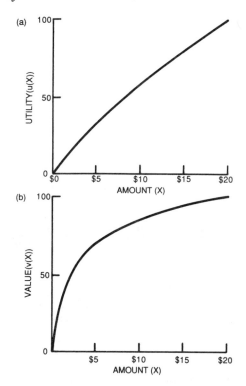

FIGURE 9.9. Concave (a) utility and (b) value functions of a single individual. The greater concavity of the value function suggests that the person is actually risk seeking rather than risk averse, in the true senses of the terms.

her to experience greater satisfaction as a student at Central rather than at Ivy State. Actually, there is no guarantee that this would be the case. In fact, in terms of expected utility theory per se, there is no necessary connection whatsoever between utility assignments and the satisfaction the decision maker might ultimately experience with the outcomes in question. All that *does* matter is that, when the assignments are used in computing the expected utilities of simple prospects, the orders of those expectations agree with the decision maker's stated preferences among the prospects.

Although expected utility theory does not care about the connection between utility assignments and reality, decision makers certainly do. In particular, the usefulness of a decision analysis is seriously jeopardized if utility assignments fail to faithfully represent the decision maker's actual satisfaction with the pertinent outcomes. And there is good reason to expect that discrepancies might exist (see Christensen-Szalanski, 1984). Utility (and value) assessments rest on the decision maker's responses to questions about hypothetical situations. Essentially, the decision maker offers predictions of how he or she would respond in circumstances that are sometimes quite unfamiliar. Like all predictions, they could be wrong.

Why do our utility and value assessments sometimes go awry as predictions? Most real-world decision outcomes—money being a notable exception—entail multiple specific outcomes that matter to us. For instance, your new job can usefully be seen as

New job = (Modest pay, Problem-solving duties, Congenial colleagues, City, ...)

and your old job as

Old job = (Good pay, Routine duties, Aloof colleagues, Suburbs, ...)

where the items in parentheses are various aspects of your jobs, each of which affects your satisfaction. Our utility and value assessments are partly the result of our **entailment predictions**, that is, the specific outcomes that we anticipate will be entailed by the overall outcomes. And those predictions could be off base. For example, you might like your new job more than your prior value assessment suggested because you had failed to foresee how congenial your colleagues would be.

When we make utility and value assessments, we also make predictions about ourselves, **reaction predictions**. That is, we predict how we would be affected by the specific outcomes entailed by an overall outcome. *Those* predictions could be in error, too. So, perhaps another reason your previous appraisal of your new job was so deficient is that you thought your reaction to working in a city (a new experience for you) would be worse than it really is.

Consider cases when we say things like, "Gee, I don't know *which* one I like," for instance, when comparing two outfits in a clothing store. This often means that we doubt our ability to anticipate what the options entail, for example, whether each outfit will be appropriate for most of our future social engagements. We also sometimes mean that we question our ability to forecast our reactions, such as whether each outfit will continue to satisfy our fickle fashion tastes.

A decision analysis from medicine

An understandable response to the previous illustration of decision analysis is this: "Felicia Pine's law school problem was important to her. But it isn't very significant in the grand scheme of things. It's not very complicated either; she should have been able to solve her problem by herself. What can decision analysis do for more 'serious' decision problems—anything?" Actually, decision analysis is thought to be worth all the effort it demands only in complex situations where the stakes are high. Our second illustration, which is described in outline only, suggests the power the decision analytic approach is believed to provide. It is taken from a medical context and was reported by Dunn and Pauker (1986). The focus of the analysis is a 64-year-old man who has previously had one of his kidneys removed. Lately, he has been experiencing increasingly severe problems with the remaining kidney. His case was referred to Dunn and Pauker for decision analytic consultation.

After observing the patient for some time, the physicians feel that there is an 80% chance that his kidney has been invaded by cancer. Figure 9.10 shows the decision tree that was developed. The major branches emanating from the square choice node identify the options that were considered. The numbers in parentheses are the corresponding expected utilities. (More on these later.) The branches growing from each choice alternative, beginning at a circular chance node, describe the various events that might occur if that alternative were selected. The number in parentheses adjacent to a given event is the probability assigned to that event. In most instances, these probabilities are proportions derived from records of former patients in similar situations. In others, they represent the expert opinions of the physicians. The tips of the branches describe the significant outcomes. The associated numbers in parentheses are the utilities of those outcomes, taken altogether. (More on these later, too.)

Let us examine the three alternative actions:

The first option is **OBSERVE**. That is, the physicians will continue observing the development of the patient's condition. If the patient does have cancer, it can be expected to worsen. If so, this might become obvious, and the situation will be reevaluated. Then again, the presence of the cancer might *not* become more apparent; the patient will continue to suffer from untreated malignancy. Finally, if the patient does not have cancer, all is well and good.

The second alternative is **EXPLORE**. That is, exploratory surgery is undertaken. The various branches within the **EXPLORE** section of the decision tree indicate what would happen, contingent on preceding events. In the exploratory surgery, a sample of tissue will be removed from the patient's kidney. It will then be subjected to a biopsy. This is a test to determine if the kidney is indeed cancerous. The notation "**BIOPSY+ (.995)**" means that, if cancer is present, there is a 99.5% chance that the biopsy will be positive, that is, will indicate that cancer is present. In the event of a positive biopsy, the surgeons will immediately continue the surgery, performing a nephrectomy, removing the patient's remaining kidney. Any surgical procedure carries a risk of perioperative death; that is, the patient might die during the procedure. In this case, the patient could die from the exploration necessary for the biopsy or from the nephrectomy. If the patient survives the surgery **(LIVE)**, there is still the possibility of morbidity, illness due to complications from the entire procedure.

The third option is preplanned **NEPHRECTOMY**. That is, the surgeons would simply remove the patient's kidney, without taking the extra time required to test the kidney for the presence of cancer.

Some comments on the outcomes and their utilities: As suggested above, each path through the decision tree results in possibly several outcomes that have significance for the decision maker. Consider the path **EXPLORE/CANCER/BIOPSY+/LIVE/MORBIDITY**. The indicated outcomes are "Cancer(?), No Kidneys, Complications." That is, the patient will

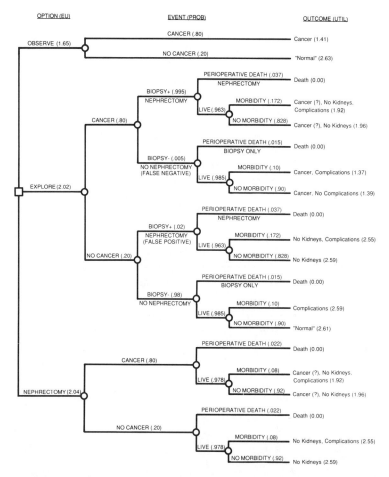

OPTION (EU)   EVENT (PROB)   OUTCOME (UTIL)

OBSERVE (1.65)

CANCER (.80) — Cancer (1.41)

NO CANCER (.20) — "Normal" (2.63)

EXPLORE (2.02)

CANCER (.80)

BIOPSY+ (.995) NEPHRECTOMY

PERIOPERATIVE DEATH (.037) NEPHRECTOMY — Death (0.00)

LIVE (.963)

MORBIDITY (.172) — Cancer (?), No Kidneys, Complications (1.92)

NO MORBIDITY (.828) — Cancer (?), No Kidneys (1.96)

BIOPSY– (.005) NO NEPHRECTOMY (FALSE NEGATIVE)

PERIOPERATIVE DEATH (.015) BIOPSY ONLY — Death (0.00)

LIVE (.985)

MORBIDITY (.10) — Cancer, Complications (1.37)

NO MORBIDITY (.90) — Cancer, No Complications (1.39)

NO CANCER (.20)

BIOPSY+ (.02) NEPHRECTOMY (FALSE POSITIVE)

PERIOPERATIVE DEATH (.037) NEPHRECTOMY — Death (0.00)

LIVE (.963)

MORBIDITY (.172) — No Kidneys, Complications (2.55)

NO MORBIDITY (.828) — No Kidneys (2.59)

BIOPSY– (.98) NO NEPHRECTOMY

PERIOPERATIVE DEATH (.015) BIOPSY ONLY — Death (0.00)

LIVE (.985)

MORBIDITY (.10) — Complications (2.59)

NO MORBIDITY (.90) — "Normal" (2.61)

NEPHRECTOMY (2.04)

CANCER (.80)

PERIOPERATIVE DEATH (.022) — Death (0.00)

LIVE (.978)

MORBIDITY (.08) — Cancer (?), No Kidneys, Complications (1.92)

NO MORBIDITY (.92) — Cancer (?), No Kidneys (1.96)

NO CANCER (.20)

PERIOPERATIVE DEATH (.022) — Death (0.00)

LIVE (.978)

MORBIDITY (.08) — No Kidneys, Complications (2.55)

NO MORBIDITY (.92) — No Kidneys (2.59)

FIGURE 9.10. Decision tree characterization of the problem of how to treat a 64-year-old male patient with one kidney whose remaining kidney is now performing poorly. See text for details. Adapted from Dunn and Pauker (1986), Figure 11, with permission from the Society for Medical Decision Making.

be alive, but it is uncertain that the cancer was completely removed or that it will not shortly reappear. The patient will also have to function with no kidneys, relying completely on dialysis machines to remove wastes from his blood. Moreover, he will suffer from complications arising from the surgery. Taken as a whole, however, this situation is better than death. So it is not unreasonable that the assigned utility of 1.92 is higher than the 0.00 associated with death. On the other hand, this array of outcomes is much worse than the "Normal" existence of a 64-year-old man with one poorly functioning kidney who undergoes no surgery. This "good" outcome is assigned a utility of 2.63, as indicated at the tip of the **OBSERVE/NO CANCER** path.

The utility measures used in this decision analysis were derived from a method that is different from that used in Felicia Pine's analysis. The present utilities are called *quality adjusted life years*. Essentially, they can be understood as life expectancies, adjusted for the discomfort the patient might experience due to various negative outcomes. Compare, for instance, the second and the last paths through the **EXPLORE** part of the tree. As we saw before, the second path has outcomes "Cancer(?), No Kidneys, Complications." The last is described as essentially "Normal." Based on mortality tables, the three negative outcomes associated with the second path objectively will reduce the life expectancy from the 2.61 years indicated for the "normal" 64-year-old man with one bad kidney. But those years also will be filled with more pain and aggravation. The utility assessment method used by Dunn and Pauker takes this into account by reducing statistical life expectancies on the basis of patients' reports of how much they say pain and suffering reduce the quality of their lives.

The expected utility for each alternative indicated in the decision tree is calculated as usual by multiplying the utility of the outcomes at the end of each path by the path probability and then summing the results. The probability for a path—a joint probability—is simply the product of the probabilities along that path (see Chapter 5). For instance, the probability of the fifth path in the EXPLORE section of the tree is

P(CANCER & BIOPSY-/NO NEPHRECTOMY & LIVE & MORBIDITY)

$$= (0.80) (0.005) (0.985) (0.10)$$
$$= 0.000394.$$

As indicated in the decision tree, the resulting expected utilities are

EU(**OBSERVE**) = 1.65

EU(**EXPLORE**) = 2.02

and

EU (**NEPHRECTOMY**) = 2.04

Thus, according to the expected utility choice principle, the **OBSERVE** option should be eliminated from consideration. The expected utilities for **EXPLORE** and **NEPHRECTOMY** are so close together that it is possible that the difference reflects only measurement error.[3] Thus, according to the analysis, it is a toss-up between exploratory surgery and an immediate, planned removal of the patient's remaining kidney.

Appraisals of decision analysis

Does decision analysis work? More precisely, does using decision analysis tend to leave decision makers better off than other decision proce-

---

[3]The computations here differ slightly from those of Dunn and Pauker (1986), although the conclusions do not.

dures? It might surprise you to learn that no one can answer that question, despite the fact that decision analysis has been around for many years. Ideally, the best way to answer such a question would be to randomly assign large numbers of decision problems to various decision procedures, including decision analysis, and then compare the satisfactoriness of the outcomes yielded by the decisions produced. This evaluation strategy is simple in concept. In practice, however, it has proved to be so difficult to execute that no one has actually done so.

There are several reasons decision procedures are hard to test. A major one is that few people will consent to having their serious decisions made by randomly assigned procedures. Instead, they prefer to follow what they believe to be the best procedure. (Would you want a decision about surgery on *your* father to be made by a randomly selected decision method?) Moreover, even when decision makers agree in advance to follow a certain procedure, they often reserve—and exercise—the right to override the decisions recommended by the procedure. For instance, if a decision technique says that Job A should be selected over Job B, the decision maker might disagree and choose Job B anyway. In essence, such individuals reject the previously adopted decision procedure in favor of their own intuitive one.

From one vantage point, overriding the recommendations of one's chosen decision aiding procedure makes no sense. If an alternative decision method always produced the same decisions you would make if left to your own devices, why do you need it in the first place? From another perspective, the decision makers' behavior is more understandable. What is so bothersome to some users of various decision-aiding technologies, including decision analysis, is that they do not understand how the procedures arrive at their recommendations. It is unclear why the recommendations conflict with their own choices. And since people understand how they make their own decisions (or at least they think they do), they embrace those decisions instead.

Expert systems are computer programs that accomplish various tasks usually performed by people, for example, medical diagnosis. The name comes from the fact that the rules according to which expert systems operate seek to mimic those that real experts appear to employ. An appealing feature of many contemporary expert systems is that they not only accomplish the intended task, but that they also explain their reasoning. For instance, one of the best known expert systems for medical diagnosis provides the user with a detailed, written account of how it uses the various signs and symptoms of the patient to arrive at its diagnoses (Buchanan and Shortliffe, 1984). Decision analysts might be well-advised to follow suit, to devise a means of clearly explaining how decision analyses reach their conclusions (Holtzman, 1989).

In view of the fact that there is virtually no hard evidence that decision analysis leads to better outcomes, why is it practiced? Most proponents of decision analysis emphasize what are thought to be its inherent advantages for the decision process. As the arguments go, if the *process* is good, then the *products* of the process must be good, too (see also Howard, 1980; Kassirer and others, 1987; Ulvila and Brown, 1982). Three aspects of the decision process are usually mentioned:

The first aspect consists of the formal parts of the decision process. These pertain to how various elements of the decision situation are seen to be logically and sometimes causally connected to one another. For instance, characterizing the situation in a decision tree is thought to be enlightening and useful in and of itself. However, the most important formal advantage of decision analysis is that value and uncertainty considerations are integrated via expected utility rules.

The second aspect of the decision process concerns the psychological forces that bear on the decision maker. Among the advantages decision analysis has been suggested to provide in their regard are ones pertaining to the following:

Information	Decision analysis should prevent the decision maker from being overwhelmed by information, for example, all the considerations in the kidney cancer problem described above.
Order	Decision analysis imposes orderliness. One simply cannot accomplish an analysis without being systematic.
Discipline	Decision analysis demands hard, disciplined thinking. Presumably, other procedures allow—perhaps even encourage—chaotic thought.
Reasoning	Decision analysis promotes clarity and explicitness of reasoning. Indeed, it is impossible to perform a decision analysis unless the decision maker makes clear statements about relationships, beliefs, and values.
Insight	Decision analysis facilitates insight, such as the recognition of elements of the decision problem that might have gone unnoticed otherwise. This is often cited as *the* main advantage of decision analysis, even more important than features like the expected utility combination rule.

The third aspect of the decision process sometimes said to be affected by decision analysis concerns social relationships between the decision maker and others. For instance, decision analysis provides a structure for organizing discussions of decision problems, thereby perhaps facilitating communication. Because of its explicitness, decision analysis also implies that the rationales for decisions can be scrutinized more carefully by others, permitting errors to be identified and corrected in advance. Relatedly, decision analyses are sometimes used as a tool for defending a decision or a recommendation, for example, to a board of directors or a court of law.

As you might expect, these claims for decision analysis have not gone uncontested. They are also counterbalanced by the inherent disadvantages of decision analysis (see also Fischhoff, 1980; Williams, 1987). First, while many of the presumed benefits of analysis for various aspects of the decision process seem eminently plausible, rarely have they been carefully documented. And, as you have no doubt gathered from our simple illustrations, decision analysis is often time consuming, difficult, and expensive to apply.

SUMMARY

Expected utility decision principles have essentially the same form as expected value principles. The difference is that expectations are taken over utilities or subjective values, rather than amounts of some objectively defined quantified outcome. Utility theory is a reasonable first approximation of decision making under uncertainty in many situations. For instance, it is often found that there is a strong association between individuals' decisions and expected utilities for the alternatives as computed with those individuals' utility functions. However, more sensitive tests have revealed persistent and systematic discrepancies between how the theory says people will decide and how they in fact decide.

Despite its limitations as a description of how people actually decide, interest in expected utility theory remains high. This is largely because of arguments that conclude that people *should* decide in accordance with the prescriptions of the theory. Decision analysis is a body of techniques for assisting people to make decisions, particularly in situations where the stakes are high. The arguments for expected utility theory as a guide to appropriate decision making provide the cornerstone for most decision analytic practice.

KEY TERMS

Allais Phenomenon/Paradox
Axiom
Bernoullian utility
Certainty equivalent
Combination rule
Concave
Convex
Decision analysis
Diminishing marginal value
Entailment prediction
Expected utility
Expected utility choice principle
Expected utility evaluation principle
Expert system
Linear
Logical esthetics
Material trap

Measurable value function
Money pump
Necessary condition
Postulate
Reaction prediction
Risk premium
St. Petersburg Paradox
Structuring
Subjective expected utility
True/relative risk attitude
Utile
Utility
Utility function
Utility theory
Value function
von Neumann–Morgenstern utility
    function

ADDITIONAL READING

Anderson and Shanteau (1970); Beach, Campbell, and Townes (1979); Cooper (1987); Dickson (1981); Fishburn (1981); Galanter (1962); Goodman and others (1979); Hershey, Kunreuther, and Schoemaker (1982); Pauker and Pauker (1977); Shafer (1986); Siedel (1986); Slovic and Tversky (1974).

EXERCISES AND STUDY QUESTIONS

1. (Optional) Thelma makes decisions according to expected utility. However, her utility function for money is linear. Thus, she always chooses among monetary prospects in a manner that is consistent with expected value maximization. Show why this is so.

2. "Bernie Griswold" runs a small driveway paving company. Every day he goes down to the local union hall to hire the workers he needs for that day. If it rains on a particular day, Mr. Griswold cannot pave any driveways. But if he goes ahead and hires the workers anyway, he has to pay them a nominal fee of $200 for the entire group, and he gets nothing for his efforts. On the other hand, if it does not rain that day, Mr. Griswold stands to clear $1000. If on a particular day he sends out no crews, he neither makes nor loses money.

    (a) Construct a decision tree representing the choice facing Mr. Griswold on a given day.

    (b) Suppose Mr. Griswold makes the decision about sending out crews according to the expected value choice principle. What is the threshold probability for rain, p_t, such that, if the probability is above p_t, he sends out no crews; otherwise he does?

    (c) Suppose Mr. Griswold makes decisions according to expected utility. Would you expect his critical rain probability to be the same as, larger than, or smaller than the number you derived in part (b)? Explain.

3. Consider the Allais Paradox problem, perhaps the "Uncle Harvey" version described in the chapter.

    (a) What would you consider to be a plausible hypothesis for why so many people choose between the alternatives in a manner that appears to violate expected utility theory?

    (b) Describe a good strategy for testing your hypothesis in part (a).

4. (Optional) Show that the monotonicity principle is a necessary condition for decision making according to expected utility.

5. Devise and perform a small experiment to test whether a friend's decision behavior is consistent with the substitutability principle implied by expected utility theory.

6. (Optional) Show the sufficiency of the Luce and Raiffa principles for choice according to expected utility. That is, given the stated conditions and that a person's decision behavior always agrees with Principles P1 to P7, show that that individual's choices among prospects can be described as expected utility maximization.

7. Find a friend who can assume the role of someone looking for a summer job. In this exercise you will lead your friend through a simple decision analysis.

    (a) Have your friend bring to mind five potential jobs. He or she should make the jobs as concrete and realistic as possible. (It would help if the jobs *were* real.) To facilitate realism, ask your friend to describe the jobs to you in detail, although you need not record those details.

(b) Ask your friend to rank order the jobs from the most to the least attractive. For the purposes of the remainder of the exercise, label the jobs J_1 through J_5, where the former is the most attractive job and the latter is the least.

(c) Your next task is to obtain your friend's utility for each of the jobs. You should do this by adapting the procedure used in Felicia Pine's law school decision analysis. Some hints: Show your friend lotteries structured as follows:

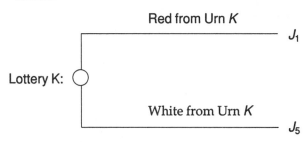

Urn K contains 100 poker chips, K of which are red and the remainder white. It would probably be helpful to your friend if you displayed the contents of the urn graphically. Your friend should indicate what K must be in order for him or her to be indifferent between job J_2 and Lottery K. Suppose your friend says that K is 60. Thus, the probability of getting job J_1 in the lottery would be 60%. Suppose the utility of job J_1 is set to be $u(J_1) = 100$ and that of J_5 is set at $u(J_5) = 0$. Assuming that your friend expresses indifferences in a manner consistent with expected utility theory, what must you infer to be the utility of job J_2? You should repeat the implied procedure to obtain the utilities of jobs J_3 and J_4 also.

(d) Now have your friend imagine the following situation: Job J_1 is no longer available. Job J_4 has been offered, and the offer will remain open until the summer starts. Job J_3 has also been offered, but it must be either accepted or rejected by tomorrow. (Your friend's ethics do not allow him or her to accept a job and then later reject it.) Your friend will not know about job J_2 for another week. So the problem is this: Should your friend accept or reject job J_3?

In this part of the exercise, you should indicate the prescription of (subjective) expected utility (EU) theory. That is, determine which option should be taken to maximize EU. Clearly, to do this, you need to first determine your friend's probability judgment that job J_2 indeed will be offered. It might help to draw a decision tree, too.

(e) Before communicating the results of your analysis in part (d), find out what alternative your friend thinks he or she *should* take. Ask your friend to explain how that intuitive decision was made. Compare those responses to the prescription derived from your analysis. Do the decisions and the apparent logic underlying them agree or disagree? Explain.

(f) Offer a critique of your decision analysis. That is, discuss its strengths and weaknesses, relative to how your friend might make decisions when left to his or her own devices.

8. Recruit another friend to serve as your subject.

(a) Assess your friend's utility function for money in the range $0 to $20, using the following *certainty equivalents technique*:

First, your friend states a certainty equivalent for Gamble $G1$ = (H, $20; T, $0), where H indicates that heads appears on the toss of a balanced coin. (Be sure your friend concedes that the coin toss is just as likely to result in heads as tails.) Call that amount $CE1.

Next, your friend states a certainty equivalent for Gamble $G2$ = (H, $CE1; T, $0). For instance, Gamble $G2$ = (H, $8; T, $0) if the previous response had been $CE1 = $8. Call this new certainty equivalent $CE2.

Finally, your friend reports a third certainty equivalent, this time for Gamble $G3$ = (H, $20; T, $CE1). Call it $CE3.

(i) Set $u(\$0) = 0$ and $u(\$20) = 100$. Assuming that your friend responded to the questions as if deciding according to expected utility, what must be the utilities for $CE1, $CE2, and $CE3?

(ii) Sketch the graph of your friend's utility function.

(iii) Would you characterize your friend's apparent risk attitude in this context, as risk aversion, risk neutrality, or risk seeking?

(b) Now assess your friend's value function for money in the $0 to $20 range, using the *exchange method* (Dyer and Sarin, 1979; Krzysztofowicz, 1983). The questions you must ask your friend are difficult, so be patient and be certain that he or she understands what you want done:

First, ask your friend to imagine starting with nothing and then being given $10. Your friend should "store away" how that exchange of $0 for $10 felt. Call that sensation *exchange value* $D(10-0)$.

Next, your friend should imagine starting with $10, but now exchanging that amount for a gift of $20. Again, the satisfactoriness of the exchange should be stored away, exchange value $D(20-10)$.

Now ask your friend to compare the previous two sensations, that is, $D(10-0)$ and $D(20-10)$. Which was stronger, or were they the same?

(i) Suppose that your friend says that $D(10-0)$ was greater than $D(20-10)$. Would you conclude that your friend's value function for money in the $0 to $20 range is concave, linear, or convex? Explain.

(ii) Is the shape of the implied value curve the same as that of the utility curve you derived previously? If there is a difference, how would you interpret that difference in terms of your friend's risk attitude?

(iii) Devise additional questions to ask your friend that will enable you to actually sketch his or her value function, setting boundary value assignments of $v(\$0) = 0$ and $v(\$20) = 100$. Again, compare the value function to the previous utility function. What are the implications for conclusions about your friend's feelings about risk?

9. Ask a friend to bring to mind five different graduate or professional schools he or she would seriously consider attending. Have your friend rate the schools on a 0 to 100 point scale (least to most appealing). Then have your friend explicitly list as many features as possible that would be entailed in attending each school. After that, your friend should rate the attractiveness or unattractiveness of each feature. Finally, have your friend repeat the initial overall school rating task. Do the new and original ratings differ? Which ratings seem more comfortable to your friend? What conclusions do you draw from this exercise in entailment and reaction prediction?

10. We have discussed value and utility assessments being wrong in the sense that entailment and reaction predictions can be in error. But is it also meaningful to speak of a person's feelings toward risk being wrong? If so, how? For example, if you tend to be very risk aversive in your financial dealings, would it be legitimate for your decision analyst to convince you to be more daring?

10

Cousins of Expected Utility

The man who insists upon seeing with perfect clearness before he decides, never decides.

—Frédéric Amiel

After reading the last two chapters, you might easily have said, "Well, now I know how people *don't* decide: They don't follow expected value. Nor do they consistently abide by expected utility. But I'm still left wondering how people *do* make decisions. Where should I turn?" At one time, decision scholars felt similar frustration. The remaining chapters describe some of the explanations they have since discovered. As we will see, several tacks have been taken in the quest for deeper understanding. One approach has been to modify expected utility (EU) theory so that it more adequately accounts for what people actually do when confronted with their decision problems. The results have been theories that can be thought of as close "cousins" of EU theory. The first section of this chapter briefly discusses the resemblances and variations among the members of this family of theories. The bulk of the chapter is the second section, which examines the currently most prominent family member—prospect theory.

A PERSPECTIVE ON MODIFIED VERSIONS OF EXPECTED UTILITY THEORY

Recall that expected utility theory, as a description of how people decide, makes two general claims. The first is that we take two things into account when deciding: our values for potential outcomes and the chances of those outcomes actually being delivered. The second claim concerns how such considerations of value and uncertainty are combined into the ultimate decision. According to EU theory, this is done interactively, with value differences assuming greater significance when coupled with greater likelihoods, and vice versa. In such broad outline, these claims are uncontroversial, some would even say they are obvious. However, at some point the claims must be made precise, for example, specifying exactly *how* value and uncertainty combine with each other. Then things cease being so obvious. As we have also seen, various intuitively appealing specific claims are clearly wrong, for instance, as implied by phenomena such as the Allais Paradox.

The family of decision theories that have taken their inspiration directly from EU theory retain the above basic claims about value, uncertainty, and their combination. However, they differ in their detailed assertions. Expected utility theory makes one set of specific claims, for example, that uncertainty is characterized in a form equivalent to probabilities (Chapter 5), and that these are combined multiplicatively with measures of value that behave like utilities. We have noted only a sample of the demonstrations that various of these precise claims are often wrong. Most cousins of EU theory are essentially the original version of EU theory, but with particular specific claims weakened or relaxed. Typically, the claims that are modified are altered because people's behavior clearly violates them.

Many decision theories closely related to EU theory have been proposed and in some instances tested (see, for example, Anderson and Shanteau, 1970; Fishburn, 1982; Karmarkar, 1978; Machina, 1982; Quiggin, 1985). The general strategy implicit in building such theories is well represented by the most prominent example, Kahneman and Tversky's (1979) prospect theory, to which we turn now.

PROSPECT THEORY

Picture yourself on a television quiz show called "Peril." The host gives you a choice between two prizes, the first of which is actually a lottery:

Peril Prize 1:   50% chance of a three-week tour of England, France, and Italy; 50% chance of nothing
Peril Prize 2:   One-week tour of England, no strings attached

Which would you choose?

Now imagine that you are a contestant on another quiz show, "Risk." Again, you are offered a choice between two alternatives, both of which are lotteries:

Risk Prize 1:   5% chance of a three-week tour of England, France, and Italy; 95% chance of nothing
Risk Prize 2:   10% chance of a one-week tour of England; 90% chance of nothing

Once more, which would you pick?

Suppose that you made your decisions according to expected utility theory and that you chose the guaranteed one-week tour of England on Peril. This would be interpreted as implying that

$$EU(\text{Peril Prize 2}) > EU(\text{Peril Prize 1}).$$

This is equivalent to saying that

$$u(\text{One-week tour}) > (0.50)\ u(\text{Three-week tour}) + (0.50)u(\text{Nothing})$$

where u denotes your utility function for vacations. Now suppose that on the Risk show you chose the three-week lottery over the one-week lottery. This means that

$$EU(\text{Risk Prize 1}) > EU(\text{Risk Prize 2})$$

which in turn amounts to saying that

$$(0.05)u(\text{Three-week tour}) + (0.95)u(\text{Nothing})$$
$$> (0.10)u(\text{One-week tour}) + (0.90)u(\text{Nothing})$$

But, multiplying through by 10 and rearranging terms, we see that this is equivalent to

$$(0.50)u(\text{Three-week tour}) + (0.50)u(\text{Nothing}) > u(\text{One-week tour})$$

which directly contradicts our previous conclusion. Thus, you must not have made your choices on the Peril and Risk shows according to expected utility.

Kahneman and Tversky (1979) presented the alternatives described above to a large number of subjects. They found a predominant pattern of preferences similar to that suggested. This pattern is illustrative of ones that contradict expected utility theory, but can be explained by Kahneman and Tversky's **prospect theory**. Prospect theory actually makes two quite distinct sets of claims about how people decide. In this chapter we will focus on only one, its assertions about the issues addressed by expected utility theory. We discuss the other claims in Chapters 12 and 13.

Overview

As do all theories similar to EU theory, prospect theory contends that both the magnitudes of outcomes as well as their probabilities affect people's decisions. As suggested in the following schematic, the theory says that there are three phases in the decision process:[1]

Phase 1: Translation:	Outcome → Subjective Value
	Probability → Decision Weight
Phase 2: Combination:	Values and Weights → Prospect Value
Phase 3: Decision:	(a) Prospect Value → Evaluation
	or
	(b) Prospect 1 Value versus Prospect 2 Value → Choice

That is, the decision maker examines each prospect and first translates the pertinent outcomes and probabilities into corresponding subjective values and decision weights, respectively. After this is done, the values and weights are combined or synthesized into a subjective value for the prospect as a whole. Finally, the decision itself is dictated by the prospect values. In an evaluation situation, an uncertain prospect, for example, a gamble, is considered equivalent to a sure thing whose value is identical to the prospect's value. In a choice situation, the prospect that has the highest value is the one that is picked. Effectively, the same viewpoint is implicit in EU theory. However, prospect theory differs in its claims as to precisely what occurs in the translation and combination phases. In our discussion of prospect theory's details, we will first examine the translation claims and then the proposed combination rules.

Details of the theory

Decision weights In contrast to expected utility theory, prospect theory does not maintain that probabilities combine directly with values. Instead, the decision maker first somehow transforms probabilities into psychological **decision weights**. The latter are then applied to the values.

---

[1]It also proposes that there is another phase that precedes all three of the present ones. We discuss that phase in Chapters 12 and 13.

See 332, -

Prospect theory proposes that there are characteristic relationships between the probabilities associated with various potential outcomes and the weights those probabilities have in the decision process. Some of the theory's weighting claims are abstract and thus difficult to understand at first. However, you should try to bear with the abstractness until their implications are illustrated more concretely.

Figure 10.1 shows a characteristic probability–weight function, as proposed by prospect theory. The first thing to note about this function is that low probabilities tend to be overemphasized and high ones underemphasized. In Chapter 6, we examined the correspondence between actual proportions and people's estimates of those proportions. We saw that there tend to be systematic kinds of miscalibration and discrepancies between actual and estimated proportions. It might seem that prospect theory simply takes note of those previously acknowledged relationships. Not so; the weighting claim of prospect theory is quite distinct. It says that, *given* a perception of various probabilities, those perceived probabilities will be used by the decision maker differently than EU theory says they will. The second feature that stands out in Figure 10.1 is the *crossover probability a*, the point where probabilities and weights coincide. Prospect theory is vague about exactly where the crossover occurs, but it is definitely lower than *a* = 50%. Some of prospect theory's other weighting proposals cannot be recognized easily in a graph such as Figure 10.1. We consider some of them now.

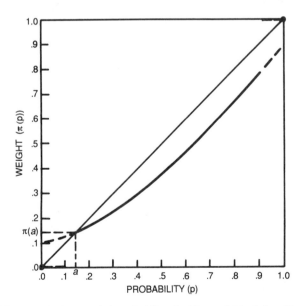

FIGURE 10.1. A characteristic probability–decision weight relationship, according to prospect theory. Probability *a*, which is unspecified, is the crossover probability, where overweighting changes to underweighting. Note that near probability .0 weights drop to .0, and near probability 1.0 they leap to 1.0, although it is ambiguous precisely where these discontinuities occur.

Discontinuity. Notice in Figure 10.1 that, as probability p gets close to 0, the corresponding decision weight $\pi(p)$ does not tend toward 0 smoothly. Instead, somewhere at the low end of the scale, there is a sharp dropoff, with the weight plunging to 0. Conceptually, this means that there is a dramatic difference between the decision impact of an event that is considered impossible ($p = 0$) and one that is merely remote ($p \approx 0$). Nevertheless, prospect theory also maintains that *some* small but nonzero probabilities are ignored. That is, although the pertinent events are not impossible, they are treated as if they were. There is a similar **discontinuity** at the opposite end of the scale. Unfortunately, the theory is imprecise as to where these discontinuities occur. That is why, in Figure 10.1, there are dashes at each end of the curve and on the upper and lower axes, to acknowledge the implied ambiguity.

Subadditivity. Take two probabilities p_1 and p_2, and add them, yielding probability

$$p_3 = p_1 + p_2$$

If decision weights were *additive*, the weight for the new probability would be the sum of the weights for the original ones:

$$\pi(p_3) = \pi(p_1) + \pi(p_2)$$

For instance, we would observe that

$$\pi(25\%) = \pi(10\%) + \pi(15\%)$$

The probability-weight relationship proposed by prospect theory does not exhibit additivity. In particular, for small probabilities, it is claimed that weights are *subadditive*, as represented by the extreme flatness at the lower end of the curve shown in Figure 10.1. For instance, the weight for probability 0.002 is less than twice that for probability 0.001:

$$\pi(0.002) < 2 \times \pi(0.001)$$

You might be inclined to say that such probabilities are so ridiculously small that they can be ignored. In fact, however, they are on the order of the probabilities involved in typical insurance decisions.

Subcertainty. Except for guaranteed or impossible events, prospect theory asserts that the weights for complementary events do not sum to 1. This is one implication of the **subcertainty** feature of the theory's probability–weight relationship, which says that, for all probabilities p with $0 < p < 1$,

$$\pi(p) + \pi(1 - p) < 1$$

Recall Gamble $G^* = (25\%, \$8; 75\%, \$2)$ considered by Minerva Avery in Chapter 9. Subcertainty implies that the weights associated with the $8 and $2 prizes will sum to less than 1: $\pi(0.25) + \pi(0.75) < 1$.

Regressiveness. In general, the concept of **regressiveness** says that extreme values of some quantity do not deviate very much from the average value of that quantity. The relative flatness of the probability–weight curve shown in Figure 10.1 is a special type of regressiveness. In particular, it asserts that people's decisions are not as responsive to changes in uncertainty as the associated probabilities are. Another aspect of this regressiveness is the claim that nonextreme high probabilities are underweighted, that is,

$$\pi(p) < p$$

and that low ones are overweighted:

$$\pi(p) > p$$

A "high" probability is one that is above the crossover probability a, as indicated in Figure 10.1.

Subjective value   In its present state of development, the main thrust of prospect theory is restricted to a narrow class of prospects. One restriction is that the outcomes of the prospects are quantified. For instance, the theory's combination rules are intended to account for such things as choices among investments that are characterized solely according to their financial returns, or evaluations of public health policies purely in terms of the numbers of lives they might save. As indicated above, prospect theory proposes that the overall subjective value of a prospect depends on probability-determined decision weights and the subjective values of potential outcomes. The theory makes specific claims about the form of the relationship between various amounts of an outcome and their subjective values.

Figure 10.2a shows one hypothetical example of a value function for money, of the type anticipated by prospect theory. Figure 10.2b shows another. Actually, both value functions belong to the same person, "Glenn Cleaver." The assertion that a single individual can have more than one value function is one of prospect theory's most distinctive features. The value function in Figure 10.2a applies when Mr. Cleaver is thinking about the amount of money he will earn or lose this year on a small mutual fund account he owns. The function in Figure 10.2b applies when he is reflecting on his merit salary increase for next year. Let us examine prospect theory's claims about value functions, including why Mr. Cleaver's two monetary value functions look the way they do.

Figure 10.2c shows a generic prospect theory value function. The function has three noteworthy characteristics. The first pertains to the decision maker's reference point. According to prospect theory, in a given situation, there is a focal amount of the pertinent outcome such that, psychologically, smaller amounts are considered losses and larger amounts gains. That focal amount is the reference point. Recently, Glenn Cleaver has done a lot of reading about mutual funds. Based on that reading, he has concluded that a decent mutual fund should give him a return of about $100 for the size of investment he has in the fund already. Thus, any return over $100 would be quite pleasing. On the other hand, a return of less than $100, even if not objectively a loss of wealth, would be regarded by Mr. Cleaver as a loss. That is why $100 serves as Mr. Cleaver's reference point for mutual fund returns. In the case of salary improvements, Mr. Cleaver expects that the average

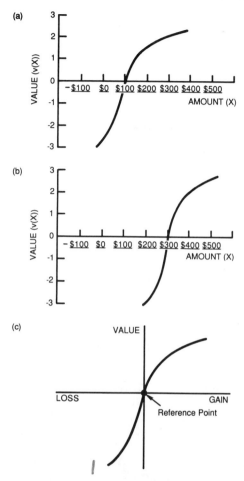

FIGURE 10.2. Representative value functions, according to prospect theory: (a) for mutual fund earnings or losses by Glenn Cleaver; (b) for Mr. Cleaver's salary change; (c) for the generic case of any quantified outcome.

employee in his classification will get a raise of about $300. Hence, $300 is his salary reference point. Implicit in prospect theory is the claim that the absolute amount of a given outcome is unimportant to decision makers. What *is* important is the magnitude of that amount relative to the reference point. Thus, effectively, subjective value is defined on the sizes of gains and losses, that is, how far above or below the reference point an amount happens to be.

The second distinctive feature of prospect theory's value function is that the shape of the function changes markedly at the reference point. As indicated in Figure 10.2, for gains the value function is concave, exhibiting diminishing marginal value (Chapter 9, pp. 268–69). That is, the significance of constant increases in gains becomes less and less as the starting point for those increases becomes larger. A complementary phenomenon is presumed to occur in the domain of losses, as indicated by the convexity of the value function to the left of the reference point. That is, constant changes in the negative direction away from the reference point also assume diminishing significance the farther from the reference point the starting point happens to be.

Kahneman and Tversky (1979, p. 278) have suggested that the implied notion of **diminishing marginal significance** is an instance of a general psychological principle observed in many other contexts. For example, most people find it easier to detect the difference in brightness between 15- and 25-watt light bulbs than between 115- and 125-watt bulbs. Measured value functions for money often do exhibit diminishing marginal significance (see, for example, Galanter, 1962; Krzysztofowicz, 1983). However, it has not been demonstrated that there is indeed a common basis for value functions and such psychophysical phenomena as brightness discrimination. The foundations might well be different.

The final outstanding characteristic of prospect theory's value function is that it is steeper for losses than for gains. That is, gains and losses of identical magnitude have different significance for people; the losses are considered more important. This makes intuitive sense from a functional perspective. A primary motive of virtually every organism is survival. Hypersensitivity to threats, for example, losses, would serve that motive well. There is considerable evidence of such sensitivity among a variety of species (see Fisher and Fisher, 1969).

Combination rules   How do decision weights and outcome values combine to determine the subjective value of a prospect? According to prospect theory, the way this occurs depends on the nature of the prospect. In its present state of development, prospect theory's combination rules only apply to what are called *simple prospects*. These are prospects in which there are at most two nonnull outcomes. An outcome is *nonnull* if it differs from the decision maker's reference point.

Consider the following **absolute representation** of a prospect:

$$(p, \underline{X}; q, \underline{Y}; r, \underline{RP})$$

where, as is customary in list notation, $\underline{X}$, $\underline{Y}$, and $\underline{RP}$ are particular amounts, with associated probabilities p, q, and r, respectively. The outcome $\underline{RP}$ is the decision maker's reference point, for example, $100 for Glenn Cleaver when he is considering mutual funds. According to prospect theory, what we can call the **effective representation** of the above prospect is

$$(p, \underline{X} - \underline{RP}; q, \underline{Y} - \underline{RP}; r, \underline{RP} - \underline{RP}) = (p, x; q, y; r, 0)$$

That is, the amounts that are effective for the decision maker are not the actual sums that would be awarded to or taken away, but are instead the differences between those sums and the decision maker's reference point. For example, the mutual fund prospect represented absolutely as

$$(35\%, \underline{\$225}; 40\%, \underline{-\$50}; 25\%, \underline{\$100})$$

would be seen by Glenn Cleaver as effectively

$$(35\%, \$225 - \$100; 40\%, -\$50 - \$100; 25\%, \$100 - \$100)$$

that is,

$$(35\%, \$125; 40\%, -\$150; 25\%, \$0)$$

Most of the remainder of our discussion about simple prospects is in terms of their effective representations of the form

$$(p, x; q, y; r, 0)$$

where we follow the convention that outcome x is at least as great as outcome y, that is, $x \geq y$. Of course, the probabilities are such that $p + q + r = 1$. Moreover, it is understood that one or two of those probabilities might be 0. As implicit in the above examples, we will follow the convention that absolute representations of prospects are denoted with the pertinent amounts underlined.

Regular prospects are simple prospects in which either or both of two conditions are present. One condition is that the prospect can yield a null outcome, identical to the reference point. The following is an example of a regular prospect:

$$P_1 = (30\%, \$250; 40\%, \$150; 30\%, \$0)$$

So is

$$P_2 = (75\%, \$175; 25\%, \$0)$$

The other condition that qualifies a prospect as regular is that one outcome is *positive*, that is, above the reference point, and another is *negative*, that is, below the reference point. Thus, according to this criterion, the following are regular prospects, too:

$$P_3 = (15\%, \$75; 10\%, -\$50; 75\%, \$0)$$

and

$$P_4 = (35\%, \$110; 65\%, -\$40)$$

It sometimes helps to visualize prospects as in Figure 10.3. The horizontal axis in each of these **probability mass graphs** shows the potential outcomes of the given prospect. The probability *mass bar* above each amount indicates the corresponding probability for that amount, as marked along the vertical axis. Figure 10.3a shows regular prospect $P_1 = (30\%, \$250; 40\%, \$150; 30\%, \$0)$. Regular prospect $P_4 = (35\%, \$110; 65\%, -\$40)$ is depicted in Figure 10.3b.

The combination rule for regular prospects says that the **subjective prospect value (V)** of regular prospect

$$P = (p, x; q, y; r, 0)$$

is the following:

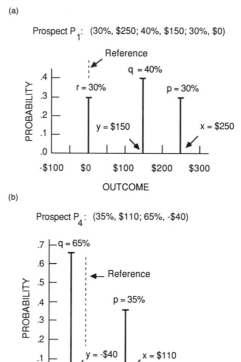

FIGURE 10.3.   Probability mass graph representations of simple prospects considered regular in prospect theory.

$$V(P) = \pi(p)v(x) + \pi(q)v(y) + \pi(r)v(0)$$
$$= \pi(p)v(x) + \pi(q)v(y) \tag{10.1}$$

since $v(0) = 0$, that is, the value of a null outcome is 0. Thus, the value of prospect P_1 above would be

$$V(P_1) = \pi(0.30)v(\$250) + \pi(0.40)v(\$150)$$

More concrete examples are given below. Observe that the rule expressed in Equation 10.1 has the same form as an expected utility, with the role of probabilities being assumed by probability-determined decision weights and that of utilities by the decision maker's values for the outcomes.

As you no doubt guessed, there are nonregular prospects, too. They come in two varieties: A **strictly positive prospect** is one whose worst possible outcome is positive, that is, better than the reference point amount. In contrast, the *best* possible outcome of a **strictly negative prospect** is negative. Specific examples are

$$P_5 = (30\%, \$200; 70\%, \$20)$$

which is strictly positive, and

$$P_6 = (40\%, -\$50; 60\%, -\$125)$$

which is strictly negative. Figure 10.4 shows schematic representations of these examples.

According to prospect theory, the subjective values of strictly positive and negative prospects are determined differently from those of regular prospects. The value of strictly positive prospect

$$P = (p, x; q, y)$$

with $x > y > 0$, is given by

$$V(P) = v(y) + \pi(p)[v(x) - v(y)] \tag{10.2}$$

The intuition behind this characterization is compelling, as suggested by the following argument. Consider strictly positive prospect

$$P_5 = (30\%, \$200; 70\%, \$20)$$

shown in Figure 10.4a. The decision maker is guaranteed to gain at least $y = \$20$. So the only uncertainty is whether the additional amount

$$x - y = \$200 - \$20 = \$180$$

will be gained also. The probability of this happening is simply the probability associated with $x = \$200$, $p = 30\%$. In effect, Equation 10.2 says that the decision maker anchors on the guaranteed gain y. The prospect's overall

(a)

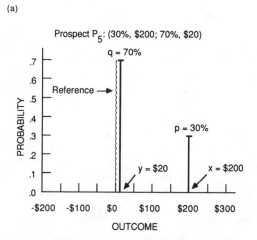

FIGURE 10.4. Probability mass graph representations of simple prospects considered nonregular in prospect theory: (a) a strictly positive example; (b) a strictly negative example.

(b)

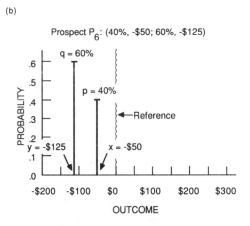

Prospect P_6: (40%, -$50; 60%, -$125)

FIGURE 10.4. (continued)

subjective value increases in relation to the magnitude and chance of another potential gain beyond the guarantee, $x - y$:

$$V(P_5) = v(\$20) + \pi(0.30)[v(\$200) - v(\$20)]$$

An analogous situation occurs with strictly negative prospects. Now let prospect

$$P = (p, x; q, y)$$

be strictly negative, that is, $y < x < 0$. Then its subjective value is described by

$$V(P) = v(x) + \pi(q)[v(y) - v(x)] \qquad (10.3)$$

The underlying intuition is the same as before, as suggested when we consider strictly negative prospect $P_6 = (40\%, -\$50; 60\%, -\$125)$, which is represented in Figure 10.4b. The decision maker is sure to lose $50; that is, $x = -\$50$. With probability $q = 60\%$, another $75 will be lost, too; $y - x = -\$125 - (-\$50) = -\$75$.

Decisions   Once the decision maker arrives at his or her subjective values for the given prospects, those values are used to make the decision. Suppose an evaluation decision is required. For instance, suppose that the monetary value of Glenn Cleaver's mutual fund account, as indicated on the account statement, is $1000. The new dividends and share values have not been posted. So, let us say that, from Mr. Cleaver's viewpoint and ignoring the $1000 statement value, his account is actually the regular prospect

$$P_1 = (30\%, \$250; 40\%, \$150; 30\%, \$0)$$

when represented effectively, or

$$P_1 = (30\%, \underline{\$350}; 40\%, \underline{\$250}; 30\%, \underline{\$100})$$

in absolute terms, since Mr. Cleaver's reference point is a gain of $100. Let us say Mr. Cleaver is asked to indicate the smallest amount he would accept in exchange for his fund account.[2] From Figure 10.2a, we see that

$$v (\$250) = v (\underline{\$350}) \approx 2.3$$
$$v (\$150) = v (\underline{\$250}) \approx 1.9$$

and, of course,

$$v(\$0) = v(\underline{\$100}) = 0$$

And assuming that Figure 10.1 describes Mr. Cleaver's decision weights, the subjective value of his account is found to be

$$V(P_1) = \pi(0.30)v(\$250) + \pi(0.40)v(\$150)$$
$$\approx (0.25) \, (2.3) + (0.30) \, (1.9)$$
$$= 1.145$$

Also note in Figure 10.2a that an effective gain of about $55 has a value of

$$v(\$55) = v(\underline{\$155}) \approx 1.145$$

Thus, according to prospect theory, Glenn Cleaver would sell his account for no less than $155 above the statement value, that is, a total of $1155.

Now suppose a choice decision is demanded. For example, suppose Glenn Cleaver is trying to decide whether to buy the above mutual fund,

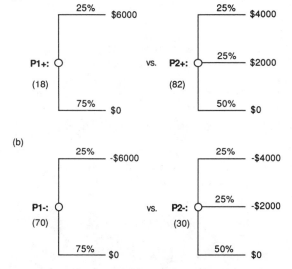

FIGURE 10.5. Prospect pairs used by Kahneman and Tversky (1979, p. 278) to demonstrate the reflection effect. Numbers in parentheses indicate the percentages of subjects who selected the given alternatives.

[2]The present example is for illustration only; mutual funds are not actually sold this way.

which is equivalent to the regular prospect P_1 or another one, equivalent to the strictly positive prospect

$$P_5 = (30\%, \$200; 70\%, \$20)$$

Prospect theory says Mr. Cleaver will choose the latter fund only if

$$V(P_5) = v(\$20) + \pi(0.30)[v(\$200) - v(\$20)]$$

is greater than

$$V(P_1) \approx 1.145$$

You might find it useful to substitute decision weights and values from Figures 10.1 and 10.2 to confirm that the theory predicts that he would pick the first fund.

The evidence

How good at describing how people actually decide are the aspects of prospect theory we have considered so far? Kahneman and Tversky (1979) have performed numerous experiments whose results are consistent with each of the claims made by prospect theory. Consider, for example, the choices subjects exhibited in the vacation decision problems described previously (pp. 284–85). These preferences are taken as instances of a general **certainty effect**, whereby people overweight guaranteed outcomes, for instance, the no-strings-attached, one-week tour of England offered on the Peril show, relative to outcomes that are merely probable, for example, the lottery providing a 10% chance of the same vacation offered on the Risk program. The certainty effect results from the discontinuity and subcertainty features of prospect theory's probability–decision weight relationship depicted in Figure 10.1.

Before any theory can be accepted generally, it must withstand the scrutiny of thorough testing from every perspective. Several investigators have taken up the challenge in the case of prospect theory. It is useful to examine briefly how some of those tests have proceeded and how prospect theory has fared. Most studies have focused on prospect theory's implications for differences between how people decide in contexts of gains versus losses, relative to their reference points. These are the kinds of studies we examine presently.

Decisions within the gain and loss domains   Consider Prospects $P1+$ and $P2+$, shown in Figure 10.5a. Now make a decision: Which would you prefer to own? It is easy to verify that both Prospect $P1+$ and Prospect $P2+$ have expected value $1500. Nevertheless, it is doubtful that you were indifferent between them. If you are like most of Kahneman and Tversky's (1979, p. 278) subjects, you chose Prospect $P2+$. Let us say that that *was* your choice. Should we conclude that you decided according to the principles implicit in prospect theory?

Suppose you did choose via prospect theory's tenets. Since the prospects you considered are regular, Equation 10.1 says that your subjective values for those prospects must have been

$$V(\text{Prospect } P1+) = \pi(0.25)\, v(\$6000)$$

and

$$V(\text{Prospect } P2+) = \pi(0.25)v(\$4000) + \pi(0.25)v(\$2000)$$

respectively. And since you picked Prospect *P2+*, this means that it must have been the case that

$$\pi(0.25)v(\$6000) < \pi(0.25)v(\$4000) + \pi(0.25)v(\$2000)$$

which is equivalent to

$$v(\$6000) < v(\$4000) + v(\$2000)$$

But is this reasonable to expect? Yes it is, provided that, as claimed by prospect theory, your value function for gains is concave, exhibiting diminishing marginal significance. To see why, notice that the above relation is the same as

$$v(\$6000) - v(\$4000) < v(\$2000) - v(\$0)$$

since $v(\$0) = 0$. In words, this says that a gain of $2000 means more to you when you start from nothing than when you start from $4000. Thus, your choice of Prospect *P2+* seems completely consistent with prospect theory.

Now examine Prospects *P1−* and *P2−* in Figure 10.5b. Given the opportunity, everyone would reject both of these options. However, most people, with the understanding that they *have* to choose one of them, select Prospect *P1−* (Kahneman and Tversky, 1979, p. 278). By the same argument as above, this choice is consistent with prospect theory, too, assuming that the value function for losses is convex. You should be able to convince yourself that expected utility theory makes the same predictions in these situations as does prospect theory, if the decision maker's utility function is concave for gains and convex for losses (Chapter 9, pp. 244–48). You should be aware that utility functions with concave and convex regions have been suggested for some time, although they have not been proposed to have precisely the form of prospect theory's value function (for example, Friedman and Savage, 1948; Markowitz, 1952). So, although the choice patterns observed in the present situations are compatible with prospect theory, by themselves they are not definitive evidence for the theory. So let us turn to another test.

Picture yourself in Paris (probably a pleasant chore), as a subject in the experiment by Cohen, Jaffray, and Said (1987). Figure 10.6a illustrates a typical task. On the one hand, you are offered

$$\text{Gamble } G_{p=\frac{1}{4}} = (\tfrac{1}{4}, \text{ FF } 1000; \tfrac{3}{4}, \text{ FF } 0)$$

You are told that, in this prospect, you will win 1000 French francs (FF 1000) if a diamond is drawn at random from a deck of cards (probability $p = \frac{1}{4}$); otherwise, you win nothing. On the other hand, you can accept a gift of some

(a)

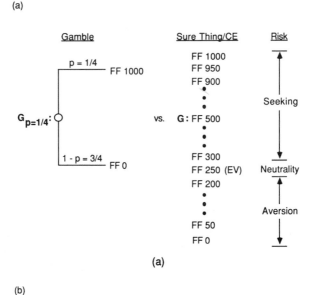

(a)

(b)

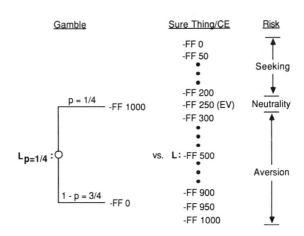

FIGURE 10.6. Illustrative prospect choices presented to subjects by Cohen, Jaffray, and Said (1987): (a) for gains; (b) for losses. Certainty equivalents (CE) were inferred from the point in the sure thing list where preference for the gamble changed to preference for the sure thing. Certainty equivalents above the expected value (EV) indicate risk seeking, those below risk aversion.

amount of money between FF 1000 and FF 0. Suppose the gift is FF 900. Surely you would take the gift. But if the gift were only FF 100, you might well prefer the gamble. Presumably, there is some gift between FF 1000 and FF 0 such that you would be indifferent between the gamble and the gift. In our previous terminology, that gift would be your certainty equivalent for the gamble, $CE(G_{p=\frac{1}{4}})$; that is,

$$CE(G_{p=\frac{1}{4}}) =_P \text{Gamble } G_{p=\frac{1}{4}}$$

where $=_P$ implies indifference. Essentially, Cohen, Jaffray, and Said estimated $CE(G_{p=\frac{1}{4}})$ by having the subject choose between the gamble and each of the 21 amounts FF 0, FF 50, …, FF 1000, where the increments are in units of 50 francs. The certainty equivalent is the point, going up or down the list of gifts, where preference for the gift changes to preference for the gamble.

Recall that a person is said to exhibit risk aversion if he or she rejects a risky prospect in favor of a sure thing that is identical to or less than the expected value of that prospect (Chapter 8, pp. 230–31). Thus, in the present situation, your behavior would be risk aversive if your certainty equivalent for Gamble $G_{p=\frac{1}{4}}$ were less than its expected value:

$$CE(G_{p=\frac{1}{4}}) < EV(G_{p=\frac{1}{4}}) = \text{FF } 250.$$

According to prospect theory, decision makers like yourself will often be risk aversive for prospects with the form of Gamble $G_{p=\frac{1}{4}}$. This prediction follows from two considerations. The first is the concavity of the value function for gains, which should always contribute to risk aversion for gains. The other consideration is the relationship between probabilities and decision weights. Reexamine the probability–weight function shown in Figure 10.1. Now compare Gamble $G_{p=\frac{1}{4}} = (\frac{1}{4}, \text{FF } 1000; \frac{3}{4}, \text{FF } 0)$ and the sure thing FF 250, the expected value of that gamble. Notice in Figure 10.1 that probabilities above the crossover probability are underweighted. Thus, assuming that the crossover is lower than $p = \frac{1}{4}$, you will underweight the prize probability of the FF 1000 in the gamble. Your affinity for the sure thing should also be enhanced by the fact that the probability of the sure thing, 100%, is *not* underweighted.

Cohen, Jaffray, and Said (1987) actually had subjects make decisions like those illustrated in Figure 10.6a for several gambles, all involving gambles similar to Gamble $G_{p=\frac{1}{4}}$, but with differing values of p, the probability of winning 1000 francs. The specific values were $p = \frac{1}{2}, \frac{1}{3}, \frac{1}{4},$ and $\frac{1}{6}$. The filled points in Figure 10.7 show the percentages of subjects whose certainty equivalents indicated risk aversion. If the subjects' decisions were generally risk averse, then each of those points would have been above the 50% mark denoted by the horizontal dashed line. Clearly, risk aversion was not the norm.

Each subject in the Cohen, Jaffray, and Said experiment also considered gambles and sure things that involved losses. These alternatives were mirror images of ones implying gains. For example, loss Gamble $L_{p=\frac{1}{4}}$ in Figure 10.6b parallels gain Gamble $G_{p=\frac{1}{4}}$ in Figure 10.6a. Again, the subject indicated a certainty equivalent, somewhere in the range from a loss of 1000 francs (–FF 1000) to a loss of nothing (–FF 0). An argument symmetric to the one described above for prospects involving gains leads to the expectation

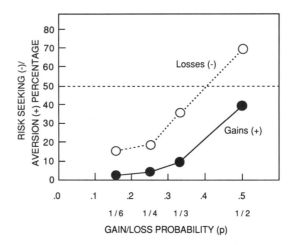

FIGURE 10.7. Percentages of certainty equivalents indicating risk seeking or risk aversion, as a function of gain or loss probability *p* in Gamble G_p or Gamble L_p. Based on results reported by Cohen, Jaffray, and Said (1987), Table 2, with permission from Academic Press and the authors.

that, according to prospect theory, decisions entailing losses commonly should be risk seeking. That is, the decision maker should tend to accept risky prospects over sure things that are identical to or better than the expected values of those prospects. The open points in Figure 10.7 indicate that this prediction held true only when the probability of a 1000-franc loss was $p = \frac{1}{2}$.

The present results seem incompatible with prospect theory. Notice, however, that each of the plots of risk-taking percentages shown in Figure 10.7 declines as the probability of the gain or loss in the pertinent gamble decreases. This pattern is actually in accord with what prospect theory predicts. Recall that high probabilities are underweighted (see Figure 10.1). However, this underweighting weakens as the probabilities become smaller. And, eventually, underweighting becomes overweighting. This characteristic of prospect theory's probability–weight relationship implies that, in the context of gains, as gain probabilities become smaller, risk aversion should weaken, eventually becoming risk seeking. In parallel fashion, in the domain of losses, as loss probabilities tend toward 0, risk seeking should evolve into risk aversion. The fact that the two plots shown in Figure 10.7 are for the most part below 50% might not betray a fundamental flaw in prospect theory. Instead, it might be due to the degree of curvature in subjects' value functions. Or it could be an indication that the crossover point at which probability underweighting changes to overweighting is higher than originally hypothesized.

The reflection effect Consider once more the pairs of prospects shown in Figure 10.5. Observe that the pair consisting of Prospects *P1*+ and *P2*+ is identical to the pair comprised of Prospects P1– and P2–, except that the signs of the outcomes are reversed. For example, the gain of $6000 in Prospect P1+ is replaced by a loss of $6000 in Prospect P1–. Recall that Prospect P2+ is generally chosen over Prospect P1+, and that Prospect P1– is typically preferred to Prospect P2–. Kahneman and Tversky (1979) have labeled such reversals of preferences in response to reversals in the signs of the outcomes the **reflection effect** (p. 268); the preferences are mirror images of each other. Several elements of people's decision making apparatus, as proposed in prospect theory, should contribute to such reflections. One is the claim that value functions are concave for gains but convex for losses. Another contributor, coupled with the reversal in value function shape across the reference point, is the over- and underweighting of probabilities. Numerous examples cited by Kahneman and Tversky (1979) suggest that the reflection effect is a common occurrence and thus buttresses the case for prospect theory generally. But how well has the prediction of reflections held up under closer examination?

According to prospect theory, the decision weight and value functions shown in Figures 10.1 and 10.2 should be characteristic of every decision maker. If so, the decisions of every individual person should reflect. However, in Kahneman and Tversky's (1979) experiments, which demonstrated the reflection effect, comparisons were made "between subjects" (Hershey and Schoemaker, 1980, p. 398). That is, the subjects who made decisions between prospects involving gains (for example, Prospect P1+ versus Prospect P2+) were different from those who decided among prospects entailing losses (for example, Prospect P1– versus Prospect P2–). Is it indeed the case that *individual* decision makers' choices reflect?

The experiment by Cohen, Jaffray, and Said (1987) sheds some light on the present issue, too. Every subject in the experiment made decisions of the forms illustrated in both Figures 10.6a and 10.6b, that is, parallel decisions involving both gains and equivalent losses. Interestingly, there was virtually no consistent relationship between subjects' decisions within the gain and loss domains. The relationships among subjects' certainty equivalents are one illustration. The correlation (r) between two variables is one measure of how strongly related those variables are. It ranges from +1 to –1. Essentially, a correlation of r = +1 means that there is a perfect positive relationship, such that the larger one variable is, the larger is the other. A correlation of r = –1 implies the opposite; that is, larger values of the first variable always occur with smaller values of the second one. A correlation of r = 0 typically means that there is no consistent relationship at all between the variables. Table 10.1 shows the correlations between subjects' certainty equivalents for parallel gain and loss prospects, for example, Gambles $G_{p=\frac{1}{4}}$ and $L_{p=\frac{1}{4}}$, as shown in Figure 10.6. Observe that, for all probabilities of winning or losing 1000 francs, the correlations were practically 0. Because, according to prospect theory, value functions have different shapes above and below the reference point, perfect correlations should not have been expected. But they certainly should not have been nil.

TABLE 10.1   Correlations between Certainty Equivalents for Parallel Gain and Loss Gambles G_p and L_p

PROBABILITY (P)	CORRELATION
1/2	−0.080
1/3	−0.080
1/4	−0.070
1/6	0.002

Source: Cohen, Jaffray, and Said (1987), Table 4, with permission from Academic Press and the authors.

One would also expect that, if the reflection effect were a common occurrence, subjects' risk-taking behavior would change character on either side of the reference point. In particular, according to prospect theory, we should typically observe that individuals will make risk-averse decisions among prospects involving gains, but risk-seeking ones when those prospects entail losses. Interestingly, Cohen, Jaffray, and Said found only a weak association between individual subjects' risk-taking behavior in the loss and gain domains. So did Hershey and Schoemaker (1980).

An appraisal

So what is the status of prospect theory? As suggested by the present examples, the empirical evidence on the aspects of prospect theory discussed in this chapter is mixed; some experiments support the theory, others do not. On balance, however, the consistent findings seem to outweigh the negative ones. What this probably means is that many of the claims made by the theory are correct, while others are in error. Only additional and more definitive studies will clarify the picture.

Leaving aside the question of evidence, it is also worth commenting on the character of prospect theory itself. Prospect theory is attractive because it impressively accounts for a number of decision phenomena that expected utility theory cannot. It also ties together in a coherent package various suggestions about decision behavior that have been around for some time, for example, the notions of reference points, concave and convex value functions, and decision weights. But like every theory, cast against its strengths, prospect theory also has weaknesses, including the following:

Ambiguity: As you have surely noticed, in its present stage of development, prospect theory is vague on a number of significant issues. One concerns the location of the probability–decision weight crossover point. Another pertains to the fuzziness of decision weights near 0 and 1. For instance, will a probability of 0.1% be overweighted, or will it be rounded to 0% and effectively ignored? We have seen that these ambiguities make it difficult to test the theory. Moreover, such vagueness is inherently unattractive in any theory.

Depth: One might also say that prospect theory—actually, all theories in the class associated with expected utility theory—suffers from a problem of depth. Take the proposed probability–decision weight relationship (Figure 10.1). Various features of this relationship are crucial to the theory; that is how it explains many decision phenomena. Such explanations are indeed an important accomplishment. But you have undoubtedly asked yourself questions like the following: *Why* do decision weights behave the way they do? For instance, why are high probabilities underweighted? Why does the crossover probability occur below 50%? Psychologically, what does *weighting* mean in the first place? Unfortunately, prospect theory does not address such fundamental questions.

Complexity: Some observers (for example, Shafer, 1987) have also commented on the complexity of prospect theory. It is possible that human decision processes are so complicated that they demand a complicated theory to account for them. But many hope that a more elegant and more accurate theory will someday present itself. Perhaps future refinements of prospect theory will constitute that theory. And those refinements must, of course, include extensions such that the theory applies to prospects that entail more than just two nonnull outcomes

SUMMARY

In some way or another, almost all theories of decision making under uncertainty suggest that the decision maker trades off uncertainty against value. Expected utility theory describes value versus uncertainty tradeoffs in terms of utilities for outcomes being weighted by their probabilities, that is, Probability × Utility. There are numerous cousins of expected utility theory, with prospect theory being the most prominent. The differences between expected utility theory and its cousins typically entail relaxations of some of the strong specific claims made by the former. These relaxed claims allow the newer theories to explain phenomena expected utility theory cannot, for example, the Allais Paradox.

KEY TERMS

Absolute representation
Certainty effect
Decision weight
Diminishing marginal significance
Discontinuity
Effective representation
Probability mass graph
Prospect theory

Reference point
Reflection effect
Regressiveness
Regular prospect
Strictly negative prospect
Strictly positive prospect
Subcertainty
Subjective prospect value

ADDITIONAL READING

Bell and Farquhar, (1986); Kahneman and Tversky (1982a); Karmarkar (1979); Larson (1980); Schneider and Lopes (1986); Schoemaker (1982); Sugden (1986).

EXERCISES AND STUDY QUESTIONS

1. Recall Ms. A, whose utility function for money in the range $0 to $10 is shown in Figure 9.2 (p. 246). Suppose that Ms. A is presented with Prospect $P = $ (30%, $7; 70%, $1) and the sure amount $1.80. She is asked to indicate which she prefers, if either. What would be her decision under the following conditions?
    (a) She decides according to expected utility.
    (b) She decides according to the principles of prospect theory, where we can assume that the pertinent part of her value function coincides with the utility function in Figure 9.2, and that the curve shown in Figure 10.1 describes how she weights various probability values.

2. (a) A few minutes ago, Glenn Cleaver (pp. 288–89) learned that his company has been having a bad year, and thus merit salary increases will be smaller than expected. His division's budget has been set, and so he knows that his salary increase will be $250. Mr. Cleaver has also been offered a transfer to another division. He is unsure of the salary situation in that other division. However, his best information leads him to conclude that, if he took the new job, there is a 35% chance that his salary would increase by $275, but a 65% chance that it would go up by only $200. Suppose that Mr. Cleaver has to make a decision right now and that he does so according to the principles of prospect theory, with Figures 10.1 and 10.2b representing his decision weight and value functions, respectively. Will Mr. Cleaver stick with his old job, or will he transfer to the new position?
    (b) Suppose that Mr. Cleaver has a week to mull over his new job offer. In what way might he be expected to decide differently, according to prospect theory?

3. (Optional) Suppose a decision maker is considering choices between prospects of the form $P = (p, x; 1 - p, 0)$, with $x > 0$, and sure things that are identical to the expected values of those prospects, that is, $ST = px$. An example would be (25%, $30; 75%, $0) versus $7.50.
    (a) According to prospect theory, under what conditions will the decision maker's choices be risk averse and when might they not?
    (b) Similarly, according to prospect theory, when will the decision maker's choices definitely reflect and when is reflection less certain to occur?

4. Consider reference points in prospect theory:
    (a) Propose a plausible hypothesis for what induces a decision maker to adopt one reference point rather than another.
    (b) Outline an experiment whereby you could test your hypothesis.
    (c) In your opinion, is it rational for a person to have multiple reference points?

5. In Chapter 8, we learned about how parking tickets are handled in "Chance City." The violator is offered a choice between paying a fine of $5 or playing a gamble in which there is a 50% chance of having to pay a $10 fine and a 50% chance of having to pay nothing. It was indicated that most people choose the gamble, an instance of risk-seeking behavior. On the other hand, virtually all Chance City drivers buy auto insurance, too, which is risk aversive behavior. How would prospect theory explain this state of affairs?

Expected Value Versus Risk

Everything is sweetened by risk.

—Alexander Smith

Picture yourself as a regional public health officer. In recent years, your area has suffered over a thousand deaths from a certain infectious disease, which we will call "degracy." You have received two proposals for programs to reduce the degracy toll. One is from "Margaret Lopez," the other from "Aubrey Kim." Both programs involve various vaccination, sanitation, and educational activities. Only one of the programs can be funded. Since both cost about the same amount of money, you conclude that the basis for your decision should be the number of lives each program would save. Accordingly, you ask a panel of experts to give you their probability judgments about the efficacy of the programs. Following are the approximate list representations of the alternatives, reflecting the experts' opinions:

Lopez: (10%, 0; 10%, 200; 20%, 400; 50%, 500; 10%, 600)

and

Kim: (20%, 100; 10%, 200; 60%, 400; 10%, 500)

In these representations, the quantities are the numbers of lives that would be saved each year. For instance, it is indicated that there is a 10% chance that the Lopez program would save no lives, a 10% chance that it would save 200 lives a year, and so on. So how should you make your decision? How *would* you do so?

It is sometimes argued that decisions like yours should be made according to expected values. If you accepted those arguments, you would pick the Lopez program since, as you can verify, EV(Lopez) > EV(Kim), where EV denotes the expected number of lives saved annually by the respective programs. A case can also be made that you ought to decide according to expected utilities. As we saw in Chapter 9, this could lead you to pick the Kim program if your utility function for lives saved is concave. One reason this might be so is that, for you, the marginal significance of saving additional lives diminishes as the total number of lives already saved increases. In the last couple of chapters, we have learned that people's decisions often deviate systematically from the prescriptions of expected utility theory. Thus, if you made your funding decision intuitively, there is a good chance that your strategy would not be well-described as expected utility maximization, regardless of what you "should" do. Instead, you might perhaps decide according to the concepts in prospect theory or similar principles.

There is yet another perspective that has been adopted for decision problems similar to the present one. This alternative perspective, to which the present chapter is devoted, does not always lead to decisions that conflict with those yielded by the strategies we have considered so far. However, that point of view *is* different and offers useful insights. Moreover, many people say that it provides an especially easy and natural way to think about decision problems. It rests on a simple observation: the typical uncertain decision situation involves two major considerations. The first is the promise of potential gain, for example, that some number of lives will be saved. The other is the specter of loss—risk; for instance, that some number of lives might *not* be saved, or that *more* people are killed. For reasons described below, the possibility of gain is roughly captured by expected values. That is why this alternative approach is called the expected value (EV) versus risk perspective.

As suggested by your public health problem, the EV versus risk perspective has considerable generality. However, it captures the essence of financial decisions especially well. For instance, the "Fletchers," a couple choosing investments for their retirement, are naturally attracted by retirement plans that offer the possibility of high income when they are no longer working. And they are leery of schemes that might leave them penniless. It is perhaps because of the prevalence and seriousness of such situations that the principles we discuss presently mainly have their origins in the field of finance. That is also one reason we will emphasize prospects in which the outcomes are monetary.

The first section of the chapter starts with an assumption that is essential for almost all analyses of decision making within the EV versus risk perspective. The second section discusses several proposals for decision principles appropriate for this context. You already know what expected values are. However, we have discussed the concept of risk only in general terms. Greater precision is required to make EV versus risk concepts applicable and testable. Accordingly, the third section discusses how the idea of risk has been concretely operationalized. The fourth section reviews evidence about how well various EV versus risk principles describe how people actually decide. And the fifth ties together the various threads that run through the findings.

A FUNDAMENTAL ASSUMPTION: MONOTONICITY

The expected value of a prospect incorporates *all* its potential outcomes, not just the gains. Nevertheless, a prospect's EV is often taken as an indicator of its long-run gain potential. If the EV is positive, then in a specific sense the prospect does indeed promise an expected gain (see, for example, Chapter 8, pp. 225–27). Cast against a prospect's EV is its riskiness. On pages 316–32, we discuss in some detail exactly what is meant by "risk" in the present context. But for the moment, it suffices to recognize that the technical meanings of the term correspond closely to its everyday connotation—the possibility of loss.

According to the view to be described presently, every prospect can be represented in terms of two of its features, its expected value and its risk. It sometimes helps to visualize such prospects by their locations in an expected value-risk plane. Consider an example. The Fletchers are faced with two investment opportunities. They are, respectively,

$$\text{Plan } A = (\text{EV}_A, \text{R}_A)$$

and

$$\text{Plan } B = (EV_B, R_B)$$

where EV and R symbolize the expected values and risk levels of the opportunities. Graphically, those prospects are characterized as the points A and B in Figure 11.1.

Within the EV versus risk perspective, it is ordinarily assumed that the decision maker's preferences are **monotone** in both expected value and risk. Specifically, higher expected values are always preferred to lower ones, all other considerations being equal. Also, less risk is preferred to more. These assumptions are emphasized in Figure 11.1 by the arrows in the upper-left corner pointing downward and to the right. Thus, roughly, prospects increase in their attractiveness as we move to the lower right in the expected value–risk plane.

SOME PROPOSED DECISION PRINCIPLES

At a rudimentary level, the monotonicity assumption is one principle by which people are claimed to make decisions. Other proposed decision principles are more versatile, as we see now.

Acceptability thresholds

One possible decision rule says that prospects should be rejected out of hand whenever they fail to surpass either or both of two **acceptability thresholds**. An **expected value threshold (EV$_t$)** is a sum of money (or

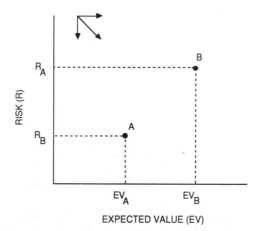

FIGURE 11.1. The expected value-risk plane. Each prospect, such as Prospect A or B, is characterized in terms of its expected value (EV) and its risk level (R). Preferences are assumed to be monotone in expected value (more is better) and risk (less is better).

whatever the relevant outcome is) such that, if a prospect's expected value falls below that point, it is automatically eliminated from consideration. For instance, the Fletchers might reject both Plan *A* and Plan *B* because neither offers an expected retirement income that is sufficiently high. If a prospect is more risky than an operative **risk threshold (R_t)**, it is rejected too. As suggested by Figure 11.2a, EV and risk thresholds define regions of acceptable and unacceptable prospects.

Threshold rules are instances of **noncompensatory decision principles.** For example, suppose a decision maker has a risk threshold R_t, and that the riskiness of Prospect *Q* exceeds that threshold, as in Figure 11.2a. This means that, no matter how good Prospect *Q*'s expected value is, that fact cannot offset or "compensate" for its unacceptable riskiness; it will be rejected. Imagine that a decision maker has both a risk threshold and an EV threshold. Thus, to be acceptable, a prospect must overcome two hurdles. The implied noncompensatory rule is an instance of a **conjunctive decision principle;** acceptable prospects must conjunctively satisfy two criteria.[1]

Dominance

Consider arbitrary acceptable Prospect $P = (EV_P, R_P)$ in Figure 11.2b. Suppose the decision maker has the opportunity to choose between Prospect

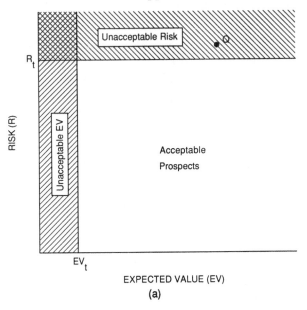

FIGURE 11.2. (a) Acceptable and unacceptable regions of prospects defined by expected value (EV_t) and risk (R_t) thresholds. (b) Preference relationships of Prospect $P = (EV_P, R_P)$ to prospects with better and worse expected values and risk levels.

[1]In general, the term "conjunction" implies joining.

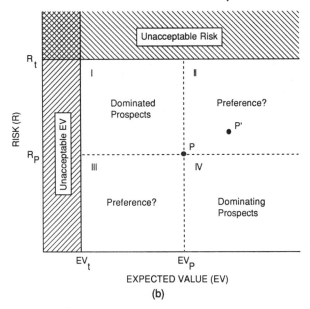

FIGURE 11.2. (continued)

P and some other acceptable prospect. Four categories of alternatives can be distinguished, according to whether their expected values and risk levels are better or worse than those of Prospect *P*. The prospects in Region I are worse in both respects; that is, they are dominated by Prospect *P*. Accordingly, the decision maker clearly should select Prospect *P* over any of them. On the other hand, Prospect *P* is itself dominated by the options in Region IV, and hence should be rejected in favor of any of those. The implied **EV–risk dominance principle** is eminently reasonable. But it provides no help in choosing between Prospect *P* and any of the alternatives in Regions II and III. More generally, dominance is not a guide for choices between prospects that bear a lower-left to upper-right relationship to each other in the expected value–risk plane. These are the choices that pose special problems; in choosing one alternative over the other, the decision maker achieves an advantage in one respect, but at a cost in the other. For example, compare Prospect *P* to Prospect *P'*, which is in Region II. If the decision maker were to choose Prospect *P'*, this would provide a better expected value, but greater riskiness.

The dominance concept is so simple and compelling that it might seem to have no practical value. After all, no one would ever knowingly choose a dominated prospect. But "knowingly" is the key word. In lots of practical situations it is very difficult to tell whether one prospect does indeed dominate another. Take the problem of assembling and choosing among portfolios of financial securities. Imagine, for instance, that the Fletchers are considering Portfolios *P*1 and *P*2 consisting of various numbers of shares in the indicated companies:

Portfolio *P*1: (150 IBM; 100 AT&T; 200 General Motors)

Portfolio $P2$: (110 Digital; 160 Beatrice; 250 Detroit Edison)

For convenience (and this will surely be untrue), we will assume that the costs of the portfolios are essentially the same. Suppose the Fletchers can characterize each of the stocks according to its expected value and riskiness; for example,

$$IBM = (EV_{IBM}, R_{IBM})$$

and

$$Beatrice = (EV_{Beatrice}, R_{Beatrice})$$

But what the Fletchers really need is the following characterization:

$$Portfolio\ P1 = (EV_{Portfolio\ P1}, R_{Portfolio\ P1})$$

and

$$Portfolio\ P2 = (EV_{Portfolio\ P2}, R_{Portfolio\ P2})$$

that is, the expected value and riskiness of each entire portfolio. It would then be immediately obvious whether one of the portfolios dominates the other.

So the task facing the Fletchers (or any portfolio manager) is to determine the expected value and riskiness of an entire portfolio from the expected values and risk levels of the various stocks comprising that portfolio. A major complication in this endeavor is that the future prices and earnings of the stocks are not independent of one another. For instance, if IBM stock declines in value, there is a good chance that General Motors stock will decline, too, although this is not guaranteed. There exist techniques of financial portfolio analysis that, in essence, amount to ways of determining dominance in situations like this (see Markowitz, 1959, for the classic ideas underlying these techniques). These methods are regarded as valuable guides in financial management. Thus, in practice, the dominance principle is far from useless.

Lexicographic rules

Lexicographic decision rules are one means of choosing between two prospects, neither of which might dominate the other. According to the *risk-priority lexicographic rule*, the decision maker first compares the prospects with respect to risk, because he or she considers risk to be more important than expected value. If one alternative has lower risk than the other, it is chosen; expected value is ignored. On the other hand, if the options are equivalent with respect to riskiness, the alternative with the higher expected value is picked. The *EV-priority* form of the lexicographic rule is essentially the same, except that the procedure starts with a comparison on expected values.

As a concrete example, suppose the Fletchers follow a risk-priority lexicographic decision rule. Consider Investment Plans W, X, Y, and Z in Figure 11.3, where it is assumed that all the plans are in the acceptable region.

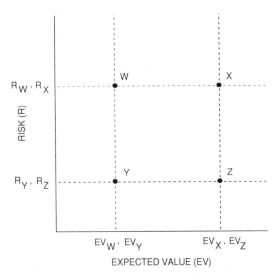

FIGURE 11.3.   Prospects illustrating a lexicographic decision rule. See text for details.

Plan *Y* has lower risk than either Plan *W* or Plan *X*, so it would be chosen over either of them. On the other hand, the risk levels of Plans *Y* and *Z* are identical; there is no basis for choice between them on that score. The Fletchers would then compare their expected values. Since Plan *Z* has the better expected value, it is the one that is chosen.

The adjective "lexicographic" is appropriate for the present rules. Lexicography is the task of compiling a dictionary. Words are placed in a dictionary in alphabetical order. Thus, in deciding whether Word 1 should precede Word 2, the words are compared on their first letters. If the words differ in that letter, the precedence is determined; the word whose starting letter is closer to the beginning of the alphabet is placed earlier in the dictionary. If their first letters agree, a comparison is made on the second letters. Again, if a difference exists on the second letters, the precedence is resolved. Otherwise, a comparison is made on the third letter. And so on. In form, lexicographic decision rules operate the same way. In lexicography, the letter positions in words correspond to the risk and expected value dimensions in decisions between prospects. The priority of A's, B's, C's, and so on, is dictated by the accepted order of the alphabet. In the decision rules for prospects, priority is dictated by whichever the decision maker considers more important, risk or expected value.

Compensatory rules

Lexicographic decision rules clearly are noncompensatory; strength on one dimension cannot compensate for weakness on another. Noncompensatory rules are often seen as unreasonable. For instance, suppose that

Investment Plan P_1 is riskier than Investment Plan P_2. The Fletchers (and their financial planner) might very well consider it possible for the sellers of Plan P_1 to, say, decrease its price such that it is indeed a wiser selection than Plan P_2. Depending on what we mean by "risk," this is equivalent to saying that an advantage in expected value *should* be able to offset a disadvantage in riskiness.

There are innumerable ways that a decision maker might in fact **trade off** expected value against riskiness. Such tradeoff mechanisms are sometimes described via **compensatory decision rules**, the simplest of which are **additive decision rules**. Consider the following special case:

$$W = EV - kR \tag{11.1}$$

In this equation, W is the *worthiness* of a prospect that has expected value EV and riskiness R. The constant k is a **risk weight**, which summarizes how important risk is to the decision maker, relative to expected value. As a matter of fact, k can be thought of as an index of the decision maker's risk attitude; the larger k is, the more risk averse the individual happens to be. Concrete examples should facilitate the interpretation of the additive expected value–risk rule.

Suppose that the Fletchers's feelings about prospects can be represented by the following instance of Equation 11.1, with $k = 2$:

$$W = EV - 2R \tag{11.2}$$

Figure 11.4a is a graphical depiction of how the Fletchers trade off expected value and risk against each other. The horizontal expected value axis is marked off in thousands of dollars. The vertical axis is in units of risk, which we continue to leave unspecified for the moment. The two straight lines shown in the plane are *isoworthiness contours*.[2] This means that all the prospects represented along a given line are equally worthy. For example, the worthiness of each prospect along the leftmost contour is indexed as 10. Consider Prospect A, which has $EV_A = 20$ and $R_A = 5$. By Equation 11.2, its worthiness is

$$W_A = 20 - 2(5) = 10$$

Similarly, Prospect B has $EV_B = 40$ and $R_B = 15$, and thus

$$W_B = 40 - 2(15) = 10$$

Any prospect that lies on a contour to the left of that containing a given prospect is less worthy. On the other hand, any prospect on a contour to the right is more worthy.

Consider another couple planning for retirement, the "Miltons." Their additive EV–risk rule is

$$W = EV - 4R \tag{11.3}$$

---

[2]The stem iso- implies "same."

(a)

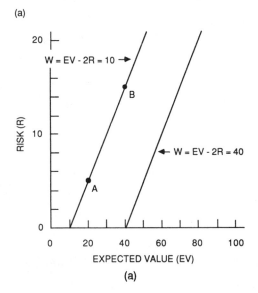

(a)

(b)

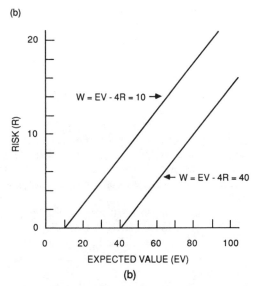

(b)

FIGURE 11.4. Isoworthiness (equal-worth) contours for prospects when expected value and risk compensate for each other additively: (a) for the Fletchers; (b) for the Miltons, who are more risk averse than the Fletchers.

Two of their isoworthiness contours are shown in Figure 11.4b. In comparing the rules for the Fletchers and the Miltons (Equation 11.2 versus Equation 11.3), notice that the risk weight is twice as large for the Miltons as for the Fletchers. This means that the Miltons are more risk averse. Suppose that the riskiness of a prospect increases by some amount, say, 10 units. For both the Fletchers and the Miltons, there is some increase in expected value that would leave the worthiness of the prospect unchanged. However, that compensating increase in expected value must be greater for the Miltons than for the Fletchers—twice as large to be exact. You should be able to convince yourself of this risk weight interpretation by comparing various changes along the corresponding isoworthiness contours in Figures 11.4a and 11.4b.

Generality

We have been discussing various decision principles, for instance, lexicographic and compensatory rules, as they apply to situations in which the person's major considerations are expected value and risk. However, it is important to realize that these principles apply more generally, too. That is, the dimensions could be almost anything, and there could be more than two. A couple of examples: If you are looking for a boyfriend or girlfriend, the dimensions might be "wit" and "looks." If you are seeking a new house, the pertinent considerations might include "location," "condition," and "price." (Some say that the only considerations should be "location," "location," and "location.") Regardless, the previous principles would be applied essentially the same as described above.

CHARACTERIZING RISK

Let us now address the question we have been deferring: What is risk? In what follows, we will discuss the problem in terms of decision situations where the outcomes are quantitative, for example, monetary. However, you should keep in mind that the underlying ideas are broader. You should consciously think about their extensions to other situations, for instance, in choosing medical treatments, where the outcomes might be the loss of bodily functions, or in selecting a spouse, where the potential outcomes include a lifetime of domestic misery.

As indicated previously, most people agree that the general concept of risk connotes the prospect of loss. However, for the purposes of applying the various principles we have been discussing—either as guides for how decisions should be made or as descriptions of how decisions in fact are made—much more precision is required. For instance, if the Fletchers wanted to determine whether financial Portfolio P1 dominates Portfolio P2, that is, has both better expected value and riskiness, they must be able to say unambiguously what riskiness is.

Risk has been characterized in many ways. Taken alone, every risk measure that has been applied in some way reflects what most of us would agree is risk. But we would also agree that no single one of those indicators fully represents what risk is. So it is probably useful for you to think of the various risk measures we will discuss as reflections of particular *aspects* or *components* of risk. The complete concept of risk is undoubtedly some combination of these (and perhaps other) components. It is an interesting problem determining exactly what that combination happens to be (see, for example, Fishburn, 1984). Typically, however, in specific applications and studies, individual measures of the type we examine below have proved sufficient. In effect, decision makers and investigators have said, "We know that risk is a broader concept. But for the present purposes, *this* is what we will mean by the term 'risk': ...."

Various aspects of risk are most easily understood in terms of probability mass graph representations of prospects, such as those we used in our discussion of prospect theory (Figures 10.3 and 10.4, pp. 292 and 293). By definition, a **random variable** is some quantity that takes on alternative values with specified probabilities. The number of heads that would be observed in three successive tosses of a coin is one example. The height of a randomly selected adult male living on your block is another. The outcome of a monetary prospect is clearly a random variable, too. In the present view, a prospect is simply the distribution of the random variable defined by the outcomes of that prospect. As we will see, various risk measures correspond to particular features of such distributions.

Reference points

As agreed, risk entails loss. Before we can examine specific risk measures, we must establish what a loss is. Traditionally, in defining risk indicators, loss has meant essentially what it means within prospect theory. That is, a prospect yields a loss if it results in an outcome that falls short of a specified reference point. In practice, three different reference points have been distinguished:

Reference Point 1: Expected value According to the first standard, a loss is experienced when the actual result of a prospect is an outcome that is less than the expected value of that prospect. Consider, for example, Investment Plan *A* in Figure 11.5. A real investment plan would, of course, yield an income that could take on hundreds of different values, for example, $527, $1245, and so on. For simplicity, we round the potential incomes to the nearest $1000. As indicated, Plan *A* promises the Fletchers an expected income of $800 per year. Thus, if the Fletchers adopted the expected value as their reference point, any income less than $800 would be experienced as a loss.

Reference Point 2: Zero According to a second standard, a loss is any outcome less than zero, an objective loss. For instance, from this perspective, Investment Plan *A* would provide a loss for the Fletchers only if it really did leave them with less money than they had in the first place.

Reference Point 3: Target The decision maker easily can have a target outcome or *aspiration level* that is quite different from either the expected value of a prospect or zero. That target might be self-imposed, or it could be set by an external agent, for example, one's superior. For instance, in the business world no firm wants to lose money. However, the firm's "goal" is

(a)

Investment Plan A

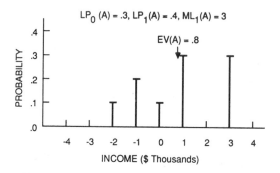

(b)

Investment Plan B

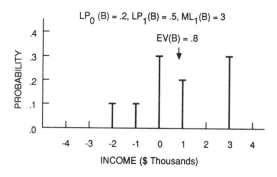

FIGURE 11.5. Investment plan probability mass graphs illustrating loss probability (LP) and maximum loss (ML) risk measures. See text for details.

not to avoid losing money. Instead, for every venture there is a positive target level of financial return, say, 20% or 30% on the initial investment. Anything less would be seen as a loss. And the employee who accepts a proposition resulting in such a loss is held accountable for it. In the previous example, the Fletchers might, for various reasons, consider $1000 a legitimate target income from an investment of the size required for Plan A.

Risk Indicators

We are now in a position to describe the major risk indicators that have been employed.

Indicator 1: Loss probability The first risk measure we consider is a simple one—the probability that a loss of some kind will be incurred. Clearly, the **loss probability (LP)** for a prospect is simply the sum of the probabilities for all potential outcomes that happen to fall below the decision maker's reference point. For an example, return to Figure 11.5. Although this is unlikely, suppose the Fletchers adopt zero income as their reference point. Then the loss probabilities of Investment Plans A and B would be

$$LP_0(A) = 0.1 + 0.2 = 0.3$$

and

$$LP_0(B) = 0.1 + 0.1 = 0.2$$

where the subscripts identify the reference point. Thus, Plan A would be the more risky alternative. But suppose, as seems more reasonable, that the Fletchers's reference point is an income of $1000. As easily seen, in that case the loss probabilities would be $LP_1(A) = 0.4$ and $LP_1(B) = 0.5$, and we would come to a different conclusion about the relative riskiness of the two plans.

Indicator 2: Maximum loss   Our second risk aspect is the **maximum loss** (**ML**), the largest possible loss a prospect can yield. Suppose that, in a given situation, the decision maker's reference point is denoted RP and that an arbitrary outcome is indicated by X. Then the corresponding **relative loss** (**L**) is simply

$$L = RP - X$$

that is, the difference between the reference point and what was actually obtained. For instance, suppose that, as before, the Fletchers's reference income is $1000. Then an absolute loss of $1000 would be a relative loss of $1000 - (-\$1000) = \$2000$. Notice that, as shown in Figure 11.5, the maximum losses of Investment Plans A and B are identical, $3000. However, the losses are quite different for Plans C and D, shown in Figure 11.6, $ML_1(C) = \$3000$ and $ML_1(D) = \$5000$, respectively. Thus, by this measure, Investment Plan D is considerably riskier than its competitor.

Indicator 3: Expected loss   By now you know that the expected value of a prospect is the sum of the potential outcomes of that prospect, each multiplied by its probability.[3] It sometimes helps to describe such concepts in equation form. As above, suppose we represent the outcomes of a given Prospect Q by the random variable X. Then the expected value of that prospect is simply the expected value or **expectation** of the random variable, which is often denoted as follows:

$$EV(P) = E(X) = \sum_{\text{All } X} P(X)X \qquad (11.4)$$

Implicit in these remarks is that the notion of an expectation is more general than its application to prospects; any random variable has an expectation, which is simply the sum of all the possible values of that random variable, each value multiplied by its probability.

---

[3]We will continue to restrict our attention to prospects in which only a finite number of distinct amounts might occur; continuous random variables for which this is not the case are beyond the scope of this text.

(a)

Investment Plan C

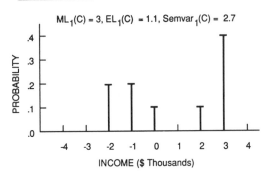

(b)

Investment Plan D

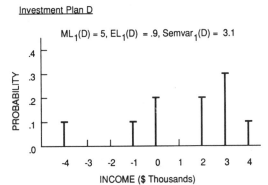

FIGURE 11.6. Investment plan probability mass graphs illustrating maximum loss (ML), expected loss (EL), and semivariance (Semvar) risk measures. See text for details.

Our third risk measure is something of a combination of the previous two, along with the expectation idea. The **expected loss (EL)** of a prospect is the expectation of the losses, restricted to those cases where the outcome is actually less than the decision maker's reference point. (The specific formula for the expected loss is given on page 323.)

For examples, refer to Figure 11.6. Suppose that the Fletchers's reference income is $1000. We would find that the expected loss for Investment Plan C is $EL_1(C) = 1.1$ and that of Plan D is $EL_1(D) = 0.9$, where, as indicated in the figure, the units are in thousands of dollars. So, by this measure, Plan C is riskier, a conclusion that disagrees with our previous inference from maximum losses.

To summarize: If we use maximum loss as our measure of risk, then the representations of Investment Plans C and D are

$$\text{Plan } C = (EV = 0.8, ML_1 = 3.0)$$

and

$$\text{Plan } D = (EV = 1.2, ML_1 = 5.0)$$

However, if risk is indicated by expected loss, the representations are

$$\text{Plan } C = (EV = 0.8, EL_1 = 1.1)$$

and

$$\text{Plan } D = (EV = 1.2, EL_1 = 0.9)$$

Observe that, in the latter representation, Plan D dominates Plan C; it has a better expected value and is less risky. Such was not the case with the previous risk measure. Thus, we see that the way we characterize risk can make a world of difference in our decision.

Indicator 4: Below-reference semivariance Suppose, as before, that the Fletchers have a reference income of $1000 for the class of investments they are considering. Picture two scenarios. In the first, the Fletchers experience an objective loss of $1000, an outcome that is $2000 below their reference income. In the second, they lose $3000, which falls short of the reference by $4000. Since, relative to their reference point, the Fletchers lost twice as much money in the second scenario, would they feel twice as bad about that loss? It is possible that they would feel *more* than twice as bad.

The above scenarios illustrate the motivation behind our fourth risk indicator, the **below-reference semivariance (Semvar)**, whose formula is given on page 323. The essence of the semivariance is that a given loss contributes to the riskiness of a prospect not in relation to the size of the loss itself, but to the *square* of that loss. And if the loss is greater than one unit, the square is larger than the loss itself. Thus, effectively, the risk significance of a loss grows explosively as the magnitude of the loss increases.

The investment plans in Figure 11.6 again provide good examples. The semivariance of Plan C is $Semvar_1(C) = 2.7$, and that of Plan D, $Semvar_1(D) = 3.1$. So, in contrast to what was indicated when we used expected loss as our measure of risk, we now conclude that Plan D is riskier than Plan C. The reason for the difference is that the semivariance places special emphasis on the extreme loss of $4000 that is possible with Plan D.

Indicator 5: Variance Our final risk measure, the variance, has been used more often than any of the others. For instance, it is the one traditionally used in financial portfolio analysis (see Elton and Gruber, 1987; Markowitz, 1959). The variance of a random variable is an index of the extent to which the values of that random variable tend to differ from one another, and hence from their expected value. This highlights the interpretation of the expected value as an average (see Chapter 8). Figure 11.7 illustrates the idea. Notice that all four of the investment plans described there have the same expected income, EV = $1000. However, they differ substantially in the variability of the actual incomes they might provide. Plan E has no variability at all; it guarantees $1000—nothing more, nothing less. The potential incomes from the remaining plans vary, but they all lie between –$1000 and $3000. Nev-

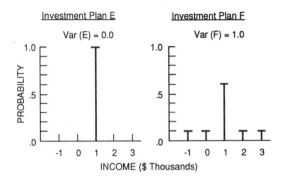

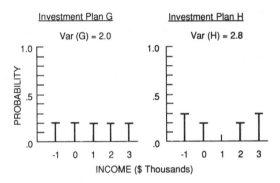

FIGURE 11.7. Investment plan probability mass graphs illustrating the variance (Var) as a measure of risk. See text for details.

ertheless, the intuitive impression is that the variability grows from Plan *E* through Plan *H*. Moreover, many observers would say that the riskiness of the plans increases from Plan *E* through Plan *H*, too; the plans offer progressively less assurance of an income in the vicinity of $1000. That is, riskiness increases with variability.

The quantity known as the variance is a way of capturing the above risk intuitions numerically. The formula for the variance is given on page 323. The larger the variance, the greater the risk. As examples, the variances of the above investment plans are, respectively, Var(E) = 0, Var(F) = 1.0, Var(G) = 2.0, and Var(H) = 2.8. These values are in accord with our previous intuitions about the relative riskiness of the prospects.

The variance is both similar to but different from the semivariance. One point of similarity is that losses contribute to indicated riskiness in relation to the squares of the losses, not the magnitudes of the losses themselves. But note that the reference point for the variance is restricted to the expected value of the prospect. However, the most striking difference between the variance and all the previous risk indicators, including the semivariance, is that the variance is affected by *all* the outcomes of a prospect, not just those that fall below the reference point. In that respect, since the concept of risk implies loss, the variance is a contaminated risk measure.

Computational formulas (Optional) If you have had a course in elementary statistics, the application of the computational formulas for various risk indicators will be straightforward. If you have not had such a course, ask a more experienced friend to help you work your way through the formulas. As practice exercises, you could verify the calculations of the indicators cited in the previous examples.

Expected loss: In the previous notation, the expected loss of arbitrary Prospect Q would be

$$\mathrm{EL_{RP}}(P) = \sum_{X < RP} Q(X)L$$

$$= \sum_{X < RP} P(X)(RP - X) \tag{11.5}$$

where RP is the decision maker's reference point and, as implied, the losses are $L = RP - X$.

Below-reference semivariance: For Prospect Q,

$$\mathrm{Semvar_{RP}}(Q) = \sum_{X < RP} P(X)(X - RP)^2 \tag{11.6}$$

where RP is the decision maker's reference point. The larger the semivariance, the greater the riskiness. An equivalent expression is

$$\mathrm{Semvar_{RP}}(Q) = \sum_{X < RP} P(X)L^2 \tag{11.7}$$

where, as you will recall, $L = RP - X$ is the loss implied by outcome X.

Variance: For arbitrary Prospect Q, the **variance (Var)** is given by

$$\mathrm{Var}(P) = \sum_{\mathrm{All}\,X} Q(X)(X - EV)^2 \tag{11.8}$$

EVIDENCE

How well do the various expected value versus risk principles we have discussed account for how people actually decide? There has been surprisingly little systematic study of decision behavior within the EV versus risk perspective, despite its popularity within such practical fields as finance. However, a few studies are suggestive of conclusions that might be further substantiated by future investigations.

Conjunctive acceptance

Conrath (1973) intensively studied the decision making of a certain corporation's executive committee and its staff over a long period of time. For convenience, let us refer to their employer as Corporation X. The decisions under consideration concerned whether Corporation X should invest in the development of specific new products. Analyses of how the executives responded to real proposals that arose in the course of their business, as well as to large numbers of hypothetical ones presented by the investigator, led Conrath to the following characterization of how the executive committee makes its decisions.

The critical quantities in the committee's decision procedure are these:

r = actual rate of return on investment
e = expected rate of return on investment
C = critical rate of return on investment
$p = P(r < C)$, that is, the probability of a return rate less than the critical rate

Thus, the committee thinks about proposals in terms of the *rates* of return on investment (profits), rather than the magnitudes of those returns themselves. For instance, in evaluating a $100,000 investment that yielded a profit of $15,000, the important thing is not the $15,000, but rather the rate of return $r = \$15,000/\$100,000 = 15\%$. The expected return rate e can be taken as the expected value of r. Effectively, the critical rate C is the company's reference point. Thus, if $C = 30\%$, as is commonly the case at Corporation X, then any return $r < 30\%$ is effectively regarded as a loss, for example, less than $30,000 on an outlay of $100,000. The probability $p = P(r < C)$ is hence a measure of risk, a loss probability.

The executive committee's decision rule is such that new product Proposal P is accepted if, for that proposal, both

$$\text{(a)} \quad e \geq e_t = C + 3p$$

and

$$\text{(b)} \quad p \leq p_t = 10\%$$

otherwise, the proposal should be rejected. Thus, e_t and p_t are, essentially, expected value and risk thresholds, respectively.

As a concrete though fictional example, suppose that "Ralph Bland," the manager of Corporation X's widget division, proposes to spend $250,000 developing a new type of widget, and that the critical rate of return established by the executive committee is in fact $C = 30\%$. The company's analysts carefully construct a probability distribution of the amount of money they can expect Mr. Bland's widget project to yield over the life of the product. This is equivalent to a distribution in terms of the rate of return, r. The analysts conclude that the probability of a return rate less than $C = 30\%$ is only 5%; that is,

$$p = P(r < C = 30\%) = 5\%$$

which is less than the risk threshold $p_t = 10\%$. So the project is indeed acceptable on that score. However, the expected value of the return rate distribution is

$$e = 40\%$$

which is less than the threshold expected return rate,

$$e_t = 30\% + 3(5\%) = 45\%$$

Thus, Mr. Bland's widget proposal is rejected; Corporation X will stick with its old widget.

The decision method described above clearly is a special type of conjunctive decision procedure. As indicated, the risk dimension is identified with p, a loss probability, where a loss is a return rate r less than $C = 30\%$. The risk threshold is $p_t = 10\%$. The expected value dimension is described in terms of the expected rate of return, e. What is special about this conjunctive decision rule, which prevents us from considering it a pure one, is that the expected value threshold depends on the risk of the alternative under consideration. Corporation X's executives demand a higher expected return on investment for riskier projects. In effect, they are trading off risk against expected value.

Additive compensation

Greer (1974) presented 20 realistic, even if hypothetical, investment opportunities to executives at 27 major "Fortune 500" corporations. The executives were to treat the opportunities as if they were available to their own firms. Greer then constructed a model of investment decision making in which the overall worthiness (W) of an opportunity could be represented in the form described previously by Equation 11.1, which is reproduced here for easy reference:

$$W = EV - kR \tag{11.1}$$

Recall that EV is the expected value of a given prospect and R its riskiness. Also, the risk weight k indexes the decision maker's feelings about risk. Greer's risk measure was the standard deviation, which is simply the square root of the variance. His measure of risk attitude for a firm reflected, among other things, the size of the loss probability the executive would tolerate for the firm. There were indeed systematic discrepancies between executives' actual decisions and predictions made by Greer's model. However, the accuracy of the model was fairly good.

To be concrete, consider a typical decision problem. In one alternative, the firm could earn $123,000 for sure, for example, by keeping its money in the bank. On the other, it could invest in a proposition that promised a 50% chance of a return of $194,000 and a 50% chance of a $91,000 return. Over all such problems and all firms, the correlation between the numbers of risky options chosen by the executives and by the model was $r = 0.63$. When Hoskins (1975) replaced the standard deviation as the risk measure by the semivariance, the model did even better.

Is less risk always preferred to more?

Suppose a decision maker is confronted with a choice between two prospects that have identical expected values. Within the expected value versus risk perspective, there remains only one basis for choice, their riskiness. As indicated at the outset of our discussion, conventional wisdom says that the decision maker will choose the alternative that entails less risk. After all, why would anyone want to lose something? Contesting this seemingly obvious prediction is **portfolio theory**, as proposed by Coombs (1975). For two prospects to have the same expected value but different levels of riskiness, the possibility of loss in the riskier alternative must be compensated for by a greater potential gain. According to portfolio theory, every individual has an "optimal level of tension between this push and pull" of "greed and fear" (Coombs and Huang, 1970, pp. 23–24). Hence, each person has a maximally preferred level of risk, which might not be the absence of risk altogether.

There have been numerous tests of portfolio theory. Most have yielded results consistent with the theory. Often those results conceivably also could be explained by such competitors as expected utility theory, especially if one admits the possibility of utility functions consistent with either risk-aversive or risk-seeking behavior. But sometimes results from portfolio theory tests have directly contradicted those alternative theories. If we were to summarize all the available evidence, it appears that in a reliable minority of circumstances some people indeed do have intermediate ideal risk levels. However, there is little reason to expect such to be the case for lots of people or in circumstances where the stakes are serious, for example, as opposed to recreational gambling situations (see Lehner, 1980).

A SYNTHESIS

What conclusions should we draw from studies of decision making within the EV versus risk perspective? First, you should recognize that the claims made from this point of view do not always conflict with those made by other kinds of theories, for example, prospect theory. Comparing the alternative perspectives is something like comparing apples and oranges because they are so different. However, in principle, we ought to be able to contrast the accuracy of their predictions for how people will decide. Unfortunately, only rarely have investigators succeeded in devising situations in which theories within the two perspectives make clearly different predictions. Often people's decisions can be described equally well within either framework. For instance, if a person decides in such a way that expected value and risk compensate for each other, this individual's behavior is likely to be well described by utility theory, too. In such cases, as far as accounting for the observed decisions is concerned, it is largely a matter of taste which perspective we accept. Nevertheless, some researchers maintain that the EV versus risk perspective seems closer to the way decision makers literally think, especially in business. Moreover, people sometimes *say* that they make decisions in stages, for example, first eliminating out of hand alternatives that are too risky, and then making tradeoffs between risk and expectations in choosing among the options that remain. It is hard to reconcile these reports solely within the framework of, say, utility theory or prospect theory.

The previous remarks highlight themes that will recur in the remaining pages of this book. They turn on the idea that it is probably naive to expect that any single rule will fully describe how people decide. An inescapable conclusion is that people employ a variety of methods for making decisions. So, rather than pursuing an elusive equation that will explain everything, a more sensible goal might be to discover rules that are reliably used at least sometimes. Then there would be several important auxiliary goals. The first is to characterize the relative frequency with which various procedures are used. For instance, it would be useful to know, say, relatively how often people follow prospect theory rather than lexicographic rules, and vice versa. It seems quite plausible—indeed there is evidence of it—that a given individual will use several different ways of deciding. A crucial problem, then, is determining the higher-level principles that guide the person in selecting decision procedures—literally, deciding how to decide. This issue is sometimes described as understanding the rules of *contingent processing* (Payne, 1982). That is, contingent on what conditions will a person, for instance, decide according to expectations, and when will he or she do something else? Finally, there is the question of individual differences. There is at least some evidence that different decision makers exhibit characteristically different inclinations to approach decision problems in particular ways (Henderson and Nutt, 1980; McKeeney and Keen, 1974). For example, whereas for a given class of problems, 80% of the time you might follow procedures similar to prospect theory, in the same circumstances your best friend might most often use a conjunctive procedure of the type described by Conrath (1973). Pursuing these issues is a major challenge of decision research for the next several years.

SUMMARY

Within the expected value versus risk perspective, each alternative is characterized in terms of its expected value and its riskiness. When it is positive, the expected value of a prospect is its promise of reward. Cast against that promise is the threat of loss the prospect entails—risk. Several decision principles within the expected value versus risk perspective capture the notion that a prospect with a low expected value can compensate for this weakness by having little risk. However, this perspective also easily accommodates noncompensatory decision principles. An example is that in which, if the riskiness of an alternative exceeds a risk threshold, it will be rejected, no matter how good its expected returns are. There is evidence that some decision makers in fact do make decisions in noncompensatory ways.

KEY TERMS

Acceptability threshold
Additive decision rule
Below-reference semivariance
Compensatory decision rule
Conjunctive decision principle
EV–risk dominance principle
Expectation
Expected loss
Expected value threshold
Lexicographic decision rule
Loss probability

Maximum loss
Monotone
Noncompensatory
Portfolio theory
Random variable
Relative loss
Risk threshold
Risk weight
Trade off
Variance

ADDITIONAL READING

Fishburn (1977); Keller, Sarin, and Weber (1986); Libby and Fishburn (1977); Lopes (1983, 1984); Payne (1973, 1975); Payne, Laughhunn, and Crum (1980); Ranyard (1976).

EXERCISES AND STUDY QUESTIONS

1. Reconsider the Lopez and Kim anti-degracy public health programs described at the beginning of the chapter. Recall that, in terms of lives saved annually, the list representations of these programs were Lopez: (10%, 0; 10%, 200; 20%, 400; 50%, 500; 10%, 600) and Kim: (20%, 100; 10%, 200; 60%, 400; 10%, 500).

   (a) Construct probability mass graph representations of the alternatives.

   (b) Determine the expected values of the programs, that is, the expected numbers of lives saved each year.

   (c) Suppose that your reference point is RP = 300 lives saved annually. Determine the following risk measures for the Lopez and Kim programs: (i) loss probability, (ii) maximum loss, (iii) (optional) expected loss, (iv) (optional) below-reference semivariance, and (v) (optional) variance.

   (d) For some of the above risk measures, the Lopez program dominates the Kim program and thus clearly should be chosen. For which measures is that the case?

   (e) Suppose that your reference point is RP = 200 lives saved and that your expected value and maximum loss risk thresholds are EV_t = 300 lives and ML_t = 150 lives, respectively. Which program, if either, would be acceptable to you?

   (f) Again assume that your reference point is RP = 200 lives saved and that your expected value threshold is EV_t = 300 lives. However, your maximum loss risk threshold is ML_t = 225 lives. Suppose that you make decisions using a risk-priority lexicographic rule. Which program would you choose, if either?   Which would you pick if you used an expected value-priority lexicographic rule?

(g) Assume the same conditions as in part (f) with respect to the reference point and thresholds. Also suppose that you decide between programs according to the following additive compensatory rule:

$$W = EV - kML$$

where W is the subjective worthiness of a given program, from your point of view, EV is the expected number of lives saved, ML is the maximum loss of the program, and k is the risk weight that reflects your risk attitude. Which program would you choose if k were to take on the following values: (i) $k = 2$, (ii) $k = 1$, and (iii) $k = \frac{1}{2}$?

(h) For each of the values of k indicated in part (g), sketch isoworthiness contours. In which case are you indicated to be most risk averse?

2. Suppose that Bertrand is a risk seeker, even when making serious financial decisions, and that he trades off risk against expected value additively (pp. 314–16). What would his isoworthiness contours look like? How would they appear if he were indifferent to risk?

3. Suppose that a decision maker has a risk threshold. Could you explain that person's behavior within the context of expected utility theory? If so, how?

4. Judy manages her parents' retirement investments. Her reference point for investments that have a certain cost is an income of $1000. Conservative Investment A has an expected income of EV_A = $1500. It also guarantees a minimum income of $700. Thus, its maximum loss is ML_A = $1000 − $700 = $300. In contrast, the expected income of Investment B is EV_B = $2000. We want to gauge Judy's attitude toward risk in the present context. So we ask her, "What is the guaranteed income from Investment B that would make it equally attractive as Investment A?" Imagine two possible responses: "$500" and "$200."

(a) Intuitively, which response indicates greater risk aversion?

(b) Suppose we can assume that Judy makes her investment decisions in a manner that is well described by an additive compensatory rule:

$$W = EV - kML$$

where W is subjective worthiness, EV is expected income, ML is the maximum loss of an investment, and k is the risk weight that quantifies Judy's risk attitude. For each of Judy's responses in part (a), determine the implied value of k. Does the difference in the k's agree with your previous intuitions about Judy's risk attitudes?

5. Recruit two different friends to serve as subjects. Ask each to assume the role of Judy in Problem 4, acting as the investment manager for his or her own parents.

(a) Ask each friend for the smallest guaranteed income that would make Investments A and B equally attractive. Which friend is indicated to be more risk averse? (Optional: Derive the implied risk weights k.)

(b) Using the methods described in Problem 8a, Chapter 9, measure your friends' utility functions for investment income in the $0 to $2000 range. Compare the curvatures of the resulting utility functions. Does the indicated difference in your friends' risk attitudes agree with your conclusion in part (a)? If the conclusions are not the same, discuss plausible explanations for the discrepancy.

6. (Optional) (a) According to prospect theory, losses have diminishing marginal significance. This seems inconsistent with using the semivariance (and also the variance) as a measure of the riskiness of a prospect. How so?

   (b) How might the semivariance be modified to construct a risk measure that better agrees with prospect theory's notion of diminishing marginal significance?

7. (Optional) It was indicated (p. 321) that traditional approaches to financial portfolio analysis (pp. 310–12) have used the variance as a measure of riskiness. In view of the considerations discussed in Problem 6, as well as other shortcomings of the variance as a measure of risk, those approaches seem flawed. Would you consider such flaws to be serious? How would they alter portfolio investment decisions, as compared to what those decisions would be like if a risk measure such as that implied in Problem 6(b) were used? What do you suspect would be the major drawback to performing traditional portfolio analysis using this alternative indicator of risk?

12

Personal Representations: Their Character

Beauty is in the eye of the beholder.

—Margaret Wolfe Hungerford

Last Thursday, "Herbert King" visited "Autorama," the local "Zipmobile" dealership, and spoke with sales representative "Martha Malloy." Within hours, he was driving home in his new $15,000 Zipmobile. The next day, "Carl Anderson" listened to the same sales pitch from Ms. Malloy. However, unlike Mr. King, he did not buy a Zipmobile. Instead, he went down the street and spent his $15,000 on a "Hummer." Why the difference? In the previous chapters, we have learned about many factors that might account for the opposing decisions of Messrs. King and Anderson. In this chapter and the next, we consider several others, all concerning representations.

We have made extensive use of standard **external decision representations** in the past several chapters, for example, decision trees, ordered lists, and payoff matrices. On many of those occasions, you probably felt that the representations were helpful; they allowed you to better understand the given situations. Indeed, that is why those representations have become indispensable tools for decision analysts and others who try to help people make better decisions. But the fact that the standard representations are helpful also highlights a crucial point: They differ from the way you *normally* view decision problems, your own *personal* representations.

A **personal** or **internal representation** is the decision maker's individual conception of the decision situation with which he or she is faced. It does not encompass everything in the decision maker's mind, however, only those aspects that affect the resulting decision. We were able to take "mental snapshots" of the thoughts of Herbert King and Carl Anderson as they strolled around Autorama with Martha Malloy. Table 12.1 shows a sample of those thoughts, which are suggestive of what we can expect to find in personal decision representations. The representations of Messrs. King and Anderson have much in common, but they are also quite different. It is easy to imagine those representational discrepancies contributing to their different decisions.

Three questions about personal representations arise. The first is about *content*. Any given decision situation entails seemingly countless features. The decision maker cannot possibly pay attention to them all, that is, include them in his or her representation. Nor would the decision maker want to. So which features *will* affect the decision? For instance, every car has literally thousands of physical parts, to say nothing of such intangibles as its esthetics and prestige value. As suggested by the mental snapshots of Herbert King and Carl Anderson, only a handful of features are likely to dictate a car-buying choice. The second representation question concerns form, or *character*. The car-shopping reflections displayed in Table 12.1 are *indicative* of Messrs. King and Anderson's representations, but are not the representations themselves. The latter are psychological entities that, as we will see, are sometimes hard for even the decision maker to describe. What are the distinctive characteristics of people's personal representations, char-

TABLE 12.1 Mental Snapshots at Autorama

Customer Herbert King:

1: "Wow, this is a pretty seedy-looking place!"
2: "She seems very nice, genuinely interested in her customers."
3: "Gosh, this is a gorgeous car! But I wish they had a better selection of colors."
4: "Billy never had a bit of trouble with *his* Zipmobile."
5: "I sure *hope* this thing is reliable. In *my* job I can't afford to be running back and forth getting stuff fixed."
6: "Ed would really be impressed. This is a lot better than that heap *he's* got!"
7: "Can I *afford* $15,000, with the wedding and all...?"
8: "She's right: This *is* a great car!"

Customer Carl Anderson:

1: "Service department looks okay, even if the showroom is no great shakes."
2: "Decent fuel economy—to start with, at least."
3: "Colleen was right. The sales people in this place are really pushy. Why won't this woman keep quiet?"
4: "I really like the smell of new cars. Exciting!"
5: "One good thing you can say for Zipmobiles is that they are made right here."
6: "All the books say the resale value of Zipmobiles is really low. I wonder if it's gonna stay that way?"
7: "At least it's cheap."
8: "Maybe I'd better look at the Hummer before I decide."

acteristics that explain some of the puzzles of decision behavior? The third representation question is about *moderation*. As implied by Table 12.1, different individuals' representations of the same situations tend to disagree. Why? What are the factors that influence or moderate personal representations?

Several aspects of the content question are addressed in this chapter. However, most of our discussion about content is in Chapter 13, along with a survey of various moderation effects. The emphasis of the present chapter is on the character of personal decision representations. The first section discusses representation scope, for instance, how many of the objective features of a situation are likely to be considered by the decision maker. The second section concerns the nature of the elements of personal representations, for example, how coarse or fine they are. The third section examines the interconnections among those elements.

How do the present issues relate to the previous chapters? Decision making normally proceeds in two broad phases, a **representation phase** followed by a **combination phase**. As the name suggests, in the representation phase, the decision maker constructs his or her characterization of the situation at hand. The resulting representation is likely to incorporate several different considerations.[1] Seldom does every one of them favor the same decision. For example, although Herbert King eventually did buy a Zipmo-

---

[1]In prospect theory, the construction of representations is referred to as "editing."

bile, as indicated in Table 12.1, some of his reflections argued against that decision. In virtually every decision problem that arises, the various considerations contained in the representation somehow must be combined in order to produce a final decision. That is what occurs during the combination phase.

In earlier chapters, we have assumed that the decision maker's likelihood judgments are critical elements in almost all decision representations. Such was the case when Herbert King wondered about the Zipmobile's reliability and Carl Anderson investigated its potential resale value. Chapters 2 to 7 were an in-depth study of this most pervasive and important aspect of representations. Value is also a consideration in every decision representation. For instance, Herbert King was disposed toward the Zipmobile partly because he *likes* sales representative Martha Malloy; on the other hand, her style *irritates* Carl Anderson. Whereas Herbert King considers the Zipmobile to be *expensive*, Carl Anderson regards it as a *bargain*. Value was a recurring theme throughout Chapters 8 to 11. Prospect theory and other models make specific claims about value and, hence, about representations. Thus, we see that the previous chapters indeed have shed light on representational problems. However, the particular representation questions studied there are different from those examined in this chapter and the next. And the emphasis of the past several chapters has clearly been on combination. To wit, *the* critical problem addressed by the likes of utility theory, prospect theory, and expected value versus risk principles is how likelihood and value combine to produce people's choices and evaluations.

In practical terms, how important are the various aspects of decision behavior we have distinguished? That is, when people make decisions that ultimately fail, how likely is it that the errors leading to those failures find their origins in, say, judgmental processes, valuation procedures, combination mechanisms, or representational phenomena? Unfortunately, the question has not been systematically studied. However, as you will probably become convinced in Chapters 12 and 13, there is good reason to suspect that faulty representations account for many of our bad decisions.

SCOPE

Once a decision is made, eventually the decision maker will experience a specific set of outcomes that are considered significant—an *eventual reality*, as suggested on the left side of Figure 12.1a. Imagine that we can look into Herbert King's future life with his new Zipmobile. The complete list of his experiences is almost endless. However, the outcomes shown on the left side of Figure 12.1b are illustrative. Thus, we see that the car always got good mileage; he did not care much about its looks one way or the other; paying for the car proved to be a strain; the car was big enough for his growing family; it was not especially reliable, more than once leaving his wife stranded on cold, lonely roads at night; and he got virtually nothing when he traded it in on a new car.

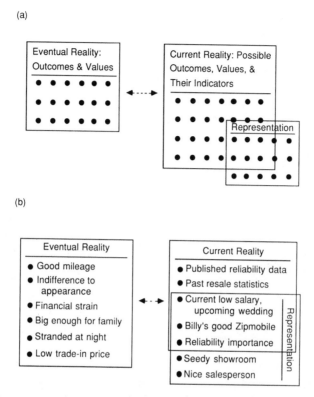

FIGURE 12.1. Representations, current realities, and eventual realities: (a) the generic case, (b) for car buyer Herbert King. See text for details.

No one knows what the eventual reality of a decision will be. However, at the moment of decision, there is a *current reality* which is imperfectly related to the eventual reality, as suggested by the dashed arrows in Figure 12.1. The current reality consists of possible outcomes and values, including the ones that eventually would be experienced. It also contains indicators that allow one to evaluate the chances of those possibilities. Thus, as indicated in Figure 12.1b, one element of Herbert King's current reality when considering the Zipmobile consisted of published reliability data, for example, in the magazine *Consumer Reports*. Those data would not have perfectly predicted that Mrs. King would be stranded on the night of March 12, but they might have given some inkling of the chance of such events.

The **scope** of a representation is its extent, relative to the current reality. As suggested in Figure 12.1, the typical representation overlaps the current reality only partially; some elements of the current reality are included in the representation and some are not, and vice versa. The discrepancies can be quite consequential. For instance, Herbert King might have avoided the shockingly low trade-in value of the Zipmobile had he simply bothered to look for past resale statistics. And the balance in favor of buying the Zipmobile might have been tipped by the good impression made by sales representative Martha Malloy. In this section we consider two questions about the scope of personal representations. The first concerns size: How much of the current reality is likely to be included in the typical representation? Given that not every element of the current reality can be represented, the second question is about selectivity: What kinds of elements have especially good chances of being included or excluded from personal representations?

Size: Aspects of the alternatives

Imagine that you are moving to a new city and are looking for a new apartment. You are under no pressure to make a quick decision; you have as much time as you wish to make up your mind. You go to see an apartment broker who has listings for the whole city. You could make your decision on the basis of the listings alone. But you are also free to visit any of the apartments you like. Question: How thoroughly will you investigate all the seriously considered apartments before you pick one?

Research by Payne (1976) suggests that you would decide on the basis of surprisingly little of the available information. Payne asked his subjects to choose among either two, six, or twelve hypothetical apartments. Information was available about each apartment with respect to either four, eight, or twelve aspect dimensions, for example, rent, cleanliness, landlord attitude, and noise level. The subject was allowed to inspect as much or as little information as desired. When subjects had to choose between only two apartments and had access to only a small amount of information about each, they examined almost everything before deciding. However, as the number of alternative apartments and the amount of available information on each option increased, the subjects were progressively less thorough in their inspections. For example, one subject, when faced with deciding among twelve apartments for which information on eight aspect dimensions was available, looked at only slightly more than 25% of that information before deciding.

Payne's results illustrate a commonly observed characteristic of representations of alternatives: They seem to be small. That is, they appear to include remarkably few of the alternatives' aspects, features that are capable of significantly affecting the decision maker's eventual satisfaction with those alternatives. Why are representations so minimal? One reason is that, as we saw in Chapter 7, people have limited cognitive capacity. There are only so many distinct items of information, commonly called **chunks**, that we can process at any one time, for instance, at the moment of decision. That number is generally thought to be around seven (Miller, 1956).

Size: The alternatives themselves

In many—perhaps most—discussions of choice, the decision maker is portrayed as choosing between two or more alternatives that have essentially the same character. For instance, in Payne's (1976) apartment study, the subject was always presented with at least two different apartments. However, it is easy to imagine situations in which a renter is offered only one apartment. The options are then to either accept that apartment or keep looking for a better one, two qualitatively distinct alternatives.

Beach and Mitchell (1978) intensively studied the decision behavior of executives in their normal work settings. They found that the executives rarely had to choose among two or more business opportunities presented at the same time. More often, they had to either accept or reject individual proposals brought to them sporadically. Conrath (1973), who closely monitored the investment decision making of Corporation X's executive committee (Chapter 11), found the same. We will see later that people behave differently depending on the nature of the decision task before them. This is a representational issue because often the decision maker has the freedom to solicit competing alternatives, even when asked to accept or reject one particular opportunity. For instance, an apartment seeker could simply refuse to give a rental agent a decision about a given apartment before examining others. The observations of Beach and Mitchell and of Conrath suggest that such behavior is not especially common, however. Instead, decision makers frequently will retain the simpler single-option representation of the situations as presented to them.

Recall from Chapter 1 that, besides choice and evaluation, there is another type of decision task with which people are sometimes faced—construction. That is, the decision maker is not presented with specific alternatives and asked to either select from them or evaluate them. Instead, he or she is free to use the available resources to assemble the *ideal* alternative. The example we discussed in Chapter 1 was that in which a business woman had the opportunity to tailor a personal computing system that was most appropriate for her needs. A broad view of virtually all real-world decision problems suggests that they evolve as indicated here:

Stage 1: Discovery or generation of alternatives
Stage 2: Evaluation or choice

In most scholarship on decision making, the focus has been on Stage 2 almost exclusively. For example, recall that Conrath (1973) was concerned with how an executive committee came to accept or reject an investment proposal presented by a staff member. But how did the staff member arrive at the proposal in the first place? Somehow, in what is called Stage 1 above, he either discovered that the proposal already existed or he developed it anew. Suppose that a given individual solves an entire decision problem by generating a single alternative in Stage 1. Then, in effect, the entire affair is an instance of construction decision making. Stage 2 occurs only if more options are assembled.

The discovery and generation of alternatives can be viewed as a representation issue. If the decision maker does not create or recognize the existence of an alternative, obviously that alternative cannot be chosen. It would be naive to expect that decision makers routinely create or identify the best possible alternative in every decision problem that arises. However, the available evidence suggests that we often do not even come close.

A study by Gettys and others (1987) is illustrative. In this study, subjects were reminded that their university had a serious parking problem. They were then given the following instructions:

> Suppose you are a member of a student organization which is researching this problem for officials of the University. Your task is to suggest as many possible solutions to the committee as you can. These solutions need not be "perfect"; often good solutions are derived from ideas which at first seem silly. The university officials will worry about how to pay for any solutions suggested and how to convince the involved parties to accept the decision. Your task is simply to think of all possible solutions which might be effective.

The subjects were allowed as much time as they desired.

Over 300 different alternatives were generated by the subjects. These alternatives could be classified into seven major categories, as shown in Table 12.2. Several aspects of the results are pertinent. First, whereas the average subject proposed about eleven specific alternatives, only about three of the seven major categories were represented by those alternatives. Suppose the seven categories are taken as the true extent of the potential alternatives. The typical individual's representation of the decision situation covered only about 50% of that extent. There would be little cause for concern if the excluded alternatives generally were bad ones, options the subjects would never choose if brought to their attention. But this was not the case.

In a second experiment, Gettys and others (1987) asked subjects to avoid reporting worthless alternatives. They also provided subjects with incentives for either the number of alternatives generated or their quality. Interestingly, these incentives had virtually no effects. It is also interesting that subjects were largely unaware of the smallness of their representations. Subjects were asked to estimate how many high-quality alternatives they might have overlooked. An independent panel of experts evaluated the quality of various classes of alternatives. The analyses suggested that the average subject missed about 70% to 80% of the actual high-quality alterna-

TABLE 12.2 Categories of Alternative Solutions to the University Parking Space Shortage

CATEGORY	DESCRIPTION
1	Use available parking space more efficiently, for example, segregate cars according to size.
2	Increase available space for parking, for example, make all future buildings multistory to conserve land.
3	Reduce demand for parking, for example, increase parking fees.
4	Change parking priorities, for example, reduce service vehicle parking.
5	Provide faculty and staff with nearby housing.
6	Frivolous and other options, for example, reduce student population.
7	Combinations of alternatives in Categories 1 to 6.

Source: Gettys and others (1987), Appendix.

tives, whereas the subjects themselves estimated that they omitted only about 25%.

Selectivity: Concreteness

Consider an experiment by Northcraft and Neale (1986). Subjects were asked to assume the role of an advisor for a fictitious real estate development firm, "Sunburst Investments." (You might want to try the role yourself.) At the outset, each subject was told that in Sunburst's local area "there are always construction projects available, usually returning anywhere from 15% to 20%," and that interest rates on investment savings accounts were 10% to 15%. The subject was then told about Sunburst's dilemma, which is outlined in Table 12.3. A year ago, the company started building a tennis club, with an initial construction budget of $6.73 million. Given that budget, Sunburst could have expected a rate of return on investment of 14% to 19% when it sold the completed building. However, after having spent $1.97 million during the first year of construction, unforeseen increased costs led to a revised budget of $8.29 million. This yielded a best estimate of 7.5 percent as the revised rate of return for the second year. Sunburst has been offered $1.76 million to turn over the partially completed tennis club project to another company. Should Sunburst commit the remaining $6.32 million required to complete the project, or should they accept the offer to abandon it?

If Sunburst sells the tennis club project, they will have lost $210,000 **out of pocket**, the difference between what the other company would give them and what they have already spent. Suppose they then deposit the uncommitted $6.32 million in an investment savings account that pays 11% interest. Then the following is a summary of the financial consequences of the "Abandon" decision after one year:

–$210,000	Out-of-pocket loss
$695,000	Savings account interest
	(11% of $6.32 million)
$485,000	Net

TABLE 12.3   Details of Tennis Club Construction Project

ITEM	AMOUNT
Original 2-year budget	$6.73 million
Estimated effective 2-year rate of return	14% to 19%
Spent after 1 year	$1.97 million
Needed to finish	$6.32 million
Revised 2-year budget	$8.29 million
Revised effective second-year rate of return	7.5%
Offer for unfinished project	$1.76 million

Source: Northcraft and Neale (1986), Table 1, with permission from Academic Press and the authors.

But suppose Sunburst completes the project. Then they would expect to clear 7.5% of their $6.32 million second-year investment, $474,000. So the following summarizes the one-year financial consequences of the "Continue" alternative:

-$0   Out-of-pocket loss
$474,000   Estimated investment return
———————
$474,000   Net
$11,000   Opportunity cost

Thus, if the Continue option were selected, Sunburst would be forfeiting the opportunity to make an additional $11,000 = $485,000 – $474,000. As indicated, such amounts are known as **opportunity costs**.

Two versions of the Sunburst case were presented to subjects by Northcraft and Neale. In the *Implicit Opportunity Costs* (IOC) version, besides the initial statement about local construction project availability and savings interest rates, subjects received essentially the information presented in Table 12.3. In the *Explicit Opportunity Costs* (EOC) version, subjects also read an additional paragraph. That passage explicitly indicated how much money would be earned if the $6.32 million needed to finish the tennis club were instead deposited in a savings account at 11% interest (similar to what was outlined above) or else invested in another construction project with an estimated 18% rate of return. Also, in this version, each subject was asked to describe two specific things he or she might do with the uncommitted $6.32 million if the tennis club project were abandoned. In all cases, subjects indicated whether they would recommend that Sunburst continue with the tennis club project or sell it. The subjects were also asked, in essence, to describe how they thought about the alternatives. Every one of the subjects, in both the IOC and the EOC conditions, mentioned the out-of-pocket costs. However, whereas only 15% of those in the IOC conditions mentioned opportunity costs, 85% of those in the EOC conditions did so. It is thus not surprising that the latter individuals were significantly more inclined to recommend abandonment.

The Sunburst Investments experiment illustrates a general phenomenon, sometimes called **concreteness effects**. Some aspects of a decision situation are explicitly and concretely displayed for the decision maker, for example, the amount Sunburst has already spent on the tennis club project and how much the other company would pay for it. Other aspects, however, are more remote and must be inferred, sometimes with great effort, for example, opportunity costs. Under many circumstances, people are not inclined to draw such inferences. Instead, the representation they use for decision purposes departs very little from the information that is immediately available.

Selectivity: Projection in time

Should you wear a seat belt when driving your car? One way you could represent this decision problem corresponds to the decision tree shown in Figure 12.2a. That is, every time you get into your car, you might compare the relative merits of fastening and not fastening your seat belt. As suggested, a major consideration is that wearing the belt is a nuisance. According to statistics reported by Slovic, Fischhoff, and Lichtenstein (1978), the chance that a beltless driver will suffer a disabling injury in a single auto trip is minuscule, about 1 in 100,000. From this point of view, wearing your seat belt hardly seems worth the bother.

Now rethink your choice from the perspective afforded by the decision tree in Figure 12.2b. There the problem is cast not in terms of a single trip, but rather as a decision about whether you will routinely buckle up for the rest of your life. In effect, you ask yourself to make a policy decision for an entire class of essentially identical episodes projected indefinitely into the future. Slovic, Fischhoff, and Lichtenstein estimate that, over the course of 50 years of driving, the typical person will take about 40,000 trips. This implies that the chance of a non-seat-belt user suffering at least one disabling injury is about 33%. These are disturbing odds for most people. Thus,

(a) Single Episode (1 Trip)

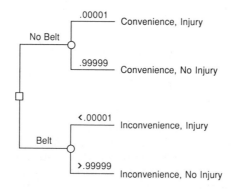

(b) Lifetime Policy (50 Years, 40,000 Trips)

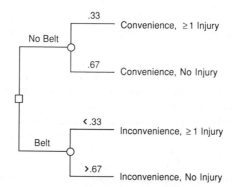

FIGURE 12.2. Decision tree representations of the seat belt decision: (a) from a single-episode perspective, that is, one trip; (b) from the perspective of a lifetime policy, in other words, whether to routinely wear a seat belt.

wearing a seat belt looks much more appealing when considered from a long run rather than an episodic point of view. Nearly four times as many subjects said they intended to wear seat belts when they were induced to adopt the former perspective instead of the latter.

Beach and Mitchell (1987) have proposed an *image theory* of decision behavior. This theory says that an important basis for many decisions is the decision maker's **projection** or image of what might result in the future from those decisions. Strictly speaking, at the moment of decision, *all* the potential outcomes from a decision occur in the future. However, those outcomes differ in how *far* into the future they might be experienced. The seat belt example suggests that people's unaided personal representations might seriously neglect outcomes that are more remote in time, for instance, injuries that occur over a lifetime rather than on a single trip. There is at least some evidence that people reliably differ in tendencies to make distant future projections (for example, Savickas, Silling, and Schwartz, 1984). This might partly explain why Herbert King failed to even think about the Zipmobile's resale value whereas Carl Anderson did.

Nondecisions

Let us stay with the seat belt issue. When you first read the last section, you might well have said to yourself, "I never really thought about seat belts in just that way." Perhaps you were referring to how the problem was cast as a decision tree or in terms of the long run rather than the short run. However, your remark might have meant that, when you get into your car, seat belts do not even cross your mind. In your own representation of the situation, there is actually no decision to be made; you do what you habitually do, without reflection. These observations highlight the fact that many actions we might *think* people take because they *decide* to do so are pursued for other reasons. They are, instead, due to *nondecisions*; they are not undertaken with the intention of producing more satisfying outcomes than afforded by alternative actions (see Chapter 1).

Erroneously assuming that a person represents a given situation as a decision problem can be costly. Suppose that, before reading the previous discussion on seat belts, you generally did not use them. However, after viewing the options as depicted in Figure 12.2b, you declare, "That settles it. From this day on, I'm buckling up all the time." Nevertheless, a week later your best friend observes that you still rarely wear a seat belt. He concludes that you have become a backslider; you have rescinded your decision to change your ways. He assumes that, whenever you get into your car, you make a conscious decision to either adhere to or reject your previous commitment. In trying to understand your behavior, your friend speculates about why you changed your mind. Perhaps you no longer believe the statistics about injuries. Maybe you have concluded that using the seat belt is more inconvenient than you had realized. In trying to set you back on the right path, your friend intends to reemphasize the considerations that led you to make a commitment in the first place.

Of course, your friend is wrong about your motivations. Normally, you do not even recognize the opportunity to use your seat belt. Out of habit, automatically you simply start the car and go on your way. If you *had* been conscious of the seat belt option, you would have taken it. It would be pointless for your friend to try to reemphasize to you the wisdom of buckling up. Instead he should simply bring the seat belt to your attention. In effect, by reminding you that the seat belt is there, he would induce you to again represent the situation as a decision problem. And, given your previous commitment, there is a good chance that you would make the right choice.

The present analysis of the seat belt problem is essentially the reason that buzzers that sound whenever the driver starts a car without the seat belt being fastened are effective—for a while, at least. Similar analyses underlie the advice that people who want to reduce their smoking should remove their cigarettes from their customary places; this makes taking a smoke a deliberate decision rather than a nonconscious, habitual act. Marketing researchers also acknowledge the possibility that at least some *apparent* purchase decisions are actually nondecisions (Olshavsky and Granbois, 1979; Ursic, 1980). In such cases, attempts to change buying patterns by altering the presumed decision process have little chance of success.

NATURE OF THE ELEMENTS

We have discussed the kinds of features that tend to be included and excluded from decision representations. In this section we consider how the included features are symbolized in the decision maker's mind.

Coarseness

Decision makers often are provided with finely detailed information about the available alternatives. However, the elements of typical decision representations are rather coarse. An illustration of the implied **coarseness principle** is provided by Russo and Dosher (1983). On each trial, subjects were asked to choose the more deserving of two hypothetical applicants for a college scholarship. Every applicant was described by three factors: adjusted family income, high school grade point average (GPA), and total Scholastic Aptitude Test (SAT) score. An illustrative pair was the following (for the moment, ignore the information in parentheses, which was not presented to the subjects):

FACTOR	APPLICANT A	APPLICANT B	(ADVANTAGE)
Income	$7920	$6420	(B)
GPA	3.51	3.43	(A)
SAT	1440	1260	(A)

Observe that neither of these applicants dominates the other, if one assumes that, all other things being equal, the student who has less income is more deserving of financial aid. Russo and Dosher found considerable evidence that subjects encoded the differences between applicants very crudely. Thus, instead of taking note that Applicant A was exactly $1500 richer than Applicant B, the subjects acknowledged nothing more than that Applicant B had an income advantage over Applicant A. So, effectively, the subjects' representations were equivalent to the parenthesized advantages shown in the last column above.

Another example of coarse representations comes from medicine. Levi (1986) studied how nuclear medicine specialists diagnose heart disease using a technique called nuclear ventriculography. How the technique actually works is unimportant for present purposes. What *is* of interest is how the physicians express, and presumably encode, their opinions about patients' chances of having heart disease. Normally, the physician is required to report only that disease is "unlikely," "equivocal," or "likely." Additional coarseness examples abound in other professional areas, for example, financial analysis (Bouwman, 1982).

Why are personal representations so coarse? Two hypotheses suggest themselves. The first is that decision makers are incapable of making reliable fine distinctions. This seems implausible, however. Levi (1986) demonstrated that, when nuclear medicine specialists were asked to make significantly finer distinctions than customary, the refinements within previous broad diagnostic categories were consistently related to whether patients actually had heart disease. If the physicians were capable of only crude distinctions, this would not have occurred. It seems that there must be limits to the discriminations people are able to make. But the distinctions implicit in typical representations seem far from those limits.

A more reasonable explanation for coarseness is that decision makers acknowledge distinctions only to the degree of fineness required by the decision rules that will be applied to their representations. Russo and Dosher (1983), for instance, found that subjects often used a rule no more sophisticated than awarding a scholarship to the student who had the greater number of advantages. In conventional medical practice, the physician who must actually treat a patient with heart disease might need nothing more than a three-category diagnosis in order to decide how to proceed. However, approaches to decision making such as maximizing expected utility require sharper distinctions in order for the decision maker to trade off value against uncertainty. So, if medicine moves toward methods akin to decision analysis (Chapter 9), more precise statements of uncertainty will be required. Levi's (1986) results suggest that physicians indeed will be able to comply with those requests. There is no reason to think that the same is untrue of decision representations generally.

Gain versus loss encoding

Recall that prospect theory says that the decision maker evaluates outcomes relative to some reference point. Specifically, outcomes are categorized as gains if they are better than the reference point and losses if they are worse. There is considerable evidence consistent with the view that this is how outcomes are characterized or **encoded** in people's personal representations of decision situations. A crucial issue that has undoubtedly occurred to you is what determines the decision maker's reference point.

Typically, people report that outcomes that are lower than the reference point *feel* markedly worse than those that are higher. Sometimes these feelings are objectively based, since the immediate outcomes have very real practical implications beyond themselves. Consider, for example, a manager who has been told that the company's goal for his division is a profit of $500,000 (see Payne, Laughhunn, and Crum, 1980). Then, when he considers various options for how to run his division, his reference point will be $500,000, not $0—and with good reason. If the division fails to make $500,000, there will be concrete adverse effects, including, perhaps, the manager's firing. At other times, the basis for reactions to exceeding or missing reference points seems purely internal. For instance, an experienced crossword puzzle fan who fails to solve a puzzle below her customary difficulty level feels awful, despite the fact that she never even mentions her hobby to anyone else.

Decision makers' expectations (in the everyday sense of the term, not the expected value sense) are the common denominator for many reference point phenomena (Kahneman and Tversky, 1979). For a variety of reasons, the decision maker comes to view some particular outcome as the most reasonable one to expect. If the outcome that is actually achieved falls short of that expectation, it is experienced as a loss; if the actual outcome surpasses that standard, it feels like a gain. That is, in many instances, the reference point is the decision maker's expectation of what will happen.

One frequently adopted reference point is the decision maker's **adaptation level**, the level to which he or she has become accustomed. Consider, for instance, a prosperous business woman who normally makes about $15,000 per month. Any income that is markedly different from that level is surprising. If it is less, she is highly displeased, if more, quite satisfied. Another common reference point is the person's **aspiration level**. For instance, a mediocre student who has, contrary to his custom, studied especially hard for a test expects a grade of about 90. Any lesser score would be a blow, even if still a passing grade. Other reference points are socially determined. Suppose you are a golfer and that your playing partners normally achieve scores of around 85. If you score 95, you will feel rather badly, and your friends will razz you about your performance. But if your friends are duffers who generally get—and hence expect—scores around 100, you will feel pretty good about your 95.

Affective versus cognitive encoding

Picture yourself as a university professor. In early February, as a member of your department's admissions committee, you examine the credentials of all the applicants. Later that month, during the committee meeting, the case of "Jane Bowen" comes up. The chairperson asks you,

"Well, what did you think of Ms. Bowen?" You respond, "She's really good! I think we ought to let her in." Another member of the committee then says, "Oh, really? What did you like about her?" Embarrassingly, you are stuck. You cannot say a thing about Jane Bowen other than that you thought she was a good prospect.

There are at least two plausible explanations for what happened to you in the Jane Bowen incident. Both explanations might apply, and both emphasize that decision representations sometimes do not consist solely of features corresponding to the "facts" of the situation. The first explanation is purely **cognitive**, that is, concerning the way information is mentally processed. It says that you cannot remember anything about Jane Bowen because, when you were examining her application, you made no attempt to memorize the details of her case, but only the appraisal supported by those details. For the same kinds of reasons, you might remember that most of the people at a recent party were from out of town, without remembering very much about any of them individually.

The second explanation follows from proposals made by Zajonc (1980; Zajonc and Markus, 1982). It says that the elements of decision representations are encoded in two ways, cognitively as well as **affectively**, in terms of the associated feelings. This is because the very aim of decision making is to achieve satisfactory outcomes, that is, to create positive affect. Furthermore, the hypothesis says that cognitive and affective codes can exist fairly independently of one another. Thus, generally we should not expect to be able to reliably explain our feelings about objects or people on the basis of facts we know about them.

The above viewpoint is supported by a fascinating study by Kunst-Wilson and Zajonc (1980). Subjects were shown slides of several geometric figures, five times each. The exposures were extremely fast, $\frac{1}{1000}$ of a second. Later, the subjects were shown pairs of figures at a leisurely pace. In each pair, one of the figures was among those flashed on the screen previously; the other was not. The subject had two tasks. The first was to indicate which figure was "new" and which was "old." The second was to rate which figure he or she liked better. Sixty percent of the time, subjects liked the old figures more than the new ones. This was not unexpected because it is an established fact that, within limits, the more often people see a given stimulus, the more they like it, a phenomenon called the *mere exposure effect* (Zajonc, 1968). Nevertheless, consistent with the hypothesis of independent cognitive and affective encoding, subjects could explicitly discriminate new from old figures at no better than a chance level.

CONNECTIONS AMONG THE ELEMENTS

We have discussed some important characteristics of individual decision representation elements. In this section, we pursue the question of how those elements are related to one another.

Disjointedness

Recall the concreteness phenomenon, as illustrated by the neglect of opportunity costs (pp. 339–40). There decision makers fail to acknowledge relationships that really do exist among various aspects of the decision situation, but which are not overtly displayed. This suggests a generalization, that the elements of personal decision representations largely are isolated from one another. That is, representations often are **disjointed**. Several commonly observed decision phenomena seem to agree with this conclusion.

Consider the following decision situations, which were devised by Tversky and Kahneman (1981, p. 454):

Situation 1

Imagine that you face the following pair of concurrent decisions. First examine both decisions, then indicate the options you prefer.

Decision (i). Choose between:
    A. a sure gain of $240
    B. 25% chance to gain $1000, and
       75% chance to gain nothing
Decision (ii). Choose between:
    C. a sure loss of $750
    D. 75% chance to lose $1000, and
       25% chance to lose nothing

Situation 2

Now imagine that you have a choice between these alternatives:

    E. 25% chance to win $240, and
       75% chance to lose $760
    F. 25% chance to win $250, and
       75% chance to lose $750

If you are like the typical participant in Tversky and Kahneman's experiments, in Situation 1 it seemed entirely reasonable to take the sure gain, Option *A*, in Decision (i), and the gamble, Option *D*, in Decision (ii). Moreover, you were firmly convinced that you should select Option *F* in Situation 2. But let us examine the situations more closely.

In Situation 1, there are actually four composite options, as summarized in Table 12.4. Suppose, for example, that you pick Option *A* in Decision (i). This means that you will add $240 to whatever you might lose in Decision (ii). So, if you choose Option *D* in Decision (ii), this is equivalent to selecting the resultant prospect in which you have a 75% chance of –$1000 + $240 = –$760 and a 25% chance of $0 + $240 = $240. But this is the same as Option *E* in Situation 2. The remaining composite options can be understood

TABLE 12.4   Alternatives and Choice Percentages in Situations 1 and 2

SITUATION 1			SITUATION 2	
OPTION	CHOICE%	RESULTANT PROSPECT	OPTION	CHOICE %
A & C	?	−$510	—	—
A & D	73	(25%, $240; 75%, −$760)	E	0
B & C	3	(25%, $250; 75%, −$750)	F	100
B & D	?	(6.25%, $1000; 37.5%, $0; 56.25%, −$1000)	—	—

Source: Constructed from Problems 3 and 4, Tversky and Kahneman (1981, p. 454).

similarly. We thus realize that, in terms of what can ultimately happen to your pocketbook, composite Options (A & D) and (B & C) in Situation 1 are identical to Options E and F in Situation 2, respectively. However, the choice percentages reported by Tversky and Kahneman (1981) in the two situations were dramatically different. Why?

We see in Table 12.4 that Option (B & C), equivalent to Option F, probabilistically dominates Option (A & D), equivalent to Option E (Chapter 8, pp. 220–22). This is obvious in the table and in the original presentation of Situation 2. It is thus no surprise that every subject chose Option F over Option E. Tversky and Kahneman (1981) surmised that this dominance was obscured in Situation 1. Instead, in that situation subjects seemed to **segregate** Decisions (i) and (ii), to treat them as unrelated to each other, despite the instructions. Tversky and Kahneman suggest that decision segregation is common. That is, people tend to overlook the relationships that actually exist between the various decisions that face them. In the present example, the relationships are simple. And segregation led subjects to make a pair of choices that many would consider to be a mistake, that is, picking a dominated alternative. It is unsettling to imagine what might happen in more realistic situations, which are far more complicated, for example, selecting stocks for a financial investment portfolio.[2]

Why do people segregate the above decisions? At one level, the segregation can be seen as simply a special case of concreteness. The decision maker fails to draw the conclusions that are underneath the information explicitly presented. In general, this might happen because inferential thinking is too effortful. Or maybe the decision maker does not know *how* to make the required inferences. This seems unlikely in the present case, however, because most of the inferences are so easy to perform, for example, adding $240 to all the outcomes. The most plausible explanation for the segregation observed by Tversky and Kahneman is suggested when we imagine that the experiment is changed as follows. Suppose that Decision (i) is to be executed immediately, but Decision (ii) a year later. It is now obvious that the decisions *should* be segregated. The implicit principle is that decisions ought to be segregated when the effects of outcomes from the first decision are

---

[2]Recall from Chapter 11, pp. 310–12, that an important class of portfolio analysis techniques consists of ways to detect dominance relations.

dissipated before those from the second come into play. From this perspective, the mistake Tversky and Kahneman's subjects made was inappropriately applying this most sensible *dissipation principle*.

Structuredness

Cast against the notion that decision representations are normally disjointed, there are many arguments that those representations are highly **structured**. According to this view, the elements in cognitive representations are elaborately interconnected (Anderson, 1985; Glass and Holyoak, 1986). At least four classes of relationships are observed: associational, contingency, derivational, and process.

An **associational relationship** is one that is generated purely by frequent co-occurrence. The classic example of a cognitive association is that which is built up between nonsense syllables in the psychological laboratory. For instance, suppose you are exposed to the syllable YOQ paired with REZ in a list including lots of other such pairs. After a surprisingly small number of exposures to the list, you will be able to immediately rattle off REZ when the experimenter presents YOQ and asks you to report its companion. The foundations and implications of such associations have long been an important topic in psychology (Anderson and Bower, 1973).

On a more practical level, associations are exploited throughout everyday life. Advertisers, in particular, assume that association principles apply to decision representations, and there is no reason to doubt that assumption. That is why the Ford Motor Company planned an extensive advertising campaign to build an association between a new Ford van and the United States space shuttle, which had a striking physical resemblance to each other. Apparently, it was anticipated that, when shoppers considered buying the Ford van, the association with the space shuttle would be activated, including all the positive connotations that entailed. Not surprisingly, the proposed advertising campaign was dropped when the space shuttle "Challenger" was destroyed in a tragic accident.

Associational relationships probably are rarely involved in people's conscious deliberations about how to decide. Indeed, it may well be the case that decision makers ordinarily are unaware that such associations exist or how they came about. For example, a car buyer not only might deny that his attraction to a particular vehicle has been affected by associations built up by television commercials, but resent the very idea. In contrast, each of the remaining types of relationships can easily be invoked at a conscious level.

The basic notion of a **contingency relationship** is one we have studied extensively in this book. In the case of discrete events, we say that event A is contingent on event B if the probability of event A is different, depending on whether event B does or does not occur, that is, $P(A \mid B) \neq P(A \mid B^c)$. In the case of quantities, quantity Q is contingent on quantity R if there is any reliable relationship between the two. Thus, a graph of Q versus R would look systematic instead of a jumbled mess. There is extensive evidence that decision representations often include many assumed contingency relationships. A simple example is taken from consumer behavior. People often assume that, the more expensive a product is, the better is its quality (see, for example, Woodside, 1974).

Assumptions about contingencies might explain several apparent anomalies in decision behavior. Take Payne's (1976) experiment, discussed on p. 336. Recall that the subjects in that study often chose among hypothetical apartments after examining only a fraction of the available information. They could well have assumed that complete inspections of the information were unnecessary. They might ask, for instance, "Based on my experience, or even common sense, how many dirty apartments are likely to have good landlords?" In other words, perhaps the subjects' representations were much larger than they seemed. It is just that many elements were inferred through assumed contingency relationships rather than being based on direct observation.

A **derivational relationship** is one whereby one fact is concluded to be a necessary, logical consequence of others. For instance, in Northcraft and Neale's (1986) "Sunburst Investments" study, the subjects had all the information they needed to determine opportunity costs by simple arithmetic, had they been so disposed. Various concreteness effects suggest that derivational relationships might be less common than other types of representation relationships, perhaps because they take so much effort to create.

A **process relationship** is part of a presumed chain of actions whereby one event literally leads to the occurrence of another. As suggested in Chapter 7, there is every reason to believe that the most frequent image people have of a given situation is one consisting of such chains. That is, the world is viewed in terms of "actors"—people or otherwise—constantly affecting one another. We all seem to have our theories as to the scripts governing the activities of the participants, theories that are shaped by our personal experiences. An example from medical decision making is illustrative.

Politser (1982) presented physicians with accuracy information about two commonly used tests for colon cancer, using the statistics that are commonly reported in medical journals, for example, Sensitivity = P(Positive results | Cancer) (see Chapter 5, p. 128). He then asked the physicians how they would interpret various patterns of results from repetitions of each of the tests for a given patient. One task was essentially the following (p. 162):

> Two different tests are performed on the same specimen. Suppose we find a positive followed by a negative test result. Would this finding: (a) Increase the likelihood of cancer (compared to the likelihood of cancer before either test); (b) Not change the likelihood of cancer; or (c) Decrease the likelihood of cancer?

Politser found that the physicians had an especially hard time interpreting—and presumably deciding on the basis of—test results when simply provided with the accuracy statistics. However, their interpretations improved significantly when they were also told about the biological underpinnings for those statistics, that is, the effects of enzymes on hemoglobin and other agents. Part of the reason for this improvement might be that biological explanations allow statistical information to become more easily integrated with physicians' customary representations of medical decision problems, representations that emphasize biological processes.

A consensus view

In summary, should we expect the typical decision representation to be disjointed or highly structured? The weight of the evidence leans toward the latter conclusion. If that conclusion *is* warranted, how can we explain such things as concreteness and decision segregation? We have seen one plausible explanation of segregation in the Tversky and Kahneman (1981) demonstration, the dissipation principle. In the next chapter we will discuss a conceptual framework that makes sense of both concreteness and segregation.

SUMMARY

People's decisions are made in two broad phases. In the first, the decision maker constructs a personal conception of the decision situation, a representation. In the second, the decision maker combines the considerations in that representation to arrive at the decision. Previous chapters emphasized the combination issue. The present chapter focused on the form or character of representations. The following are among the major generalizations we can draw about representations: (1) they are often limited in scope; (2) they are dominated by concrete, explicitly presented information; (3) their elements tend to be coarse and often affective, not merely cognitive; and (4) those elements typically are richly interconnected with one another, in several different ways.

KEY TERMS

Adaptation level
Affective code
Aspiration level
Associational relationship
Chunk
Coarseness principle
Cognitive code
Combination phase
Concreteness effect
Contingency relationship
Derivational relationship
Disjointed representation
Encoding

External representation
Integration
Internal representation
Opportunity costs
Out-of-pocket costs
Personal representation
Process relationship
Projection
Representation phase
Scope
Segregate
Structured representation

ADDITIONAL READING

Kahneman and Tversky (1983); Montgomery (1983); Slovic, Fischhoff, and Lichtenstein (1982).

EXERCISES AND STUDY QUESTIONS

1. A vaccine for a certain common, serious disease was introduced several years ago. In several surveys, physicians have indicated that they generally hold quite favorable opinions of the vaccine. Nevertheless, the vaccine is still greatly underutilized. Apparently, despite their favorable opinions, physicians seldom recommend that their patients receive the vaccine. What is a plausible decision representation explanation for this curious situation? (This item is based on a real problem in medicine.)

2. Describe a real-world setting in which sellers seem to take advantage of the tendency for buyers to represent decision situations concretely.

3. There are two major treatments for throat cancer, radiation therapy and surgical removal of the larynx or voice box. Suppose you are a medical decision counselor assisting throat cancer patient "James Miner" in choosing a treatment. What would be your major concerns about how Mr. Miner represents the decision problem, and how would you address those concerns?

4. Officials at "Briercliff College" are debating whether to change their grading system. Currently, only whole letter grades are allowed: A, B, C, D, and F. In the proposed change, instructors would be allowed to append + and − signs to the A through D grades, so that a student could, for instance, get a grade of B+ in chemistry instead of just a B. "Henry LeCount," Dean of Instruction, opposes the proposal, claiming that such fine distinctions are meaningless to graduate school admissions committees. That is, the distinctions would not be useful in the graduate student selection process. Evaluate the pros and cons of Dean LeCount's assertion. How could you test its validity?

5. The curriculum committee in your psychology department is considering a proposal for a new course called "The Psychology of Early Adulthood." Among the members of the committee are the department chairperson, a regular professor, and a student. Would you expect these individuals' representations of this decision problem to be essentially the same, or would you expect substantial differences? Explain. If you expect major differences, what are they?

6. This chapter has suggested that people sometimes make decisions that turn out worse than necessary because their decision representations are faulty in specific ways. Consider one of those representation inadequacies. Imagine that you are a decision analyst, a counselor, or some other individual who tries to assist people in making important decisions. Outline a strategy whereby you might help your clients to improve their representations with respect to the deficiency you have singled out.

7. As implied in this and previous chapters, people make bad decisions for at least two kinds of reasons: (1) because they construct poor representations and, (2) because they combine information improperly, for example, in a manner that disagrees with expected utility principles. Reflect on your own decision making experiences. Do you think that your decision failures more often have been due to inadequate representations or faulty information combination?

13

Personal Representations: Their Contents and Moderation

Things are not always what they seem.
—Phaedrus

In Chapter 12, we saw that personal decision representations can encompass a wide variety of elements. In many cases, those elements correspond more or less directly to objective features of the decision situation, for example, Herbert King's noticing the seediness of the Autorama showroom and his concern about the Zipmobile's reliability. However, there are also instances in which representation elements are *instigated* by objective aspects of the situation, but are actually quite distinct, for instance, anticipated psychological regret over making a decision that turns out badly. The second section of this chapter reviews some of the most commonly observed examples of such extraneous representation elements. In the previous chapter, we also learned about some of the typical characteristics of personal representations, for example, concreteness. Although these characteristics do indeed seem to be the norm, they are by no means universal. This raises the question of why representations vary. That is, what are the factors that moderate decision representations? This question is interesting in its own right. But it has considerable practical importance, too. For, if we understand what causes representations to differ from one another, we have discovered an avenue for improving representations and hence decisions. The third section of the chapter discusses several important representation moderators. However, before considering either extraneous elements or the moderation of representations, it is useful to place the issues in the context of the simplified characterization of the human cognitive system introduced in Chapter 7 (pp. 210–13). That is the topic of the first section.

REPRESENTATIONS AND THE COGNITIVE SYSTEM

Figure 13.1 is a schematic depiction of aspects of the cognitive system and the situation confronting a decision maker. As suggested in Chapter 12, there is an eventual reality encompassing all the outcomes that would ultimately occur and would matter to the decision maker, if a particular decision were made, for example, a car buyer's experiences with a given car during the time he owns it. There is also a current reality, which includes entities that exist at the time of the decision and that bear some relationship to the eventual reality, say, statistics on the reliability of the particular car model. In addition, there are typically one or more displays of the situation, which normally are external representations of the options, for example, advertisements, opinions of friends, available cars themselves.

The decision maker's representation of the decision situation resides in the working register. As indicated in Chapter 7, the capacity of the working register is quite limited. These limitations alone should contribute to some of the representational phenomena discussed in Chapter 12. One is the small size of representations. Another is concreteness. The latter follows because

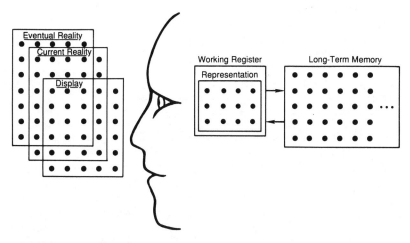

FIGURE 13.1. Schematic depiction of various aspects of the decision situation and the decision maker's cognitive system.

deriving relationships that are not explicitly presented consumes cognitive capacity in and of itself.

The decision maker's representation can easily include elements that are not contained in the situational display. In the typical sequence of events, some of the display elements are introduced into the working register and become a part of the representation. But also recall from Chapter 7 that the presence of an item in the working register tends to affect what else enters the register subsequently, too. Items in long-term memory that are related to that initial item increase their probability of being drawn into the working register, and hence into the decision representation. As we also saw, this effectively *suppresses* the chances of unrelated items doing the same. Through priming, analogous effects on the subsequent entry of items from external displays occur also. The present mechanisms constitute additional contributors to concreteness. Various of the effects we consider in this chapter are other plausible products.

EXTRANEOUS REPRESENTATION ELEMENTS

Extraneous decision representation elements are ones that are remote from the displays of the given decision situation. As suggested above, they sometimes are taken directly from long-term memory. For instance, when a car shopper sees a Zipmobile, he immediately recalls the good experiences he has had in friends' Zipmobiles, experiences that now become a part of his car-buying decision representation. On the other hand, other extraneous elements are likely to be the product of inferences derived in the working register, drawing on the presented information as well as that collected from long-term memory. Undoubtedly, extraneous elements occur in infinite diversity. In this section, we highlight several that are likely to appear in some form in decision situations of all types.

Justifiability

Decision makers sometimes have a dual task. First they must make decisions. Then they must justify those decisions to others. Imagine the situation of "Dave Glass," a section head for a computer software firm. He has been given the authority to hire junior programmers. However, he has found that his own boss, "Lorraine Shell," has a habit of asking him questions like, "Why did you hire this guy?" So, when Mr. Glass mulls over his hiring decisions, he not only takes into account how well a programmer might do the work that needs doing, but also how easy it would be to justify to Ms. Shell why he chose that person. The distinction is significant because justifiability to Lorraine Shell might disagree with the wisdom of a hiring decision on other grounds.

Justifiability is a consideration that can arise in a surprising variety of decision representations (see also Slovic, 1975; and Slovic, Fischhoff, and Lichtenstein, 1982). Take the problem of ambiguity, which was discussed in Chapter 2 (pp. 31–33). Recall the classic experimental situation used to study ambiguity (see Ellsberg, 1961). The decision maker is presented with the following gambles:

Gamble G1: (50%, $10; 50%, $0)

and

Gamble G2: (?%, $10; ?%, $0)

When Gamble G1 is played, the player draws from a bookbag containing 100 poker chips, 50 of which are red and 50 of which are white. Before the drawing, the player designates which color will be winning and which losing. Thus, if the player designates red as the winning color and then selects a red chip, he or she wins $10, otherwise, nothing. The sole difference between Gambles G1 and G2 is that, in the latter, the player knows only that there are 100 red and/or white poker chips in the bookbag. The actual distribution is unknown; it is what is formally called "ambiguous." People generally avoid ambiguity. That is, when given the choice between gambles like Gambles G1 and G2 above, most individuals select the less ambiguous alternative. The same occurs in more realistic practical decision situations, for example, when patients choose between alternative medical treatments (Curley, Eraker, and Yates, 1984). Curley, Yates, and Abrams (1986) hypothesized that justifiability is a partial explanation for ambiguity avoidance.

Picture a decision maker confronted with Gambles G1 and G2. Suppose the decision maker recognizes that there is in fact no way that Gamble G2, the ambiguous alternative, can be biased against the player, since the player chooses the winning color. Suppose the decision maker also believes that, nevertheless, most people would consider it unwise—and hence unjustifiable—to choose the more ambiguous of two options. One scenario that might motivate this feeling is the following: Suppose the decision maker picks the ambiguous alternative and ultimately discovers that the ambiguous bookbag contains no winning chips at all. Others who observe this scene, as well as the decision maker, might then feel vindicated in having considered the ambiguous choice to be unjustified; it was too reckless. What this reasoning neglects is the possibility that the urn contains no *losing* chips.

Curley, Yates, and Abrams (1986) tested this justifiability hypothesis by varying the conditions for playing and disclosing the contents of the ambiguous bookbag in choice situations like that involving Gambles G1 and G2. Subjects made their decisions privately, but in a room containing several other individuals. They were told that they might get to play their chosen gambles after the experiment was completed. Some of the subjects were instructed that they would play their gambles out of the sight of the remaining subjects; others were told that play, and hence their choices, would be public. Some of the subjects were also informed that, after the chosen gamble was played, the contents of the ambiguous bookbag would be revealed; others were told that no one besides the experimenter, not even the subject, would ever know the contents.

Figure 13.2 displays the results of the experiment. Observe that, consistent with the justifiability hypothesis, ambiguity avoidance was greater when subjects anticipated the presence of others when their decision was to be revealed. Also in agreement with that hypothesis, this tendency was especially pronounced when they expected the contents of the ambiguous bookbag to be disclosed. Thus, justifiability does appear to have been an element of the subjects' decision representations. But clearly more is involved in ambiguous decision making; note that, even under the best of circumstances, at least 69% of the subjects avoided ambiguity.

Wastefulness

Arkes and Blumer (1985, pp. 133–134) presented different versions of the Printing Press Problem to two groups of subjects. The Truck Version was as follows:

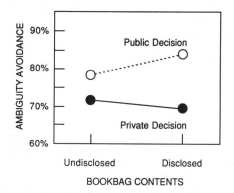

FIGURE 13.2. Percentages of subjects choosing the less ambiguous of two alternatives, as functions of whether the contents of the ambiguous urn were to be disclosed and whether decisions were to be revealed publicly. Adapted from Curley, Yates, and Abrams (1986), Figure 3, with permission from Academic Press.

As the owner of a printing company, you must choose whether to modernize your operation by spending $200,000 on a new printing press or on a fleet of new delivery trucks. *You choose to buy the trucks, which can deliver your products twice as fast as your old trucks at about the same cost as the old trucks.* One week after your purchase of the new trucks, one of your competitors goes bankrupt. To get some cash in a hurry, he offers to sell you his computerized printing press for $10,000. This press works 50% faster than your old press at about one-half the cost. You know that you will not be able to sell your old press to raise this money, since it was built specifically for your needs and cannot be modified. However, you do have $10,000 in savings. The question is should you buy the computerized press from your bankrupt competitor? [Italics added.]

The Press Version of the problem is essentially the same, except for the italicized statement. In particular, in the alternative version, instead of having spent $200,000 on new trucks, you have spent it on the new printing press, which is twice as fast as your old press but costs the same to operate. The Press Version also indicates that your competitor's computerized press is 50% faster and half as expensive to run as your new $200,000 press and that your new press cannot be sold. Again, the question is whether you would buy your competitor's press for $10,000. Almost 77% of the subjects said they would buy the computerized press in Truck Version of the problem, but only 53% in the Press Version.

The relative reluctance of subjects to purchase the computerized press in the Press Version illustrates the **sunk cost effect**. Standard economic analyses imply that a decision maker should ignore costs that have been incurred already, since they can have no bearing on the outcomes of decisions concerning the future. However, as in the present case, people actually do tend to take such sunk costs into account. Thaler (1980) shows how this tendency is consistent with prospect theory's claims about value function shapes, in particular, that they are steeper for losses than for gains. Arkes and Blumer (1985) suggest that another contributor to the sunk cost effect is that decision makers do not wish to appear wasteful by abandoning previous commitments, for example, by scrapping the new $200,000 press in the Press Version above. That is, a significant extraneous element in their decision representations is the appearance of wastefulness. Subjects' stated reasons for their choices in the Printing Press Problem were consistent with this conclusion.

Fairness

Thaler (1985, p. 206) asked subjects to put themselves in the following restful scenario (alternative versions of particular parts of the situation are indicated in parentheses). Try it yourself:

You are lying on the beach on a hot day. All you have to drink is ice water. For the last hour you have been thinking about how much you would enjoy a nice cold bottle of your favorite brand of beer. A companion gets up to go make a phone call and offers to bring back a beer from the only nearby place where beer is sold, a fancy resort hotel (a small, run-down grocery store). He says that the beer might be expensive and so asks how much you are willing to pay for the beer. He says that he will buy the beer if it costs as much or less than the price you state. But if it costs more than the price you state he will not buy it. You trust your friend, and there is no possibility of bargaining with the bartender (store owner). What price do you tell him?

When the beer was to be bought from the fancy resort hotel, the median acceptable price stated by Thaler's subjects was $2.65. That price was substantially less, $1.50, when the vendor was the run-down grocery store. (Would you have responded similarly?)

Why such a marked difference in acceptable prices? After all, the beer would be the same, as would the atmosphere in which it is consumed, that is, on the beach, and not in either a luxurious bar or the parking lot of a tacky grocery store. Thaler argues that fairness is a critical consideration taken into account in this beer problem, as well as in transactions generally. And a major determinant of the perceived fairness of a price is the cost to the seller. Under normal circumstances, a single bottle of beer sells for $0.25 to $0.75 in a supermarket. Thus, it is certainly aggravating being charged, say, $2.50 for a beer at the beach. However, this price is tolerable in a resort hotel, in view of the expenses of maintaining the hotel. But the implied profit margin on a $2.50 beer bought from a run-down grocery store would be too outrageous to bear.

Consider another situation devised by Thaler (1980, p. 50). It can be described as follows (alternative forms of specific parts of the situation are noted in parentheses):

> You set off in your car to buy a certain clock radio (color television set) at what you believe to be the cheapest store in your area. When you arrive, you find that the radio (set) costs $25 ($500), a price consistent with your expectations. As you are about to make the purchase, a reliable friend comes by and tells you that the same radio (television set) is selling for $20 ($495) at another store ten minutes away. Would you go to the other store to buy the radio (television set)?

People are much more inclined to go to the other store in the clock radio version of this problem than in the television version. You might well feel that way yourself.

At one level of analysis, different inclinations to go to the other store seem irrational. After all, in each case, a savings of $5 would be achieved. And $5 is $5. But from another point of view, $5 is *not* always just $5. Thaler (1980) suggests that the explanation for the different inclinations lies in the shape of the consumer's value function for money. Recall that, according to prospect theory, such functions exhibit diminishing marginal significance. Thus, the difference

$$v(-\$20) - v(-\$25)$$

which corresponds to the $5 saving on the radio, is larger than the difference

$$v(-\$495) - v(-\$500)$$

which is associated with the same saving on the television set.[1] This value function explanation seems highly compelling. However, it also seems plausible that an additional explanation is that the decision maker's representation of this situation includes fairness, as in the beer problem. In the clock radio case, the competing store offers the customer a saving of $5/$25 = 20%. In the television situation, the saving is only $5/$500 = 1%. A merchant who generally sells his goods at a deeper discount (20%) is fairer to those customers than one who offers only a modest discount (1%). Hence, that first merchant is more deserving of patronage.

Regret and elation

Our last illustration of extraneous decision representation elements is implicit in the following scenario: "Biff Lumpkin" is the general manager for the "Baytown Bruisers," a professional football team. In the first round of last year's player draft, Mr. Lumpkin was torn between picking defensive backs " 'Stonehead' Ferguson" and "Spike Rudman." He selected Ferguson, and Rudman went to the "Oil City Drivers." As it turned out, Ferguson was a "bust" this year. He played so poorly that the coach could seldom allow him to stay in a game for more than two or three plays. But Baytown still had to keep him on the roster and pay him lots of money because of his lucrative, no-cut contract. On the other hand, Rudman was an immediate star for the Drivers, and was a unanimous selection for the All-Star Rookie Team at cornerback.

Not surprisingly, Biff Lumpkin feels a certain amount of regret over having drafted Ferguson instead of Rudman. ("Rats! I could kick myself!") As in Mr. Lumpkin's case, regret is often involved in appraising the quality of decisions after the fact. But is it possible that regret also affects how decisions are made in the first place? There have been numerous suggestions that it does (Bell, 1982; Fishburn, 1982; Lee, 1971; Loomes and Sugden, 1982; Sugden, 1985). The essential idea is that the decision maker's representation of a given alternative does not stand alone. Instead, it is affected by the other alternatives that are included in the decision representation, too. Thus, in evaluating whether an outcome from a particular alternative is good or bad, the decision maker asks (and answers) the question, "What outcome would I have experienced if I had taken some other action?" If the outcome from the competing alternative would have been better, the decision maker would feel **regret**. If that outcome would have been worse, the decision maker would experience **elation**, as if he or she had "escaped" a tragic fate. The theories differ from one another considerably in detail. However, all maintain that, in the process of making a decision, the person takes into account potential regret or elation from the available alternatives.

---

[1]You might want to refer back to a graph of the loss side of a prospect theory value function to convince yourself of this, for example, Figure 10.2, p. 289.

What evidence is there that anticipated regret and elation are indeed common constituents of decision makers' representations? Bell (1982, 1985) notes that decision analysis clients sometimes refuse to follow the dictates of expected utility axioms even when they fully understand them (see Chapter 9, pp. 254–63). His impression is that this occurs partly because the axioms ignore such considerations as regret. Bell, as well as Loomes and Sugden (1982), also show how numerous common phenomena are consistent with decision making according to anticipated regret and elation, including many that have been cited as support for prospect theory. One example is the Allais Paradox (pp. 251–52). Recall that, in one situation, the decision maker chooses a guaranteed $1,000,000 award over a gamble of the form

$$(10\%, \$5,000,000; 89\%, \$1,000,000; 1\%, \$0)$$

In a second situation, the gamble

$$(10\%, \$5,000,000; 90\%, \$0)$$

is selected over the gamble

$$(11\%, \$1,000,000; 89\%, \$0)$$

A regret explanation of this choice pattern says that the decision maker anticipates being overwhelmed by remorse in the event of choosing the gamble in the first situation and ending up with nothing. ("Oh, no! Why was I so greedy?!") Such regret would not mitigate against the selection of the $5,000,000 gamble in the second situation, because both alternatives admit the possibility of gaining nothing. ("I probably would have lost anyway.") (See also DeGroot, 1970, p. 94.) Most of the phenomena argued to be consistent with regret theories, however, are also claimed as indications for other theories, for instance, prospect theory. This highlights the need for more definitive tests.

FACTORS THAT MODERATE REPRESENTATIONS

What determines the form a representation will take on a specific occasion? Several factors are known to be relevant. In this part of the chapter we examine some of the moderating factors that have received the most attention.

Framing

"But I was *framed*, Judge! You've *got* to believe me!"

We have heard the above protest in countless B movies and television crime stories. The just-convicted defendant insists that he is innocent. However, according to him, the evidence was arranged by the real culprit in such a way that it led the jurors to believe that the defendant committed the crime. The term **framing** is used similarly to refer to variations in the presentation of a decision situation such that the decision maker constructs markedly different representations of that situation.

A good example of framing effects was reported by McNeil and others (1982). Subjects were asked to imagine that they had lung cancer and that they had a choice between two treatments, surgery and radiation. They were then given the following information about the alternative treatments (p. 1260):

> Surgery for lung cancer involves an operation on the lungs. Most patients are in the hospital for two or three weeks and have some pain around their incisions; they spend a month or so recuperating at home. After that, they generally feel fine.
> Radiation therapy for lung cancer involves the use of radiation to kill the tumor and requires coming to the hospital about four times a week for six weeks. Each treatment takes a few minutes and during the treatment, patients lie on a table as if they were having an x-ray. During the course of the treatment, some patients develop nausea and vomiting, but by the end of the six weeks they also generally feel fine.
> Thus, after the initial six or so weeks, patients treated with either surgery or radiation therapy feel about the same.

Subjects were next presented with information about their chances of surviving or dying after the alternative treatments. For about half the subjects, this information was presented in a death or *mortality* frame, illustrated by the following:

> Of 100 people having surgery, *10* will die during treatment, *32* will have died by one year and *66* will have died by five years. Of 100 people having radiation therapy, none will die during treatment, *23* will have died by one year and *78* will have died by five years.

The remaining subjects received equivalent information in a life or *survival* frame, such as the following:

> Of 100 people having surgery, *90* will be alive immediately after the treatment, *68* will be alive after one year and *34* will be alive after five years. Of 100 people having radiation therapy, all will be alive immediately after treatment, *77* will be alive after one year and *22* will be alive after five years.

Each subject was then asked, "Which treatment would you prefer?"

The subjects included hospital patients (none of whom had cancer), physicians, and graduate students. Figure 13.3 shows the percentages of patients and physicians who chose radiation therapy after being exposed to the survival probabilities in either the mortality or the survival frame. The framing effect is clear. The mortality frame made radiation therapy much more attractive. This makes sense if immediate as compared to deferred death is especially unappealing; radiation therapy carries no risk of immediate death although it is less efficacious in the long run. One might have expected the physicians to be less affected by the frame than the patients. In fact, the opposite was true.

Other examples of framing effects are easy to find in everyday life. In fact, one might view salesmanship or marketing in general as largely resting

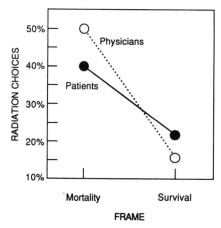

FIGURE 13.3. Percentages of patients and physicians choosing radiation over surgical treatment for lung cancer, as a function of presentation frame. Source: B. J. McNeil and others (1982), Table 2. Reprinted with permission from *The New England Journal of Medicine*, Volume 306, page 1261, 1982.

on attempts to frame purchasing situations favorably from the perspective of the seller. An especially striking example is a device used by some real estate sales representatives to close a difficult sale. The representative asks hesitant customers to adopt the decision-making aid attributed to Benjamin Franklin, to make a list of the pluses and minuses of buying the house in question. The representative first helps the customers to list the pluses, but then leaves it up to them to supply the minuses. As one famous seller put it, "I have yet to have a person come up with more than two or three on the no side" (Sumichrast and Shafer, 1987, p. 148).

Exactly how do framing effects arise? Different effects probably result from a variety of cognitive mechanisms. In the cancer treatment case, the underlying mechanism might be the same as that responsible for concreteness. On the other hand, it is also plausible that the positive and negative frames call up different associations from long-term memory. In effect, they cause the decision maker to think about different things. The real estate sales ploy seems to directly rely on the fact that information already in the decision maker's working register inhibits the entry of other information.

Physical displays

Consider the pairs of gambles described in Figure 13.4. In each case, the spinner on a wheel-of-fortune is spun. If the spinner stops on the dark part of the wheel, the amount indicated at the top is won; otherwise, nothing. If you are like many people, you would be inclined to choose Gamble *A* over Gamble *B* in Figure 13.4a, and Gamble *E* over Gamble *A* in Figure 13.4b.

The pairs shown in Figure 13.4 are only two in a series that were presented to subjects by Tversky (1969). The complete series is shown in Table 13.1. Note that the probabilities of winning money in Gambles *A* and *B* were 7/24 and 8/24, respectively. However, in the display actually

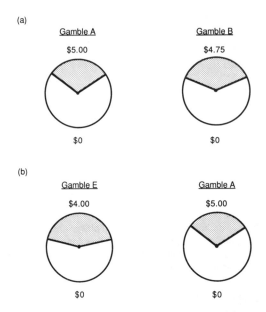

FIGURE 13.4. Illustrative pairs of gambles presented to subjects. Source: Tversky (1969), Table 1. © 1969 by the American Psychological Association. Adapted by permission from the publisher and author.

presented to subjects, that is, Figure 13.4a, those numerical values were not explicitly offered. The subject could only estimate them from the corresponding areas on the wheels-of-fortune. Tversky anticipated that subjects would have difficulty perceptually discriminating such small probability differences. Accordingly, they would focus on the payoff differences in order to make their decisions. Therefore, Gamble *A* would be favored over Gamble *B*. But notice in Figure 13.4b that the probability difference between Gambles *E* and *A* is very obvious. This was expected to compensate for the payoff difference, thus disposing subjects toward Gamble *E*. Subjects were asked to choose repeatedly between the gambles in various pairs. Table 13.1 presents the percentages of occasions Subject 1 chose the top over the bottom gamble in each successive pair listed. Thus, for instance, it is shown that 75% of the time Gamble *A* in fact was picked over Gamble *B*, and that Gamble *E* was favored over Gamble *A* 85% of the time.

An interesting phenomenon is implicit in Table 13.1. Suppose that we denote probabilistic preference by an arrow. Then Subject 1's choice pattern can be represented as follows:

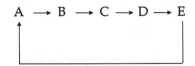

TABLE 13.1 Series of Paired Gambles Presented to Tversky's (1969) Subject 1, along with Their Expected Values (EV) and His/Her Choice Percentages

GAMBLE	EV	Choice %: TOP OVER BOTTOM
A: (7/24, $5.00)	$1.46	75%
B: (8/24, $4.75)	$1.58	85%
C: (9/24, $4.50)	$1.69	80%
D: (10/24, $4.25)	$1.77	85%
E: (11/24, $4.00)	$1.83	85%
A: (7/24, $5.00)	$1.46	—

Source: Tversky (1969), Table 2. Copyright © 1969 by the American Psychological Association. Adapted by permission from the publisher and author.

That is, this individual's preferences constituted an **intransitive cycle**. The basis for this intransitivity lies at least partly in the display. The adjacent Gambles *A* through *E* in Table 13.1 are not easily distinguished in terms of probability, but are according to payoffs. Thus, probability differences do not enter the representations of adjacent gambles, for example, Gambles *A* versus *B*. However, they are a significant part of the representations for nonadjacent pairs, for instance, Gambles *E* versus *A*.

Tversky's experiment illustrates two important general conclusions. The first is simply that the physical display of the situation can have marked effects on what enters a decision representation and in what form. Tversky assumed, for instance, that his results would have been different had he displayed gamble probabilities numerically. The second conclusion is that the character of the display can be manipulated such that the resulting representation either enhances or degrades the quality of the decisions that are induced.

Computerized decision aids

Decision and computer scientists have devoted a considerable amount of effort building computerized **decision support systems** that are intended to assist people to make better decisions. These computer programs take many forms.[2] However, two kinds of decision support programs, in particular, should achieve their effects in large measure via their influence on their users' decision representations. The first of these are programs that draw decision trees on a computer screen as well as perform the calculations involved in decision analyses (Chapter 9). We have noted several times that the mere construction of a decision tree can have a dramatic effect on how

[2] Descriptions and reviews of specific programs can be found in current issues of such scholarly journals as the *Journal of Behavioral Decision Making* and such trade magazines as *BYTE, PC Magazine,* and *MacUser.*

one thinks about a decision problem. The other class of program emphasizes a different type of display, as suggested by the following example.

Return to Carl Anderson, who bought a Hummer rather than a Zipmobile in Chapter 12. Let us imagine that, instead of making his decision by himself, Mr. Anderson had used one of several readily available **decision matrix** computer programs. Figure 13.5 shows Mr. Anderson's computer screen at the point where he actually made his decision. The format of the decision matrix displayed there is typical. Notice that the alternatives are listed down the left side of the display: the Zipmobile, the Hummer, and the Zephyr. The main columns of the display correspond to various aspect dimensions Mr. Anderson has said are important to him, for example, fuel economy and the quality of dealer service. The entries in the main body of the display are Carl Anderson's ratings of how good a particular car is on a given dimension, with 0 corresponding to "Worst Possible" and 100 "Best Possible." Thus, the 75 in the Zipmobile–Fuel Economy cell indicates that Mr. Anderson considers the Zipmobile's fuel economy to be good, but inferior to that of the Hummer. The numbers in the last column on the right are the scores assigned by the program to each car. The car with the highest score is the one that is recommended for purchase, in this case, the Hummer. The score for a given car is simply the sum of all the ratings for that car, each multiplied by the weight (WT) for the relevant dimension, shown at the top

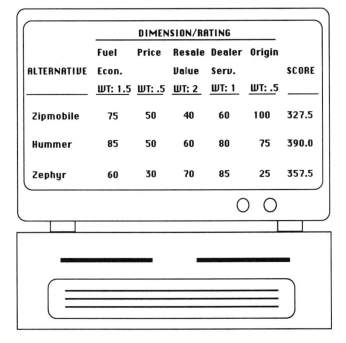

ALTERNATIVE	DIMENSION/RATING					SCORE
	Fuel Econ. WT: 1.5	Price WT: .5	Resale Value WT: 2	Dealer Serv. WT: 1	Origin WT: .5	
Zipmobile	75	50	40	60	100	327.5
Hummer	85	50	60	80	75	390.0
Zephyr	60	30	70	85	25	357.5

FIGURE 13.5. Computer screen displaying the decision matrix for Carl Anderson's car-buying decision. See text for details.

of the display. This is one form of **additive rule**, similar to the additive expected value–risk models discussed in Chapter 11 (pp. 313–16). For instance, the score for the Zipmobile is

$$\text{Score} = (1.5)\,(75) + (0.5)\,(50) + (2)\,(40) + (1)\,(60) + (0.5)\,(100)$$
$$= 327.5$$

How should programs such as Carl Anderson's affect decision representations and hence decisions? Because the working register has limited capacity, there are only so many items of information a person can keep in the forefront of his or her mind. Thus, under normal circumstances, at the *very* moment of decision, an important consideration easily could be excluded from the decision maker's effective representation, for example, that the Zephyr's resale value is significantly better than the Hummer's. The mere fact that the entire decision matrix is on the computer screen reduces the chance of this possibility. In effect, the display enlarges the decision maker's personal representation. The program also ensures that certain specific features are included in the representation that dictates the decision and that certain others are *excluded*. Thus, when Carl Anderson agrees to follow the recommendation of his program, he feels he is assured that his decisions will be affected by the fuel economy, price, resale value, dealer service, and origin of the car—and nothing else. In particular, his decisions will *not* be influenced by such things as his disdain for the pushiness of the Zipmobile sales representative, a consideration he thinks has no place in rational decision making, but might easily inject itself into his unaided personal decision representation.

A comment on the concept of aspect importance: Aspect dimension weights such as those shown in Figure 13.4 are sometimes taken to indicate the importance of those dimensions. The reason is that the larger the weight, the more will differences along that dimension affect the scores assigned to the alternatives. For instance, notice that there is a 20-point rating difference between the Zipmobile and the Hummer on both resale value and dealer service. You can verify that, since the weight for resale value is 2, the resale value difference makes the Hummer score 40 points higher than the Zipmobile score. However, because the weight for dealer service is only 1, the same dealer service difference leads to only a 20-point score advantage for the Hummer. This first sense of importance is called **effect importance**.

The second type of importance is **inclusion importance**. If Carl Anderson made decisions without the aid of his computer program, sometimes a given aspect would be included in his representation of a car buying decision, and sometimes it would not. For instance, there might be, say, an 80% chance that resale value would be in the representation and a 25% chance that attitude toward the sales representative would. Thus, these two aspects differ in their inclusion importance. It should be clear from the example that effect and inclusion importance are likely to be related to each other, but are quite distinct. One consequence of most computerized decision-aiding programs is that they make every **inclusion probability** either 100% or 0%.

The task: choice versus evaluation

Picture young "Dr. Killian," who has just finished her training. She believes that her best chance of establishing herself in town is to buy the practice of a retiring physician. Imagine two scenarios. In the first, Dr. Killian has a choice between the practices of "Drs. Zens and Patrick." Both are offered for about the same price and are approximately the same size. Dr. Killian chooses Dr. Patrick's practice. In the second scenario, neither Dr. Zens nor Dr. Patrick has stated a firm price for his practice. Instead, each requests bids. After careful study, Dr. Killian forms in her mind a maximum price she is willing to pay for each practice. In view of her choice in the first scenario, we would expect that Dr. Killian's maximum bid would be higher for Dr. Patrick's practice than for Dr. Zens's. Not necessarily, however, if we can generalize from results such as the following.

Figure 13.6 shows two of the gambles Lichtenstein and Slovic (1971) asked their subjects to consider. For instance, in Gamble I, the player has a 99% chance of winning $4 and a 1% chance of losing $1. What is distinctive about the gambles is that Gamble I, called a "P bet," offers a high probability of a modest gain, whereas Gamble II, known as a "$ bet," promises a large gain, but at only a moderate probability. In one task, subjects indicated which of the gambles they preferred to play. In a second task, the same subjects were to imagine that they had the opportunity to play each of the gambles, analogous to owning a lottery ticket. They then stated the smallest amount for which they would be willing to sell that opportunity. Typically, subjects indicated that they would prefer the P bet (Gamble I) to the $ bet (Gamble II). Surprisingly, however, they stated higher average selling prices for the $ bet. Such decision patterns are known as instances of the **preference reversal phenomenon.**

Exactly why preference reversals occur is the focus of intense study. But there is little doubt that reversals are real, in the sense that they are found under a variety of carefully controlled conditions (Grether and Plott, 1979). Moreover, they have been documented in at least one practical situation

FIGURE 13.6. An illustrative P bet (Gamble I) and $ bet (Gamble II) presented to subjects. Source: Lichtenstein and Slovic (1971), Table 1. Copyright 1971 by the American Psychological Association. Adapted by permission from the publisher and authors.

where the stakes are high, on the floor of a Las Vegas casino (Lichtenstein and Slovic, 1973). One contributor to preference reversals seems to be the mode of expression (Goldstein and Einhorn, 1987). Specifically, in the choice situation, the decision maker can express his or her appraisal in either of only two ways, for example, picking either Gamble I or Gamble II. On the other hand, in the evaluation situation, the decision maker has a wide range of potential expressions, for instance, a price for Gamble I anywhere between $4 and –$1, the latter implying that the owner of the gamble would *pay* someone a dollar to take the gamble rather than keep it.

The leading hypothesis for why most preference reversals occur remains a representational one offered by Lichtenstein and Slovic (1971). According to this view, the choice task induces a representation of the alternatives that emphasizes the probabilities, perhaps due to the physical display. For instance, in Figure 13.6, the first thing you probably noticed is that there is a larger part of the wheel associated with winning in Gamble I, the P bet, than in its competitor. Thus, the probabilities entered your representation first. As we have seen, because of the nature of the cognitive system, this access priority diminishes the chances that other items will enter the representation, for example, the exact values of the payoffs. In the evaluation task, because the required decision is more precise, in some sense you *are* forced to pay attention to the amounts. In addition, that task should encourage a representation that highlights the outcomes because the decision is in the same units, monetary.

Creativity aids

In some decision problems where the alternatives are not explicitly presented, in principle it is quite easy to generate them all. Such was the case for Brenda Summers who, in Chapter 1, had the task of assembling an ideal personal computing system for her business. For simplicity, suppose that her system will consist of a computer, a printer, and a video monitor, and that there are three kinds of computers available, four types of printers, and five different monitors. Then there are a total of

$$60 = 3 \times 4 \times 5$$

distinct systems that can be created from these components. It would be laborious for Ms. Summers to actually put all these systems together and examine them, but quite straightforward to do so (an ideal task for a computer, ironically). In contrast, many practical decision problems are such that no one has any idea how many feasible alternatives exist. And there is no foolproof way to generate every one of them. The parking space problem of Gettys and others (1987) discussed in Chapter 12 was a good example. As we saw in that case, any given individual's representation is likely to include only a few of the alternatives that person would consider attractive if they were explicitly presented. There is reason to expect that a number of aids to creativity should be helpful in generating appealing decision alternatives (see also Stein, 1974, 1975). Three of the more important ones are mentioned here.

Aid 1: Objectives   People initiate a decision episode because they are experiencing a problem; there are certain concrete objectives they feel they need to realize. An especially good approach to generating decision alternatives proceeds in two stages. First, the decision maker should list the specific objectives that ought to be met by the alternative that is ultimately selected. Then, *one objective at a time*, the decision maker should try to think of alternatives that might satisfy each objective.

An experiment by Pitz, Sachs, and Heerboth (1980) provides a good illustration of the efficacy of the above strategy. Subjects were presented with hypothetical personal decision problems. One was about "Sally," a new student at a small liberal arts college. Sally has been assigned a roommate named "Jackie," who smokes marijuana in their room twice a week. This is a problem for Sally because drug use is against her principles, and because Jackie is very obnoxious and inconsiderate when she is high. The task for Pitz, Sachs, and Heerboth's subjects was to identify feasible options for Sally to consider. Subjects were randomly assigned to several different conditions, distinguished by how the alternative-generation task was to be approached. In one basic approach, subjects were initially presented with example alternatives, which might serve as stimulants for their imaginations, for example, "Try to find another student with whom to trade rooms." In the second basic approach, the subjects were given Sally's objectives, for instance, "Avoid unpleasant feelings," "Be consistent with your moral and ethical principles." There were two variants of this strategy. In one, all the objectives were presented in a single list. In the other, each objective was shown on a separate page. There were also control conditions, for example, when subjects were free to generate alternatives for Sally any way they liked. On average, when presented with objectives one at a time, subjects generated 6.47 alternatives. Under all other conditions, the average number of options produced was only 5.79, significantly fewer.

Aid 2: Deferred criticism   There is evidence that people sometimes have trouble being creative because, as they try to bring to mind solutions to a problem, they also censor those ideas. That is, they do not report ideas because those ideas seem too outlandish to have much potential. The problem is that this "on-line" criticism is sometimes too harsh. Ideas that have good potential never see the light of day because they are rejected before they are carefully considered.

The creativity stimulation technique known as **brainstorming** is predicated largely on the assumption that deferring criticism is advantageous (Osborn, 1963). In that method, a person confronted with a problem is encouraged to try to generate as many potential solutions to the problem as possible, with little concern for whether those ideas are silly or even preposterous. He or she is explicitly told to withhold criticism of ideas until some later time. There is evidence that such approaches have three effects (see, for example, Johnson, Parrott, and Stratton, 1968; Sappington and Farrar, 1982). First, they do cause people to propose more solutions. Second, the *average* solution that is offered has lower quality. But, third, the *best* solutions are better. This final effect is especially important for decision making. This is because, if a really good alternative is among those considered, people have a number of devices at their disposal to determine that that alternative really *is* a good one, for example, expected utility. Gettys and others (1987) found direct evidence for the kinds of effects described above in their study concerning the generation of alternative solutions to a parking space shortage (Chapter 12).

Aid 3: Help! The final aid to generating alternatives is a simple one: Ask other people to help. That is, the decision maker should get other individuals to try to think of alternatives too. Common sense says this is a good idea. ("Two heads are better than one.") However, the potential benefits are even greater than most of us suspect. As an example, suppose that somewhere out in the cosmos there is some good alternative for a given decision problem. However, as suggested in the first row of Table 13.2, let us say that there is only a 10% chance that any given individual would think of that alternative. But suppose we ask a number of other people to independently generate alternatives. As indicated in the second row of the table, there is a 19% chance that the good alternative will be identified by at least one of two people set to the task. If there are five people working on it, there is a 41% chance that someone will generate that idea. If 50 people are generating ideas, it is virtually certain that at least one of them will propose our target alternative.

Should the decision maker's helpers indeed work independently of one another, or should they meet as a group? In some variants of brainstorming, group interaction is encouraged. The expectation is that the ideas of one individual would inspire others' ideas. Group interaction might be helpful when the different individuals bring different kinds of expertise to the task (Bouchard, 1971). However, there is a fair amount of evidence that more often group interaction inhibits the production of ideas, especially when the group members do not know one another very well (see Weisberg, 1986, Chapter 4). This is thought to be due partly to social discomfort. Also, as indicated in the Pitz, Sachs, and Heerboth (1980) study, we have seen that

TABLE 13.2 Probability That a Given Alternative Will Be Generated by at Least One Person in a Collection of Individuals Working Independently, as a Function of the Number of Individuals

TOTAL NUMBER OF INDIVIDUALS	GENERATION PROBABILITY
1	10.0%
2	19.0%
5	41.0%
10	65.1%
50	99.5%

Assuming 10% probability that any one individual will generate the alternative.

illustrative alternatives, such as those that would be generated by one's group partners, do not encourage the production of other options. Such inhibition is probably another instance in which any item that happens to occupy the decision maker's working register prevents the entry of other items that are unrelated to it.

Experience and expertise

An operational definition of an expert decision maker is one whose decisions ordinarily turn out better than those of the typical decision maker. Expert versus nonexpert differences are an important issue generally. There is evidence that a major distinction between expert and nonexpert decision makers is that they represent decision situations differently. In particular, experts' representations seem to be bigger, taking into account more of the available information. They appear to be different in character, too. Several studies support these conclusions (but also see Johnson, 1988).

Summers, Taliaferro, and Fletcher (1970) asked college students to predict the socioeconomic growth of hypothetical underdeveloped countries. The countries were characterized in terms of four dimensions, for example, amount of foreign investment in the country. Only about a quarter of the subjects reliably based their judgments on all four dimensions. Representations of such limited scope are typical of what is found with inexperienced decision makers. In another study, Phelps and Shanteau (1978) examined quality assessments of breeding pigs made by college-trained, expert livestock judges. In one experiment, hypothetical pigs were described to the judges verbally in terms of 11 dimensions that are considered important in the breeding business, for example, body weight, ham thickness, and quality of nipples. The judges clearly were able to make assessments that were reliably influenced by all 11 pig features, almost three times as many as the Summers, Taliaferro, and Fletcher study with amateurs would have led us to expect.

Are comparisons like these indications that experts are simply "smarter" than the rest of us, possessing a sheer greater capacity for processing information, for example, wider perceptual spans or better memories? There may be an element of truth to such a hypothesis, although there is remarkably little support for it (Anderson, 1985, Chapter 9). There is more evidence that experts are experts because of their specific, sometimes trained, experiences. First, experts have better knowledge at their disposal than novices do; they have learned more things and different *kinds* of things. It also seems plausible that, when a person is first introduced to a task, it takes a while to become accustomed to what various aspects of the situation mean and to develop a routine for synthesizing that information. These effects might well account for the differences observed in the Summers, Taliaferro, and Fletcher study and in Phelps and Shanteau's experiment with hypothetical pigs. Another effect of trained experience seems even more powerful, the effect on representation content and structure. A classic experiment in general cognitive psychology provides a good illustration.

Chase and Simon (1973) gave three chess players, a master, a Class A player, and a beginner, 5-second glimpses of chess boards supposedly depicting the middle stages of real chess games. Some of the boards in fact *were* from actual games; others were simply random configurations. The task of the subjects was to reconstruct the board positions from memory. The master clearly was better at remembering real game boards. But he was actually *inferior* at recalling the random boards. Detailed analyses by Chase and Simon showed that the superior performance of the master on the real boards was due to his organizing the locations of the pieces into larger cognitive units or *chunks* than those used by the other subjects. Moreover, those chunks could be understood in terms of their significance in chess strategy. For example, in some chunks pieces were bound to one another by relations of mutual defense or by their roles in attacks over small distances. Appreciation for such relations is thought to develop with experience and study and is an integral part of chess expertise. The deficient performance of the master on the random boards might have been due to his searching for structures that normally could be expected, but which rarely occur in random configurations (see also Adelson, 1984).

Generalized to the domain of decisions, we might expect experience to have the kinds of effects schematized in Figure 13.7. In each panel, the points in the rectangle correspond to various objective aspects of the decision situation, the current reality. Ovals identify chunks that are included in the decision maker's representation of that situation. Lines between points symbolize relations that are acknowledged by the representation. At Experience Level 0, the chunks are small. With increasing levels of experience, the chunks effectively increase in size by encompassing not isolated elements, but instead elements that are linked with others. Eventually, even the chunks themselves develop interrelationships.

This view is consistent with the results of a second experiment by Phelps and Shanteau (1978). Expert livestock judges made quality assessments of pictures of real breeding pigs. The subjects reported that, fundamentally, they judged pigs on a small number of high-level dimensions, for example, size, meat quality, and breeding quality. They could make a judgment of a real pig very easily on the basis of just a few of its features because they recognized that, in real life, such characteristics are highly correlated with one another and, more importantly, with the high-level dimensions. (How many heavy pigs with light bone structure is one likely to see?)

Note that the panels in Figure 13.7 are distinguished by experience rather than by expertise. These constructs are not necessarily the same thing. As an extreme example from a different domain, we all recognize that not every golfer who has played the game for 20 years is an expert golfer. For an expert decision maker, as compared to an experienced nonexpert, the relations contained in the more mature representations should better correspond to relations that actually exist. The elements included in the representation might well be different, too. Unfortunately, in most studies of expertise in decision making, it is difficult to distinguish what is due to expertise per se and what is due to mere experience. This is because the

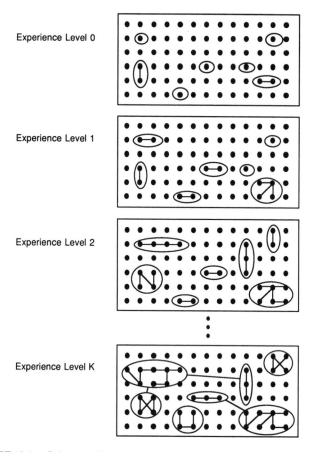

FIGURE 13.7. Schematic illustration of representation evolution through experience. Points correspond to various features of the decision situation. Chunks (ovals), and hence representations, grow in size through the development of relationships among representation elements.

experienced decision makers who are studied invariably are selected because of their presumed expertise. Nevertheless, novice–expert studies in other domains suggest that the following effects of expertise on decision representations might be anticipated (for example, Murphy and Wright, 1984; Schoenfeld and Herrmann, 1982): First, because they have learned what is significant and what is not, experts make distinctions that novices or experienced nonexperts ignore. For instance, to a layperson, a pig is a pig is a pig. But to an expert livestock judge, there is probably no such thing as "just a pig." Also, novices' representations of alternatives will remain closely tied to the information that is explicitly presented, for example, ham thickness. In contrast, the representations that eventually develop in experts' minds will be in terms of higher-level, more abstract principles or concepts, for instance, breeding quality.

Experienced and inexperienced decision makers can be expected to differ in another way that is related to representations: The experienced ones should be faster. Indeed, individuals who have made lots of decisions in a given area often report that they do not really "think" about what they do. What appears to happen over time is suggested in the following schematic:

First Occasion: Situational conditions →
                   Conscious deliberation →
                   Real decision

                        .
                        .
                        .

Nth Occasion: Situational conditions →
                   Situational classification →
                   Apparent decision

Thus, the first several times the decision maker encounters a given type of situation, for example, a beginning admissions officer considering the first few applicants, he or she consciously deliberates the problem and decides. Eventually, however, the decision maker concludes that he or she has encountered virtually all the different circumstances that can arise. From that point on, the task changes to one of classification rather than true decision making. Every new situation is classified as essentially the same as some previous one. Then the same decision made in that previous situation is adopted as the apparent decision in the current case.

These observations are related to the final expertise-related phenomenon we discuss. Slovic, Fleissner, and Bauman (1972) asked stock brokers and business students to evaluate various stocks. The companies issuing the stocks were described to the subjects in terms of numerous factors typically used in investment analyses, for example, whether the firm's profit-margin trend was increasing or decreasing. Using standard statistical procedures, the researchers determined the factors that were consistently used by the subjects, as well as how they were used. They found systematic discrepancies between how the subjects actually employed various factors and how the subjects *described* how they made their evaluations. These **self-insight failures** were significantly greater for the brokers than for the students (see also Benner and Tanner, 1987). Perhaps, over time, brokers get to the point where stock evaluation becomes virtually automatic, as suggested above. If that is indeed the case, it is less surprising that they cannot accurately report what they do.

Stress

Sometimes we have the luxury of making decisions under seemingly ideal, relaxed conditions. At other times, we must decide under duress. Figure 13.8 illustrates how such differences in stress can be expected to affect the quality of our decisions.[3] By **psychological stress** is meant an unpleasant emotional state instigated by threats to one's welfare (see Janis and Mann, 1977; Lazarus, 1966). It proves useful to distinguish **ambient stress** from **task stress**. The former is due to conditions affecting the decision maker's comfort, irrespective of what he or she is doing, for example, heat, cold, noise, and fatigue. The latter is peculiar to the decision problem itself. One example is time pressure. Another is the magnitude of the stakes, for instance, when deciding whether to authorize potentially fatal heart surgery for one's son as opposed to deciding what to have for dinner. Motivation is thought to contribute to the inverted-U relationship between stress and decision quality, especially in the case of task stress. For example, if the stakes are low or if there is plenty of time available, the decision maker might not take the task seriously enough to do it well. That is part of the reason decision quality is hypothesized to be deficient on the left side of the curve shown in Figure 13.8. However, the stress–decision quality relationship is also mediated by several cognitive factors, at least two of which involve representational effects.

For ambient stress in particular, at high levels of stress the decision maker becomes distracted from the decision problem. Attention is partly diverted to the task of eliminating the source of the threat or his or her reactions to it, that is, with coping. This appeared to have been the case indirectly, for instance, in Anderson's (1976) study of small businesses damaged in a devastating flood. Owner–managers who reported high levels of stress also exhibited greater incidences of classic emotional coping mechanisms, for example, withdrawal, hostility, aggression, and seeking refuge in groups. In addition, these individuals were less successful in rebuilding their businesses.

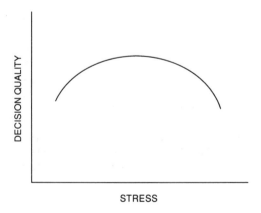

FIGURE 13.8. Characteristic relationship between stress level and decision quality.

[3]The depicted relationship is sometimes called the **Yerkes–Dodson Law.**

The other two cognitive effects of increased stress are well illustrated in a pair of experiments by Wright (1974). The task of the subjects was to rate how likely they would be to buy each of several automobiles described as anywhere from "greatly below average" to "greatly above average" along several dimensions, for example, price, ease of handling, styling. In one experiment, Wright varied the time subjects were allowed to make their decisions, that is, he manipulated task stress. In the other, he varied the amount of noise in the experimental room, thereby manipulating ambient stress. Thus, in this experiment, subjects in the low-stress group made their decisions in the presence of soft background music. In the moderate-stress condition, a tape of a radio talk show, including commercials, was played at low volume. High stress was created by playing the same tape more loudly.

Wright then constructed statistical models of how each subject went about the decision task. He discovered that stress affected the extent to which subjects' behavior was well described by the best model he could devise. For both time pressure and noise, the greater the stress, the less adequately could the best model account for how the subject decided. This suggests a generalization that is also supported by other evidence (for example, Rothstein, 1986), that stress reduces the consistency of the decision maker's behavior, causing him or her to be more erratic.

Wright (1974) also found that, as stress increased, subjects' decisions were affected by fewer of the available features of the cars. In the case of noise, the increasingly focused attention did not emphasize any particular type of features. In contrast, when the source of the stress was time pressure, heightened stress led subjects to emphasize the negative aspects of the cars, for instance, high maintenance costs. Similar attention restriction effects have been found in other decision studies (Ben Zur and Breznitz, 1981; Janis and Mann, 1977; Rothstein, 1986). The difference between the effects of ambient stress (for example, noise) and task stress (for instance, time pressure) makes sense. Suppose the decision maker realizes that there may be insufficient time to make an ideal decision. A rational strategy for dealing with this situation is to base decisions on the most important considerations. As suggested by prospect theory's value function, which is steeper for losses than for gains, this implies that special emphasis should be placed on negative features. In contrast, methods of coping with ambient stress should not be so carefully reasoned; ambient stress should mainly disrupt normal functioning.

How, precisely, do the previous representational effects contribute to the inverted-U stress–decision quality relationship? The mechanism that has received the most support is known as the **Easterbrook** (1959) **Hypothesis** (Hockey and Hamilton, 1983). This hypothesis makes two claims. Specialized to decision making, the first claim is that, consistent with what we have seen, as stress increases, attention focuses on an increasingly narrow range of situational features. The second claim is that the narrowing of attention proceeds according to the significance of the features for decision quality. As suggested in Figure 13.9a, there is an ideal range of feature attention, encompassing precisely those features that are required to support

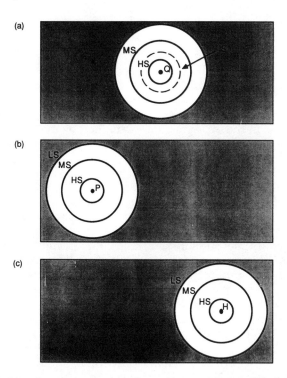

FIGURE 13.9.   Attention-narrowing effects of increased stress (LS - low stress, MS - moderate stress, IS - ideal stress, HS - high stress): (a) assuming that attention narrows according to the significance of features for decision quality (the Easterbrook Hypothesis); (b) assuming narrowing according to personal significance of features; (c) assuming narrowing according to attentional habits. Q = most significant feature for decision quality; P = most significant feature personally; H = feature with the highest probability of being attended under nonstressful conditions.

a good decision. Under low stress, the decision maker's attention scope includes not only the essential features, but many superfluous ones, too. As stress increases, attention constricts, eliminating the excess baggage. Thus, for a while, decision quality improves. As stress continues to increase, however, the scope of attention becomes so small that it excludes features that are needed for high-quality decision making.

The Easterbrook Hypothesis is compelling and compatible with much of the evidence. However, modifications might be needed to better explain what actually happens in decision making. For instance, in studies such as Wright's (1974), in the presence of task stress, attention seems to narrow according to the personal significance of situational features, such as aspects of the alternatives that are seen as negative (Figure 13.9b). It may or may not be the case that *personally* significant features are the ones that are *really* most important for good decisions.

There is also indirect evidence suggesting that narrowing proceeds according to the decision maker's attentional habits (see Zajonc, 1965). Thus, stress increases attention to features the decision maker habitually emphasizes and reduces even further attention to features the decision maker rarely notices (Figure 13.9c). For example, suppose that, under relaxed conditions, there is a 70% chance that Feature A would be included in a person's decision representations in a certain area, and a 20% chance that Feature B would also be included. Then, under stressed conditions, we might expect Feature A's inclusion probability to rise above 70% and Feature B's to sink even lower than 20%. Interestingly, one effect of this process is that, within limits, increased stress should improve the quality of experts' decisions, but degrade that of others. This is because, for the experts, the habitually attended features would coincide with the truly important features. For the nonexperts, the habitually attended features are useless, if not outright misleading. That is one reason they are not experts.

SUMMARY

Decision representations include many extraneous elements that are only indirectly tied to the objective situation. Instead, those elements are drawn from long-term memory or are effectively created by the decision maker. One example is the potential justifiability of a decision to other people. Other extraneous elements include considerations for wastefulness, fairness, and potential regret from decisions that go sour.

Among the most striking of the factors that affect how decision makers create representations are framing effects. Depending on how the facts are presented, a decision maker can be induced to form markedly different representations of the same situation and thus arrive at diametrically opposed decisions. Other important moderators of representations are experience, expertise, and stress.

KEY TERMS

Additive Rule
Ambient stress
Brainstorming
Decision matrix
Decision support system
Easterbrook Hypothesis
Effect importance
Elation
Framing
Inclusion importance

Inclusion probability
Intransitive cycle
Justifiability
Preference reversal phenomenon
Psychological stress
Regret
Self-insight failure
Sunk cost effect
Task stress

ADDITIONAL READING

Bronner (1982); Fischhoff (1983); Isen and Geva (1987); Johnson (1984); Kahneman and Tversky (1983); Keller (1985); Levin and Others (1985); montgomery (1977); Puto (1987); Slovic and Lichtenstein (1983); Tversky and Kahneman (1981); Zachary (1986); Zakay and Wooler (1984).

EXERCISES AND STUDY QUESTIONS

1. Consider Game A, which proceeds in two stages. In Stage 1, the player selects a ball at random from an urn containing 14 red balls and 6 green balls. If a red ball is drawn, the player goes on to Stage 2; otherwise, the game is over. In Stage 2, the player draws at random from an urn containing 6 blue balls and 14 white ones. If a blue ball is drawn, the player wins $1; otherwise, nothing. Game B is the same as Game A except for the compositions of the urns. In Game B, the Stage 1 urn contains 7 red balls and 13 green ones. There are 12 blue balls and 8 white ones in the Stage 2 urn.

   (a) Suppose a person is given a choice between Games A and B and that he or she chooses according to expected utility theory. Which game would that individual pick?

   (b) On representational grounds, which alternative would you expect the typical person to choose? Explain.

   (c) Offer the choice of Games A and B to several friends and ask them to think out loud as they mull over what to do. Do their choices and reflections concur with your expectations? If there are discrepancies, how would you explain them?

   (d) What real-world situations do you see as being analogous to Games A and B?

2. Suppose that "George Lowe" makes decisions as if according to the principles of prospect theory. Could his choices exhibit intransitivities, that is, instances in which Prospect A is chosen over Prospect B, Prospect B over Prospect C, but Prospect C over Prospect A? Could he do so if he decides by taking anticipated regret and elation into consideration?

3. Describe a distinction between the kinds of features that are likely to be in an experienced rather than a novice decision maker's representations and which can lead to markedly different decisions.

4. Five marketing executives are hard at work in their separate offices trying to generate alternative approaches that might be taken for selling a new product. Suppose that there is a 5% chance that any one of these individuals will hit on what we might call "Strategy D." What is the probability that, out of the entire group, at *least* one of them will come up with that approach?

5. Imagine that you have invited your boss and his wife to your house for dinner Saturday night. You have a big decision to make: "What should I serve?" Devise and carry out a plan that would help you to generate a large pool of alternative main dishes, at least one of which has a good chance of pleasing your guests.

6. "Lloyd Vaughn" has been the chief purchasing agent for a large manufacturer for 25 years. One of his duties is evaluating supply contracts offered to the company by various vendors. Mr. Vaughn is about to retire. "Sheila Metz" has been assigned by the company to develop a computerized system that will do contract evaluation after Mr. Vaughn retires. Ms. Metz hopes to build the system in such a way that it mimics the way that Mr. Vaughn accomplishes the task. Ms. Metz interviews Mr. Vaughn extensively in order to learn his procedure. There is reason to expect Ms. Metz's computerized system to have limited success. Why? What advice can you offer Ms. Metz to improve her chances of building a good system?

7. The purpose of this exercise is to simulate the application of Carl Anderson's decision matrix program described on pages 366–67 (see von Winterfeldt and Edwards, 1986). Ask a friend to serve as the decision maker. Your friend's problem is to pick an elective, nonrequired course for next term. Proceed as follows:

    (a) Have your friend list three reasonable alternatives, such that it is not immediately obvious which course ought to be selected, for example, English 350, History 400, and so on. Also ask your friend to rank order those three courses in terms of how attractive they appear at the moment.

    (b) Request that your friend identify up to five aspect dimensions that are significant for his or her satisfaction with a course, for example, quality of the instructor, time of day.

    (c) Next you should have your friend indicate the importance of those dimensions as follows:

    (i) Rank order the dimensions from most to least important.

    (ii) Assign the most important dimension a weight of 10.

    (iii) Assign weights from 1 to 10 to the remaining dimensions in proportion to their importance relative to the most important dimension. For instance, if a dimension is 40% as important as the most important dimension, its weight should be 4.

    (d) Ask your friend to rate each course with respect to each aspect dimension, with the convention that 100 indicates the best possible standing on that dimension and 0 the worst. If necessary, your friend should take the time to do the research required to justify a rating, for example, looking up previous course evaluations.

    (e) Compute the score for each alternative course, using the following additive rule:

$$\text{Score} = \text{Weight1 Rating1} + \text{Weight2Rating2}$$
$$+ \dots + \text{Weight5Rating5} \qquad (13.1E)$$

    (f) Compare the rank ordering of courses according to the scores from part (e) to the preliminary preference ordering of the courses indicated in part (a). If there is a difference, ask your friend which seems more reasonable, and why.

    (g) What aspects of the above decision procedure seem most and least attractive? Explain.

8. Imagine "John Sparks" in two different decision situations. In the first, Mr. Sparks must choose a business suit from several possibilities. In the other, he must select all the components that will go into his personal computer system. Now imagine that, in each instance, Mr. Sparks is subjected to severe time pressure. The Easterbrook Hypothesis suggests that the effects of this time pressure should be different in the two situations. How so?

Answers to Selected Exercises and Study Questions

CHAPTER 1: AN OVERVIEW

1. Adam was faced with a choice decision: either answer the phone or do not. He chose to not answer and was quite pleased with himself. Actually, however, Adam's decision was a failure; the alternative he rejected would have yielded a better outcome. The fundamental problem highlighted by Adam is that we often (typically?) do not know whether our decisions fail or succeed. That is because we do not—often cannot—find out the results of the actions we might have taken, but did not. We might thus, like Adam, maintain the fantasy that we are more effective decision makers than we really are.

3. One example would be planning houses. Many people think about what their ideal houses would be like. Some even try to sketch them, hoping one day to actually build them. They then find on tours of their communities that there are lots of real, existing houses they find more attractive than their own "dream houses." There are at least two reasons for such failures in construction decision making. The first is that often we are not very good at bringing to mind all the alternatives that can actually be assembled. The other is that we do not fully understand our own values, for example, our esthetic tastes, in the housing illustration.

4. Comment: The essential issue concerns the costs and benefits of likelihood versus deterministic judgment.

CHAPTER 2: ASSESSMENT

2. Qualitative judgments are easier to report than quantitative judgments. Also, many practical situations require nothing more than relative likelihoods, for instance, "This product will last longer than that one." So qualitative judgments might be closer to the kind of real-world judgment in which one is interested.

3. One hypothesis suggests that different considerations are taken into account when people make absolute judgments, for example, when the chances of the Yankees and the Blue Jays are considered one at a time, instead of when they make relative judgments, for instance, when the comparative chances of the Yankees and Blue Jays winning are deliberated. Thus, consistency between quantitative and qualitative judgments such as those demanded of Dan should not be expected all the time.

4. P' (Replacement) = 0.20. Odds less than 1 correspond to probabilities less than 50%.

6. One problem with such biases is that they confound two different decision-making considerations, likelihood and value. There exist formal methods for properly integrating these considerations, for example, in decision analysis (Chapter 9). The observed confounding frustrates the intent of such procedures, perhaps invalidating them. Thus, rather than helping, physicians might be behaving contrary to their patients' interests.

Some consumer advocates maintain that one of the most important roles for the patient rather than the physician is the making of value assessments. However, through value-induced biases, the physician implicitly imposes his or her values on the patient, usurping the value assignment role. For example, who is to say that the risk of pneumonia is more serious than, say, the risk of complications from pneumonia vaccines?

7. In a proper application of the procedure used in this problem, corresponding significant outcomes of the prospects should be identical. That is not the case here. In particular, Bruce is not indifferent to each of the alternative events themselves, "State wins" and "State loses." Since, as a State booster, Bruce prefers State to win, the consequence "$10 plus State wins" is more attractive than simply "$10." This suggests the conclusion that P' (State wins) < 65%.

8. (a) People would probably conclude from the second message that appendicitis is a more serious problem than they would in response to the first message. In part, this is because, as we will learn in Chapter 6, people overestimate the commonness of deaths from such highly publicized events as tornadoes. So you would use the second message.

   (b) One suggestion is that people form absolute and relative likelihood judgments in fundamentally different ways.

9. (b) EV(Protect) = $2000, EV(Do nothing) = $3750.

   (c) EV(Protect) = $1200, EV(Do nothing) = $750.

10. (b) EV(Fuller) = 9.0 min, EV(Sumpter) = 9.6 min.

   (d) Although the average arrival time is shorter with Fuller, there is never a chance that Fuller will arrive at the scene of an accident within 3 minutes; Fuller's shortest arrival time is 8 minutes. On the other hand, 20% of Sumpter's arrival times are 3 minutes in length. It is not unreasonable to expect that, over the course of a year, several people in the town would die because they received medical attention 8 rather than only 3 minutes after emergency service was requested. From the perspective of saving those individuals' lives, Sumpter clearly would be the better company to receive the service contract. On the other hand, note that Sumpter's worst arrival time (15 min) is longer than Fuller's worst (12 min). So the major issue is whether Sumpter's 5-minute advantage at short times is more important than Fuller's 3-minute advantage at long times. At least some emergency care specialists maintain that it is.

CHAPTER 3: ANALYSIS

1. Bert. The covariance graphs for each of them should indicate the same bias and slope (nil). But, whereas Bert's graph will contain no scatter, Ernie's will contain a lot.
2. (a) It rewards the person according to the size of the probability judgment assigned to the event that ultimately occurs.
   (b) It should encourage extreme judgments, that is, near 1.0 and 0.0.
   (c) *Hint:* If the person says $f = 1.0$ on an occasion for which the target event does not happen, what is the value of the logarithmic score?
3. Usually, but not always.
4. It should look very similar to that of a diabolical clairvoyant.
7. (a) Arlene's judgment is the historical base rate $h = 0.9$, a particular constant judgment. The sample base rate is $\bar{d} = 23/25 = 0.92$. Thus, we have $\overline{PS} = (0.92)(0.08) + (0.9 - .92)^2 = 0.0740$.
   (b) In this case Arlene's constant judgment is $c = 1.0$. So $\overline{PS} = (0.92)(0.08) + (1.0 - 0.92)^2 = 0.0800$.
   (c) Since Arlene's judgment is always $c = 0.0$, $\overline{PS} = (0.92)(0.08) + (0.0 - 0.92)^2 = 0.9200$.
8. (a) (ii) $\overline{PS} = 0.2104$; (iii) Bias $= -0.116$, Slope $= 0.123$, Scat $= 0.0222$.
   (b) (ii) $\overline{PS} = 0.2640$; (iii) Bias $= -0.0338$, Slope $= 0.100$, Scat $= 0.0640$.
9. (a) (iii) $\overline{PS} = 0.2135$, VI $= 0.2275$, DI $= 0.1004$, CI $= 0.0864$.
   (b) (ii) $\overline{PS} = 0.2640$, VI $= 0.2452$, DI $= 0.0464$, CI $= 0.0652$.

CHAPTER 4: ACCURACY

2. If the physicians were overconfident, the calibration curve would be rotated $0°$-$45°$ clockwise from a pivot at the 50%–50% point on the 1:1 diagonal. In fact, the calibration curve is displaced largely to the right of the diagonal. This suggests a bias to overpredict pneumonia.
3. Generalizing from the results reported by Yates, McDaniel, and Brown (in press), the most plausible expectation is that the brokers' judgments will be more scattered.
4. It should be less than 2%.
5. Notice that most of the 2% surprises were in the 1% credible interval defined by the 99th percentile and the upper bound, $(q_{0.99}, \text{UB}]$. This implies that

the subjects tended to underestimate the values of the quantities being considered.

6. One possibility concerns the existence, immediacy, and clarity of feedback about the quality of our judgments. Feedback is probably much more deficient in clinical psychology than, say, in heart surgery.

9. A reasonable hypothesis to entertain is that the previous practices of Drs. Cass and Kulick were in areas where the prevalences of pneumonia differed greatly.

CHAPTER 5: COHERENCE

2. (a) By the definition of mutual exclusivity, arprosy and blemia cannot co-occur. Thus, P(Arprosy & Blemia) = 0%. More than likely, Jane has confused the concept of mutual exclusivity with that of independence. This confusion is quite common and probably is due to the similar connotations of the terms.

   (b) Mean P' (Arprosy or Blemia) < Mean P' (Arprosy) + Mean P' (Blemia), since people's probability judgments for disjunctions of mutually exclusive events tend to be smaller than the sums of their probability judgments for the events considered alone. A less plausible, although not unreasonable, expectation is that Mean P' (Arprosy) > Mean P' (Arprosy or Blemia) or that Mean P' (Blemia) > Mean P' (Arprosy or Blemia) by generalizing from studies of disjunction errors.

3. The result Trent has in mind is the commonly observed overjudgment of conjunctive probabilities, that is,

$$P'(A \& B) > P'(A|B)P'(B)$$

This result concerns relations among three judgments made by a given individual. It does not directly concern what actually happens in the world. Thus, it is quite possible that the stock broker's judgments P' (Gain|Dividend) and P' (Dividend) are themselves so low that, even though P' (Gain & Dividend) > P' (Gain|Dividend)P' (Dividend), P' (Gain & Dividend) is still small relative to how often companies really do gain in value and pay dividends.

4. (a) You should disagree—at least tentatively. Suppose that Transaction Error E is in fact a valid cue for the presence of Weakness W. This means that the chance of that error being present differs according to whether a firm does or does not have Weakness W. Ewart's tip is that the chance of Error E is 2% when a firm has Weakness W. All that is needed for Error E to be a useful clue is that its chance of occurrence be different for firms that do not have Weakness W. To settle the usefulness question, we would need to discover what that second probability is. Andrew seems to hold the mistaken belief that the probability of Error E must be high in an absolute sense in order for it to be useful in detecting Weakness W.

   (b) In a Bayesian framework, the problem of detecting Weakness W amounts to determining whether P(Weakness W|Error E) is different from P(Weakness W). That is, should observing Error E change one's prior probability that a firm has Weakness W?

Let us abbreviate Weakness W by W and Error E by E. In the present situation, Bayes's Theorem implies that P(Weakness W|Error E) = $\{P(E|W)P(W)\}/\{P(E|W)P(W) + P(E|W^c)P(W^c)\}$. Since $P(W^c) = 1 - P(W)$, this reduces to P(Weakness W|Error E) = $\{P(E|W)P(W)\}/\{[P(E|W) - P(E|W^c)]P(W) + P(E|W^c)\}$.

We know that P(Error E|Weakness W) = $P(E|W)$ = 2%. Suppose it is also true that Error E is just as common in firms without Weakness W, that is, P(Error E|No Weakness W) = $P(E|W^c)$ = 2%. The above equation then becomes P(Weakness W|Error E) = $\{P(E|W)P(W)\}/\{0 + P(E|W^c)\}$ = $P(W)$ = P(Weakness W). That is, in agreement with intuition, when P(Error E|Weakness W) = P(Error E|No Weakness W), discovering Error E would have no effect on the probability that a firm's control system has Weakness W. But to the extent that there *is* a difference between these probabilities, the prior and posterior probabilities of Weakness W will differ from each other, too. We would then say that Error E is *diagnostic* for Weakness W.

8. On the side of importance: Having incoherent judgments amounts to having two strikes against you. First, if your judgments are incoherent, then at most only some of your judgments can be accurate. So you will suffer whatever costs that degree of inaccuracy brings. Second, if your incoherence makes you the victim of a material trap, then you are guaranteed to not come out ahead in those transactions—no matter what events actually happen.

On the side of unimportance: It is conceded that *if* you are victimized by a material trap, "your goose is cooked." But that "if" is a big one. Nobody knows just how many material traps are out there in the world just waiting to take advantage of people with incoherent opinions. Perhaps there are none. There is also the issue of costs. Are the consequences of being victimized in naturally occurring material traps serious, especially in comparison to all the trouble we would have to go through to protect against them? No one can say for sure.

CHAPTER 6: FORMAL PROCEDURES

1. (b) Label the first two events as follows: A = "The winner of the next state gubernatorial (governor's) election will be a Democrat" and B = "The winner of the next U.S. presidential election will be a Democrat." Thus, the third event is the conjunction of the first two: $A\&B$ = "The winners of both the next state gubernatorial and the next U.S. presidential elections will be Democrats."

The signed sum model makes differential predictions, depending on whether Stacey sees the events A and B as "likely" or "unlikely." The following table shows the predictions, where the ordering is in decreasing likelihood:

EVENT A	EVENT B	PREDICTED ORDERING
Likely	Likely	[A&B, A, B] or [A&B, B, A]
Likely	Unlikely	A, A&B, B
Unlikely	Likely	B, A&B, A
Unlikely	Unlikely	[A, B, A&B] or [B, A, A&B]

3. (a) For the marginal proportion method, your calibration graph would contain a single point at $(f_j, d_j) = (0.40, 0.40)$. There would be two points in the reliability diagram when you use the conditional proportion method, at (0.30, 0.30) and (0.50, 0.50).

   (b) The conditional proportion method would yield the better mean probability score. This is because the calibration will be the same as before (perfect), but the discrimination will be better.

5. (a) You should be able to show that, according to the correct method for judging contingency, variables 1 and 2 are contingent if $a \times d \neq b \times c$; otherwise, they are noncontingent. According to the sum-of-diagonals strategy, contingency exists when $a + d \neq b + c$. Thus, in principle, we can construct an infinite variety of ways in which the rules lead to conflicting conclusions by making $a \times d \neq b \times c$, but $a + d = b + c$, or the other way around.

   An especially interesting set of circumstances is that where there really is no contingency and the marginal proportions for both variables are different from 50%. An example is the table in which the frequencies are as follows: S & D –9; S & D^C – 90; S^C & D – 1; and S^C & D^C – 10, where S indicates the presence of Symptom S and D the presence of Disease D. (Construct the contingency table yourself.) It is unclear whether the stated conditions, that is, no contingency and marginal proportions different from 1/2, are sufficient to guarantee conflicting conclusions. But they often do yield such conclusions.

6. Imagine that, although both Mercedes and Charles start with the belief that there is no contingency, Mercedes holds that belief more firmly. This implies that it should take stronger evidence to change Mercedes's mind than Charles's. There are forms of analysis according to Bayes's Theorem that make precise how the same evidence should have differential impact on Mercedes and Charles. The spirit of those analyses can be appreciated by expressing Mercedes's and Charles's opinions in terms of contingency tables that contain no dependencies, but which have different absolute numbers of cases, with many more in Mercedes's table. Effectively, the new evidence is simply added to Mercedes's and Charles's original tables.

8. Imagine two young detectives, "Meredith Mast" and "Jimmy Roundtree." Each is on duty at different times. However, during their first couple of days on the job, both pay close attention to how individuals suspected of car theft are dressed and whether or not they are eventually found guilty or are cleared. In particular, they note whether each individual is wearing a certain jacket currently in fashion. Following is a contingency table where, in each cell, the first number is the frequency observed by Detective Mast among the first 12 cases she sees. The number after the first slash is the frequency noted by Detective Roundtree in his first 12 cases. The final number is the frequency recorded in the police department for the entire year:

	Fashionable Jacket?	
Case Disposition	Yes	No
Guilty	5/2/50	2/5/50
Cleared	1/4/50	4/1/50

Suppose that each detective is subject to the primacy effect in contingency judgment. Then, on the basis of their early observations, they conclude and act on the assumption that there is a contingency between the suspect's dress and his or her guilt in opposite directions. Moreover, they never pay close enough attention to subsequent cases to notice that there really is no contingency at all. Small samples of cases can differ dramatically from the populations from which they come. So there is nothing to prevent the occurrence of a situation like the present one.

9. (b) Geneva's opinion will probably change in the direction of her believing it more likely than 50–50 that oil is present. This is a classic pseudodiagnosticity situation.

CHAPTER 7: SUBSTANTIVE PROCEDURES

1. According to the availability heuristic, a medical student would consider it probable that he has Disease *D*, say, to the degree that it is easy for him to recall previous instances of Disease *D*. Because he is currently studying Disease *D*, it is certainly not hard to think of Disease *D* cases. So that part of the availability heuristic fits. On the other hand, especially if Disease *D* is rare, the only reason the student ever heard of Disease *D* in the first place is that it is on the course syllabus. Thus, it seems unlikely that the student's belief that he has Disease *D* rests on a memory-based metacognition. Instead, studying Disease *D* simply makes that disease a prominent member of the set of possible explanations for the student's assorted aches and pains.

5. Let us say that the task is to judge your chances of being elected either captain or co-captain of your bowling team, the event "Captain or Co-Captain." The argument assumes that, when you attempt to arrive at a judgment of P' (Captain or Co-captain), you start with a judgment of one of the marginal events, for example, P' (Captain). This serves as an initial judgment of P' (Captain or Co-captain), say, P' (Captain or Co-captain)$_{Initial}$. You then bring the second event to mind and try to adjust P' (Captain or Co-captain)$_{Initial}$ in view of your considerations about that second event. However, the adjustment is inadequate. That is, P' (Captain or Co-captain)$_{Final}$ is too close to P' (Captain or Co-captain)$_{Initial}$, in other words, "too small."

6. You should be sensitive to the strong possibility of value and overconfidence biases. For instance, there might well be a tendency for all your colleagues to be overly optimistic of profitability, since that is a desirable outcome. The individuals who are directly responsible for making and selling a particular product should be especially susceptible to such overoptimism. One of your strategies for making judgments might be to have your staff and others construct scenarios whereby a product either does well or *poorly*. The generation of one scenario tends to inhibit the production of others. So, it is perhaps a good idea to have individuals construct their scenarios independently of one another.

CHAPTER 8: BEDROCK PRINCIPLES

1. No, because the outcomes of applying to Central and Ivy State are dependent on different events, the decisions of the admissions committees at the separate schools.

2. Ordered lists:

   Go: (Storm, $0 and possibly death; No storm, $5000)
   Stay: (Storm, $0; No storm, $0)

   Matrix:

	Weather	
Action	Storm	No Storm
Go	$0/Death	$5000
Stay	$0	$0

4. There are sometimes circumstances in which the decision maker's preferences do not admit the possibility of dominance. As an example, suppose that an individual is considering cars that differ only in size (large versus small), and color (red versus blue). Imagine that this person prefers blue cars when they are large, but red ones when they are small. Then none of the four kinds of cars that are possible can dominate any of the others. The problem in such situations is that the appeal of a particular level of a feature dimension depends on the status of the other dimension. Dominance applies only when such dependency does not exist.

5. (b) EV = $1. Thus, the game is unfair.

6. (b) In ordered list form, the options are: Tasty Treats: (0.40, –$2000; 0.20, –$500; 0.40, $5000) and Dandy Dude: (0.35, –$2000; 0.20, –$500; 0.45, $5000). Both the probabilistic dominance and the expected value choice principle are applicable. Since the Dandy Dude option dominates the Tasty Treats opportunity, according to the dominance rule, the former alternative should be picked. Incidentally, whenever both rules apply, the dominance and EV choice principles never conflict with each other.

7. (a)

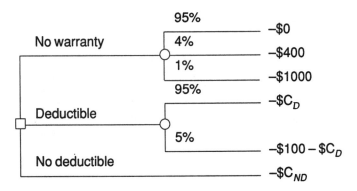

(b) Suppose that we ignore the presence of the no-deductible warranty. Then the most Al should be willing to pay for the deductible warranty is the amount required to equate the expected values of buying that warranty and having no warranty at all. This leads to the conclusion that $C_D = \$21$. That is, Al should be willing to pay up to $21 for the deductible warranty.

(c) With one exception, all the outcomes in this decision problem are negative. Suppose we can accept the generalization that, in the domain of losses, people are risk seeking. Then, since there is less risk in having the limited warranty than in having no warranty, we should expect Al to be willing to pay less than $21 for the warranty.

But now consider another argument: Sound City is highly unlikely to offer the deductible warranty for $21 or less. They would figure that they could not afford to, since, in the long run, they would probably lose money that way. If we could assume that many people find the warranty attractive at the price Sound City charges, then a not unreasonable expectation is that Al is just like those customers, and hence would be willing to pay more than $21 for the warranty. You should note that this argument does not imply that the only way for Sound City to make money on their limited warranty is that *most* people consider the warranty worth more than $21. They only need a "large number" of such individuals.

8. The expected probability score for reporting judgment f_R is

$$EV(f_R) = P'(A)PS(f_R, A) + P'(A^c)PS(f_R, A^c)$$

$$= f_T(f_R - 1)^2 + (1 - f_T)(f_R)^2$$

Note that we can describe the relationship between the true and reported judgments as

$$f_R = f_T + \Delta$$

where the difference Δ is 0 if the judgments are the same. Replacing f_R by $f_T + \Delta$, the expected score can be reduced to

$$EV(f_R) = f_T(1 - f_T) + \Delta^2$$

which clearly is minimized when $\Delta = 0$, that is, when the person reports truthfully.

9. (a)/(c) Elwood Keeser's bonus system should induce his brokers to report judgments that are more extreme than before.

CHAPTER 9: EXPECTED UTILITY

2. (b) According to the expected value choice principle, Mr. Griswold should send out work crews only if EV(Send) ≥ EV(Don't send). Let $p = P(\text{Rain})$. Then EV(Send) = $p(-\$200) + (1 - p)(\$1000)$ and EV(Don't send) = 0. Thus, crews should be sent out only if $p \le p_t = \frac{5}{6}$.

(c) It has been found that, most often, people tend to be risk averse. So it is most reasonable to expect Mr. Griswold to be risk averse, too. If so, he will prefer a sure amount to any prospect that has an expected value identical to that sure amount. When $P(\text{Rain}) = \frac{5}{6}$, the expected value of sending work crews is $0. So Mr. Griswold would definitely prefer *not* to send crews out. For him to change his mind, the expected value of the "Send crew" option would have to be larger than $0. That is, the probability of rain would have to be less than $\frac{5}{6}$.

4. To show necessity, we assume that the decision maker decides according to expected utility. The decision maker is then presented with the antecedents of the monotonicity condition. We must then demonstrate that the decision maker would make the decision articulated in the conclusion of the condition. The antecedents of the monotonicity condition are (a) that p and q are probabilities such that $p \geq q$, (b) that Prospect $P = (p, \text{BEST}; 1 - p, \text{WORST})$, and (c) that Prospect $Q = (q, \text{BEST}; 1 - q, \text{WORST})$. The conclusion says that the decision maker will not choose Prospect Q over Prospect P.

Let the decision maker's utility function be denoted by u, with $u(\text{BEST}) > u(\text{WORST})$. Then EU(Prospect P) = $pu(\text{BEST}) + (1 - p)u(\text{WORST})$ and EU(Prospect Q) = $qu(\text{BEST}) + (1 - q)u(\text{WORST})$. Suppose that the conclusion were not true. This would be equivalent to saying that EU(Prospect Q) > EU(Prospect P). If you work through the algebra, you will see that this amounts to saying that $q[u(\text{BEST}) - u(\text{WORST})] > p[u(\text{BEST}) - u(\text{WORST})]$. And since $u(\text{BEST}) > u(\text{WORST})$, this implies that $q > p$. But by assumption, $p \geq q$. So the conclusion must be true.

6. See Luce and Raiffa (1957, p. 29).

7. (d) *Decision tree:*

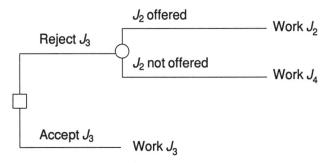

Decision rule: Your rule says that your friend should reject J_3 only if EU(Reject J_3) $\geq$ EU(Accept J_3); otherwise, he or she should accept that position. EU(Reject J_3) is given by

$$\text{EU}(\text{Reject } J_3) = P'(J_2 \text{ offered})u(J_2) + [1 - P'(J_2\text{offered})]u(J_4)$$

and

$$\text{EU}(\text{Accept } J_3) = u(J_3)$$

So all you must do is simply insert the required probability judgment and utility assessments, and your recommendation follows.

(f) Among the advantages of the decision analysis might be the following:

(i) It decomposes the overall decision task into smaller problems that might be more manageable.

(ii) The analysis forces your friend to be more careful and systematic than he or she might be ordinarily.

(iii) Assuming that your friend wishes to have his or her decision be consistent with the principles underlying expected utility maximization, the particular rule for combining value and likelihood considerations assures this. (It is assumed that the judgment and utility elicitation procedures are valid, too.)

(iv) Consistently applying the combination rule used in the analysis to all decision problems under uncertainty would prevent your friend from being victimized by material traps that exploit violations of expected utility principles. (You might well question whether this is a serious risk in the present situation, however.)

The following are some of the (potential) shortcomings of your decision analysis:

(i) It is difficult and time consuming to perform.

(ii) Your friend might find the required assessment procedures so alien and uncomfortable that they do not accurately represent his or her true feelings.

(iii) Decisions fail, that is, turn out less satisfactory than they might have, for many different reasons. Some sources of decision failures are such that there is no reason to expect a decision analysis to affect them. For example, there is nothing in the analysis *per se* to enhance your friend's ability to make a more accurate judgment of the chance that job J_2 will be offered. It is also conceivable that, if he or she actually had the opportunity to work at both job J_2 and job J_3, the latter would be *more* satisfying, not less. That is, there is nothing in a decision analysis that should improve the correspondence between a person's utility assessments and his or her actual satisfaction with the relevant outcomes.

8. (a) (i) $u(\$CE1) = 50$, $u(\$CE2) = 25$, and $u(\$CE3) = 75$.

(b) (i) If $D(10{-}0) > D(20{-}10)$, your friend has almost literally told you that a gain of \$10 is more significant when starting from \$0 than from \$10. Assuming that this is generally characteristic of your friend's valuations for money, his or her value function must be concave.

(iii) Let the value function be denoted by v, with $v(\$0) = 0$ and $v(\$20) = 100$. Suppose that you identify the intermediate amount of money \$$M$ such that your friend says that the exchange of \$0 for \$$M$ is equivalent to the exchange of \$$M$ for \$20. We can interpret the exchange values as $D(M{-}0) = v(\$M) - v(\$0)$ and $D(20{-}M) = v(\$20) - v(\$M)$, with $D(M{-}0) = D(20{-}M)$. Clearly, $v(\$M) = 50$. That is, \$$M$ is the valuewise midpoint of the range from $0 to $20. Other points on the value curve could be gotten by, for instance, seeking valuewise midpoints of the ranges $0–$M and $M–$20.

CHAPTER 10: COUSINS OF EXPECTED UTILITY

1. (a) According to Figure 9.2, $u(\$7) \approx 93$ and $u(\$1) \approx 41$. Thus, $EU(P) = (0.3)(93) + (0.7)(41) \approx 57$. But $u(\$1.80) \approx 57$, too. So we should expect Ms. A to be essentially indifferent between Prospect P and the sure thing.

   (b) By Figure 10.1, the relevant decision weights are $\pi(0.3) = 0.23$ and $\pi(0.7) = 0.57$. Assuming a reference point of $0, Prospect P is strictly positive. Accordingly, its subjective value is $V(P) = 41 + (0.23)(93 - 41) = 53$, which is less than the subjective value of the sure thing, $V(\$1.80) \approx 57$. We should therefore anticipate that Ms. Avery would take the sure thing.

2. (a) According to Figure 10.2b, Mr. Cleaver's reference point is $300. So both the old and the new job are strictly negative prospects. $V(\text{Old job}) = v(-\$50) = v(\underline{\$250}) \approx -2.3$. The absolute representation of the new job offer is ($\underline{\$200}$, 65%; $\underline{\$275}$, 35%), and the effective representation is (–$100, 65%; –$25, 35%). In any case, the subjective value of the new job is $V(\text{New job}) = v(\underline{\$275}) + \pi(0.65)[v(\underline{\$200}) - v(\underline{\$275})] \approx -1.8 + (0.52)[-3.00 - (-1.8)] = -2.424$. Thus, Mr. Cleaver will stick with his old job.

   (b) After a week, Mr. Cleaver is likely to have adapted to the weakened financial condition of his employer. If so, his reference point will have shifted from $300 to perhaps $250, the salary increase he is assured of having in his old job. In that case, the new job offer would not be a strictly negative prospect and would be evaluated differently than before. Depending on exactly what new form his value function takes, he might arrive at a different decision.

3. See Hershey and Schoemaker (1980).

5. One factor is the probability of a large loss. In the case of the parking ticket gamble, this probability is 50%, which is above the crossover point in prospect theory. Hence, the probability of losing $10 is underweighted, making the gamble appear attractive, relative to the $5 fine. In the case of car insurance, the chance of an accident is very small, far below the crossover point. Hence, that probability is overweighted, making uninsured driving look very unappealing.

CHAPTER 11: EXPECTED VALUE VERSUS RISK

1. (b) EV(Lopez) = 410 lives, EV(Kim) = 330 lives.
   (c) (i) LP(Lopez) = 0.2, LP(Kim) = 0.3; (ii) ML(Lopez) = 300 lives, ML(Kim) = 200 lives; (iii) EL(Lopez) = 40 lives, EL(Kim) = 50 lives; (iv) Semvar(Lopez) = 10,000, Semvar(Kim) = 9000; (v) Var(Lopez) = 28,900, Var(Kim) = 18,100.
   (d) Loss probability and expected loss.
   (e) The Kim program, but not the Lopez program.

   (f) Risk-priority: Kim; EV-priority: Lopez.

   (g) (i) Kim, (ii) Kim, (iii) Lopez.

   (h) When k is highest, that is, $k = 2$. When $k = \frac{1}{2}$, you care so little about the greater risk of the Lopez program that you choose it anyway.

2. Risk-seeking: His isoworthiness contours would slant to the left rather than the right. Risk neutral: Contours would be vertical.

4. (a) The $500 response, since she is willing to give up only $200 = $700 − $500 rather than $500 = $700 − $200 in guaranteed income in exchange for the improvement of $500 in expected income.

   (b) Take the case when Judy's response is $500. The implied maximum loss is $ML_B = \$500$. Thus we have

$$W_A = \$1500 - k(\$300) = W_B = \$2000 - k(\$500)$$

which implies that $k = \frac{5}{2} = 2.5$. When Judy's response is $200, $k = 1.0$, which is indicative of less risk aversion.

6. (a) The semivariance implies that the marginal significance of a loss *increases* rather than decreases.

   (b) Instead of being squared, the losses could be raised to a power less than 1.0. See Fishburn (1977).

7. The fact that the variance is "contaminated," taking into account both gains as well as losses, means that there will be more random error in taking the riskiness of investments into account. Because the variance entails increasing rather than decreasing marginal significance, the riskiness of prospects with large potential losses will be overstressed. This would lead to overly conservative investment behavior.

CHAPTER 12: PERSONAL REPRESENTATIONS: THEIR CHARACTER

1. One representational hypothesis is analogous to that proposed on pages 342–43 for why you might appear to have rescinded your decision to wear your seat belt when you really had not. Specifically, sympathethic physicians who *might* recommend the vaccine to their patients could fail to do so because, at the time of their consultations with their patients, the possibility of recommending the vaccine never comes to mind. In other words, their failure to recommend the vaccine is a nondecision (see Young, Yates, and Curley, 1986).

3. You would certainly want to make sure that Mr. Miner's representation includes the best judgments of each treatment's chance of eliminating the cancer. Surgery has a better probability of arresting cancer than does radiation therapy. But is that advantage large enough to compensate for the loss of Mr. Miner's larynx? Ultimately, only Mr. Miner will be able to answer that question. But Mr. Miner has never been deprived of his own voice. So his expectation of how badly he would feel about using an artificial voice box might be better or worse than the eventual reality. Thus, you might try to assist Mr. Miner in simulating the experience, by listening to artificial voice boxes and perhaps practicing how

one interacts with other people when using the device (see McNeil, Weichselbaum, and Pauker, 1981).

6. You might have chosen any number of problems. However, there exist decision-aiding strategies that serve as models for addressing representational difficulties. One representation problem people have when they make decisions in areas that are new to them is that they have little idea of what the significant outcomes might be. An example is having a first child. To an extent, a new parent's experiences will be unique. However, if 50 "old" parents were to list all their significant experiences, the combined list is likely to include the majority of those a 51st old parent might add. Thus, the combined list could serve as a valuable aid in assisting a couple to make a wise decision about having children, in the near future or ever (see Beach, Townes, and Campbell, 1978).

CHAPTER 13: PERSONAL REPRESENTATIONS: THEIR CONTENTS AND MODERATION

1. (a) That person should be indifferent, since the potential prizes, as well as their probabilities, are identical.

   (b/c) In its essentials, this experiment was conducted by Ronen (1973). Most subjects preferred Game A, the one that offered the higher probability of continuing to the second stage. Subjects' remarks indicated that they did so because they wanted to stay in the game as long as possible. This suggests that their representations of the decision situation included "staying in the game" as an extraneous element.

2. No, in the case of prospect theory. This is because, according to prospect theory, every prospect is assigned a unique value that is equivalent to a location on a numerical scale. Since numbers are transitive, Mr. Lowe's choices must be transitive, too. Yes, in particular versions of regret/elation theory. This is because the value of a prospect is not unique, but is instead relative to the prospect to which it is being compared.

3. One example would be significant outcomes that are only remote possibilities. For instance, a first-time homeowner chooses Contractor A over Contractor B to put a new roof on his house because he offers a better warranty. Shortly thereafter, the new roof starts leaking. To his dismay, the homeowner discovers that Contractor A has gone bankrupt (making his warranty useless), but that Contractor B is still in business. The homeowner's decision did not fail because his likelihood judgments for bankruptcy were inaccurate. In fact, the possibility of bankruptcy never occurred to the homeowner, since he never personally heard of a contractor going broke. In contrast, the potential of bankruptcy would have been a major consideration for a more experienced property owner, perhaps leading to the choice of Contractor B.

6. Mr. Vaughn probably has limited self-insight into how he evaluates contracts, since he has done the task so many times.

7. (g) Reexamine Equation 13.1E in the item statement, the *additive rule* for determining the score for a given decision alternative. That rule might very

well not be descriptive of how the decision maker actually values the alternatives. In particular, the rule implies the following about how a person evaluates elective courses. Suppose that Courses *A* and *B* are identical with respect to all significant aspect dimensions except "instructor quality," which has a weight of 5. On that dimension, Course *A* is 10 rating points better than Course *B*. The additive rule implies that the overall score of Course *A* is 50 points better than Course *B*, regardless of the status of the courses on the remaining dimensions. Is this indeed the way every individual would feel? Probably not. For instance, would the 10-point instructor quality difference mean the same to you if Courses *A* and *B* were both terrible on all other dimensions as it would if they were average on all those dimensions? (See also Keeney and Raiffa, 1976; Yates and Jagacinski, 1979.)

References

ABELSON, R. P. (1976). Script processing in attitude formation and decision making. In J. S. Carroll and J. W. Payne (eds.), *Cognition and social behavior* (pp. 33–52). Hillsdale, NJ: Erlbaum.

—— AND LEVI, A. (1985). Decision making and decision theory. In G. Lindzey and E. Aronson (eds.), *Handbook of social psychology* (3rd ed., pp. 231–309). New York: Random House.

ADELSON, B. (1984). When novices surpass experts: The difficulty of a task may increase with expertise. *Journal of Experimental Psychology: Learning, Memory, and Cognition*, **10**, 483–495.

AJZEN, I. (1977). Intuitive theories of events and the effects of base-rate information on prediction. *Journal of Personality and Social Psychology*, **35**, 303–314.

ALLAIS, M. (1953). Le comportement de l'homme rationnel devant le risque: Critique des postulats et axiomes de l'êcole americaine. *Econometrica*, **21**, 503–546.

ALLOY, L. B., AND TABACHNIK, N. (1984). Assessment of covariation by humans and animals: The joint influence of prior expectations and current situational information. *Psychological Review*, **91**, 112–149.

ALPERT, M., AND RAIFFA, H. (1982). A progress report on the training of probability assessors. In D. Kahneman, P. Slovic, and A. Tversky (eds.), *Judgment under uncertainty: Heuristics and biases* (pp. 294–305). New York: Cambridge University Press.

ANDERSON, C. R. (1976). Coping behaviors as intervening mechanisms in the inverted-U stress-performance relationship. *Journal of Applied Psychology*, **61**, 30–34.

ANDERSON, J. R. (1985). *Cognitive psychology and its implications* (2nd ed.). San Francisco: Freeman

—— AND BOWER, G. H. (1973). *Human associative memory*. New York: Wiley.

ANDERSON, N. H. (1981). *Foundations of information integration theory*. New York: Academic Press.

—— (1986). A cognitive theory of judgment and decision. In B. Brehmer and others (eds.), *New directions in research on decision making* (pp. 63–108). Amsterdam: Elsevier.

——, AND SHANTEAU, J. C. (1970). Information integration in risky decision making. *Journal of Experimental Psychology*, **84**, 441–451.

ARKES, H. R., AND BLUMER, C. (1985). The psychology of sunk cost. *Organizational Behavior and Human Decision Processes*, **35**, 124–140.

———, AND HAMMOND, K. R. (eds.). (1987). *Judgment and decision making*. New York: Cambridge University Press.

———, AND HARKNESS, A. R. (1983). Estimates of contingency between two dichotomous variables. *Journal of Experimental Psychology: General*, **112**, 117–135.

———, AND ROTHBART, M. (1985). Memory, retrieval, and contingency judgments. *Journal of Personality and Social Psychology*, **49**, 598–606.

———, AND OTHERS. (1981). Hindsight bias among physicians weighing the likelihood of diseases. *Journal of Applied Psychology*, **66**, 252–254.

———, AND OTHERS. (1987). Two methods of reducing overconfidence. *Organizational Behavior and Human Decision Processes*, **39**, 133–144.

——— AND OTHERS. (1988). Eliminating the hindsight bias. *Journal of Applied Psychology*, **73**, 305–307.

BANDLER, W., AND KOHOUT, L. J. (1985). Probabilistic versus fuzzy production rules in expert systems. *International Journal of Man–Machine Studies*, **22**, 347–353.

BARCLAY, S., AND BEACH, L. R. (1972). Combinatorial properties of personal probabilities. *Organizational Behavior and Human Performance*, **8**, 176–183.

BAR-HILLEL, M. (1973). On the subjective probability of compound events. *Organizational Behavior and Human Performance*, **9**, 396–406.

——— (1980). What features make samples seem representative? *Journal of Experimental Psychology: Human Perception and Performance*, **6**, 578–589.

——— (1983). The base rate fallacy controversy. In R. W. Scholz (ed.), *Decision making under uncertainty* (pp. 39–61). Amsterdam: North-Holland.

BAYES, T. (1958). Essay towards solving a problem in the doctrine of chances. *Biometrika*, **45**, 293–315. (Reprinted from *Philosophical Transactions of the Royal Society*, 1763, **53**, 370–418.)

BEACH, L. R., AND MITCHELL, T. R. (1978). A contingency model for the selection of decision strategies. *Academy of Management Review*, **3**, 439–449.

———, AND ——— (1987). Image theory: Principles, goals, and plans in decision making. *Acta Psychologica*, **66**, 201–220.

———, BARNES, V. E., AND CHRISTENSEN-SZALANSKI, J. J. J. (1986). Beyond heuristics and biases: A contingency model of judgemental forecasting. *Journal of Forecasting*, **5**, 143–157.

———, CAMPBELL, F. L., AND TOWNES, B. D. (1979). Subjective expected utility and the prediction of birth-planning decisions. *Organizational Behavior and Human Performance*, **24**, 18–28.

———, TOWNES, B. D., AND CAMPBELL, F. L. (1978). *The optional parenthood questionnaire: A guide to decision making about parenthood*. Washington, DC: National Alliance for Optional Parenthood.

BELL, D. E. (1982). Regret in decision making under uncertainty. *Operations Research*, **30**, 961–981.

——— (1985). Disappointment in decision making under uncertainty. *Operations Research*, **33**, 1–27.

———, AND FARQUHAR, P. H. (1986). Perspectives on utility theory. *Operations Research*, **34**, 179–183.

BEN ZUR, H., AND BREZNITZ, S. J. (1981). The effect of time pressure on risky choice behavior. *Acta Psychologica*, **47**, 89–104.

BENNER, P., AND TANNER, C. (1987). How expert nurses use intuition. *American Journal of Nursing*, **87**(1), 23–31.

BERNOULLI, D. (1954). Exposition of a new theory on the measurement of risk (L. Sommer, trans.). *Econometrica*, **22**, 23–36. (Original work published in 1738.)

BEYTH-MAROM, R. (1982). How probable is probable?: A numerical translation of verbal probability expressions. *Journal of Forecasting*, 1, 257–269.

——— (1982). Perception of correlation reexamined. *Memory and Cognition*, 10, 511–519.

———, AND FISCHHOFF, B. (1977). Direct measures of availability and judgments of category frequency. *Bulletin of the Psychonomic Society*, 9, 236–238.

———, AND ———. (1983). Diagnosticity and pseudodiagnosticity. *Journal of Personality and Social Psychology*, 45, 1185–1195.

BLATTENBERGER, G., AND LAD, F. (1985). Separating the Brier score into calibration and refinement components: A graphical exposition. *American Statistician*, 39, 26–32.

BOUCHARD, T. J. (1971). Whatever happened to brainstorming. *Journal of Creative Behavior*, 5, 182–189.

BOUWMAN, M. J. (1982). The use of accounting information: Expert versus novice behavior. In G. R. Ungson and D. N. Braunstein (eds.), *Decision making: An interdisciplinary inquiry* (pp. 134–167). Boston: Kent.

BRANDSTATTER, H., DAVIS, J. H., AND STOCKER-KREICHGAUER, G. (1982). *Group decision making*. New York: Academic Press.

BRANSFORD, J. D., AND FRANKS, J. J. (1971). The abstraction of linguistic ideas. *Cognitive Psychology*, 2, 331–350.

BRIER, G. W. (1950). Verification of forecasts expressed in terms of probability. *Monthly Weather Review*, 78(1), 1–3.

BRONNER, R. (1982). *Decision making under time pressure*. Lexington, MA: Lexington Books.

BRYANT, G. D., AND NORMAN, G. R. (1980). Expressions of probability: Words and numbers. *New England Journal of Medicine*, 302, 411.

BUCHANAN, B. G., AND SHORTLIFFE, E. H. (eds.). (1984). *Rule-based expert systems: The MYCIN experiments of the Stanford heuristic programming project*. Reading, MA: Addison-Wesley.

CARLSON, B. W., AND YATES, J. F. (in press). Disjunction errors in qualitative likelihood judgment. *Organizational Behavior and Human Decision Processes*.

CASTELLAN, N. J. (1977). Decision making with multiple probabilistic cues. In N. J. Castellan, D. B. Pisoni, and G. R. Potts (eds.), *Cognitive theory* (Vol. 2, pp. 117–147). Hillsdale, NJ: Erlbaum.

CENTOR, R. M., DALTON, H. P., AND YATES, J. F. (1984, November). *Are physicians' probability estimates better or worse than regression model estimates?* Paper presented at the Sixth Annual Meeting of the Society for Medical Decision Making, Bethesda, MD.

CHAPMAN, L. J., AND CHAPMAN, J. P. (1967). Genesis of popular but erroneous psychodiagnostic observations. *Journal of Abnormal Psychology*, 72, 193–204.

CHASE, W. C., AND SIMON, H. (1973). Perception in chess. *Cognitive Psychology*, 4, 55–81.

CHESLEY, G. R. (1978). Subjective probability elicitation techniques: A performance comparison. *Journal of Accounting Research*, 16, 225–241.

——— (1982). *Interpretation of uncertainty expressions*. Unpublished manuscript, Dalhousie University, Halifax, Nova Scotia, Canada.

CHRISTENSEN-SZALANSKI, J. J. J. (1984). Discount functions and the measurement of patients' values: Women's decisions during childbirth. *Medical Decision Making*, 4, 47–58.

———, AND BUSHYHEAD, J. B. (1981). Physicians' use of probabilistic information in a real clinical setting. *Journal of Experimental Psychology: Human Perception and Performance*, 7, 928–935.

————, AND OTHERS. (1983). Effects of expertise and experience on risk judgments. *Journal of Applied Psychology*, **68**, 278–284.

COHEN, J., AND HANSEL, C. E. M. (1958). The nature of decisions in gambling: Equivalence of single and compound subjective probabilities. *Acta Psychologica*, **13**, 357–370.

————, DEARNALEY, E. J., AND HANSEL, C. E. M. (1956). The addition of subjective probabilities: The summation of estimates of success and failure. *Acta Psychologica*, **12**, 371–380.

COHEN, L. J. (1977). *The probable and the provable.* New York: Oxford University Press.

COHEN, L. J. (1979). On the psychology of prediction: Whose is the fallacy? *Cognition*, **7**, 385–407.

COHEN, M., JAFFRAY, J., AND SAID, T. (1987). Experimental comparison of individual behavior under risk and under uncertainty for gains and for losses. *Organizational Behavior and Human Decision Processes*, **39**, 1–22.

CONRATH, D. W. (1973). From statistical decision theory to practice: Some problems with the transition. *Management Science*, **19**, 873–883.

COOMBS, C. H. (1975). Portfolio theory and the measurement of risk. In M. F. Kaplan and S. Schwartz (eds.), *Human judgment and decision processes* (pp. 63–85). New York: Academic Press.

————, AND HUANG, L. (1970). Tests of a portfolio theory of risk preference. *Journal of Experimental Psychology*, **85**, 23–29.

————, AND ———— (1976). Tests of the betweenness property of expected utility. *Journal of Mathematical Psychology*, **13**, 323–337.

————, DAWES, R. M., AND TVERSKY, A. (1970). *Mathematical psychology.* Englewood Cliffs, NJ: Prentice-Hall.

COOPER, W. S. (1987). Decision theory as a branch of evolutionary theory: A biological derivation of the Savage axioms. *Psychological Review*, **94**, 395–411.

CROCKER, J. (1981). Judgment of covariation by social perceivers. *Psychological Bulletin*, **90**, 272–292.

CURLEY, S. P., ERAKER, S. A., AND YATES, J. F. (1984). An investigation of patients' reactions to therapeutic uncertainty. *Medical Decision Making*, **4**, 501–511.

————, YATES, J. F., AND ABRAMS, R. A. (1986). Psychological sources of ambiguity avoidance. *Organizational Behavior and Human Decision Processes*, **38**, 230–256.

DANNENBERG, A. L., SHAPIRO, A. R., AND FRIES, J. F. (1979). Enhancement of clinical predictive ability by computer consultation. *Methods of Information in Medicine*, **18**, 10–14.

DAWES, R. M. (1979). The robust beauty of improper linear models in decision making. *American Psychologist*, **34**, 571–582.

———— (1988). *Rational choice in an uncertain world.* San Diego: Harcourt, Brace, Jovanovich.

DEGROOT, M. H. (1970). *Optimal statistical decisions.* New York: McGraw-Hill.

DIAMOND, G. A., AND FORRESTER, J. S. (1983). Metadiagnosis: An epistemologic model of clinical judgment. *American Journal of Medicine*, **75**, 129–137.

DICKSON, G. C. A. (1981). An empirical examination of the willingness of managers to use utility theory. *Journal of Management Studies*, **18**, 423–434.

DOHERTY, M. E., AND OTHERS. (1979). Pseudodiagnosticity. *Acta Psychologica*, **43**, 111–121.

DOLAN, J. G., BORDLEY, D. R., AND MUSHLIN, A. I. (1986). An evaluation of clinicians' subjective prior probability estimates. *Medical Decision Making*, **6**, 216–223.

DOWIE, J. (1976). On the efficiency and equity of betting markets. *Economica*, **43**, 139–150.

DUNN, V. H., AND PAUKER, S. G. (1986). An ambiguous renal cyst in a patient with a prior nephrectomy: What to do when there is only one more to lose. *Medical Decision Making*, 6, 49–62.

DYER, J. S., AND SARIN, R. K. (1979). Measurable multiattribute value functions. *Operations Research*, 27, 810–822.

———, and ——— (1982). Relative risk aversion. *Management Science*, 28, 875–886.

EASTERBROOK, J. A. (1959). The effect of emotion on cue utilization and the organization of behavior. *Psychological Review*, 66, 183–201.

ECHTERNACHT, G. J. (1972). The use of confidence testing in objective tests. *Review of Educational Research*, 42, 217–236.

EDDY, D. M. (1982). Probabilistic reasoning in clinical medicine: Problems and opportunities. In D. Kahneman, P. Slovic, and A. Tversky (eds.), *Judgment under uncertainty: Heuristics and biases* (pp. 249–267). New York: Cambridge University Press.

EDWARDS, W. (1961). Behavioral decision theory. *Annual Review of Psychology*, 12, 473–498.

——— (1962). Dynamic decision theory and probabilistic information processing. *Human Factors*, 4, 59–73.

EINHORN, H. J., AND HOGARTH, R. M. (1978). Confidence in judgment: Persistence of the illusion of validity. *Psychological Review*, 85, 395–416.

———, AND ——— (1981). Behavioral decision theory: Processes of judgment and choice. *Annual Review of Psychology*, 32, 53–88.

ELLSBERG, D. (1961). Risk, ambiguity, and the Savage axioms. *Quarterly Journal of Economics*, 75, 643–669.

ELTON, E. J., AND GRUBER, M. J. (1987). *Modern portfolio theory and investment analysis* (3rd ed.). New York: Wiley.

ERICSSON, K. A., AND SIMON, H. A. (1980). Verbal reports as data. *Psychological Review*, 87, 215–251.

ESTES, W. K. (1976). The cognitive side of probability learning. *Psychological Review*, 83, 37–64.

FAMA, E. F. (1965). The behavior of stock-market prices. *Journal of Business*, 38, 34–105.

FELLER, W. (1968). *An introduction to probability theory and its applications*, Vol. 1 (3rd ed.). New York: Wiley.

FISCHHOFF, B. (1975). Hindsight ≠ foresight: The effect of outcome knowledge on judgment under uncertainty. *Journal of Experimental Psychology: Human Perception and Performance*, 1, 288–299.

——— (1980). Decision analysis: Clinical art or science? In L. Sjoberg, T. Tyszka, and J. Wise (eds.), *Decision analysis and decision processes*. Lund, Sweden: Doxa.

——— (1983). Predicting frames. *Journal of Experimental Psychology: Learning, Memory, and Cognition*, 9, 103–116.

———, AND BEYTH, R. (1975). "I knew it would happen": Remembered probabilities of once-future things. *Organizational Behavior and Human Performance*, 13, 1–16.

———, AND BEYTH-MAROM, R. (1983). Hypothesis evaluation from a Bayesian perspective. *Psychological Review*, 90, 239–260.

———, AND MACGREGOR, D. (1982). Subjective confidence in forecasts. *Journal of Forecasting*, 1, 155–172.

———, SLOVIC, P., AND LICHTENSTEIN, S. (1977). Knowing with certainty: The appropriateness of extreme confidence. *Journal of Experimental Psychology: Human Perception and Performance*, 3, 552–564.

———, ———, AND ——— (1978). Fault trees: Sensitivity of estimated failure probabilities to problem representation. *Journal of Experimental Psychology: Human Perception and Performance*, 4, 330–344.

———, ———, AND ——— (1979). Subjective sensitivity analysis. *Organizational Behavior and Human Performance*, **23**, 339–359.

FISHBURN, P. C. (1970). *Utility theory for decision making*. New York: Wiley.

——— (1977). Mean-risk analysis with risk associated with below-target returns. *American Economic Review*, **67**, 116–126.

——— (1981). Subjective expected utility: A review of normative theories. *Theory and Decision*, **13**, 139–199.

——— (1982). Nontransitive measurable utility. *Journal of Mathematical Psychology*, **26**, 31–67.

——— (1984). Foundations of risk measurement: I. Risk as probable loss. *Management Science*, **30**, 396–406.

——— (1986). The axioms of subjective probability. *Statistical Science*, **1**, 335–358.

———, AND KOCHENBERGER, G. A. (1979). Two-piece von Neumann-Morgenstern utility functions. *Decision Sciences*, **10**, 503–518.

FISHER, G. L., AND FISHER, B. E. (1969). Differential rates of GSR habituation to pleasant and unpleasant sapid stimuli. *Journal of Experimental Psychology*, **82**, 339–342.

FONG, G. T., KRANTZ, D. H., AND NISBETT, R. E. (1986). The effects of statistical training on thinking about everyday problems. *Cognitive Psychology*, **18**, 253–292.

FREEDMAN, D. A., AND PURVES, R. A. (1969). Bayes' method for bookies. *Annals of Mathematical Statistics*, **40**, 1177–1186.

FRIEDMAN, M., AND SAVAGE, L. J. (1948). The utility analysis of choices involving risk. *Journal of Political Economy*, **56**, 279–304.

FRYBACK, D. G., AND THORNBURY, J. R. (1976). Evaluation of a computerized Bayesian model for diagnosis of renal cyst vs. tumor vs. normal variant from excretory urogram information. *Investigative Radiology*, **11**, 102–111.

GABRIELCIK, A., AND FAZIO, R. H. (1984). Priming and frequency estimation: A strict test of the availability heuristic. *Personality and Social Psychology Bulletin*, **10**, 85–89.

GALANTER, E. (1962). The direct measurement of utility and subjective probability. *American Journal of Psychology*, **75**, 208–220.

GETTYS, C. F., AND OTHERS. (1987). An evaluation of human act generation performance. *Organizational Behavior and Human Decision Processes*, **39**, 23–51.

GINOSSAR, Z., AND TROPE, Y. (1987). Problem solving in judgment under uncertainty. *Journal of Personality and Social Psychology*, **52**, 464–474.

GLASS, A. L, AND HOLYOAK, K. J. (1986). *Cognition* (2nd ed.). New York: Random House.

GODFREY, M. D., GRANGER, C. W. J., AND MORGENSTERN, O. (1964). The random-walk hypothesis of stock market behavior. *Kyklos*, **17**, 1–30.

GOLDBERG, L. R. (1970). Man versus model of man. *Psychological Bulletin*, **73**, 422–432.

GOLDSTEIN, W. H., AND EINHORN, H. J. (1987). Expression theory and the preference reversal phenomenon. *Psychological Review*, **94**, 236–254.

GOODMAN, B., AND OTHERS. (1979). Prediction of bids for two-outcome gambles in a casino setting. *Organizational Behavior and Human Performance*, **24**, 382–399.

GREER, W. R. (1974). Theory versus practice in risk analysis: An empirical study. *Accounting Review*, **49**, 496–505.

GREGORY, W. L., CIALDINI, R. B., AND CARPENTER, K. M. (1982). Self-relevant scenarios as mediators of likelihood estimates and compliance: Does imagining make it so? *Journal of Personality and Social Psychology*, **43**, 89–99.

GRETHER, D. M., AND PLOTT, C. R. (1979). Economic theory of choice and the preference reversal phenomenon. *American Economic Review*, **69**, 623–638.

HABBEMA, J. D. F., HILDEN, J., AND BJERREGAARD, B. (1978). The measurement of performance in probabilistic diagnosis: I. The problem, descriptive tools, and measures based on classification matrices. *Methods of Information in Medicine,* **17**, 217–226.

HACKING, I. (1975). *The emergence of probability.* London: Cambridge University Press.

HADAR, J., AND RUSSELL, W. R. (1969). Rules for ordering uncertain prospects. *American Economic Review,* **59**, 25–34.

HALMOS, P. R. (1944). The foundations of probability. *American Mathematical Monthly,* **51**, 493–510.

HAMILTON, D. L., AND ROSE, T. L. (1980). Illusory correlation and the maintenance of stereotypic beliefs. *Journal of Personality and Social Psychology,* **39**, 832–845.

HAMMOND, K. R., AND OTHERS. (1975). Social judgment theory. In M. Kaplan and S. Schwartz (eds.), *Human judgment and decision processes* (pp. 271–312). New York: Academic Press.

HASTIE, R., AND PARK, B. (1986). The relationship between memory and judgment depends on whether the judgment task is memory-based or on-line. *Psychological Review,* **93**, 258–268.

HENDERSON, J. C., AND NUTT, P. C. (1980). The influence of decision style on decision making behavior. *Management Science,* **26**, 371–386.

HENDERSON, J. M., AND QUANDT, R. E. (1971). *Microeconomic theory: A mathematical approach* (2nd ed.). New York: McGraw-Hill.

HERSHEY, J. C., AND SCHOEMAKER, P. J. H. (1980). Prospect theory's reflection hypothesis: A critical examination. *Organizational Behavior and Human Performance,* **25**, 395–418.

————, KUNREUTHER, H. C., AND SCHOEMAKER, P. J. H. (1982). Sources of bias in assessment procedures for utility functions. *Management Science,* **28**, 936–954.

HICKMAN, W. B. (1957). *Corporate bonds: Quality and investment performance* (Occasional Paper 59). Cambridge, MA: National Bureau of Economic Research, Inc.

HLATKY, M., BOTVINICK, E., AND BRUNDAGE, B. (1982). Diagnostic accuracy of cardiologists compared with probability calculations using Bayes' Rule. *American Journal of Cardiology,* **49**, 1927–1931.

HOCH, S. J. (1984). Availability and interference in predictive judgment. *Journal of Experimental Psychology,* **10**, 649–662.

———— (1985). Counterfactual reasoning and accuracy in predicting personal events. *Journal of Experimental Psychology: Learning, Memory, and Cognition,* **11**, 719–731.

HOCKEY, R., AND HAMILTON, P. (1983). The cognitive patterning of stress states. In R. Hockey (ed.), *Stress and fatigue in human performance* (pp. 331–362). New York: Wiley.

HOGARTH, R. M. (1981). Beyond discrete biases: Functional and dysfunctional aspects of judgmental heuristics. *Psychological Bulletin,* **90**, 197–217.

HOLMES, D. S. (1970). Differential change in affective intensity and the forgetting of unpleasant personal experiences. *Journal of Personality and Social Psychology,* **15**, 234–239.

HOLTZMAN, S. (1989). *Intelligent decision systems.* Reading, MA: Addison-Wesley.

HOSKINS, C. G. (1975). Theory versus practice in risk analysis: An empirical study: A comment. *Accounting Review,* **50**, 835–838.

HOWARD, R. A. (1980). An assessment of decision analysis. *Operations Research,* **28**, 4–27.

HOWELL, W. C. (1971). Uncertainty from internal and external sources: A clear case of overconfidence. *Journal of Experimental Psychology,* **89**, 240–243.

———— (1973). Representation of frequency in memory. *Psychological Bulletin,* **80**, 44–53.

HUNT, V. B., AND OTHERS. (1983, October). *Calibration of clinicians' probability estimates.* Paper presented at the Fifth Annual Meeting of the Society for Medical Decision Making, Toronto.

ISEN, A. M., AND GEVA, N. (1987). The influence of positive affect on acceptable level of risk: The person with a large canoe has a large worry. *Organizational Behavior and Human Decision Processes*, **39**, 145–154.

JANIS, I. L., AND MANN, L. (1977). *Decision making.* New York: Free Press.

JENSEN, F. A., AND PETERSON, C. R. (1973). Psychological effects of proper scoring rules. *Organizational Behavior and Human Performance*, **9**, 307–317.

JOHNSON, D. M., PARROTT, G. L., AND STRATTON, R. P. (1968). Production and judgment of solutions of five problems. *Journal of Educational Psychology Monograph Supplement*, **59** (6, Pt. 2).

JOHNSON, E. J. (1988). Expertise and decision making under uncertainty: Performance and process. In M. T. H. Chi, R. Glaser, and M. J. Farr (eds.), *The nature of expertise* (pp. 209–228). Hillsdale, NJ: Erlbaum.

JOHNSON, M. D. (1984). Consumer choice strategies for comparing noncomparable alternatives. *Journal of Consumer Research*, **11**, 741–753.

JOHNSON-LAIRD, P. N. (1983). *Mental models.* Cambridge, MA: Harvard University Press.

JONIDES, J., AND NAVEH-BENJAMIN, M. (1987). Estimating frequency of occurrence. *Journal of Experimental Psychology: Learning, Memory, and Cognition*, **13**, 230–240.

KAHNEMAN, D., AND TVERSKY, A. (1972). Subjective probability: A judgment of representativeness. *Cognitive Psychology*, **3**, 430–454.

————, AND ———— (1973). On the psychology of prediction. *Psychological Review*, **80**, 237–251.

————, AND ————. (1979). Prospect theory: An analysis of decision under risk. *Econometrica*, **47**, 263–291.

————, AND ————. (1982a). The psychology of preferences. *Scientific American*, **246**(1), 163–169.

————, AND ———— (1982b). The simulation heuristic. In D. Kahneman, P. Slovic, and A. Tversky (eds.), *Judgment under uncertainty: Heuristics and biases* (pp. 201–208). New York: Cambridge University Press.

————, AND ———— (1983). Choices, values, and frames. *American Psychologist*, **39**, 341–350.

————, SLOVIC, P., AND TVERSKY, A. (eds.). (1982). *Judgment under uncertainty: Heuristics and biases.* New York: Cambridge University Press.

KAPLAN, M. F., AND MILLER, C. E. (1983). Group discussion and judgment. In P. B. Paulus (ed.), *Basic group processes* (pp. 65–94). New York: Springer-Verlag.

KARMARKAR, U. S. (1978). Subjectively weighted utility: A descriptive extension of the expected utility model. *Organizational Behavior and Human Performance*, **21**, 61–72.

———— (1979). Subjectively weighted utility and the Allais Paradox. *Organizational Behavior and Human Performance*, **24**, 67–72.

KASSIRER, J. P., AND OTHERS. (1987). Decision analysis: A progress report. *Annals of Internal Medicine*, **106**, 275–291.

KEENEY, R. L., AND RAIFFA, H. (1976). *Decisions with multiple objectives: Preferences and value tradeoffs.* New York: Wiley.

KELLER, L. R. (1985). The effects of problem representation on the sure-thing and substitution principles. *Management Science*, **31**, 738–751.

————, SARIN, R., AND WEBER, M. (1986). Empirical investigation of some properties of the perceived riskiness of gambles. *Organizational Behavior and Human Decision Processes*, **38**, 114–130.

KEREN, G. (1987). Facing uncertainty in the game of bridge: A calibration study. *Organizational Behavior and Human Decision Processes*, **39**, 98–114.

KLATZKY, R. L. (1980). *Human memory: Structures and processes* (2nd ed.). San Francisco: Freeman.

KLAYMAN, J., AND HA, Y.-W. (1987). Confirmation, disconfirmation, and information in hypothesis testing. *Psychological Review*, **94**, 211–228.

KOEHLER, R. A. (1971). A comparison of the validities of conventional choice testing and various confidence marking procedures. *Journal of Educational Measurement*, **8**, 297–303.

KONG, A., AND OTHERS. (1986). How medical professionals evaluate expressions of probability. *New England Journal of Medicine*, **315**, 740–744.

KORIAT, A., LICHTENSTEIN, S., AND FISCHHOFF, B. (1980). Reasons for confidence. *Journal of Experimental Psychology: Human Learning and Memory*, **6**, 107–118.

KRZYSZTOFOWICZ, R. (1983). Strength of preference and risk attitude in utility measurement. *Organizational Behavior and Human Performance*, **31**, 88–113.

KUNST-WILSON, W. R., AND ZAJONC, R. B. (1980). Affective discrimination of stimuli that cannot be recognized. *Science*, **207**, 557–558.

LANGER, E. (1975). The illusion of control. *Journal of Personality and Social Psychology*, **32**, 311–328.

LARSON, J. R. (1980). Exploring the external validity of a subjectively weighted utility model of decision making. *Organizational Behavior and Human Performance*, **26**, 293–304.

LAZARUS, R. S. (1966). *Psychological stress and the coping process*. New York: McGraw–Hill.

LEARY, M. R. (1981). The distorted nature of hindsight. *Journal of Social Psychology*, **115**, 25–29.

LEE, K. L., AND OTHERS. (1986). Predicting outcome in coronary disease: Statistical models versus expert clinicians. *American Journal of Medicine*, **80**, 553–560.

LEE, W. (1971). *Decision theory and human behavior*. New York: Wiley.

LEHNER, P. E. (1980). A comparison of portfolio theory and weighted utility models of risky decision making. *Organizational Behavior and Human Performance*, **26**, 238–249.

LEVI, A. S., AND PRYOR, J. B. (1987). Use of the availability heuristic in probability estimates of future events: The effects of imagining outcomes versus imagining reasons. *Organizational Behavior and Human Decision Processes*, **40**, 219–234.

LEVI, K. R. (1985). A signal detection framework for the evaluation of probabilistic forecasts. *Organizational Behavior and Human Decision Processes*, **36**, 143–166.

——— (1986). *Numerical likelihood estimates from physicians and linear models*. Unpublished doctoral dissertation, University of Michigan, Ann Arbor.

LEVIN, I. P., AND OTHERS. (1985). Framing effects in judgment tasks with varying amounts of information. *Organizational Behavior and Human Decision Processes*, **36**, 362–377.

LIBBY, R., AND FISHBURN, P. C. (1977). Behavioral models of risk taking in business decisions: A survey and evaluation. *Journal of Accounting Research*, **15**, 272–292.

LICHTENSTEIN, S., AND FISCHHOFF, B. (1977). Do those who know more also know more about how much they know? The calibration of probability judgments. *Organizational Behavior and Human Performance*, **20**, 159–183.

———, AND ——— (1980). Training for calibration. *Organizational Behavior and Human Performance*, **26**, 149–171.

———, AND SLOVIC, P. (1971). Reversal of preferences between bids and choices in gambling decisions. *Journal of Experimental Psychology*, **89**, 46–55.

————, AND ———— (1973). Response-induced reversals of preferences in gambling: An extended replication in Las Vegas. *Journal of Experimental Psychology*, **101**, 16–20.

————, FISCHHOFF, B., AND PHILLIPS, L. D. (1982). Calibration of probabilities: The state of the art to 1980. In D. Kahneman, P. Slovic, and A. Tversky (eds.), *Judgment under uncertainty: Heuristics and biases* (pp. 306–334). New York: Cambridge University Press.

————, SLOVIC, P., AND ZINK, D. (1969). Effect of instruction in expected value on optimality of gambling decision. *Journal of Experimental Psychology*, **79**, 236–240.

LICHTENSTEIN, S., AND OTHERS. (1978). Judged frequency of lethal events. *Journal of Experimental Psychology: Human Learning and Memory*, **4**, 551–578.

LINDLEY, D. V., TVERSKY, A., AND BROWN, R. V. (1979). On the reconciliation of probability assessments (with discussion). *Journal of the Royal Statistical Society: Series A*, **142** (Part 2), 146–180.

LIPSEY, R. G., STEINER, P. O., AND PURVIS, D. D. (1987). *Economics* (8th ed.). New York: Harper & Row.

LOCKSLEY, A., AND STANGOR, C. (1984). Why versus how often: Causal reasoning and the incidence of judgmental bias. *Journal of Experimental Social Psychology*, **20**, 470–483.

LOFTUS, E. F., AND PALMER, J. C. (1974). Reconstruction of automobile destruction: An example of the interaction between language and memory. *Journal of Verbal Learning and Verbal Behavior*, **13**, 585–589.

LOOMES, G., AND SUGDEN, R. (1982). Regret theory: An alternative theory of rational choice under uncertainty. *Economic Journal*, **92**, 805–824.

LOPES, L. L. (1981). Decision making in the short run. *Journal of Experimental Psychology: Human Learning and Memory*, **7**, 377–385.

———— (1983). Some thoughts on the psychological concept of risk. *Journal of Experimental Psychology: Human Perception and Performance*, **9**, 137–144.

———— (1984). Risk and distributional inequality. *Journal of Experimental Psychology: Human Perception and Performance*, **10**, 465–485.

LORD, C. G., LEPPER, M. R., AND PRESTON, E. (1984). Considering the opposite: A corrective strategy for social judgment. *Journal of Personality and Social Psychology*, **47**, 1231–1243.

LUCE, R. D., AND RAIFFA, H. (1957). *Games and decisions*. New York: Wiley.

MACCRIMMON, K. R. (1968). Descriptive and normative implications of the decision-theory postulates. In K. Borch and J. Mossin (eds.), *Risk and uncertainty* (pp. 3–32). New York: Macmillan.

MACHINA, M. J. (1982). Expected utility analysis without the independence axiom. *Econometrica*, **50**, 277–323.

MANIS, M., AND OTHERS. (1980). Base rates can affect individual predictions. *Journal of Personality and Social Psychology*, **38**, 231–248.

MARKOWITZ, H. (1952). The utility of wealth. *Journal of Political Economy*, **60**, 151–158.

———— (1959). *Portfolio selection*. New York: Wiley.

MARKUS, H., AND ZAJONC, R. B. (1985). The cognitive perspective in social psychology. In G. Lindzey and E. Aronson (eds.), *Handbook of social psychology* (3rd ed., pp. 137–230). New York: Random House.

MASON, I. (1982). A model for assessment of weather forecasts. *Australian Meteorological Magazine*, **30**, 291–303.

MATHESON, J. E., AND WINKLER, R. L. (1976). Scoring rules for continuous probability distributions. *Management Science*, **22**, 1087–1096.

MCKEENEY, J. L., AND KEEN, P. G. W. (1974). How managers' minds work. *Harvard Business Review*, **52**(3), 79–90.

MCNEIL, B. J., WEICHSELBAUM, R., AND PAUKER, S. G. (1981). Speech and survival: Tradeoffs between quality and quantity of life in laryngeal cancer. *New England Journal of Medicine, 305,* 982–987.

———— AND OTHERS. (1982). On the elicitation of preferences for alternative therapies. *New England Journal of Medicine, 306,* 1259–1262.

METCALF, W. O. (1973). *Starting and managing a small business of your own.* Washington, DC: Small Business Administration.

MEYER, D. E., AND SCHVANEVELDT, R. W. (1976). Meaning, memory structure, and mental processes. *Science, 192,* 27–33.

MILLER, G. A. (1956). The magical number seven, plus or minus two: Some limits of our capacity for processing information. *Psychological Review, 63,* 81–97.

MILLER, J. (1986, December 12). Troubled Willow Run schools ask 'why?' *Ann Arbor News,* pp. A1, A7.

MILNOR, J. (1954). Games against nature. In R. M. Thrall, C. H. Coombs, and R. L. Davis (eds.), *Decision processes* (pp. 49–59). New York: Wiley.

MONTGOMERY, H. (1977). A study of intransitive preferences using a think aloud procedure. In H. Jungermann and G. de Zeeuw (eds.), *Decision making and change in human affairs* (pp. 347–362). Dordrecht, The Netherlands: Reidel.

———— (1983). Decision rules and the search for a dominance structure: Towards a process model of decision making. In P. C. Humphreys, O. Svenson, and A. Vari (eds.), *Analyzing and aiding decision processes* (pp. 343–369). Amsterdam: North-Holland.

————, AND ADELBRATT, T. (1982). Gambling decisions and information about expected value. *Organizational Behavior and Human Performance, 29,* 39–57.

MORIER, D. M., AND BORGIDA, E. (1984). The conjunction fallacy: A task specific phenomenon? *Personality and Social Psychology Bulletin, 10,* 243–252.

MOSKOWITZ, H., AND SARIN, R. K. (1983). Improving the consistency of conditional probability assessments for forecasting and decision making. *Management Science, 29,* 735–749.

MOSTELLER, F. A., AND NOGEE, P. (1951). An experimental measurement of utility. *Journal of Political Economy, 59,* 371–404.

MURPHY, A. H. (1973). A new vector partition of the probability score. *Journal of Applied Meteorology, 12,* 595–600.

————, AND BROWN, B. G. (1984). A comparative evaluation of objective and subjective weather forecasts in the United States. *Journal of Forecasting, 3,* 369–393.

————, AND DAAN, H. (1985). Forecast evaluation. In A. H. Murphy and R. W. Katz (eds.), *Probability, statistics, and decision making in the atmospheric sciences* (pp. 379–437). Boulder, CO: Westview Press.

————, AND WINKLER, R. L. (1974). Subjective probability forecasting experiments in meteorology: Some preliminary results. *Bulletin of the American Meteorological Society, 55,* 1206–1216.

————, AND ———— (1977). Reliability of subjective probability forecasts of precipitation and temperature. *Applied Statistics, 26,* 41–47.

————, AND OTHERS. (1985). The use of probabilities in subjective quantitative precipitation forecasts: Some experimental results. *Monthly Weather Review, 113,* 2075–2089.

MURPHY, G. L., AND WRIGHT, J. C. (1984). Changes in conceptual structure with expertise: Differences between real-world experts and novices. *Journal of Experimental Psychology: Learning, Memory, and Cognition, 10,* 144–155.

NEIMARK, E. D., AND SHUFORD, E. H. (1959). Comparisons of predictions and estimates in a probability learning situation. *Journal of Experimental Psychology, 57,* 294–298.

NEWMAN, R. S. (1984). Children's numerical skill and judgments of confidence in estimation. *Journal of Experimental Child Psychology*, **37**, 107–123.

NISBETT, R. E., AND ROSS, L. (1980). *Human inference: Strategies and shortcomings of social judgment.* Englewood Cliffs, NJ: Prentice-Hall.

———, AND WILSON, T. D. (1977). Telling more than we can know: Verbal reports on mental processes. *Psychological Review*, **84**, 231–259.

———, ZUKIER, H., AND LEMLEY, R. E. (1981). The dilution effect: Nondiagnostic information weakens the implications of diagnostic information. *Cognitive Psychology*, **13**, 248–277.

———, AND OTHERS. (1983). The use of statistical heuristics in everyday inductive reasoning. *Psychological Review*, **90**, 339–363.

NORMAN, D. A. (1983). Some observations on mental models. In D. Gentner and A. L. Stevens (eds.), *Mental models* (pp. 7–14). Hillsdale, NJ: Erlbaum.

NORTHCRAFT, G. B., AND NEALE, M. A. (1986). Opportunity costs and the framing of resource allocation decisions. *Organizational Behavior and Human Decision Processes*, **37**, 348–356.

OLSHAVSKY, R. W., AND GRANBOIS, D. H. (1979). Consumer decision making—fact or fiction? *Journal of Consumer Research*, **6**, 93–100.

OLSON, C. L. (1976). Some apparent violations of the representativeness heuristic in human judgment. *Journal of Experimental Psychology: Human Perception and Performance*, **2**, 599–608.

OSBORN, A. F. (1963). *Applied imagination* (3rd ed.). New York: Scribner's.

OSKAMP, S. (1965). Overconfidence in case-study judgments. *Journal of Consulting Psychology*, **29**, 261–265.

PAUKER, S. P., AND PAUKER, S. G. (1977). Prenatal diagnosis: A directive approach to genetic counseling using decision analysis. *Yale Journal of Biology and Medicine*, **50**, 275–289.

PAYNE, J. W. (1973). Alternative approaches to decision making under risk: Moments versus risk dimensions. *Psychological Bulletin*, **80**, 439–453.

——— (1975). Relation of perceived risk to preferences among gambles. *Journal of Experimental Psychology: Human Perception and Performance*, **104**, 86–94.

——— (1976). Task complexity and contingent processing in decision making: An information search and protocol analysis. *Organizational Behavior and Human Performance*, **16**, 366–387.

——— (1982). Contingent decision behavior. *Psychological Bulletin*, **92**, 382–402.

———, LAUGHHUNN, D. J., AND CRUM, R. (1980). Translation of gambles and aspiration level effects in risky choice behavior. *Management Science*, **26**, 1039–1060.

PETERSON, C. R., AND BEACH, L. R. (1967). Man as an intuitive statistician. *Psychological Bulletin*, **68**, 29–46.

PHELPS, R. H., AND SHANTEAU, J. (1978). Livestock judges: How much information can an expert use? *Organizational Behavior and Human Performance*, **21**, 209–219.

PHILLIPS, L. D., AND EDWARDS, W. (1966). Conservatism in a simple probability inference task. *Journal of Experimental Psychology*, **72**, 346–354.

———, EDWARDS, W., AND HAYS, W. L. (1966). Conservatism in complex probabilistic inference. *IEEE Transactions on Human Factors in Electronics*, **HFE-7**, 7–18.

PIAGET, J., AND INHELDER, B. (1975). *The origin of the idea of chance in children* (L. Leake, Jr., P. Burrell, and H. D. Fishbein, trans.). New York: Norton. (Originally published in 1951.)

PICKHARDT, R. C., AND WALLACE, J. B. (1974). A study of the performance of subjective probability assessors. *Decision Sciences*, **5**, 347–363.

PITZ, G. F. (1975). Bayes' theorem: Can a theory of judgment and inference do without it? In F. Restle and others (eds.), *Cognitive theory* (Vol. 1, pp. 131–148). Hillsdale, NJ: Erlbaum.

————, AND SACHS, N. J. (1984). Judgment and decision: Theory and application. *Annual Review of Psychology*, **35**, 139–163.

————, SACHS, N. J., AND HEERBOTH, J. (1980). Procedures for eliciting choices in the analysis of individual decisions. *Organizational Behavior and Human Performance*, **26**, 396–408.

———— AND OTHERS. (1981). Learning conditional frequencies in a probability learning task. *Acta Psychologica*, **47**, 229–243.

POLITSER, P. E. (1982). *The evaluation of repeated medical tests: Logical and statistical considerations*. Unpublished doctoral dissertation, University of Michigan, Ann Arbor.

———— (1984). Explanations of statistical concepts: Can they penetrate the haze of Bayes? *Methods of Information in Medicine*, **23**, 99–108.

POLLATSEK, A., AND OTHERS. (1987). Understanding conditional probabilities. *Organizational Behavior and Human Decision Processes*, **40**, 255–269.

POSES, R. M., AND OTHERS. (1985). The accuracy of experienced physicians' probability estimates for patients with sore throats: Implications for decision making. *Journal of the American Medical Association*, **254**, 925–929.

PRATT, J. W. (1964). Risk aversion in the small and in the large. *Econometrica*, **32**, 122–136.

PRUITT, D. G., AND HOGE, R. D. (1965). Strength of the relationship between the value of an event and its subjective probability as a function of method of measurement. *Journal of Experimental Psychology*, **69**, 483–489.

PUTO, C. P. (1987). The framing of buying decisions. *Journal of Consumer Research*, **14**, 301–315.

QUIGGIN, J. (1985). Subjective utility, anticipated utility, and the Allais Paradox. *Organizational Behavior and Human Decision Processes*, **35**, 94–101.

RAMSEY, F. P. (1931). Truth and probability. In F. P. Ramsey, *The foundations of mathematics and other logical essays* (pp. 156–198). New York: Harcourt, Brace, Jovanovich.

RANYARD, R. H. (1976). Elimination by aspects as a decision rule for risky choice. *Acta Psychologica*, **40**, 299–310.

ROBERTS, F. S. (1979). *Measurement theory*. Reading, MA: Addison-Wesley.

ROBINSON, F. P. (1962). *Effective reading*. New York: Harper & Row.

RONEN, J. (1973). Effects of some probability displays on choices. *Organizational Behavior and Human Performance*, **9**, 1–15.

RONIS, D. L., AND YATES, J. F. (1987). Components of probability judgment accuracy: Individual consistency and effects of subject matter and assessment method. *Organizational Behavior and Human Decision Processes*, **40**, 193–218.

ROTHBART, M. (1970). Assessing the likelihood of a threatening event. *Journal of Personality and Social Psychology*, **15**, 109–117.

ROTHSTEIN, H. G. (1986). The effects of time pressure on judgment in multiple cue probability learning. *Organizational Behavior and Human Decision Processes*, **37**, 83–92.

RUNDUS, D. (1973). Negative effects of using list items as recall cues. *Journal of Verbal Learning and Verbal Behavior*, **12**, 43–50.

RUSSO, J. E., AND DOSHER, B. A. (1983). Strategies for multiattribute binary choice. *Journal of Experimental Psychology: Learning, Memory, and Cognition*, **9**, 676–696.

SAMSON, D. A., AND THOMAS, H. (1986). Assessing probability distributions by the fractile method: Evidence from managers. *Omega*, **14**, 401–407.

SANDERS, F. (1963). On subjective probability forecasting. *Journal of Applied Meteorology*, **2**, 191–201.

SAPPINGTON, A. A., AND FARRAR, W. E. (1982). Brainstorming vs. critical judgment in the generation of solutions which conform to certain reality constraints. *Journal of Creative Behavior*, **16**, 1982.

SAVAGE, L. J. (1954). *The foundations of statistics.* New York: Wiley.

SAVICKAS, M. L., SILLING, S. M., AND SCHWARTZ, S. (1984). Time perspective in vocational maturity and career decision making. *Journal of Vocational Behavior*, **25**, 258–269.

SCHAEFER, R. E., AND BORCHERDING, K. (1973). The assessment of subjective probability distributions: A training experiment. *Acta Psychologica*, **37**, 117–129.

SCHLANGER, J. L. (1985, April). Phillips Petroleum Co., Phillips Petroleum International Finance N. V., Phillips Petroleum Credit Corp. *Standard and Poor's International Creditweek*, pp. 26–27.

SCHNEIDER, S. L., AND LOPES, L. L. (1986). Reflections in preferences under risk: Who and when may suggest why. *Journal of Experimental Psychology: Human Perception and Performance*, **12**, 86–94.

SCHOEMAKER, P. J. H. (1982). The expected utility model: Its variants, purposes, evidence and limitations. *Journal of Economic Literature*, **20**, 529–563.

SCHOENFELD, A. H., AND HERRMANN, D. J. (1982). Problem perception and knowledge structure in expert and novice mathematical problem solvers. *Journal of Experimental Psychology: Learning, Memory, and Cognition*, **8**, 484–494.

SCHUM, D. (1980). Current developments in research on cascaded inference processes. In T. Wallsten (ed.), *Cognitive processes in choice and decision behavior* (pp. 179–210). Hillsdale, NJ: Erlbaum.

SEAVER, D. A., VON WINTERFELDT, D., AND EDWARDS, W. (1978). Eliciting subjective probability distributions on continuous variables. *Organizational Behavior and Human Performance*, **21**, 379–391.

SEGGIE, J. L., AND ENDERSBY, H. (1972). The empirical implications of Piaget's concept of correlation. *Australian Journal of Psychology*, **24**, 3–8.

SELVIDGE, J. E. (1980). Assessing the extremes of probability distributions by the fractile method. *Decision Sciences*, **11**, 493–502.

SHAFER, G. (1976). *A mathematical theory of evidence.* Princeton, NJ: Princeton University Press.

——— (1986). Savage revisited. *Statistical Science*, **1**, 463–501.

——— (1987). Probability judgment in artificial intelligence and expert systems. *Statistical Science*, **2**, 3–44.

——— (1987, November). *The problem of small worlds.* Paper presented at the Annual Meeting of the Judgment and Decision Making Society, Seattle, WA.

SHAKLEE, H., AND MIMS, M. (1982). Sources of error in judging event covariations: Effects of memory demands. *Journal of Experimental Psychology: Learning, Memory, and Cognition*, **8**, 208–224.

———, AND TUCKER, D. (1980). A rule analysis of judgments of covariation between events. *Memory and Cognition*, **8**, 459–467.

SHAPIRA, Z. (1981). Making tradeoffs between job attributes. *Organizational Behavior and Human Performance*, **28**, 331–355.

SHAPIRO, A. R. (1977). The evaluation of clinical prediction. *New England Journal of Medicine*, **296**, 1509–1514.

SHORTLIFFE, E. H., AND BUCHANAN, B. G. (1975). A model of inexact reasoning in medicine. *Mathematical Biosciences*, **23**, 351–379.

SHWEDER, R. A. (1977). Illusory correlation and the MMPI controversy. *Journal of Consulting and Clinical Psychology*, **45**, 917–924.

SIEDEL, G. J. (1986, January–February). The decision tree. *Bar Leader*, 18–21.

SLOVIC, P. (1962). Convergent validation of risk taking measures. *Journal of Abnormal and Social Psychology*, **65**, 68–71.

——— (1964). Assessment of risk taking behavior. *Psychological Bulletin*, **61**, 220–233.

——— (1966). Value as a determiner of subjective probability. *IEEE Transactions on Human Factors in Electronics*, **HFE-7**(1), 22–28.

——— (1975). Choice between equally valued alternatives. *Journal of Experimental Psychology: Human Perception and Performance*, **1**, 280–287.

———, AND FISCHHOFF, B. (1977). On the psychology of experimental surprises. *Journal of Experimental Psychology: Human Perception and Performance*, **3**, 544–551.

———, AND LICHTENSTEIN, S. (1983). Preference reversals: A broader perspective. *American Economic Review*, **73**, 596–605.

———, AND TVERSKY, A. (1974). Who accepts Savage's axiom? *Behavioral Science*, **19**, 368–373.

———, FISCHHOFF, B., AND LICHTENSTEIN, S. (1978). Accident probabilities and seat belt usage: A psychological perspective. *Accident Analysis and Prevention*, **10**, 281–285.

———, ———, AND ——— (1982). Response mode, framing, and information-processing effects in risk assessment. In R. Hogarth (ed.), *New directions for methodology of social and behavioral science: Question framing and response consistency, no. 11.* San Francisco: Jossey-Bass.

———, FLEISSNER, D., AND BAUMAN, W. S. (1972). Analyzing the use of information in investment decision making. *Journal of Business*, **45**, 283–301.

SMEDSLUND, J. (1963). The concept of correlation in adults. *Scandinavian Journal of Psychology*, **4**, 165–173.

SPETZLER, C. S., AND STAËL VON HOLSTEIN, C.-A. S. (1975). Probability encoding in decision analysis. *Management Science*, **22**, 340–358.

STAËL VON HOLSTEIN, C.-A. S. (1971). An experiment in probabilistic weather forecasting. *Journal of Applied Meteorology*, **10**, 635–645.

——— (1972). Probabilistic forecasting: An experiment related to the stock market. *Organizational Behavior and Human Performance*, **8**, 139–158.

——— (1977). The continuous ranked probability score in practice. In H. Jungermann and G. de Zeeuw (eds.), *Decision making and change in human affairs* (pp. 263–273). Dordrecht, Holland: Reidel.

STANDARD & POOR'S. (1985, April). International ratings. *Standard & Poor's International Credit Week.*

STEIN, M. I. (1974). *Stimulating creativity, Vol. 1: Individual procedures.* New York: Academic Press.

——— (1975). *Stimulating creativity, Vol. 2: Group procedures.* New York: Academic Press.

SUGDEN, R. (1985). Regret, recrimination and rationality. *Theory and Decision*, **19**, 77–99.

——— (1986). New developments in the theory of choice under uncertainty. *Bulletin of Economic Research*, **38**, 1–24.

SUMICHRAST, M., AND SHAFER, R. G. (1987). *The complete book of home buying.* New York: Bantam.

SUMMERS, D. A., TALIAFERRO, J. D., AND FLETCHER, D. J. (1970). Subjective vs. objective description of judgment policy. *Psychonomic Science*, **18**, 249–250.

SVENSON, O. (1981). Are we all less risky and more skillful than our fellow drivers? *Acta Psychologica*, **47**, 143–148.

SWETS, J. A., AND OTHERS. (1986). Use of probability estimates in medical communications and decisions. *Methods of Information in Medicine*, **25**, 35–42.

TALBERT, R. (1981, August 20). There's really nothing like consistency. *Detroit Free Press*, p. 11B.

THALER, R (1980). Toward a positive theory of consumer choice. *Journal of Economic Behavior and Organization,* **1,** 39–60.

——— (1985). Mental accounting and consumer choice. *Marketing Science,* **4,** 199–214.

THURING, M., AND JUNGERMANN, H. (1986). Constructing and running mental models for inferences about the future. In B. Brehmer and others (eds.), *New directions in research on decision making* (pp. 163–174). Amsterdam: Elsevier.

TIERNEY, W. M., AND OTHERS. (1986). Physicians' estimates of the probability of myocardial infarction in emergency room patients with chest pain. *Medical Decision Making,* **6,** 12–17.

TOMASSINI, L. A., AND OTHERS. (1982). Calibration of auditors' probabilistic judgments: Some empirical evidence. *Organizational Behavior and Human Performance,* **30,** 391–406.

TROUTMAN, C. M., AND SHANTEAU, J. (1977). Inferences based on nondiagnostic information. *Organizational Behavior and Human Performance,* **19,** 43–55.

TVERSKY, A. (1969). Intransitivity of preferences. *Psychological Review,* **76,** 31–48.

———, AND BAR-HILLEL, M. (1983). Risk: The long and the short. *Journal of Experimental Psychology: Human Learning and Memory,* **9,** 713–717.

———, AND KAHNEMAN, D. (1971). The belief in the "law of small numbers." *Psychological Bulletin,* **76,** 105–110.

———, AND ——— (1973). Availability: A heuristic for judging frequency and probability. *Cognitive Psychology,* **5,** 207–232.

———, AND ——— (1974). Judgment under uncertainty: Heuristics and biases. *Science,* **185,** 1124–1131.

———, AND ——— (1980). Causal schemas in judgments under uncertainty. In M. Fishbein (ed.), *Progress in social psychology* (pp. 49–72). Hillsdale, NJ: Erlbaum.

———, AND ——— (1981). The framing of decisions and the rationality of choice. *Science,* **211,** 453–458.

———, AND ——— (1982). Judgments of and by representativeness. In D. Kahneman, P. Slovic, and A. Tversky (eds.), *Judgment under uncertainty: Heuristics and biases* (pp. 84–98). New York: Cambridge University Press.

———, AND ——— (1983). Extensional versus intuitive reasoning: The conjunction fallacy in probability judgment. *Psychological Review,* **90,** 293–315.

ULVILA, J. W., AND BROWN, R. V. (1982). Decision analysis comes of age. *Harvard Business Review,* **60**(5), 130–141.

URSIC, M. (1980). Consumer decision making—fact or fiction? Comment. *Journal of Consumer Research,* **7,** 331–333.

VERPLANKEN, B., AND PIETERS, R. G. M. (1988). Individual differences in reverse hindsight bias: I never thought something like Chernobyl would happen. Did I? *Journal of Behavioral Decision Making,* **1,** 131–147.

VON NEUMANN, J., AND MORGENSTERN, O. (1947). *Theory of games and economic behavior* (2nd ed.). Princeton, NJ: Princeton University Press.

VON WINTERFELDT, D. (1980). Structuring decision problems for decision analysis. *Acta Psychologica,* **45,** 71–93.

———, AND EDWARDS, W. (1986). *Decision analysis and behavioral research.* New York: Cambridge University Press.

WALLSTEN, T. S. (1981). Physician and medical student bias in evaluating diagnostic information. *Medical Decision Making,* **1,** 145–164.

——— (1983). The theoretical status of judgmental heuristics. In R. W. Scholz (ed.), *Decision making under uncertainty: Cognitive decision research, social interaction, development and epistemology* (pp. 21–37). Amsterdam: North-Holland.

———, AND BUDESCU, D. V. (1983). Encoding subjective probabilities: A psychological and psychometric review. *Management Science,* **29,** 151–173.

———— AND OTHERS. (1986). Measuring the vague meanings of probability terms. *Journal of Experimental Psychology: General,* **115,** 348–365.

WARD, W. C., AND JENKINS, H. M. (1965). The display of information and the judgment of contingency. *Canadian Journal of Psychology,* **19,** 231–241.

WEINSTEIN, M. C., AND FINEBERG, H. V. (1980). *Clinical decision analysis.* Philadelphia: Saunders.

WEISBERG, R. W. (1986). *Creativity: Genius and other myths.* San Francisco: Freeman.

WILLIAMS, S. (1987). The limit of quantitative ethics. *Medical Decision Making,* **7,** 121–123.

WINKLER, R. L. (1972). *Introduction to Bayesian inference and decision.* New York: Holt, Rinehart, and Winston.

————, AND MURPHY, A. H. (1968). "Good" probability assessors. *Journal of Applied Meteorology,* **7,** 751–758.

WOLF, F. M., GRUPPEN, L. D., AND BILLI, J. E. (1985). Differential diagnosis and the competing hypotheses heuristic: A practical approach to judgment under uncertainty and Bayesian probability. *Journal of the American Medical Association,* **253,** 2858–2862.

WOODROOFE, M. (1975). *Probability with applications.* New York: McGraw-Hill.

WOODSIDE, A. G. (1974). Relation of price to perception of quality of new products. *Journal of Applied Psychology,* **59,** 116–118.

WRIGHT, G. (1982). Changes in the realism and distribution of probability assessments as a function of question type. *Acta Psychologica,* **52,** 165–174.

————, AND AYTON, P. (1986). Subjective confidence in forecasts: A response to Fischhoff and MacGregor. *Journal of Forecasting,* **5,** 117–123.

————, AND PHILLIPS, L. D. (1980). Cultural variation in probabilistic thinking: Alternative ways of dealing with uncertainty. *International Journal of Psychology,* **15,** 239–257.

————, AND WHALLEY, P. (1983). The supra-additivity of subjective probability. In B. P. Stigum and F. Wenstop (eds.), *Foundations of utility and risk theory with applications* (pp. 233–244). Dordrecht, Holland: Reidel.

————, AND WISHUDA, A. (1982). Distribution of probability assessments for almanac and future event questions. *Scandinavian Journal of Psychology,* **23,** 219–224.

WRIGHT, J. C., AND MURPHY, G. L. (1984). The utility of theories in intuitive statistics: The robustness of theory-based judgments. *Journal of Experimental Psychology: General,* **113,** 301–322.

WRIGHT, P. (1974). The harassed decision maker: Time pressures, distraction, and the use of evidence. *Journal of Applied Psychology,* **59,** 555–561.

WRIGHT, W. F. (1979). Accuracy of subjective probabilities for a financial variable. In T. J. Burns (ed.), *Behavioral experiments in accounting II* (pp. 1–13). Columbus, OH: Ohio State University Press.

WYER, R. S. (1976). An investigation of the relations among probability estimates. *Organizational Behavior and Human Performance,* **15,** 1–18.

YATES, J. F. (1982). External correspondence: Decompositions of the mean probability score. *Organizational Behavior and Human Performance,* **30,** 132–156.

————, AND CARLSON, B. W. (1986). Conjunction errors: Evidence for multiple judgment procedures, including "signed summation." *Organizational Behavior and Human Decision Processes,* **37,** 230–253.

————, AND CURLEY, S. P. (1985). Conditional distribution analyses of probabilistic forecasts. *Journal of Forecasting,* **4,** 61–73.

————, AND ———— (1986). Contingency judgment: Primacy effects and attention decrement. *Acta Psychologica,* **62,** 293–302.

————, AND JAGACINSKI, C. M. (1979). Reference effects in multiattribute evaluations. *Organizational Behavior and Human Performance*, 24, 400–410.

————, McDANIEL, L., AND BROWN, E. (in press). Probabilistic forecasts of stock prices and earnings: The hazards of nascent expertise. *Organizational Behavior and Human Decision Processes*.

———— AND OTHERS. (1989). Probability judgment accuracy: China, Japan, and the United States. *Organizational Behavior and Human Decision Processes*, 43, 147–71.

YOUNG, M. J., YATES, J. F., AND CURLEY, S. P. (1986, October). *Physicians' active versus default health maintenance decisions*. Paper presented at the Annual Meeting of the Society for Medical Decision Making, Chicago.

ZACHARY, W. (1986). A cognitively based functional taxonomy of decision support techniques. *Human–Computer Interaction*, 2, 25–63.

ZAJONC, R. B. (1965). Social facilitation. *Science*, 149, 269–274.

———— (1968). Attitudinal effects of mere exposure. *Journal of Personality and Social Psychology Monograph*, 9 (Part 2), 1–28.

———— (1980). Feeling and thinking: Preferences need no inferences. *American Psychologist*, 35, 151–175.

————, AND MARKUS, H. (1982). Affective and cognitive factors in preferences. *Journal of Consumer Research*, 9, 123–131.

ZAKAY, D. (1984). The influence of perceived event's controllability on its subjective occurrence probability. *Psychological Record*, 34, 233–240.

————, AND WOOLER, Z. (1984). Time pressure, training and decision effectiveness. *Ergonomics*, 27, 273–284.

Index